ROGUE CORPORATIONS

Quentin Beresford is an Adjunct Professor at Sunshine Coast University and the author of *The Rise and Fall of Gunns Ltd*, *Adani and the War over Coal* and *Wounded Country* (winner of the 2022 Queensland Premier's Award for a work of state significance), all published by NewSouth.

ROGUE CORPORATIONS

Inside Australia's biggest business scandals

QUENTIN BERESFORD

NEWSOUTH

UNSW Press acknowledges the Bedegal people, the Traditional Owners of the unceded territory on which the Randwick and Kensington campuses of UNSW are situated, and recognises their continuing connection to Country and culture. We pay our respects to Bedegal Elders past and present.

A NewSouth book

Published by
NewSouth Publishing
University of New South Wales Press Ltd
University of New South Wales
Sydney NSW 2052
AUSTRALIA
https://unsw.press/

First published 2023

10 9 8 7 6 5 4 3 2 1

A catalogue record for this book is available from the National Library of Australia

ISBN 9781742237589 (paperback)
9781742238852 (ebook)
9781742239798 (ePDF)

Internal design Josephine Pajor-Markus
Cover design Luke Causby, Blue Cork
Printer Griffin Press

CONTENTS

INTRODUCTION

In the final months of 2022, Australia was rocked by a series of corporate scandals. Two involved the hacking of customers' private data and its release onto the dark web. Telecommunications company Optus and private health insurer Medibank had to fend off an angry public as to why their sensitive personal data was not better protected from hackers. The consensus from technology experts was that these companies – along with corporate Australia generally – had been asleep at the wheel when it came to installing critical cybersecurity infrastructure. As Paul Smith, technology writer for the *Australian Financial Review*, commented acerbically, corporate Australia needed 'to get a bedside clock with a louder alarm' because it had been underfunding this area of business operations for at least a decade and ignoring the persistent warnings about the consequences.[1] The result was dire: hundreds of thousands of Australians experienced deep distress over the release, and potential misuse, of their private data. Most wanted an answer to the obvious question: why is such data held, *ad infinitum,* in the first place?

A third scandal to hit the media at much the same time occurred in an industry already plagued by scandal: casinos. Star Casino, which operated in both New South Wales and Queensland, was found not to be fit to hold a licence after an inquiry into the company's operations found allegations of money-laundering, organised crime links and fraud at the company's Sydney casino.

But any digging around will quickly reveal less publicised corporate outrages: everything from greenwashing emissions reduction targets to paying little or no tax despite eye-watering profits. It's as if we've become immune from the reality that big corporations often play by their own rules.

It was ever thus. Anyone who remembers the 1980s will recall the tales of corporate malfeasance that flooded the news media. So-called entrepreneurs had, over the decade, ridden a wave of easy money and public adulation before driving a string of companies off the financial cliff. Billions were lost. Investors suffered. The nation's reputation took a battering. The term 'corporate cowboys' entered the lexicon.

But in the wash-up of the eighties, only a few of the swashbuckling entrepreneurs went to jail; Alan Bond was the most high-profile example. Like him, many of the corporate cowboys were regarded as loveable rogues. Consequently, the warning signs about the dangers posed by corporations went unheeded.

What followed was an endless repetition of scenes from the film *Wall Street* played out in real life – business models driven by debt, glitz, greed and deceit. Many corporations simply went rogue.[2] The trail of disasters and destruction is a long one. Building manufacturer James Hardie lied about its commitment to asbestos victims, effectively trying to bin its responsibilities to provide on-going support for them. Lying was at the heart of the collapse of HIH Insurance. Owing billions, its implosion paralysed the insurance industry. Storm Financial conned people into borrowing against their assets to invest, on the pretext that they were safely providing for their retirement. Storm was only one of a number of dodgy financial services companies.

By the 2000s, unethical behaviour seemed baked into corporate business models. Convenience store giant 7-Eleven allegedly turned a blind eye to underpaying thousands of its vulnerable workers. It was only one of a number of iconic brands doing the same.

Bupa Aged Care collapsed the standards of care in its residential homes in the chase for profits. The toll of suffering across the sector led to the establishment of a royal commission. The 'big wigs' at Westpac were caught out inadvertently giving a green light to paedophiles.

But all four big banks had developed rotten cultures. Another royal commission got under way. Crown Resorts knowingly built its business model around attracting criminal elements, becoming a haven for money-laundering. The company was just too big and powerful for authorities to notice and take action. Star got caught for doing much the same.

No company was more powerful than News Corp. After a decade of waging a campaign that denied climate change, it wanted the public to believe that the disastrous 2019–20 bushfires were caused by arsonists. And recently things have only worsened for the company's tarnished reputation. And how could Rio Tinto top this list of 'cowboy' activity? By knowingly blowing up some of the most archeologically significant caves in the world. Preserving precious pre-history wasn't a company priority.

Of course, there are many well-run and ethical companies operating in Australia. But there's a dark side to corporate life, which this book explores.

I began researching bad corporation behaviour over a decade ago. In 2010, I became immersed in a project to unpack the power wielded by Gunns Ltd, Tasmania's largest employer and Australia's largest timber company. It was notorious for its capacity to wield power over many years at both state and federal levels. In 2003, it sought to add value to its forestry business by constructing a highly polluting mega pulp mill in the picturesque Tamar Valley in northern Tasmania. The proposal landed on the public as a *fait accompli*, the product of a secret meeting held between John Gay, Gunns' burly and belligerent CEO and chair, and Premier Paul Lennon, a 'hard man' of right-wing state Labor politics.

In the end, Gunns Ltd blundered its way into bankruptcy, saving the Tamar Valley from a totally inappropriate development.

My next encounter with the stark realities of corporate power was on an even larger scale. From 2016, I watched with horrified fascination the relentless efforts of Indian conglomerate Adani Ltd to gain approval from both the Queensland and federal governments for a mega coal mine in the Galilee Basin in central Queensland.

As I researched Adani's operations in India, alarm bells rang. Founder and chair Gautam Adani was a high-level political operator who, over decades, had benefitted from cosy, insider deals through his close relationship with Indian political strongman Narendra Modi, who went on to become India's Prime Minister.[3]

Adani had poor governance standards in its Indian operations and a shocking reputation for flouting environmental laws in that country.[4] Yet, the Queensland and federal governments embraced the conglomerate. The mine went ahead despite huge public protest.

This is the first book to explore corporate scandals as a continuous phenomenon of Australian society over the past four decades. Only by examining the older, well-known scandals side-by-side with the newer ones can we see the extent of the phenomenon. Taken together, hundreds of thousands of Australians have had their lives upended in the thirteen examples of corporate bad behaviour included in this book. So severe have many of the scandals been that faith in the free-market system has sometimes been called into question. And the impacts of individual scandals have often left a trail of traumatised victims. There's no shrinking from the nature of the unethical behaviour involved; it's frequently cold and calculating and contemptuous of anything but profits and status. Even though the consequences of bad corporate behaviour are there for all to see, the internal dynamics that produce this behaviour are often difficult to evaluate – unless a scandal has been the subject of official inquiry, in which case the public is let into the often sordid world of corporate culture. Such is the case in several of the examples in this book. In other cases, the dynamics of corporate culture remain opaque, making elusive any definitive judgments about some CEOs and boards.

Given the seriousness of the phenomenon of bad corporate culture, the book seeks to examine the causes of the continuous string of business scandals. It does so through a wide lens. Corporations, of course, sit within a system of power.

Australia has embraced the neo-liberal idea of allowing corporations maximum freedom with minimal responsibilities to wider society. Australia incorporated the so-called 'Friedman doctrine', the view associated with Nobel Prize–winning economist Milton Friedman, who, in the 1960s, argued that the only purpose of a corporation was to maximise shareholder wealth.[5] This is the root cause of the scandals examined in the book. The *Corporations Act 2001* stipulates that directors and executives should act in good faith and with care and diligence, that they should avoid improper use of information and position, and should disclose conflicts of interest. These obligations have not stopped the continual lurch into bad behaviour by many corporations.

In several of the case studies in this book, corporate scandals are linked to the power corporations wield, specifically their ability to capture key decision-making processes of the state to further their business models. In turn, this capacity undermines the integrity of the political system to uphold the public good. In a select number of cases, this process of undermining also assumes features of crony capitalism, a term used to describe the forging of close relations between powerful corporations and government. It's designed to deliver mutual benefits to both parties: corporations get favourable treatment in developing projects and governments derive campaign donations, opportunities for post-political careers and the ability to trumpet delivering jobs.

The fact that both state capture and crony capitalism have become normalised features of certain areas of the economy is important in understanding why some corporations go rogue. Why has gambling become rampant in society? Why did standards in aged care collapse? Why did banks betray so many of their customers? Why did the financial services industry sink into a reputational hole?

Inevitably, the question arises as the extent to which, in chasing their business models, corporations have corrupted our politics.

There's no agreed definition of corruption but it's generally seen to be a multi-layered phenomenon, beyond the simplified image of graft – politicians receiving brown paper bags stuffed with cash. None of the corporations examined in this book falls into this category. Rather, in some cases, corporations have undermined the integrity of our politics through a set of rules and practices legally set out for them. Although there are several exceptions, most of the corporations examined in the book played by these rules, but they overreach and scandals follow. My argument is that these rules – election donations, self-regulation, uncapped remuneration packages, weak lobbying regulations, the recruitment of retired politicians and limited public reporting requirements – are skewed in favour of corporate interests. Compounding the problem is weak enforcement of the limited provisions of the *Corporations Act*. With this framework in mind, I ask two overriding questions: What constitutes an ethical corporation? And why do so many fail to uphold community standards of ethical behaviour?

The book drills down into the scandals to explore the complex interplay of causes: the downside of free-market (neo-liberal) ideology; the ability of corporations to capture the state; the resort to unscrupulous corporate behaviour by senior management; and the timidity of regulators. Taken together, these elements suggest that the unspoken assumption has been that corporate interests must prevail for Australia to realise its potential.

Each scandal involved a unique interplay of causal factors; two or more factors can be found in each. In several, four are present. Within the interplay of underlying factors, I place special emphasis on the role played by corporate leaders. After all, they act like generals marshalling the troops and determining corporate strategy, often with huge ramifications for the nation. But why do boards so often fail to rein in aberrant CEOs and prevent corporations going bad? Most board members are establishment-type businessmen networked like a private club. I found board culture an intriguing issue to explore.

As mentioned, there is a plethora of corporate scandals from which to choose. The selection was based on several criteria. I wanted a historical perspective to trace patterns of causation. I wanted to draw on examples from different sectors of the economy to illustrate the breadth of the problem. I also wanted examples that highlight the serious consequences of unethical corporate behaviour. And lastly, I chose examples on the availability of source material.

Australia has been plagued by narcissistically inclined CEOs, toothless regulators, timid governments and shockingly negligent boards. But how do unethical behaviour and gross incompetence become entrenched in some of our largest and most iconic corporations? And how can we avoid the repetitious cycle of corporate scandals?

We can only begin to answer these questions by exploring the causes of the scandals that have dudded investors and cruelled the lives of countless ordinary Australians.

1

RIPPING OFF MEDIBANK AND MEDICARE: THE RISE OF CORPORATE MEDICINE

In October 2022, the ABC's *7.30* program aired a report on fraud in Medicare, Australia's widely supported universal health scheme. Investigative journalist Adele Ferguson, who has had a long and distinguished career exposing corporate abuse of power, interviewed experts in the medical profession who were talking publicly for the first time. She exposed a rotten underbelly in some of the nation's corporate medical practices: billing dead people, fabricating medical records, billing for unnecessary services. The cost to the public purse from these rip-offs is simply staggering: $8 billion a year, or 30 per cent of Medicare's total annual expenditure. Some practices were making hundreds of thousands in additional income. And they could get away with fraud on this scale because the scheme operated largely on an honour system: doctors were trusted to bill correctly. But as Ferguson's report showed, some medical practices 'see Medicare as a money pit, and they can just help themselves'.[1]

Federal Health Minister Mark Butler didn't waste any time setting up an independent inquiry into Medicare, which, at the time of writing, remains in progress. However, Ferguson's exposé was a case of *déjà vu*. One of federal Labor's most cherished reforms has been rorted from its very beginnings in the mid-1970s (as Medibank), its integrity undermined by the simultaneous rise of corporate medicine. Little had been done over the decades to learn the lessons about the fraudulent practices that developed and drove a significant section of the modern medical business model. And no figure was more central to either the rise of corporate medicine and its ethical failings than Geoffrey Edelsten. The flamboyant medical entrepreneur, a one-time darling of Australian media, was known for his gaudy tastes in cars, buxom young women and colourful clothing. He was a fixture of the 1980s fast money social set. Edelsten revolutionised medicine in Australia with his concept of 24-hour medical 'super clinics' in the mid-1980s. But Edelsten's innovative corporate medical business model was driven by greed – profits came before patients. And, in turn, the greed drove his fraudulent behaviour. He was willing to rip off the public to enrich himself. The lack of enforceable regulations allowed the culture to flourish.

Edelsten is an intriguing character. Conveniently, perhaps, he liked to refer to himself as an enigma.[2] From the time he gained notoriety for his ground-breaking super clinics, Edelsten was in the forefront of the celebrity model of entrepreneurs. with a fixation on projecting his lavish lifestyle. Edelsten was especially known for his passion for high-end cars. He gushed at the joy his stable of cars brought him: a Porsche, a Lamborghini, a Ferrari, two Maseratis, a Rolls-Royce Corniche. Two sides to Edelsten became fused in the public mind: the show-off and the disruptive innovator.

Creating a new medical business model

For a noted show-off and fraudster, Edelsten came from a very conventional background. Born in 1943, he was the grandson of Jewish European refugees fleeing anti-semitism, and the son of successful small business owners. Esther and Hymie built Melbourne's first lingerie chain. Obviously possessed of entrepreneurial flair, they were otherwise a conservative, private couple who winced at the publicity their son attracted.

One clue to Edelsten's personality came from his oldest friend, David Wolff, who had known Edelsten since childhood. He had always known his friend as a charming person – 'shy, unassuming, polite'. Why then did he court so much publicity, Wolff was asked by journalist Jane Cadzow, who was writing a profile on Edelsten. 'Without sounding too harsh,' Wolff explained, 'it's egomania.'[3]

Both Edelsten's talents and flaws emerged in the early 1970s, when he and a fellow medical graduate, Tom Wenkart, together set out to revolutionise medicine. They had burst onto the business scene seemingly out of nowhere. At medical school they were known as 'whiz kid doctors'.[4] They shared similar personality traits: intelligence, charm and ambition. Edelsten claimed that he was the ideas man behind their partnership while Wenkart was 'the fine detail partner'.[5] Together they 'wanted to focus on financial growth' through medicine.[6] But whereas Wenkart preferred to stay out of the limelight, with the consequence that little is known about his personal life, Edelsten craved attention.

Their new medical technology company, Preventicare, was groundbreaking and showed the best of entrepreneurial innovation. Some claimed it was a world-first. Doctors were offered the opportunity to rent 'typewriter-like terminals' from IBM linking them, in turn, to a $3.5 million computer at the IBM centre in Sydney. Doctors were able to courier pathology tests to specialists who would provide results at the doctor's computer terminal within hours, rather than the weeks such test results typically took. It was essentially a system of health screening made possible by technological advances in testing and analysis, journalist Margaret Rice argued: 'the new tools of diagnosis made a utopian dream – preventing illness by catching it before it started – seem possible'.[7] The technology was 'a thing of the future', gushed one doctor at a seminar dedicated to the new approach.[8] GPs could also store their patients' records on the computerised system. With the equipment installed free of charge, along with a nurse to oversee the process, doctors started signing up in droves. Six hundred signed on in the first year of operation.[9] The system had the significant advantage of efficiency by enhancing the role of the general practitioner at the centre of diagnosis and treatment.[10]

However, a few 'old school' medical practitioners believed Preventicare would increase the use of both medical and pathology services; that, in the name of efficiency, doctors might be tempted to ramp up their use of testing.[11] In her 2004 study of medical fraud, Kathryn Flynn, a PhD student and later lecturer at Wollongong University, found that Preventicare stimulated overservicing through Edelsten and Wenkart's offer of inducements to general practitioners of computers and nursing staff. As a consequence, a spike occurred in the number of pathology tests.[12] But overservicing is a problematic concept because medicine is an inexact science and, as a consequence, the term is ambiguous. Edelsten and Wenkart sparked what turned into a decades-long debate about what constitutes medical fraud. Wenkart went on to found Macquarie Health and build it into a medical empire. He was never found to have engaged in overservicing.

In their joint business venture, Edelsten and Wenkart had big plans for the future. They wanted to sign on doctors across the country and they saw the opportunity to install their computer screening system in factories and pharmacies. However, they encountered a headwind: the company had grown so quickly that it had liquidity problems purchasing the expensive equipment.[13] And private health funds baulked at paying out for rising services.[14] Even before the introduction of Medibank in 1975, the private health industry was worried about the rising incidence of overservicing.[15] Despite the glowing reception it received, Preventicare went into liquidation after fifteen months, although Wenkart revived the company several years later. Edelsten claimed that he sold out his share to Wenkart for several million dollars.[16]

Years later, Wenkart explained that while Edelsten was hard-working and dedicated, he nevertheless upset fellow doctors: 'He was colourful, he was extreme, he was not liked by the profession in general and certainly not by its conservative leaders.' Edelsten, he elaborated, wasn't popular with his creditors either because he was a 'very slow payer' and was 'pretty flippant about cash flow' with a tendency to over-extend himself. Wenkart got the impression that up-market auto dealers gleefully rubbed their hands when they saw him coming. If Edelsten had his chequebook with him when he walked into a showroom, he was likely to drive away in a fancy new vehicle: 'He's got a manic streak, there's no argument.'[17]

Dangerous spaces

When Edelsten formally broke with Wenkart after the collapse of Preventicare, his career took a decidedly different and dangerous turn. While continuing to work as a doctor and owner of several GP clinics, he was seduced into the gambling industry. He began gambling in casinos – both legal and illegal – and on horse racing, including race fixing. In his 2011 autobiography, he described these experiences as his introduction 'to a very corrupt world'.[18]

Edelsten's attraction to the destructive world of heavy gambling revealed other sides to his complex persona. He was undoubtedly a narcissistic-type personality. Corporate governance expert Brain Tayan provides insights into this personality typology. On the one hand, he writes, narcissistic CEOs have an 'inflated sense of self-importance, and excessive need for attention and admiration, and lack empathy'. But, he cautions, such traits are not dissimilar from 'confident, dynamic or transformative leaders'. The two typologies are not synonymous, Tayan adds, but it can be hard to tell them apart.[19]

Edelsten's personality straddled this definitional fault line. A noted medical innovator, he had an unmistakable need for admiration and attention, and he was a risk-taker unconcerned about abiding by the rules.

Edelsten was thrilled at trying to beat the odds and projecting an image of the successful gambler. 'I really enjoyed the fun – and the risks of gambling,' he wrote. And: 'Dressed in black leather jacket I could be seen at the races placing large amounts of money'.[20] And he was untroubled by the ethics of race fixing. In a revealing passage from his autobiography, he wrote that while he thought 'the whole thing was illegal', he was 'merely following up on an anonymous tip'.[21] The New South Wales Medical Tribunal later assessed Edelsten as someone who demonstrated 'a lack of insight into his behaviour'.[22] This lack of insight is crucial to understanding Edelsten's personality. His life would regularly take unpredictable and often disastrous turns, the consequences of which he continually brushed aside.

In 1975, flush with money from the deal with Wenkart and no doubt from gambling, Edelsten decided to open a nightclub. Spending over $1 million, he opened The Centrefold, a flashy establishment in Sydney's Kings Cross with a capacity to entertain a thousand people. It became 'a place to be seen', he wrote. And it fed Edelsten's swelling ego:

> As I strolled around the premises in the first few weeks after the grand opening, attended by models and actresses with the sound of champagne corks popping and the occasional balloon bursting, I felt like a king.[23]

How much Edelsten knew about the corrupt world he had entered cannot be gauged. But the success of his club drew the attention of notorious criminal figures. In fact, clubs were a prominent feature of Sydney's underworld. The year before Edelsten opened The Centrefold, a royal commission had been held into allegations of organised crime in clubs. Justice Athol Moffitt confirmed what many had already suspected; that organised crime had infiltrated registered clubs. The Liberal government led by Robert Askin had turned a blind eye to the problem.[24]

Edelsten became enmeshed in this world. It brought him into contact with two well-known underworld identities. One was Jack Rooklyn, the poker machine entrepreneur. He had amassed fabulous wealth from his control of 50 per cent of the New South Wales poker machine market. A key figure in the establishment sport of ocean racing, the burly Rooklyn appeared to be untouchable. However, in 1992 he was convicted retrospectively of bribing bagman Jack Herbert, a Queensland police officer, and also Terry Lewis, the corrupt Queensland police chief,[25] to protect Rooklyn's illegal gambling operations in the state.

Abe Saffron, notorious Sydney crime boss, was the other underworld figure to cross Edelsten's path.

Both Rooklyn and Saffron tried to extract payments from Edelsten to keep him free of trouble, meaning avoiding raids from the police. Edelsten claims he was aware of the awe in which both underworld figures were held, but this didn't stop him from being enticed into dealing with them. He claims to have had a phone call from Rooklyn but actually met with Saffron. As Edelsten later wrote: 'When these kinds of people intrude into your life, when they ask you to meet them, you keep the appointment'.[26] It's hard to believe that an enterprising doctor, with a busy practice, was prepared to engage with the likes of Abe Saffron who, for decades, had had allegations of corruption and criminality floating around him like a toxic odor.

Saffron was Australia's version of Al Capone; a dangerous criminal who was never convicted of anything more than tax evasion. He served one seventeen-month stint in jail. But he was a linchpin in Sydney's network of organised crime. Hovering around him like vultures were a coterie of corrupt officials – policemen, licensing authorities and none other than NSW Premier Sir Robert Askin, who protected Saffron's operations in the inner-city suburb of Kings Cross where Saffron owned just about every brothel, strip club and bar. From here, Saffron ruled over a business empire like the head of a Mafia family.[27] His criminal activities extended into arson, insurance fraud, blackmail and extortion. He built an impregnable wall around these illegal activities by letting his bovver boys do the dirty work and by having a bevy of police officers on his payroll. Just how important political protection was to this brutal operator remains unclear, with Askin's role in Sydney's corrupt underworld attracting conflicting findings.[28]

In his autobiography, Edelsten claimed that he rejected the demands of both Saffron and Rooklyn, but much of what he says in this book is widely thought to be unreliable.[29] Nevertheless, Edelsten claims that Saffron organised police raids on his club because he, Edelsten, was unknowingly operating without a liquor licence. In any event, the club became a burden, so he sold it.

While Edelsten immersed himself in the glitzy, menacing world of clubs and gambling, he was also operating as a respected doctor with on-going ambitions to be a medical entrepreneur. But by now, the risky side of his personality, marked by a self-confidence that he could get away with dodgy behaviour, seemed to have become entrenched. In fact, as early as 1974, Edelsten placed an advertisement in the *Sydney Morning Herald* seeking a young medical graduate who would be paid to 'sell services to general practitioners'. This was interpreted as Edelsten seeking to develop a system of kickbacks from GPs to use designated pathology providers. Edelsten was also operating a pathology business – Omnimann Pty Ltd – as a sideline. He could become a 'pathology provider' simply by paying his $10 fee to the Health Commission. He was identified by the phone number placed with the advertisement.[30] Although kickbacks weren't made illegal until 1977, it was clearly a shady practice.

In 1976, Edelsten's association with pathology and the rorting of Medibank was inadvertently aired in a court case. In a financial dispute between himself and another company, it was revealed that Edelsten was operating a pathology company that was extracting nearly $600 000 per month from Medibank.[31] That Edelsten remained involved in the pathology business after his split with Wenkart shows his astute understanding of the rich pickings to be had as a medical 'entrepreneur'. Pathology underwent huge growth after the introduction of Medibank. Benefits paid to the industry doubled in the first twelve months of the scheme's operation. Doctors' need for a return on the purchase of expensive equipment drove excessive testing.[32]

Claims of rorting: Universal healthcare

Despite its initial failure, Preventicare was the medical equivalent of the canary in the coalmine – a harbinger of what was to come when government-funded universal healthcare was introduced several years after Edelsten and Wenkart unleashed their innovation. The Whitlam government introduced Medibank in 1975, which was abolished by the subsequent Coalition government led by Malcolm Fraser. In 1984, the Hawke government reintroduced the scheme, renamed Medicare.

Soon after its introduction, overservicing became an entrenched part of Australia's publicly funded universal healthcare system. In the early 1980s, official estimates put the cost of overservicing at around 7 per cent of total outlays on Medibank, but others regarded this figure as the tip of the iceberg.[33]

Doctors involved in overservicing in the early years of universal healthcare engaged in one or more of several practices: ordering far more sophisticated tests than were warranted; phantom treatments; assembly-line processing; requiring more patient consultations than were necessary; upgrading the level of treatment actually provided; and finding an excuse for conducting a superfluous number of home visits. Doctors asked some patients to sign blank payment forms.[34] Yet, to compound the problem of policing, not all such practices necessarily constituted a deliberate attempt to defraud Medibank, unless the scale of the practices was abnormally high.

Overservicing was a complex problem to solve, and successive governments dragged their collective feet in tackling the problem. It was largely a case of regulatory failure. Neither Medibank nor Medicare was designed with a stringent regulatory system to manage the programs. Consequently, there was a lack of legislative powers to deal with abuse of medical benefits. Not surprisingly, therefore, the Health Department was slow to address the problem.[35]

Attempts to enhance accountability were met by powerful counter-attacks by doctors.

Given the difficulties of reining in the medical profession, health authorities became defensive, preferring 'printing cheques to claimants in the interests of "efficiency" rather than in developing expensive programs to contain the abuse of medical benefits'.[36] Medical entrepreneurs with high-risk personal profiles filled the regulatory vacuum. It was left to whistleblowers and the media to expose abuses. As revelations spilled out into the media, the public were shocked at the extent of the abuse. Claims that doctors rorted the system and were more concerned with profit than patient care were at odds with the profession's avuncular image.

Edelsten was in the forefront of developing an integrated medical business model linking general practice and the emerging profession of pathology. Regulations governing pathology contained a convenient loophole. Under the *Heath Insurance Act 1973*, pathology was only minimally regulated; the main requirement was that, for the purposes of medical rebates, a pathology provider had to be approved. However, gaining approval into the profession was as easy as becoming a member of a sporting club. Application was made via a telephone call to the Health Department requesting the relevant form, which was filled out with payment of a fee of $10. There were no questions asked.[37]

As a consequence, pathology providers proliferated. By the mid-1980s, at least 3000 were operating across the country, nearly 70 per cent of whom did hardly any pathology at all: 'The great majority of pathology companies are a mystery to the Royal College of Pathologists', according to Dr Peter Roache, a fellow of the College.[38] The sector came to be dominated by several dozen top providers, and the industry remained throughout the 1980s as 'basically unregulated by the Commonwealth'.[39] Significant loopholes existed for rogue operators.

Just how far Edelsten exploited this system is hard to determine. However, in 1977, he unsuccessfully tried to stop publication of a story in Sydney's *The Sun* newspaper that an unnamed doctor had claimed more than $3 million from Medibank. The problem for Edelsten was that the same article referred to the doctor in question as having invested in a nightclub.[40] Edelsten thought he'd been unjustifiably identified.

If the claims made by *The Sun* were only approximately accurate, it highlighted the systemic problem of overservicing in Medibank and the lack of attention from the federal government to curb the problem. Overservicing had even been given a name – 'Medibank rip-offs'.[41] In 1977, no one knew the extent of the problem, but it was assumed at the time to have only been a small number of Australia's then 20 000-strong medical profession. With only thirty cases ever having been referred to the Commonwealth Police in the first few years of the scheme, the chances of getting caught seemed slim. In all likelihood, Edelsten was a central player in the racket of ripping off Medibank.

Over the next decade, Edelsten cemented his links to the pathology industry and forged ahead with plans to transform medicine from a cottage industry into a slick, lucrative and, in his mind, efficient professional business.

The Liberace of the medical profession

In the mid-1980s, Edelsten hit upon another entrepreneurial innovation and became one of the most significant disrupters in the history of Australian medicine. In 1984, he found a way to break open the cottage industry model of medicine by redefining how GPs delivered services. At the time, all GPs were either solo operators or part of small practices. They were encased in a cultural image of 'benign father figures, devoted to their patients'.[42] However, as Edelsten realised, the reality was quite different. 'Doctors' surgeries were, to many people', he wrote, 'grim, austere places, where they sat on plastic chairs, listening to others coughing and wishing they could get the hell out of there as soon as possible.' Many were carved out of the front rooms of their family home and were ruled by a 9-to-5 mentality;[43] many doctors took Wednesday afternoons off. Outside these strict hours, patients had to wait hours in the emergency department of the local hospital or find a locum.[44]

Edelsten imagined what patients might want from a visit to their GP: 'I knew that if I offered patients a stylish home away from home, even if it was just for an hour or so, they [patients] would actually enjoy a visit to the doctor'. He introduced to the public the revolutionary idea of the 24-hour state-of-the-art super clinic, staffed with a team of doctors, offering a range of medical services, and bulk-billing their patients from Medicare so that a visit to the doctor was free. But Edelsten added a brilliant public relations touch to his disruptive idea: to make a visit to the GP not just enjoyable but fun.

The first of Edelsten's super clinics opened in Baulkham Hills in western Sydney in 1984 and expansion of the concept followed in quick time. Importantly, his were the first medical clinics in Australia to bulk-bill patients. Clinics were decked out with a grand piano, accompanied by a pianist, chandeliers and couches made of a pink material resembling mink. Gold-clad hostesses and small robots offered refreshments and educational advice to patients, who were told that 'if they wait more than 10 minutes to be attended to they are entitled to a free Instant Lottery ticket'.[45]

Edelsten's model had immediate impact. Patients flocked to the new clinics; passers-by pressed their noses into the windows of the clinics to catch a glimpse of the glitz and the glamour. Edelsten was quickly named the Liberace of medicine.[46] But opposition to the model was fierce. Traditional family GPs, fearful of losing out to 'an invasion of medical empires', bristled that Edelsten was an outsider, a non-establishment upstart.[47] Up went the cry that the clinics were 'prostituting' the profession, that Edelsten was the 'Hugh Heffner of medicine'.[48]

A more compelling criticism came from advocates of Community Health Centres, who warned that the super clinic model was based on 'overcare', rather than preventative health care, and that they were designed to maximise profit from Medicare.[49] Allegations that some of Edelsten's clinics saw a thousand patients a day were publicly aired.[50] Overall, Edelsten's thirty-two clinics saw 1.5 million patients per annum; he was 'the busiest doctor in Australia'.[51] His network of clinics was the first clear manifestation of the corporatisation of medicine in Australia.[52] And he'd developed a model that could reap maximum benefit from exploiting overservicing both through regular contact with patients and through his relationship to the pathology side of medicine.

Criticisms were brushed aside as Edelsten opened more clinics across the eastern states. The expansion was facilitated by borrowed money. Edelsten had a casual relationship with his creditors, as if in his mind the loans were somehow fictitious. Max Donnelly, the bankruptcy trustee later charged with distributing Edelsten's assets when he declared himself bankrupt in 1987, described Edelsten's approach: 'Everyone thought he was a man of great substance but there wasn't really a lot behind it', he explained. Donnelly went on to say that Edelsten had built his network of clinics on borrowed money. However, with each new loan, 'he'd make the first payment and then just didn't make any more. It was a bizarre sort of scenario'.[53]

Nevertheless, the success of Edelsten's super clinics made him rich and famous. While his model was genuinely innovative and would have been successful as a legitimate business, Edelsten continued to be dogged by claims that he was fraudulently exploiting Medicare by overservicing, gouging the system for higher payments than were warranted by continuing to exploit the loopholes in the pathology industry. Health Department records from 1985 show that Edelsten was reaping $5 million annually from Medicare payments; or in excess of $15 million in today's money.[54]

He began to project his life as a fairytale, which captured even more publicity. In 1988, he married the first of his three wives: nineteen-year-old Leanne Nesbitt. Edelsten was forty-five at the time. That marriage lasted only three years, after which Edelsten moved on to marry twenty-six-year-old Brynne Gordon. He lavished his wives with designer clothes and jewellery. Home was a fifteen-room, $6 million Sydney mansion where Edelsten housed his collection of luxury cars and where, on the sprawling front garden, he kept a helicopter for his personal use. Edelsten and his various wives were instantly recognisable whenever they went for a spin in one of the high-end cars; the personalised number plates were inscribed 'SEXY', 'GROOVY' and 'FAMOUS'.[55] To some, the Edelstens were a gauche couple, and Geoffrey 'a quintessential Sydney spiv'.[56] But much of the broader public loved the glimpses the media offered into their lives. Years later, first wife Leanne explained her belief that both she and Brynne were merely part of Edelsten's business strategy to court publicity.[57]

Attracting publicity was central to Edelsten's career. He was smart enough to make garnering media attention a key part of his business success. As one commentator noted:

> His stock in trade was sensation: the swaggering gesture, the flamboyant action, the bravura venture, all designed to turn heads, create debate, engender controversy and ensure that whatever project he was involved with was front and centre in the public eye.[58]

But he seems to have had no insight into how his craving for publicity fed the reckless side of his personality. Behind the glare of Edelsten's luminous public image, he was living multiple, separate lives: the dedicated doctor committed to the welfare of his patients; the restless and innovative entrepreneur; the clever fraudster; and the Peter Pan-like figure caught up in his own teenage fantasies.

Edelsten's fame soared even further when he purchased the struggling Sydney Swans AFL team for $6.5 million, the first private ownership deal struck in the competition. The AFL needed to draw maximum publicity to the Swans in a city dominated by rugby. Ever the showman, Edelsten fitted the bill.[59]

However, buying the Swans was just another scam for Edelsten, as Bob Pritchard, the Swans marketing manager, later explained. At a lavish party held at Edelsten's mansion on the night he became the Swan's new owner, Pritchard claimed that, amid the celebrations and the media throng, 'Geoff said to me "Mate, I don't have any money"'.[60] It was typical of Edelsten's impetuous nature to have spent big to satisfy his ego and not worry about the consequences. Somehow the money had been cobbled together and Edelsten's association with the Swans gave his surgeries additional publicity.[61] And it boosted the gaudy, fast-paced, fairy-tale lifestyle which had become an integral part of his image.

The tactic worked; the media lapped up the string of sensations. But critics were proved right: Edelsten was deploying overservicing and unethical practices as his business model. In 1984, ABC's *Four Corners* program devoted an episode to Edelsten's tattoo removal clinic, which he had recently opened as a sideline. Journalist Chris Masters examined claims that Edelsten's clinic was involved in a number of botched tattoo removals. Titled 'Branded', the episode found that Edelsten's clinic had engaged in misleading advertising about the safety of new laser technology and had failed to train staff in its safe use. As was often the case, Edelsten liked to boast about his expertise; that he was the only medical practitioner in Australia performing tattoo removal with an argon laser and that he had developed 'an unusual expertise' in the procedure.[62]

But the reality was very different. As a consequence of his actions, a number of clients received third-degree burns, were left in crippling pain and with scarring that was uglier than the original tattoo. In addition, Masters discovered that Edelsten was claiming twice the allowable rebate from Medicare by assigning a code number with a higher rebate.[63]

In fact, Masters had been given leaked documents supplied by unofficial confidential sources in the Department of Health that Edelsten was both delegating the tattoo procedures to a nurse rather than performing them himself and then also charging in excess of the Medicare schedule fee.[64] For his trouble, Masters was threatened by Edelsten's underworld figures.[65]

In 1985, Senator Chris Puplick released the contents of a leaked memo from Edelsten to his surgeries which expressed concern that

> despite awareness that patients were waiting, there appeared to be little effort in 'speeding up'. It stated that patients were not being asked to make appointments which was essential as 'patients believe if you ask them to return, that you are interested in them'. The memo went on to say that 'charm' was extraordinarily important and that utilisation of X-ray facilities was 'far from optimum'.[66]

But Edelsten faced an even more threatening problem than allegations of overservicing.

Engaging a hit man

At the time the *Four Corners* program went to air, Edelsten was dealing with one particularly troublesome tattoo client; the fallout would have grave consequences. In 1980, Raymond Keith Roach, then known as Stephen Evans, underwent tattoo removal from Edelsten which went badly wrong. Roach, who suffered from chronic anxiety and depression, unsuccessfully tried to sue Edelsten. Years of torment followed. Roach's Housing Commission flat was broken into and he was jailed for three months after Edelsten claimed that Roach had been demanding money from him in a menacing manner. Roach later denied this claim.[67]

Where the truth lies in their fractious relationship is impossible to determine, but Edelsten's reaction to Roach's anger was extreme to say the least. He contacted hit man Christopher Dale Flannery, who happened to be one of his patients, to try and fix the problem. In fact,

Flannery's wife later claimed that her husband was also a victim of a botched tattoo removal at Edelsten's clinic. She said that Flannery's wounds smelt 'really bad like dead meat', he was nauseous, dizzy and had 'lumps under one arm' and was vomiting and 'really hot'.[68] For some reason Flannery didn't take out his anger on Edelsten. In fact, Edelsten wrote in his autobiography that the two had enjoyed a frank chat about Flannery's occupation and he invoked a sense of naivety when Flannery told him that he earned $10 000 for a bashing and $50 000 for a killing. 'I knew he had to be joking', explained Edelsten, who was familiar with Sydney's underworld.[69] Joking aside, Edelsten cemented his ties to Flannery by offering the hit man a medical certificate to delay a court appearance in a murder trial so as to avoid a certain judge. In fact, the certificate that Edelsten issued stated that his tattoo removal operation had resulted in an infection that rendered him too ill to attend court.[70]

Flannery's nickname, 'Mr Rent-a-Kill', left nothing to the imagination about the potential danger he posed as 'a contract killer willing to murder for the right price'.[71] He had a violent background, having been jailed for rape in Victoria in the 1970s. On release he became a bouncer at a St Kilda nightclub before graduating to contract killing and becoming a major part of the gang wars that gripped Sydney during the 1970s and early '80s.

Unbeknown to Edelsten, his phone was being tapped by the National Crime Authority, although it's not clear which of Edelsten's nefarious activities attracted the attention of the crime-busting agency. Nevertheless, these recordings revealed Edelsten answering wife Leanne's question about Flannery: 'Bashing up people, is that all he does?' 'No, he kills people,' Edelsten replied. 'Nice young fella.'[72] Edelsten claimed that the phone call to Leanne was made 'simply to reassure her that heavy moves were being made to remove an extortionist from our lives'.[73] Edelsten didn't explain what exactly 'heavy' meant in his mind.

Not long after his dealings with Edelsten, Flannery disappeared.

On the morning of 9 May 1985, Flannery, according to his wife, left home frightened and nervous, armed with a .38 calibre pistol, probably cocked and tucked into his belt, and disappeared into thin air.[74] His body has never been found.

Dr X

By the time the Commonwealth Joint Committee on Public Accounts on Medical Fraud and Overservicing – Pathology released its report in September 1986, Edelsten's life had long been a roller-coaster ride. Wealth, glamour and media fame had sat alongside claims of medical malpractice and overservicing and his dark links to the underworld. Edelsten's notoriety rose after the *Four Corners* program into his tattoo business. Medical fraud and overservicing 'now had a colourful figure to capture public attention'.[75]

With the release of the Joint Committee's report, Edelsten's name was again splashed across the media. The committee's findings included a case study of a 'medical entrepreneur' whose activities were of great concern to both the medical profession and the government. The committee called the entrepreneur 'Dr X':

> This particular general practitioner operates a large complex commercial practice which, among other things, includes several suburban clinics. Each of these clinics refers almost all their pathology tests to Y Pty Ltd – a pathology company owned and operated by Dr X.[76]

The committee argued this integrated approach was a model designed for ripping off Medicare. The evidence suggested, they wrote, that the current record on pathology and prior corporate dealings characterise the 'profit first' motive of the group'.[77] The committee's findings add another layer of complexity in understanding the scope of Edelsten's use and abuse of pathology. He was using both his own company structure as well as Wenkart's to handle pathology testing, the clear implication being that the volume of use throughout his clinics was very high.

The day after the report was tabled in the Senate, Queensland Labor Senator George Georges identified Edelsten as Dr X in the chamber. In doing so, he said that sufficient information had been 'thrown around this chamber' to identify Edelsten as Dr X. Predictably, Edelsten denied the claim, saying that the allegations had been thrown at him because he had 'upset some of the conservatives' of the medical profession.[78] He called for an inquiry into his case. Not surprisingly, perhaps, his protestations were in vain.

However, health authorities didn't instigate charges against Edelsten. The Health Department was still struggling to devise an appropriate means to deal with overservicing. Its experiment of deploying police monitoring techniques to spy on doctors and patients was discovered by the Joint Committee and roundly condemned. And, even though the Hawke government doubled the resources devoted to fraud and overservicing in the financial year 1984–85, it took several years to train the necessary staff.[79] Doctors continued to be 'counselled' rather than prosecuted. Others argued that the slowness of this response reflected a 'capitulation in the face of pressure from the organized medical profession'.[80]

Despite the lack of concerted action by authorities, the Joint Committee report was the beginning of the end for Edelsten's reputation. In fact, by the end of 1986 his life was imploding. He was being pursued not only by the Medical Tribunal but also by the tax office, which demanded payment of $1.5 million in back taxes. Compounding the tarnishing of his public image, he had also been shafted from his position as chair of the Sydney Swans and the calls he had made to Flannery had been played to the Stewart Royal Commission into drug trafficking held between 1981 and 1983.

Edelsten declared himself bankrupt in 1987 and sold off his medical clinics. Bankrupted on several occasions throughout his life,

Edelsten was found to have 'misled both the taxation office and his creditors concerning the nature and extent of his assets'.[81]

Edelsten was now unable to maintain his flamboyant lifestyle and moved into a flat behind one of his surgeries.[82] As he said himself: 'The pressures on me were enormous, tearing away at me personally'.[83] However, the wheels of justice continued to turn.

In November 1988, Edelsten was deregistered by the New South Wales Medical Tribunal. He was found not to be a person of good character. The assessment was based on evidence that he had induced doctors in his corporate medical practice to overservice patients; in other words, to rip off Medicare. Edelsten was also found to have contacted Flannery to intimidate a former patient. And he had allowed an untrained person to perform laser surgery. In a searing assessment of his character, the Tribunal found that the root cause of Edelsten's deregistration was his own 'professional misconduct and criminal behaviour'.[84] He was banned from registering as a medical practitioner for ten years. Several years later he was deregistered in Victoria.[85]

In 1990, Edelsten was convicted on the Flannery charges and jailed. It was all too much for Leanne who, even though now divorced from Edelsten, sat behind him during the trial and wept silently as the verdict was read out.[86] A headline in the *Sydney Morning Herald* on 28 July passed on news of the judgment in the bluntest way possible: 'Verdict to End Edelsten's Flamboyant Career'.

Edelsten was humiliated in the grim walls of Sydney's Long Bay jail: 'Everyone knew who I was and at first they had all taken a great deal of mocking pleasure … in seeing a man they regarded as a high-flier reduced to this'.[87] The tone, of course, is self-pitying.

Later on, Edelsten built another fortune as a non-practising medical director of GP clinics through his new company, Allied Medical Group, which he sold in 2011 for a reported $120 million.[88] By this stage, he had developed a full-blown vertically integrated model of corporate medicine that showed his on-going drive for profits before patients. In a newspaper article in 2000 he wrote about 'the enormous economies of scale' that could be reaped by merging GP practices and vertically integrating them with radiology, pathology, visiting specialists, and day-care and in-patient hospital facilities. This model, he wrote, delivers 'extraordinary profits'.[89]

By now, his talent for entrepreneurial medicine was beyond dispute. But his personal life continued to lurch from one disaster to another. Vast wealth sparked another downfall.[90] Embarking on a spending spree, he blew an estimated $63 million on dud business ventures in the United States and on his incurable addiction to the high life. Rumours resurfaced about his connections to organised crime figures, who, it was said, delivered cash in brown paper bags 'in a bid to keep the various plates spinning'.[91] Inevitably, the creditors came knocking. Edelsten went bankrupt in the US in 2014.

In the same year Edelsten was accused in a US court of orchestrating the stabbing and bashing of a former US business partner with whom he had been feuding over business assets. While nothing came of the alleged incident, it was eerily reminiscent of the Flannery episode.

In 2015, Edelsten's third and last wife, Gabi Grecko, accused him of 'domestically abusing' her by pushing her and twisting her arm during their bitter split.[92] Grecko called the police but, finding neither of the pair injured, they did not press any charges.

And, as Edelsten aged, he seemed to grow ever more into a parody of his Peter Pan self, which became centred around his colourfully dyed hair and attention-grabbing clothing, such as a canary-yellow suit. He remained a human headline until his lonely death in 2021. His was an early example of the value of public relations to corporate success. In the days before public relations experts were embedded in corporate business models, Edelsten acted as his own one-man publicity machine. But his career was a reminder too, that entrepreneurs will find new avenues to exploit and that large-scale government programs are highly vulnerable to exploitation. In rorting Medicare,

Edelsten showed both sides of an entrepreneur: the innovative and the ruthless.

All the while, Medicare fraud has remained an unsolved problem. Despite its obvious benefits, turning such an essential service such as medicine into a profit-driven corporate model carries inherent risks. In fact, Edelsten's career stands as a warning about the capacity of smart but unethical entrepreneurs to exploit the emerging era of big government.

2

EMPIRE OF DEBT: BOND CORPORATION

In April 1988, Alan Bond visited the home of his arch business rival Robert Holmes à Court to discuss a deal to purchase the latter's share in the flagship company, Bell Resources. It must have been a strained meeting – neither liked the other. Their personalities couldn't have been more different. Holmes à Court – the tall, urbane, cerebral, quietly spoken and unflappable corporate raider who claimed lineage to British aristocracy – faced off against the gauche, brash, boisterous Bond. Born into the British working class, Bond, who had migrated to Australia with his family in 1950 as an eleven-year-old boy, loved the glare of publicity and flaunting his wealth. But both men were in the same dire predicament – how to survive the crippling sharemarket crash of six months before. Both had built corporate empires on the shifting sands of high borrowings offset by rising sharemarket prices. They were two of the biggest corporate cowboys who dominated business in the 1980s – others included John Elliott, Christopher Skase, John Spalvins, Rodney Adler, Sir Ron Brierley and Laurie Connell. But for this entire cohort, the wild 1980s decade of Australian business had ended on 19 October 1987, 'Black Monday', when the sharemarket fell off a cliff, wrecking the business model.

Only two years previously, Holmes à Court had been crowned Australia's first billionaire. During the 1970s, he had sliced his way through the establishment with daring raids on some of the country's leading companies, including, on four separate occasions, the 'holy of holies', BHP. He had developed a fearsome reputation in the game of corporate takeovers: striking swiftly but with an air of grace.[1] All the while he'd remained an enigma; building an empire and indulging in racehorses and fine art seemed to be his only interests.

Bond, of course, had been crowned a national hero following his 1983 America's Cup yachting victory and, among the credits of his sprawling conglomerate, Bond Corporation, was his status as the world's fourth largest brewer.

Bond and Holmes à Court had ridden the wave of a rising share market and enjoyed the adulation of the Australian press.[2] But now each was haemorrhaging funds. Both thought their route to emerging from the financial carnage rested on a deal over ownership of Bell Resources. For his part, Holmes à Court had Westpac breathing down his neck, threatening to throw him into a rapid liquidation sale.[3] More than any of the other corporate cowboys, he realised the grave implications of the crash.[4] Bond, on the other hand, misread the signs and was bent on expansion.[5]

Having already purchased nearly 20 per cent of Bell Resources, Bond viewed the company as a prized asset. After the crash it remained in the top ten of Australian stocks.[6] Bond's bid to gain control required him to borrow a further $400 million. He had in mind a daring scheme to rip the cash out of Bell Resources in a desperate bid to fill the black hole in his company's books. Bond was conjuring his reputation as 'the most swashbuckling' of the eighties entrepreneurs in conceiving such an audacious and fraudulent scheme, which set out to defraud Bell's shareholders and deceive regulators in a series of transactions that moved $1 billion out of Bell, funds that were never returned.

But Bond had bigger plans for the Bell Resources cash than simply staving off the collapse of Bond Corporation. He planned to use some of the cash to snare an even bigger prize – a takeover bid for Lonrho, a British company owned by one of the world's most feared corporate raiders, British tycoon 'Tiny' Rowland. Bond was in his typical gambler's mode – addicted to the thrill of chasing deals using other people's money and indifferent to the consequences.

Back at Bond Corporation headquarters on St George's Terrace, in the flashy tower Bond had emblazoned with his name, the scheme to defraud Bell's shareholders was secretly executed. Bond ran the company. He was both CEO and chair of the board. His inner circle of loyal (some might say slavish) corporate executives – Peter Beckwith, Peter Mitchell and Tony Oates – also acted as directors. All attended a meeting in October 1988 – signing off on the minutes – which discussed the intention to move ahead with a 'loan' from Bell to Bond Corporation without any consultation with Bell shareholders.[7]

The extent of the involvement of Bond's directors in defrauding Bell Resources became the subject of legal action when, years later, they faced charges. Both Mitchell and Oates pleaded guilty to misusing their positions as directors but had the more serious charge of conspiracy to defraud dropped. Beckwith died before facing any potential charges.

Over a six-week period, Oates authorised 'back-to-back' loans through a friendly intermediary.[8] The fraud was concealed by misleading Bell Resources shareholders, as well as hiding the loans from the stock exchange and the National Companies and Securities Commission (NCSC), the corporate regulator at the time.[9] Throughout the sordid saga, Holmes à Court was on the board of Bell Resources and did nothing to stop the fraud.[10] Holmes à Court died of a heart attack not long afterwards, on 2 September 1990.

In what was an essentially simple heist, $1.2 billion was poured into Bond Corporation straight out of the coffers of Bell Resources. A depleted Bell Resources collapsed and the raid failed to save Bond Corporation, which went bankrupt in mid-1991. However, the details of the fraud took eight years to emerge publicly. At much the same time that Bond Corporation went down, Bond's private company, Dallhold Investments, which had creamed millions from Bond Corporation, went into liquidation owing $500 million to creditors. The carnage for investors from Bond's reckless and criminal business dealings was on an unprecedented scale.

However, the problem for Bond was that the Bell Resources fraud was anticipated in financial circles. There was open speculation that, for the cash-strapped Bond Corporation, it may have proved too tempting a move, especially given Bond's reputation as a buccaneer businessman.[11] The NCSC launched an investigation. Some of the top people at the NCSC considered Alan Bond to be 'the biggest menace' in Australia's corporate sector.[12] But it took until 1995 to untangle the legal labyrinth that had given Bond the cover to hide behind.

What drew Alan Bond, national hero from his victory in the America's Cup a mere five years earlier, into committing the nation's greatest ever fraud? Part of the answer is straightforward – Bond was predisposed to criminal behaviour and created a culture within Bond Corporation to allow him free rein. Bond Corporation embodied all four of the drivers of bad corporate behaviour identified as the framework for this book: the downside of free-market ideology; state capture by corporations; unscrupulous corporate culture; and failed regulators. Bond Corporation was a train wreck waiting to happen. Mesmerised by the glitz and the greed, no one noticed the sheer shonkiness of Bond's business model until it was too late.

Bond as corporate psychopath

Bond's was an improbable rise to wealth and fame. His childhood in war-torn Britain was marked by deprivation and benign neglect. Father Frank, a gentle and hard-working coal-miner and builder, spent years away with British forces and returned seriously injured. His mother, Kathleen, equally hard-working, was busy earning a living. Alan and his sister, Geraldine, roamed freely, splitting their time between their outer London suburb and their Welsh relatives' coal-mining town.

For Alan, this freedom was an invitation for trouble. Young Alan was a habitual juvenile delinquent, both before and after he arrived in Australia with his family in 1950 as 'ten pound Poms'. His biographers examine this behaviour in some detail – each mentioning similar but also different incidents, depending on which witnesses to Bond's childhood had been interviewed. The composite picture is disturbing: petty thieving, truanting, trespassing, running away from home, disrespecting teachers and showing a bombastic attitude to fellow students.[13] Of course, a pattern of youthful anti-social behaviour isn't always a predictor of the fully-developed adult. But in Bond's case it was a crucial determinant. The idea that ordinary rules did not pertain to him became entrenched. He demonstrated the classic early signs of an antisocial personality: an unwillingness to conform to social norms, a disrespect for the law, and impulsivity.[14]

A particularly disturbing incident occurred when Bond was eighteen years old, married, gainfully employed as a signwriter and with a young child. His wife, Eileen, was the daughter of a respected and well-to-do Fremantle identity, William Hughes. It was therefore inexplicable that Bond could have been caught one day trying to break into several properties. As biographer Paul Barry explains: 'Bond [was caught] wearing a pair of overalls with "State Electricity Commission" emblazoned on them, and carrying a variety of screwdrivers and pliers that made him look like a meter reader'.[15]

Bond got lucky; he received nothing more than a six-month good behaviour bond. However, the incident is an illustrative one. Bond had no reason to commit robbery other than a desire to live on the edge, the pursuit of quick money and a belief that he was invincible.

Even before this incident, Frank Bond had worried about his son's character. He opined to friends that Alan would either end up a wealthy man or in jail. Of course, Bond ended up doing both.

Several explanations exist for Bond's teenage delinquent behaviour. He was determined to escape the poverty he witnessed among his coal-mining relatives, willing himself to a brighter future. And he experienced trauma as a young migrant; he was teased for being a

'Pom' and he developed a compensatory 'I'll show 'em' attitude.[16] Being small and squat and poor at school exacerbated his need to project a powerful image of himself. 'Bondy always insisted he was better and smarter than the rest of us', recalled one schoolmate.[17]

After Bond left school he found work as an apprentice signwriter. By his own later account, he had a burning desire to achieve wealth quickly. But, from the outset, Bond was attracted to shonky business practices. While working as an apprentice, he began moonlighting for work after hours, undercutting his employer. Frank started to worry that his son couldn't 'do anything by the book'.[18]

Keen to make his fortune, Bond quit his apprenticeship and started up his own painting business – Nu-Signs – in partnership with his father. His first business venture was a portend of things to come. He'd hustle for jobs by under-quoting and then struggle to make a profit. To keep the creditors at bay he'd engage in sharp practices – skipping on quality by skimping on paint. He'd also stretch out paying creditors until they were chasing him down, then only drip-feed them their money.[19] It was an early sign of his ruthlessness and lack of business ethics. When one employee asked if he would repay Nu-Signs' debts, Bond replied: 'No. It's cheap money'.[20] After seven years, Nu-Signs was teetering on the brink of bankruptcy.

The rise of Bond Corporation

Bond sold the signwriting business and launched himself as a property developer. It was a bold move for a young man with a sketchy business record. More than simply the financial rewards, his first foray into the cut-throat world of property development psychologically set him up for the future: prevailing against the odds, he saw himself as a winner.

Responding to Perth's emerging minerals boom and consequent demand for housing, Bond eyed a residential development site in the Darling Ranges east of Perth. With his steely nerve, his effervescence and his larrikin-like charm – all trademark qualities he deployed into the future – he secured the finance to pull off the scheme. And, as people queued up to buy the blocks, Bond realised his dream of becoming a millionaire by the age of twenty-one.

Bond's lightning-quick success highlighted an emerging schism in Australian business between the new breed of brash entrepreneurs and the old business establishment. The latter were, according to investigative journalist Neil Chenoweth, a 'conservative, subdued and incurably smug' clique of insiders, 'where power was marked by directorships on the big boards, the banks and finance companies, as well as institutions such as the Melbourne Club'. Bond became synonymous with a group of outsiders, who congregated with lightning speed around any new source of money. They were 'unorthodox, brash and disrespectful, but they made terrific lunch companions'.[21]

By the time he formed Bond Corporation in 1967, Bond was a swaggering, stocky twenty-seven-year-old with all the trappings of wealth: a dark blue Mercedes 600, a cruising yacht, speed boats and the first of his mansions on the Swan River. Alan and Eileen's parties were the talk of Perth. With her exuberant personality and fetching red hair, Eileen was the life of the couple's many soirees.[22] She would pay a price for her loyalty to Alan, choosing to ignore the gossip that he was fraternising with mostly beautiful, blonde and significantly younger women. When it came to women, Bond was said to have had 'more charm than 007'.[23]

Bond started buying up prime sites on St George's Terrace, Perth's financial strip. However, an all-too familiar approach emerged as his business model: act boldly and worry about the money later. As Terrance Maher, financial journalist and Bond biographer, explains: 'Again and again, he would buy something, borrow money to develop it, capitalise the development costs into the asset's value and borrow further money against the higher value'.[24]

The tactic worked. By 1974 he controlled more than sixty companies. Bond then took his next big plunge into property development. He bought a large greenfield site at Yanchep north of

Perth where he envisaged building a satellite city of 200 000 happy sun-lovers. He bought the site cheaply because there was nothing there. Hot, dry and off the beaten track, Yanchep presented Bond with the challenge of selling little more than shifting sandhills. He launched the project as Yanchep Sun City on a world stage with flashes of brilliant salesmanship alongside shady practices. One story has it that he hoodwinked British investors by spraying the sand on the development with green vermiculite to give it a lush appearance. Aerial shots used in promotional material made it appear 'as if the land that investors on the other side of the globe were buying were green pastures by the beach'.[25]

Bond was able to side-step local criticism by promoting even bigger plans for his Yanchep site. In 1971, he linked the promotion of the development to his involvement in the America's Cup. He announced plans to develop a world-class marina at the site at the same time as outlaying millions for a challenge for the Cup in 1974. Bond envisaged the site becoming the home of a defence of the Cup in 1977 in the event of the Bond syndicate winning.[26]

Thus, the legend of Alan Bond was created in the public's mind. The working-class-man-made-good took on the stuffy elites of the New York Yacht Club and challenged their immovable hold on the trophy, the 'Auld Mug'. The fact that he doggedly persisted through three failed bids before winning the Cup in 1983 is testimony to the inspirational side of Bond's high-octane personality. However, behind the tale of heroism was a calculated campaign of public relations; Bond at his most brilliant. And his status as a folk hero papered over his nefarious and criminal business conduct, while at the same time, bolstering his innate self-belief.

Bond appeared to possess a constellation of the characteristics associated with the label '(non-violent) corporate psychopath'. Not to be confused with a diagnosed clinical condition, 'corporate psychopath' has proved to be a useful tool in analysing corporate performance, especially large-scale corporate collapses. The term wasn't in use when

Bond strutted the corporate stage, but in recent years there's been an upsurge in academic and popular interest.

In 2006, two of the world's authorities on the topic, Paul Babiak and Robert Hare, published what became a standard text: *Snakes in Suits: When Psychopaths Go to Work.*[27] As they write, the constellation of personality characteristics associated with psychopaths in the workplace are often connected with narcissism or 'a pervasive pattern of grandiosity'. Bond, of course, dreamed of vast wealth and establishing a global business empire. He shared what Babiak and Hare term 'deadly charm' to con and manipulate others. With his broad smile, gleaming, pearly white teeth, and boundless optimism, Bond in full flight was said to be a near-hypnotic experience.[28]

Bond became a master at shaking vast funds out of banks. He certainly shared what Babiak and Hare identify as 'a penchant for high risk' because the psychopathically inclined corporate leader hates monotony; like an animal predator stalking game, corporate psychopaths 'go where the action is'. They are addicted to thrill-seeking. Bond loved nothing more than pulling off the next big deal … and the one after that. As Babiak and Hare further explain, corporate psychopaths lack empathy: 'people do not exist in their mental world except as objects, targets and obstacles'. As a consequence, they explain, corporate psychopaths are highly prone to committing fraud. Bond, of course, became a calculating corporate thief.

Among the CEOs included in this book, Bond displayed the most obvious links to the typology of corporate psychopath. But some of his core qualities – grand ambition, charm and ruthlessness – are also the very essence of successful corporate leaders. Whether CEOs have the propensity to steer a corporation into scandal can be hard to detect. But Bond offers one typology.

Conning his way to the top

For Bond, blue-water sailing and the America's Cup were all about making business contacts and furthering his Yanchep project. He tapped into the business culture of the sport. 'The America's Cup is as much an international marketplace as it is a boat race', acknowledged *The Bulletin* magazine.[29]

But on the eve of the 1974 challenge, all was not well at Yanchep: empty homes and unsold plots were scattered about his ambitious residential, holiday and yachting complex.[30] Residents complained about being duped over the lack of services.[31] Here was Bond at his most unscrupulous.

Yanchep was not Bond's only problem. By 1976, his burgeoning empire of debt-fuelled acquisitions nearly crumbled. Bond had made a series of moves in which his exuberance got the better of his judgment. As *The Bulletin* pointed out: '[g]oing into mining at the time of the Minerals Securities crash, concentrating on real estate during the property crash, borrowing around $90 billion with its fearsome interest bills despite his choking cash flow, moving back into iron ore mining just before the Japanese industry cut back'.[32]

Bond was basically insolvent.[33] However, his second serious brush with bankruptcy held no lessons for him or the wider business community. His survival became a heroic tale. He was applauded for being '[an] audacious high-wire juggling act'.[34] But luck was on Bond's side too. Banks were reluctant to call in loans while he was challenging for the America's Cup.

Bond's eventual snatching of the Cup in 1983 was an occasion of national jubilation. It brought two incalculable benefits. Firstly, he was anointed a national hero by no less than the Prime Minister, Bob Hawke. As the victory was sealed, an ecstatic and champagne-drenched Hawke proclaimed a national holiday to celebrate: 'Any employer who sacks a worker for not coming in today is a bum'. But Hawke was not merely acknowledging Bond's sporting achievement in a sports-obsessed nation, he also conferred legitimacy on Bond as a businessman. After all, federal Labor had embraced free market ideas in its policy of deregulating and privatising the economy to enhance the country's international competitiveness. Hawke believed that free markets that were working efficiently should be left to do their job. Hawke was channelling the advocates of neo-liberal economics whose ideas had, by then, become a force of nature, ripping apart the old Keynesian tradition of a state-managed economy.

Measures such as allowing the entry of foreign banks and removing government controls on interest rates proved transformative to the Australian economy but, in the short term, they led to a credit boom and excessive borrowing by corporate raiders such as Bond. But unquestionably, the 'big bang' in terms of deregulation occurred when Treasurer Paul Keating announced that he would licence sixteen foreign banks to operate in Australia. As financial journalist Max Walsh said of the unprecedented shake-up in the banking sector: 'This set off a tremendous battle to lend money to Australian companies ... Easy credit was the dynamic lifter of the new class of bold entrepreneur'.[35] Under the old financial system, where bankers were treated like gods, the new 'buccaneers' 'would not have been given any money for anything'.[36]

However, in hindsight, writes fellow journalist Trevor Sykes, it would have been wiser for the Hawke government to have pursued a more moderate course of deregulation because kerosene was thrown onto an already blazing economy.[37] The irrational chase by banks for market share put many investors at grave risk; nobody could step back and assess what was happening.

But the times suited Bond. In America, President Reagan had unleashed a deregulation revolution of the economy on his election in 1980, a rollback of the protections against concentrated capital put in place during the Great Depression of the 1930s. And capitalism was undergoing a seismic shift. A new dynamic had emerged in corporate America – no longer was it thought good enough to build products or develop services – the new mantra was 'to buy or be bought'.[38] An entire industry of takeover specialists rode the new merger wave. Bond became Australia's boldest rider of this wave. To cap off the '80s as an emerging new era, a culture of greed infiltrated American corporate culture – the rise of a band of financial raiders, schemers, looters and fraudsters. Bond channelled this zeitgeist.

'Bondy', at least in Hawke's mind, was synonymous with the new free-wheeling-style of private enterprise. Hawke repudiated the 'sloppy talk' that there was no place in the concerns of his government 'for the Alan Bonds of this world'.[39] The two men shared a larrikin streak and a common touch, and Hawke's embrace of Bond fitted more broadly into what one of his ministers described as the Prime Minister's 'flamboyant affinity with the big end of town'.[40] Others were more critical. Journalist John Pilger described Hawke's closeness to big businessmen – including Bond, media magnate Kerry Packer and investment banker Laurie Connell – as constituting a 'gang of mates'.[41] Indeed, at a 1987 gala event at Sydney's Regent Hotel, Hawke, in customary fashion, teared up when he told the assembled glitterati that he was proud to have as personal friends both Packer and Bond. And to the latter he said: 'Alan congrats for all your achievements and may I thank you for your generous comments about the Government'.[42]

Some saw more than just shared values between Hawke and the new, brash entrepreneurs like Bond. Political motives buttressed the Prime Minister's enthusiastic endorsement. According to Max Walsh, the 'curious alliance' between the two resulted in the traditional business establishment, the support base for the Liberal Party, being neutralised 'because its energies were being totally absorbed in defending itself from the raiders'.[43]

In this way, Bond's free-wheeling style was further boosted in a 'go-go' culture of easy money and veneration of wealth.[44] However, in their enthusiasm to embrace this turbo-charged form of capitalism, Australia's political leaders underplayed the risks to ordinary investors.

So did the media. The business magazines and the financial pages of the daily newspapers frequently depicted Bond – and other takeover entrepreneurs – as 'the most attractive investments going around'.[45]

The second advantage conferred by the America's Cup win was entrée into the world of prestigious American banks. As Bond later acknowledged, banks from across Australia and around the world showered money on Bond Corporation and Dallhold Investments. Their attitude was, he said, that 'if you could win the America's Cup then nothing was impossible'.[46] Every bank wanted Bond in their portfolio. He stayed on in the US for a month after the victory, criss-crossing the country to meet bankers and industrialists.[47] In an interview years later, Bond reflected on the impact winning the Cup had on his business career: 'we could do anything anywhere'. But, he also admitted, 'a little bit of ego' got control of him.[48]

Bond cemented his new-found celebrity status by building an even bigger mansion on the Swan River. The four-level, 240-square house 'rose out of the Swan River like a huge white fortress'.[49] Bond even paid over $3 million for the adjoining block because another Perth millionaire planned to build his own three-storey mansion on it.

Bond's garish displays of conspicuous consumption were instrumental in changing cultural mores. As one observer noted, attitudes had been turned on their head by the attention-grabbing displays of wealth that became commonplace in the 1980s. In previous decades, 'it was considered uncouth to laud wealth. New money and showcasing luxury was unseemly. Industry barons hid behind the heavy iron gates of their mansions, protected by the privacy of lush garden hedges'.[50]

Bond regarded displaying his wealth as a marketing tool to affirm his success as a businessman and, therefore, his continued access to credit. He threw parties at his mansion which the women's glossy magazines drooled over in their coverage. In this regard, Bond complemented the trend also being set by Geoffrey Edelsten in projecting an opulent lifestyle with the image of business success. Later entrepreneurs took this form of marketing to another level.

All these cultural trends came to be symbolised by the introduction in 1984 of Australia's Rich List by *Business Review Weekly.* Launched as 'Australia's 100 Richest People' it was expanded to 200 the following year, attracting ever more media interest. The new entrepreneurs, like Bond, scrambled for inclusion.[51]

In the new era of easy finance, Bond was prepared to pay huge fees to bankers for quick approvals, and he and his lieutenants raked off 'massive personal success fees every time they notched up a deal'.[52] Bond didn't know how to stop and, at the time, 'no-one cared', in the words of journalist Ian Verrender.[53]

Back in Perth, Bond was feted. Between his America's Cup win and the stockmarket crash of 1987, Bond and his corporation symbolised the celebration of a 'greed is good' culture.[54] Bond was omnipresent. Every second beer Australians drank came from Bond's breweries. Bond and Eileen – the latter now known as 'Red' – dominated the social pages, and the media revelled in their nouveau riche party set who had elbowed out Perth's staid, old-money clique. And to cement Bond's status as the man of the moment, Perth car number plates carried the insignia: 'Home of the America's Cup'.

Bond's brashness, together with his America's Cup win, turned him into one of the first national celebrity businessmen in Australia, a symbol of the country's ocker self-image. In turn, Bond broadened this image by buying heavily into art as if this conferred on him the social status that he lacked but eagerly sought. He liked to remind people that he had the biggest collection of French Impressionists in the country.[55] He also had an impressive collection of Australian colonial masters. In all, Bond developed a collection of 140 extremely valuable paintings, including works by Renoir, Toulouse-Lautrec and van Gogh. He started out as a collector to cover his boardroom with artworks to project a corporate image but developed into a serious collector with discerning tastes. But like other aspects of Bond's life, his art collection was built on other people's money – loans and finance company leases.[56]

To cap his newly acquired status, Bond was given an insider's role in running the Western Australian economy. In fact, along with Laurie Connell, Bond had effectively captured the WA government during the early to mid-1980s. These were the shadowy years of what became known as WA Inc – the forging of close ties between entrepreneurs like Bond and the WA Labor government led by the young and telegenic Brian Burke. Operating as a classic model of crony capitalism, the entrepreneurs got the inside running on projects in return for substantial political donations, although each side was careful to avoid the implication of institutional corruption. But the model ended in a series of scandals that resulted in the establishment in 1990 of a royal commission. Charges were laid against Burke and a range of other players.[57]

Under Burke, Labor had won the 1983 state election on a platform of developing closer ties with Western Australian businesses. As a pragmatist, Burke knew that his government had to neutralise the opposition from big business. The 'four-on-the floor' Perth entrepreneurs jumped on board. However, Bond and financier Laurie Connell were the key conduits between business and Burke. It was supposed to be a 'win, win' approach to politics: entrepreneurs got an inside running to develop projects and Burke would amass a war chest of campaign donations to become a forceful player in state and national politics.

Connell, the founder and director of Rothwells Bank, was a friend of both Bond and Burke. Connell, dubbed 'last resort Laurie', financed projects that mainstream banks were unwilling to back and, to attract custom, paid high rates of interest on deposits. Like Bond, he was driven by humble beginnings and a craving for wealth and recognition.[58] Like Bond, too, he was a shady operator. Despite the impressive title of 'banker', he was little more than a con artist running a Ponzi scheme masquerading as a bank.[59]

To facilitate this crony model of development, Burke bypassed Cabinet, caucus and the public service while also operating an

$11 million 'Leader's Account' from his private office. Accountable government had been abandoned. While a full account of WA Inc is not required here, the details of Bond's involvement reveal the grandiose side of his personality. Bond imagined he could run the state, as Burke later explained in the *West Australian* newspaper:

> Mr Burke said Mr Bond was 'very forthright, perhaps even brash, in telling me how the government should run the State'.
>
> 'He was brimming full of ideas and had a very firm view about the role that he thought Bond Corporation could play in the running [of] the State,' Mr Burke said.[60]

Over the next few years, a series of disastrous deals ended up costing the state in excess of $1 billion, and damaged its reputation for more than a decade. As journalist and Bond biographer Paul Barry attests, some of the biggest deals at the heart of WA Inc involved Bond and Connell in partnership. The WA Inc saga confirmed the former's ruthless opportunism. Bond cut some tidy deals for himself along the way, none more notorious than claiming a consultant's fee of $16 million for the attempted rescue of Connell's Rothwells Bank when it, inevitably, teetered towards insolvency in 1988. It would take the WA Inc Royal Commission, established in 1990, to fully uncover the sordid trashing of democratic norms that constituted the premiership of Brian Burke.

The dream of a global empire

His involvement in WA Inc showed how much Bond craved power. And, by 1987, he was 'hunting power, seemingly at any price'.[61]

Bond's deal-making during the 1980s was pursued at a dizzying pace. He launched bids for and bought and offloaded companies like a problem gambler at a casino, all the time shuffling assets and flying around the world attending meetings with obliging bankers. Bond ended up with a stake in numerous Australian and overseas mining companies: petroleum, coal, gold, diamond, nickel and gas; multiple Australian and overseas breweries; media companies in both Australia and overseas; a British airship manufacturer; high-profile retail and real estate outlets; and the Chilean national telephone company.[62]

In addition to the grab-bag of international companies, Bond had managed to get his hands on the cream of Australian big business. He had a controlling stake in businesses in the key sectors of mining, retail, brewing and media. Bond had bought his way into the business establishment.

Some of the deals brought in much sought-after cash flow, but equally, Bond's addiction to deal-making underpinned the corporate house of cards he had created. He was a bad deal-maker. He couldn't stand the thought that someone might trump him, so he often paid over the mark for a business.

Driven by little more than his plucky, irrepressible optimism, Bond paid $1 billion – well over the odds – for the Kerry Packer-owned Nine Network, which he later sold back to Packer for $300 million. Of his windfall, Packer famously enthused that 'you only get one Alan Bond in your lifetime'. And some of his purchases during the heady years were so large that he kept putting the net value of his company on the line each time he struck a big deal. He paid $1.2 billion for Castlemaine in 1985 and more than US$1.2 billion for US brewer Heileman in 1987 in his quest to become one of the world's largest brewers.

And the momentum projected an illusion of success. As one observer noted: 'Balance sheets were drawn up every year as the law required ... [but] by the time they were published and questions asked, the group had moved on'.[63]

Bond, like other corporate raiders of the '80s, subscribed to the 'theory' that inflation would inexorably lift the price of assets; and debt could be serviced by the cash flow as the value of the assets rose.[64] And academic theorists weighed in on the debate, arguing that 'synergies' were created by bringing together the different parts of conglomerate companies like Bond Corporation, and the constant threat of corporate takeovers encouraged vulnerable companies to use their resources effectively.[65]

However, the theory failed to take of account a major reversal of the share market and, therefore, the decline in the value of the assets. Equally delusional was Bond's belief in his capacity to repay his loans. By the late 1980s, his interest bill was sucking up the company's cash flow like an industrial vacuum cleaner.[66]

Bond used a variety of accounting tricks to give the impression that his empire was more profitable than it actually was, including understating the true amount of debt it had.[67] The net result was a corporate performance based on 'puffed up financial figures and rubbery bottom lines'.[68] Exacerbating the flakiness of Bond Corporation was Bond's poor grasp of management. He lacked the patience to focus on each of the myriad businesses he bought into his stable and, with no more than a poor high school record, his intellectual horizons were narrowly focused on immediate cash flow rather than the longer-term challenges of building businesses in an increasingly competitive environment. And he hadn't adjusted his operating model from his early, free-wheeling days to managing a large, complex organisation. The takeover of Bell Resources, for example, proceeded without a single document recording the fact.[69] Whether deliberate obfuscation or haphazard management, it should have been a red flag to regulators and institutional investors.

Improbably, Bond Corporation's 1980s spending spree was underwritten by some of the largest banks in Australia and the world. Just how these banks ended up lending Bond $14 billion is like entering an Alice in Wonderland fantasy world. 'Supersalesman' Alan Bond could unleash his persuasive skills on normally ruthless big banks, and they wouldn't really bother to inquire into either the validity of his proposals, the consequences of his mounting debts or his track record as a flawed businessman. Plucky as ever, Bond always said, 'get me into any bank and I'll come out with the money'. Bond was displaying a skill common to corporate psychopaths, who 'make their living by being good at fooling people'.[70]

The sheer intensity of Bond's deal-making often had his inner circle reeling with exasperation. Peter Beckwith, Bond Corporation's managing director and one of its key strategists, once explained that whenever 'the boss' returned from a business trip a shudder would go through the executive team as they were called on to patch up one crippled acquisition after another: 'It all made Alan seem as though he was invincible', Beckwith said. Beckwith tolerated Bond's chaotic approach out of friendship and loyalty. He died in 1989, whereupon Bond sought to shift the blame for his company's troubles onto his dead friend and loyal lieutenant. Even though Bond sought to apologise for his unseemly behaviour, it was another telling insight into his personality.

However, the culture at Bond Corporation was more complex than just bowing to Bond's will and trying to clean up the mess he'd create. Beckwith and the others in Bond's inner circle were active participants in the high-risk takeover culture. They were handsomely paid to be loyalists, and Bond even spared them contracts based on performance. A month after the October 1987 stockmarket crash, approval was given by shareholders to grant a payout of $41 million to Bond Corporation's handful of senior executives. In an action that amounted to corporate larceny, given the precarious position of the company after the crash, the approval was granted by the company's large shareholders over the objections of many of the thousand small shareholders attending the annual general meeting.[71]

Among the recipients of this largesse was Tony Oates, described as Bond's 'money man'. At Oates' trial over the stripping of Bell assets, his lawyer claimed that his action was not motivated by personal greed but 'a misplaced intention to save Bond Corporation at all costs'. He sacrificed his legal responsibilities 'to the imperatives of the Bond group'.[72] Equally, Oates was under pressure because of his huge remuneration package to try to ensure the survival of Bond Corporation by whatever means.

The Bond Corporation board provided little or no counterweight to the takeover strategies and risky excesses of Bond and his executive. Insights have been provided by Bill Widerberg, who was put on the board when Bond Corporation bought out Toohey's brewery. Widerberg had an impressive track record, taking the struggling Toohey's to above 50 per cent market share. For the first two years with Bond 'he really thought he had hit the corporate big time'. He was moving and shaking with captains of industry, but he began to feel something was amiss: 'Finance presentations were given regularly and the company was going swimmingly as far as the directors were concerned but we weren't being told the truth'. This lack of candour didn't become fully evident for Widerberg until early 1989 when his proposal to build a brewery in Melbourne was swiftly rebuffed by executives. 'The company couldn't afford it', he was told. When he started pressing for answers it soon 'became clear that his queries were not welcome'.

For Widerberg, his experience on the board of Bond Corporation in the 1980s mirrored a wider problem. Boards, he said, formed a small, well-guarded, inter-connected and largely unaccountable coterie. Board members were paid $50 000 a year to attend meetings, 'but they are not always well versed on the agendas. On many boards, the resolutions are written before the meeting and really you've got to commit murder to be kicked off a board'.[73]

The Bond Corporation board was an early lesson in the role boards played in corporate disasters. The company was an object lesson in poor organisational culture: Bond was both CEO and chair and he stacked his board with his loyal lieutenants. A fully independent board would never have been contemplated by the egotistical and autocratic Bond. Other companies discussed in this book fell into the same trap of poor governance, leading to disastrous outcomes.

Bond's parallel world

Throughout the years rebuilding his company, Bond lived in much the same parallel, shadowy world that he had inhabited on and off all of his life. Just as he had done as a tearaway youth and a roguish young entrepreneur, he continued to believe the rules didn't apply to him. Whether he was doing deals inside the WA Inc bubble or with other leading business figures, Bond could switch from legitimate business figure to shady operator without a hint of moral scruple. The greed and self-delusion driving Bond were clear from the mid-1980s onwards.

Bond's troubles started mounting in 1986 when he wanted to buy shares owned by the Queensland government in the lucrative Castlemaine Perkins XXXX Brewery. He had to negotiate with Premier Joh Bjelke-Petersen, a polarising, authoritarian, populist leader later known to have operated one of the most corrupt governments in Australian history. His standard retort to any probing about his government's questionable dealings was a patronising, 'Don't you worry about that'.

However, Bjelke-Petersen refused to speak to Bond about his interest in Queensland's premier brewery until Bond settled a defamation action the Premier had launched against the Nine Network, then owned by Bond. The Premier alleged that its current affairs show had aired allegations against him that he had improperly obtained overseas loans. Bond, 'without reference to his lawyers, immediately wrote a cheque for $400,000. The share deal was then addressed and he acquired the brewery'.[74]

In 1986, the Australian Broadcasting Tribunal hearing on Bond's fitness to hold a television licence came dangerously close to a finding that a $400 000 defamation settlement had elements of either extortion or bribery; that, in effect, Bond had seen the demand as little more than the cost of doing business in Queensland, given the generosity of the payout and the chances of success if the action went to court.[75]

The following year, Bond tried to bribe respected Melbourne businessman John Dahlsen, who was the chair of the Herald and Weekly Times. Dahlsen explained that in late 1987 Bond wanted to buy the *West Australian* newspaper in part because of his dislike of the state's establishment. He was willing to pay 'probably double its market value'. Bond rang Dahlsen and asked to meet in Melbourne. Dahlsen recalled:

> Apart from offering a ridiculous price, Bond offered me $1 million in cash to be paid into any overseas bank plus a large yacht to be made available at any port in the Mediterranean … However, [I] took the view that to sell a dominant newspaper in Perth, Western Australia, would absolutely devastate that community and Bond would use his editorial power for his own financial gain. I then rang Bond to say that we could not deal.[76]

But Bond embarked on his most dangerous move in mid-1988 when he decided to take on Tiny Rowland's Lonhro. Having just spent a fortune buying out Holmes à Court, Bond was looking around for a new cash cow. He wanted a company he could buy cheaply but which had liquid funds to help him cover his debts. The daring move was straight from the Bond playbook – high-risk, grandiose and autocratic. Bond was simply winging it; he was addicted to the thrill.

In key respects, Bond and Rowland were similar psychopathically inclined tycoons. Like Bond, Rowland was 'dangerously charming and dangerously energetic'. Like Bond, too, Rowland's charisma co-existed with 'a vengeful, ruthless and ferociously ambitious' side.[77] But Rowland out-competed Bond in bloody-minded ruthlessness. Some described him as 'not quite human', such was his calculating, icy cold, power-hungry reputation. Like a crocodile, he would watch and wait before jamming his jaws shut on a deal, and on any person in his way. He had taken a clapped-out mining company and turned it into a sprawling conglomerate, using it to pillage his way through Africa, where he was infamous for bending the rules, squashing opponents and, allegedly, paying off politicians.[78] Somehow, Bond missed all the cues not to mess with Rowland.

The two had met briefly in the Antibes where they 'enjoyed a tipple on the back of each other's super yachts'.[79] However, Rowland became wary when Bond started buying up shares in Lonrho and then suggested the two meet: code, as Rowland well knew, for takeover talks. Rowland then set out to destroy Bond. In November 1988, he produced a ninety-three-page booklet entitled *The Bond Group of Companies: A Financial Analysis by Lonhro plc.* Eviscerating in its thoroughly researched claims, the booklet judged Bond Corporation to be technically insolvent; that contrary to its own glowing company reports, its debts, Rowland argued, were three times the size Bond claimed and its assets were only half of what he pretended. In other words, Bond's profits 'were a fiction'.[80] Not long after, Paul Barry presented a searing look into Bond's over-leveraged empire that came to the same conclusion. The banks started to call in the loans. Bankers were suddenly forced to confront their own sheer incompetence: how the mania surrounding financial deregulation had seduced them into backing to the hilt a high-wire act like Alan Bond.

As Bond was fighting the impact of the sharemarket slide and the Rowland report, he doubled down on trying to protect his personal fortune. Concerned to shore up his equally shaky private company, Dallhold Investments, he saw a way of injecting much-needed cash into his private coffers by selling Edouard Manet's painting *La Promenade*.

The sordid saga of the painting, bought by Dallhold in November 1983 for $4.6 million, showed how blurred the lines were between his private and public companies. Soon after buying the painting, Dallhold sold it for the same price to Chemical AllStates Australia. Chemical then leased it to Bond Corporation before Chemical was taken over by Macquarie Bank in 1988. The bank offered the painting, then valued at $11 million, to Bond Corporation for $2.4 million. Bond Corporation declined and the painting was instead bought by Dallhold for $2.3 million. Dallhold sold it at auction a year later for $17 million. Bond was aware at all times of the value of the painting and had misled the shareholders of Bond Corporation about the sale.[81] Bond maintained the dealings were in line with a profit-sharing arrangement between the two companies. However, this was a fabrication according to the finding of the court which, in 1994, convicted and jailed Bond over the deal.

The collapse of the house of cards

Despite Bond Corporation suffering from the ravages of the 1987 stockmarket crash, Bond's delusions of grandeur were undimmed. A month after the crash, when he began sinking in a quicksand of debt, he imagined he could pull off yet another impossible deal: purchasing van Gogh's iconic painting *Irises*. Undeterred that he lacked the funds for such a purchase, Bond bid up the price at auction to US$54 million to shatter records for the sale of artwork. He'd backed himself to strike one more deal. He convinced Sotheby's to loan him half the purchase price, which meant holding the painting in an undisclosed location as collateral.[82] It was typical of Bond's audacious negotiating skills. In bidding up the record price, Sotheby's attracted worldwide attention and the art market was given a boost. For Bond, the purchase gave him an air of invincibility just when he needed it.[83] And, in typical Bond hyperbole, he gushed that his purchase was 'not just a painting, it's the most important painting in the world'.[84]

In the 1989–90 fiscal year, Bond Corporation recorded what was then the biggest corporate loss in Australian history – a staggering $2.25 billion. One wag was reported to have quipped that no one could possibly go broke selling beer to Australians. But Rowland's analysis had proved correct; Bond Corporation had been lying about the true position of the company. In fact, the American-based accountancy firm, Arthur Andersen, had 'cooked the books' for the company. They would do the same for HIH Insurance (see chapter 4).

Little noticed at the time, Arthur Andersen was engaged in deceptive behaviour by providing friendly audits to large corporations: massaging the books to present the company in the best possible light, often hiding the extent of company debt. And they weren't the only accountancy firm doing so, reflecting the wider ethical lapses in the accountancy profession. Determined to maintain self-regulation of standards, large segments of the accountancy profession were described at the time of the collapse of Bond Corporation as being both unfamiliar with professional standards and disinterested in mastering them. Consequently, accountancy firms were riddled with 'creative accounting'.[85]

Bond resigned as CEO and Bond Corporation was put into receivership.[86] A fire sale of its assets followed, including the Nine Network, breweries, extensive mineral interests, the Chilean telephone company, a private yacht and paintings. Bond was declared bankrupt in 1992 with personal debts of $1.8 billion.

And now the banks faced the challenge of getting their money out of Bond and Dallhold Investments. Paul Barry summed up their self-inflicted predicament: 'The banks had lent their billions on a ragbag of assets whose earnings would not pay the interest bill and whose realisable value was considerably less than Bond had borrowed against them'.[87]

Bond began the process of covering his tracks. Tony Kaye, the Western Australian correspondent for the *Australian Financial Review,* received a tip-off one Sunday morning in 1992 that Bond had been seen entering his Dallhold's office building. When he drove there, he momentarily caught sight of Bond standing near the window:

> There was Bond standing in the centre of the office foyer, orchestrating a dozen or more of his employees carrying document boxes from one side to the other. I don't know what was in those document boxes. But I do know they didn't get to the receivers, because I could hear the Bond shredding machines working overtime.[88]

Kaye's encounter was entirely serendipitous. No one knows the lengths to which Bond engaged in similar activities to keep his creditors at bay.

Bond's private empire

The publicly listed Bond Corporation was merely the front for a private empire developed by Bond to accrue and hide a personal fortune. Fifty-two per cent of Bond Corporation was, in turn, owned by Bond's private company, Dallhold Investments, which creamed off significant funds from the public company. But Dallhold itself was a front for a labyrinth of private companies owned by the Bond family which were effectively put out of reach of creditors through a structure of family trusts and offshore accounts. This legal but opaque structure funded Bond's post-bankruptcy lifestyle.[89] But Bond's entire business structure – the trusts, the overseas tax havens, the shadowy trail of private companies – shows just how calculated Bond had been in setting out to rip people off. As financial journalist Trevor Sykes has written, 'in almost every deal he did, some advantage was channelled into his private interests at his shareholders' expense'.[90] He was basically robbing investors to line his own pocket ... and then hiding the loot. Loose laws aimed at protecting the rich allowed him to embark on such a plan.

Paul Barry's dogged and revelatory investigations have produced the clearest picture of how Bond 'got away with it'.[91] His investigation shows that Bond established a number of personal offshore trusts as early as the mid-1970s, after his second brush with bankruptcy. He leveraged the rise in the use of family trusts driven by clever lawyers who transformed the instrument, originally intended to protect vulnerable people's assets, into an untouchable haven for the rich to avoid tax and creditors. In Bond's case, he used his opaque financial arrangements to avoid paying almost any tax for decades. In addition, when forced into bankruptcy, neither the police nor bankruptcy experts could untangle their complex structure to retrieve assets for creditors. It was only in 1989 that federal Labor Treasurer Paul Keating announced a crackdown on the use of offshore tax havens after the publicity about Bond's extensive use of them.[92]

In addition to offshore accounts, Bond had a mysterious Swiss banker, Jurg Bollag, who operated out of the Swiss tax-haven town of Zug, managing his affairs. Bollag's financial links with Bond were publicly exposed by Paul Barry on an ABC *Four Corners* program in 1993 and later extensively detailed in his book, *Going for Broke: How Bond Got Away with it.* Other than Bond, Bollag was the only person who knew how all the pieces of the financial puzzle, split into a secretive web of shelf companies, fitted together.

In response to Barry's revelations, both the Australian Federal Police and an independent investigator, Robert Ramsay, appointed by Bond's creditors, separately spent years chasing the links to Bond's private empire, with no success. Neither was able to compel Bollag to testify in court and Bond fought a series of legal battles to prevent that from happening. In an effort to encourage Bollag to give evidence, Australian authorities granted him indemnity from prosecution, and he was subsequently interviewed in Switzerland, but to no avail. Paul Barry wrote of Bollag: 'he had served his master well … He had not run off with Bond's money. Nor had he betrayed him to the authorities, despite the pressure to do so'.[93]

'The police finally decided they weren't going to win and they gave up' explained Barry.[94] Ramsay's role ended when creditors accepted Bond's $3.25 million settlement – against his advice.

No one knows how much money Bond got away with, but the Australian Federal Police estimated it was between $50 million and $100 million.[95]

Bond had shown how easy it was, for anyone with deep pockets, good lawyers and persistence, to successfully stash a fortune away from the prying eyes of the Taxation Department. He also exposed the weakness in Australia's bankruptcy laws. If a debtor could hold out and do a deal, creditors would want to settle or risk legal fees reducing further returns. As one expert in the field explained: 'a liquidator or trustee has not got an endless pool of cash to pursue a bankrupt'.[96]

This is exactly the approach Bond and his family took. Bond feigned bouts of mental illness and loss of IQ to delay proceedings and avoid fronting court. On one occasion he was seen holidaying and doing business in the Whitsundays the day before being admitted to hospital supposedly suffering from severe depression.[97]

When eventually forced to give evidence, Bond stated that he owned nothing but a Rolex watch.[98] But money materialised when deals with creditors needed to be done. Separate deals were struck with Bond's personal bankruptcy creditors and with Dallhold's creditors. Both included clauses preventing creditors from pursuing future legal claims against Bond family members or Bond family assets. Given his hidden assets, it's not surprising Bond insisted on this clause.

Dallhold creditors accepted a $5.8 million commercial settlement in 1994 to extinguish debts of $520 million. After several attempts, Bond struck a similar $3.25 million deal in 1995 with his personal creditors – owed about $600 million – which enabled his release from bankruptcy.[99] He was free to start again, supported by an extremely wealthy family. Henry Bosch, who as chair of the National Companies and Securities Commission led the investigations into Bond's corporate fraud, was scathing about Bond's later return to the *BRW Magazine*'s rich list in 2008. 'I think it's a defect of our system that a man can pay his creditors half a cent in the dollar and then go on to flaunt his riches.'[100]

In cutting his bankruptcy deals while protecting his hidden wealth, Bond demonstrated the same chilling lack of conscience that he showed when he rolled up to Holmes à Court's house with a plan to buy, then fleece, Bell Resources. And, like the psychopath he was, there was 'never a hint of remorse or even an acknowledgement of wrong-doing'.[101]

In beating the system, Bond exposed the inadequacy of the law for so-called white-collar criminals. He served three years for the fraud over *La Promenade* and three and a half years for Bell Resources (or one day for every million he stole). The leniency of the sentences led to outrage that government and regulators were not taking white-collar crime seriously enough.

When Bond died from the complications of heart surgery in 2015, commentators described him variously as a con man, a 'great fraudster', 'a great manipulator', and the 'man who tricked Australia'. Bond was both more talented and more dangerous than these colourful descriptors. For some, he has remained a lovable rogue. But, at his core, Bond was a corporate psychopath.

3

DREAMS OF HOLLYWOOD: CHRISTOPHER SKASE AND QINTEX

In late May 1991, the newly formed corporate regulator, the Australian Securities Commission (ASC), which had recently replaced the NCSC, wanted to teach failed businessman Christopher Skase a lesson. One of the most flamboyant of the 1980s entrepreneurs, Skase was renowned for his extravagant parties and his debonair style. But the legal system was circling Skase regarding the collapse of his company Qintex two years previously with debts of $1.5 billion. The ASC alleged that he had failed in his duties as CEO and chair, and slapped thirty-two charges against him which, if proved in court, exposed Skase to up to five years' jail.

Because Skase had feigned an excuse for missing a court appearance while travelling overseas, the agency arranged for the Australian Federal Police to arrest the recalcitrant businessman when he finally turned up in court. Skase calmly heard the charges but began to shake uncontrollably when he was led away by police. Pale and drawn, and barely holding back tears, Skase called back to Lawrence van der Plaat, his right-hand man, who would later turn against his boss: 'Just get me out, whatever you have to do, just get me out today'. He was locked away for only two hours, but emerged from his holding cell a broken man.[1] The thought of jail had terrified Skase. Instead of teaching him a lesson, the ASC had overplayed its hand; Skase doubled down on his resolve to flee the country, never to return.

Several weeks later, Skase fled to the idyllic, sun-drenched Spanish island of Majorca where he lived in the lap of luxury in his mansion, La Noria. Thereafter, Skase became the poster-boy for much of the community's anger over the excesses of the eighties and the financial losses they entailed.[2] His secretive flight from the country looked like a calculated attempt to escape the clutches of the law. And the images captured by prying journalists of his luxurious life in Spain, having left investors empty-handed, only fuelled community anger, as did his tactic of feigning illness before Spanish authorities, deployed successfully to avoid extradition to Australia.

At one level, at least, this condemnation was undeserved. Skase was a more calculating entrepreneur than the bullish, chaotic Alan Bond. By comparison, Skase was more strategic in the business empire he built. And, unlike Bond who was able to leverage his America's Cup win to open the vaults of the banks, Skase had to patiently develop a personal brand to convince the banks to back him. He can also lay claim to being a genuine visionary with his high-end Queensland and American resort developments. And he turned Channel 7 around from basket case to entertainment powerhouse. He had talents as a businessman and left a legacy.

Skase lacked the same destructive personal attributes of either Geoffrey Edelsten or Alan Bond. Those close to the Qintex boss observed that he didn't dominate conversations; that he was unfailingly courteous; and that he was not abrasive to staff. He didn't even have the stomach for bitter corporate confrontations.[3] Stealth was his preferred business *modus operandi*. Yet, he shared with Bond a deceitfulness and a willingness to push the legal boundaries to pursue his self-interest, indifferent to the consequences for his shareholders. And he was as much a captive to vaulting ambition as were Edelsten and Bond.

But like Bond, Skase's ambition exceeded normal boundaries. It encompassed an attention- or admiration-seeking narcissism – the idea that no goal is off limits.[4] Skase certainly entertained dreams bigger than his capacity to execute them.

Yet, Skase flummoxed those who thought they knew him. For some he remained a reclusive character, his personality 'somehow not quite concrete'.[5] Others noted the opposite, commenting on Skase's compelling demeanour. He could zero in on a person 'with his eyes fixed on you'.[6] He was a bit of a chameleon.

The dreamer

By his mid-thirties, Christopher Skase had been tagged a 'young tycoon', who had 'startled the media world' when, in October 1984, seemingly out of nowhere, he paid $34 million for Brisbane's Channel 0 (later Channel 10). He attracted a profile in the widely read *Bulletin* magazine, complete with a photograph that captured his youthful, movie-star looks and stylish attire. Journalist David Haselhurst noted that Skase's ambition extended well beyond the purchase of the Brisbane TV station. In fact, Skase boasted that his foray into Queensland media was merely the first step in the creation of a new, national media company. But, behind the bravado, who was Christopher Skase and what fuelled his driving ambition?

Skase's restless desire for wealth and power emerged early. Like Edelsten and Bond, he had a single-minded ambition – to be rich.[7] And, in common with Bond especially, he craved the power that came from wealth. 'If you haven't made a million before you're 30, you'll never be a player,' he said.[8]

Skase's ambitions were forged by the influence of his father, Charles, who was a well-known radio broadcaster. Through his father, Skase became captivated by the media.[9] The baritone-voiced radio announcer, who paid his son's school fees by singing after hours, encouraged his son to aim to be a media proprietor rather than an employee of a media organisation. He imbibed his father's aspirations and blended them with his own need for recognition and acceptance.[10]

Melbourne-born Skase craved access to the city's stuffy business establishment and felt aggrieved when it wasn't forthcoming early in his career. His lack of entrée stoked his ambitions. 'I copped a cold shoulder all over town', he remarked later in his career, a snub that he never forgot.[11] Like Bond in Perth, Skase found that without connections to the establishment, becoming a wealthy businessman seemed out of reach. As late as 1990, it was said that it was 'still almost impossible to buy one's way into real society in Melbourne where the old establishment ruled supreme'.[12]

Skase's beginnings were comfortable but not privileged. Educated at Caulfield Grammar in Melbourne, Skase, although bright, left after Year 12 with an uncertain future. He didn't mix easily and left without forming close friendships or with any obvious interests in life other than a desire for business success and a fascination for the media.[13] For the next fifteen years Skase single-mindedly set out to acquire the skills and contacts that would enable him to become a self-made businessman.

After leaving school, Skase took a lowly position at the establishment stockbroking firm, JB Wear. He was a long way from the dashing figure he later cut for the media, described at the time as a 'bit of a geek, with plastered-down hair and a goofy grin'.[14] Wear's offered Skase the opportunity to investigate Australian companies and the operation of the stockmarket. He compiled meticulous records as he built a useful knowledge base.

Skase resigned after a few years and took time out to see Australia. Travelling alone in an old Ford Falcon, and taking odd jobs along the way, he stumbled on what would become a major interest in the remote but stunningly beautiful North Queensland town of Port Douglas. Showing the early signs of his ability to spot trends and develop a business vision, Skase saw the opportunity for resort-style tourism in the region. It became part of the Skase mythology that he had sketched a plan right there in the sand of the resort he fantasised about building.[15]

Skase then moved into finance journalism, first at the *Sun News-Pictorial* and later at the *Australian Financial Review*. In all he spent four years as a journalist doggedly accumulating insights and contacts in the business world. He became a specialist reporter on takeovers and acquisitions,[16] a handy preparation for his later career as a corporate raider. According to a former colleague, journalist Terry McCrann, 'He would devour balance sheets – and even more the fine details of the emerging dynamic of entrepreneurial deals'.[17]

Others recalled Skase adopting a calculating view of his role as a journalist; he was in the job 'to meet people and make contacts rather than write about finance ... he used his position to build his contacts. I don't think he will be remembered for anything he wrote'.[18] Business journalist Trevor Sykes knew Skase as well as anybody during their shared time at the *Australian Financial Review.* He found him intelligent, hard-working, a quick learner and a big thinker. But flaws were evident too – Skase was reserved with an authoritarian streak – he bridled 'at anyone who checked or questioned him'.[19] Van der Plaat was among the few who thought that the 'vast ambition' and complex personality hid a dark side', although it's unclear when he came to this conclusion.[20]

Meticulous and focused, Skase was, however, a fish out of water in the highly charged world of journalism. Still a loner and socially ill at ease, he shunned the party life typical of young journalists at the time.[21] None of his colleagues grasped the ego that lay latent in the young Skase.

After four years plying his trade, Skase was ready to launch his business career. In the mid-1970s, he gathered together a group of investors he had met as a journalist and formed Team Securities Limited. With working capital of $100 000, Team Securities were active traders on the stockmarket targeting undervalued companies, which they could buy and break up. One of the companies Team Securities gained control of was a small Tasmanian firm, Ludbrooks, which had mining and retail interests but which traded at a mere 2 cents. The Team valued the company's assets in excess of $400 000. The company was soon renamed Qintex.

Skase split with Team Securities over claims that he had misled his colleagues,[22] and in the wash-up he gained control of Qintex. He now had his own fiefdom, appointing his chosen directors and becoming answerable to no one.[23] But Skase, despite his limited experience, had complete confidence in himself.[24] And he worked obsessively – regularly eighty-hour weeks. He would need to draw on these strengths because he was about to enter the turbulent financial waters of the 1980s where, for entrepreneurs on the make, the expectations dictated that each deal would be bigger than the last: 'you just had to keep growing so the debt could never catch up'.[25]

But for the next few years Skase played a low-key game. With a staff of only one and working out of his dining room, he 'threw himself into the battle to clean up Qintex and move onto its first acquisitions'.[26] His first targets were jewellery companies – old companies with both stable earnings and a potential for growth and re-direction. From that base, Skase built a chain of companies where he typically acquired a 50 per cent interest, and rationalised assets, acquiring new funds for further acquisitions down the road.[27] Said to be very cautious in his early years, Skase did a personal balance sheet every Friday night just to make sure he was in front.[28]

By the mid-1970s, Skase had spotted trends around which he planned to build his business empire. He saw the world's growing pre-occupation with information, entertainment, travel and leisure. He saw, too, the potential attraction of these industries to the Japanese, whose economy was beginning to diversify away from manufacturing to focus more on lifestyle.[29]

Like Bond, Skase had the skillset to exploit the deregulated financial environment that Hawke and Keating had created. As one observer noted:

> He was a genius at extracting money out of people [he] would understand the psychology of people – bankers, brokers, analysts – and give them exactly what they wanted to hear. He was like a

> snake charmer … after he'd extracted what he wanted … he wouldn't even recognise the person in the street.[30]

Skase also had in common with Bond a capacity to exploit the new freewheeling banking culture.[31] He established commercial credibility by attracting a level of support from recognised financial institutions, which was crucial when the group raised capital through share issues. He courted institutional shareholders and developed the practice of inviting senior representatives from all the major institutions to visit Qintex head office and grill the company's executives at least once a year.[32]

Skase borrowed from merchant bank Tricontinental Corporation, a wholly owned subsidiary of the State Bank of Victoria. CEO Ian Johns ran Tricon (as it was known) as a high-risk lending machine to fuel growth. Flamboyant and autocratic, he was looking for entrepreneurs often rejected by the banks to generate high-margin lending deals. Tricon, it was said, lent to 'the flashy end of town'.[33] It wanted to take on the big banks and had a reputation for speed in approving loans.[34] It was a policy that ended in disaster in 1990 with close to $2.5 billion in debts for Tricon and a subsequent royal commission into its collapse.

Tricon was part of the glitzy, greedy, 'irrational exuberance' of the 1980s whose fate was sealed by the 1987 stockmarket crash, although it took some years for its coffers to be exhausted. The subsequent royal commission liberally shared the blame around – Johns' management style, the regulators, government and the board. Johns was eventually jailed for seven months, not for any claims about his management oversights, but for receiving a secret commission.[35]

But in its heady days, Skase showed 'all the signs of being just what Johns wanted'.[36] Johns and Skase were also said to be good mates, so signing off on big loans was no trouble. In fact, Johns lent Qintex $25 million before checks had been completed on its ability to repay,[37] and he lent Skase's private company, Kahmea Investments, $52 million before Tricon went under.[38]

Johns may have been a pushover, but AMP was another matter. Skase achieved a long-term ambition to have AMP as a shareholder in Qintex. According to his former group investment manager, Stefan Borzecki, having such a key institution as AMP 'would confirm that Qintex had arrived ... and confound all those brokers and investors who were reluctant to touch him'.[39]

When the Qintex group collapsed, AMP Australian equities manager Merv Peacock said AMP's 'research department is good and follows closely every stock they hold but they do get it wrong occasionally' and 'got caught with Qintex'. As academic Catherine Hoyte in her study of Qintex noted: 'Skase's mirage had fooled a very careful investor'.[40]

Becoming 'Christopher'

As he tasted the first fruits of success, Skase slowly began a metamorphosis. His old acquaintances noticed the change, and not just the upgrade in his style. Former fellow finance journalist Robert Gottliebsen recalled Skase always held a modest Christmas party. However, one year

> I was unable to attend. It was my colleague Alan Kohler's first Skase Christmas party. He was horrified. He and the other guests were pressured to go up on stage and say nice things about Christopher. Nothing like that had happened in the past and I realised then that my old friend 'Chris' Skase had become Christopher Skase and was beginning to take a very different tack.[41]

Similar reflections about Skase's personality were penned by another former colleague, Richard Grenning. In 1974, he first met Skase in a Melbourne gay bar:

> He already had a reputation for cultivating only those who could be of assistance and that wasn't me. Ten years later our paths crossed again when he was the tycoon and I was the right-hand man of Queensland's 'Minister for Everything', Russ Hinze. He greeted me by name as a long-lost friend and we always pretended we couldn't remember how and where we met. I had told Hinze that Skase had a reputation as being an inordinately vain man who resented any familiarity, so Hinze casually greeted him with a 'G'day Chris' just to remind him who needed whom. You could hear Skase's well-tended teeth grinding through his neon smile as he gave me a look of pure venom.[42]

Coinciding with his greater profile as an emerging successful businessman was Skase's marriage to Pixie Frew in 1979. Frew had four daughters from a previous marriage, all of whom Skase embraced.

With her trademark honey-blond hair and a fondness for jewellery, designer clothes, gossip and parties, Pixie was likened to the glamorous, slightly frivolous 1960s actress, Zsa Zsa Gabor.[43] But, as the product of an elite Melbourne private girls' school, she offered Skase an entrée into the world of the Melbourne establishment. As one observer noted, Pixie belonged to the 1950s generation of 'golden girls' who were 'offered everything'. Many of her contemporaries married men who went on to be powerful figures in business and the Liberal Party.[44]

Yet Pixie resented any suggestion that she was a dumb trophy wife.[45] In fact, she helped strategise Christopher's corporate ascent. She gave him the vision to aim for the heights and oversaw his transformation from shy geek into the strikingly good-looking mogul of his halcyon days.[46] Under Pixie's tutelage, Skase started dressing more elegantly and wearing his hair fashionably long.[47] Pixie also excelled at arranging extravagant A-list parties, which became synonymous with the Skase/Qintex brand. She remained the loyal wife to the end, despite claims that Skase gave her little real affection, at least in public.[48] There is no suggestion that she was involved in any of Skase's actual business dealings. But she paid a high price for the excesses of the 1980s. She stayed away from Australia for a decade after Skase's death in 2001.

Skase consolidated his rise as a media player by buying parcels of shares in television stations in Perth and Hobart and regional radio.[49] Consequently, between 1981 and 1984 the value of Qintex rose from $12 million to $100 million.[50]

Success started to go to Skase's head. By the mid-1980s he and Pixie were being chauffeured around Los Angeles in white stretch limousines or flying to Hawaii to test a US$13million Canadair Challenger jet they thought they might need. Skase was emulating the lifestyle of a big business tycoon before he had the funds to carry it off.[51]

Cementing political ties

In 1984, as Skase was making his move on the Queensland media, he decided to shift Qintex headquarters to Brisbane. Pixie hated the idea of moving from Melbourne, but Christopher was convinced that Queensland was the growth state and, of course, it was where he had long planned to build his luxury resorts and condominiums. Queensland, too, had a government prepared to bend over for entrepreneurs.

Skase saw in the curmudgeonly, right-wing populist and 'bible-bashing' Premier of Queensland, Joh Bjelke-Petersen, someone with whom he could develop a symbiotic relationship. Skase was impressed by Bjelke-Petersen's 'can-do', pro-development ethos. Derided as a country bumpkin in the southern states, Bjelke-Petersen was invited by Skase to one of his soirees; Skase also donated $200 000 to the Premier's National Party.[52] Characteristically verbally challenged, Joh responded by thanking his 'old friend' 'Christopher Skates'. Such was the notoriety of the Queensland government under Joh, that

Skase must have been aware that he had entered a state mired in corruption.

Indeed, Skase seamlessly obtained the land and approvals for his Port Douglas development. He allegedly told Lawrence van der Plaat that he had secured the deal 'in return for shares and cash paid to certain individuals'.[53] While such a claim is uncorroborated, it is in keeping with the character of the Bjelke-Petersen government. The only local businesses to prosper were those politically connected to the government, or – as revealed by the Fitzgerald Inquiry set up in 1987 to examine corruption in Queensland – financially connected to its powerbrokers.[54]

The couple built a mansion in the exclusive Brisbane suburb of Hamilton Hill. Skase bought two neighbouring Queensland colonial houses overlooking the Brisbane River which he promised to restore but then demolished overnight to build an imposing, brassy mansion named Bromley. Like other eighties entrepreneurs, he felt compelled to build a family home that was a conspicuous monument to his success. Bromley was the perfect backdrop for the Skases' self-promotion through lavish entertaining. Society hairdresser Lillian Frank, a close friend of Pixie's, remembered that the Skases were 'a Hollywood couple'.[55] Rivers of champagne flowed from Bromley.[56]

Even bigger corporate parties were used as a promotional tool for the couple. Melbourne social writer Annette Allison recalled one particular party at South Bank, Brisbane, where the Skases constructed a huge igloo: 'It was terribly glamorous with silk lining and chandeliers in the marquee. The who's who of Brisbane was invited and all the Queensland politicians. Everyone was asking, "Who are these people?"', she said.[57]

The Brisbane headquarters were also constructed to complement 'brand opulence'. Costing $2 million to fit out, the public areas reflected 'postmodern decoration values' with a diverse assortment of artefacts and designs – Brazilian marble floors, Ming dynasty wall panels, a blue marble desk, and Egyptian artefacts and other objects d'art.[58] No wonder the suntanned businessman carried himself with an aura of power and confidence. Still in his thirties, he was mixing with the movers and shakers and becoming a name in his own right.

Marketing the dream

Skase was sufficiently visible on the corporate radar to be invited by News Limited's owner, Rupert Murdoch, to join him in Los Angeles for the 1984 Olympics. Here Skase rubbed shoulders with the corporate elite of America and fell for the buzz of American film and television.[59] No goal was too big for Skase; he now also harboured ambitions to be a Hollywood tycoon.

But a campaign of unrelenting brand promotion was needed to scale the heights that the Skases envisaged for themselves. They understood better than most eighties entrepreneurs that wealth was not just an aspirational lifestyle but an essential marketing tool. Image had become part of the growth dynamics of capitalism.[60] And avariciousness had seeped into the culture. Thus, opulence came to define the Skases and their company. As one journalist noted: 'Much of the image was carefully manufactured, manicured almost'.[61] Qintex projected an image of luxury and leisure, targeting the leisure class, 'that small elite section of the market in the upper income brackets'.[62]

Christopher constructed his image around a *nouveau riche* style – with his trademark white jacket, set against his suntanned olive skin, or sharp suits set off with pink shirts. At his lavish private parties he liked to be seen sipping bourbon, puffing on a cigar and entertaining guests in his honey-toned, seductive voice.[63] And he was often photographed for the media holding a champagne flute at one of his many lavish functions, surrounded by politicians, millionaires and celebrities – projecting an image of power and wealth.[64]

Pixie, too, was defined by her extravagant style. Unrestrained in her spending habits, she flaunted an endless stream of expensive jewellery, gowns, shoes and fur coats. Emulating the excesses of Imelda Marcos, the much-publicised wife of 1980s Philippines dictator Ferdinand, Pixie's wardrobe in the couple's mansion contained more apparel than she could ever wear.[65] When her husband's business empire was at its peak, she used to fly from the Gold Coast to Melbourne in a chartered jet to have her hair done. At one stage the couple owned two Rolls-Royces, a BMW sports car and a $6 million yacht called *Mirage III*, complete with Pixie's finishing touches of exclusive designer ashtrays and silverware.[66]

In their social lives, the Skases appeared to borrow inspiration from the characters and the settings of F Scott Fitzgerald's classic novel *The Great Gatsby*. The parallels with the Skases are unnervingly close. A bit like Jay Gatsby, who famously never mixed at his own parties, the stiff and straight-backed Skase never looked socially comfortable.[67]

The illusion the parties created had a clear business purpose – to impress.[68] The guests were carefully chosen: clients, journalists, investors, bankers, lawyers. They were designed to showcase 'Skase the magnificent'.[69] Most of the bankers and investors 'took the Skase bait hook, line and sinker'.[70] The Skases' hospitality was seductive. In 1985, for example, the couple's Christmas party turned heads. One hundred and fifty guests from Melbourne were flown to Brisbane on a chartered jet, which was met by twenty-seven white limousines: 'They presented glamorously – the flawless hostess with big hair; Christopher the Krug [champagne]-loving tycoon'.[71] Skase was 'The Host with the Most. The Man of the Future', as a headline described him in the *Australian Financial Review*.[72]

The results were impressive. Skase had mounted one of the most calculated, extensive and successful public relations campaigns of his era. He had used the media to project an image to three crucial sectors: the sharemarket, banks and other financial institutions, and consumers.[73] 'Everyone', it was claimed, 'wanted a piece of their lifestyle'.[74]

Today this would easily be recognised as 'personal branding'. But the concept wasn't officially recognised until 1997 when American management guru Tom Peters crystalised the emergence of the marketing technique in a seminal article, 'The Brand Called You', in *Fast Company Magazine.* The Skases had anticipated the trend and helped give it momentum.

The cultural shift ushered in by the 'new entrepreneurs' with media-driven lives had had a major impact. Just a generation earlier, CEOs were largely out of the public limelight. But, as journalist and author Gideon Haigh argued: 'business got sexy; not surprisingly, it sometimes crossed the line into sleaziness'.[75] The Skases were in the forefront of this change.

Siphoning ... or stealing?

On the surface, Skase appeared driven by insatiable ambition. This was the basis of the risk he posed to investors and financiers. But he posed another risk to these groups. Skase deceptively siphoned tens of millions of dollars from Qintex to two of his private firms – Kahmea Investments and Qintex Group Management Services. The former was used, in part, to buy shares in Qintex so that Skase could maintain personal control over the publicly listed company. Maintaining control of Qintex was the key part of Skase's strategy to build his empire. Because he was convinced of his intrinsic ability to amass wealth through the company, he aimed to control 50 per cent or more of Qintex shares. But Kahmea was also used as the Skases' private bank – a fund from which they subsidised much of their lavish lifestyle. The shuffling of money around from his public to his private companies was facilitated by lax company law. Skase was executive chair of Qintex – a position that gave him considerable sway – and both he and Pixie were the directors of Kahmea. It was the financial equivalent of letting a fox run a chicken coop.

The opaqueness of Skase's business operations extended to his

Qintex Group Management Services, which was used to pay his inner circle of executives. In each case, the payments were disguised as 'consultancy fees'. The charges later brought against Skase by the ASC mainly dealt with these transfers of money. The ASC clearly thought that they breached Skase's duties as a director of the company; that is, he stole from the public company to fund his private interests. But as the charges never came to court it's not possible to determine whether any criminality was involved. Writing in *The Australian* in 2001, Robert Gottliebsen claimed that Skase secretly moved $40 million of Qintex funds to Kahmea Investments.[76] The transfers, he wrote, were not authorised by the board but it was not clear when the practice started. All that was clear, according to Gottliebsen, was that the cheques were signed off by an independent director of Qintex.

But who was the independent director? Gottliebsen didn't reveal the name in his article, presumably not wanting to attract a libel suit. But a year later, Gottliebsen disclosed in another article that 'Sir Lenox Hewitt for years as director of Qintex signed the cheques that facilitated Skase's ambition to control the company'.[77] Sir Lenox had, for decades, been a powerful federal departmental secretary, part of a post-war coterie of 'old guard' mandarins who used to meet over lunch at Canberra's Commonwealth Club and, over a sherry, negotiated with each other before confronting their ministers.[78] Skase was careful whom he put on the board and if, as claimed, Sir Lenox did sign the cheques to facilitate Skase's accumulation of private wealth, it was an extraordinary practice for him to have engaged in, to say the least.

Creating the Mirage

Once established in Queensland, Skase moved quickly to realise his dream of becoming a tourism mogul. The concept of luxury resorts was new to Australia and some financial analysts doubted that such businesses would deliver high returns. However, Skase could see that the resorts he had in mind would become global tourist attractions. And he planned to expand his concept globally.

Skase again used clever marketing in branding his resorts on the Gold Coast and in Port Douglas as a 'Mirage' and promoting them as status symbols; bywords for luxury and indulgence. Skase spared no expense in promoting his vision of a high-class resort surrounded by condominiums. When the Gold Coast Mirage opened in September 1987, a plane full of journalists and other dignitaries was flown from Melbourne for the three days of festivities. Journalist John Beveridge was one of the invitees. The soft sell greeted him on the plane with specially made seat covers with the slogan 'Too Good to be True – Mirage'. Once on the ground, he felt the resort was akin to 'entering another world', a place where you could, however fleetingly, 'live the life of Christopher Skase'. And although Beveridge was mildly repelled by the 'tacky mix of antiques and noble savagery', he admitted that 'you couldn't help but be impressed by the scale of the latest Skase vision of building a worldwide network of luxury resorts'. The lobby featured a huge waterfall, outdoor pools ringed the complex and bathrooms featured gold-plated taps.[79]

The Port Douglas resort was an even more luxurious, sprawling complex, surrounded by hundreds of palm trees airlifted individually by chopper from a plantation bought by Skase from a failed agricultural venture. Filtered saltwater lagoons surrounded the complex, making it appear as if it was floating on water. A raft of skin treatments in specially designed bottles awaited customers in the sumptuous bathrooms. The golf course was designed by five-times British Open winner Peter Thompson. The Mirage resort transformed Port Douglas from a sleepy far-north Queensland seaside town into a sophisticated tropical playground for the rich and famous.

By now, Skase had become 'the boy wonder of corporate Australia'.[80] It was an image he further burnished when he bankrolled the struggling AFL team Brisbane Bears (later Lions), using millions of his company's money to underpin the establishment of the AFL in a stronghold of rugby league. His largesse extended to paying $700 000 over three years to high-profile goal kicker Warwick Capper, described by some as an 'overrated and fading star',[81] to lure him from the Sydney Swans to the Bears. Skase also bought Capper a menswear shop as part of the deal.[82] Capper had been a star at the Sydney Swans football club when Edelsten took over the franchise. Assistant coach of the Bears at the time, Mark Maclure, was dazzled by the power Skase exuded around the club: 'he was a wheeler and dealer'.[83]

For Skase, the adulation meant that he had achieved the social acceptance that he'd long craved. By the latter 1980s, he was, as one commentator noted, 'a man feted by governments, industry, politicians and the media and he absorbed with ease the public recognition it bestowed on him'.[84]

The media mogul

By 1987, Skase's dream to be a media and tourism mogul was well advanced. And in the same year his dream was further cemented when he purchased the Channel 7 network from Fairfax Ltd. The media at the time noted that the purchase signified Skase's 'meteoric rise to national prominence'.[85] The road to the purchase had been paved the year before by the Hawke government's changes to the media laws which, henceforth, forbade cross-ownership in both print and television but allowed up to 75 per cent audience reach in each market. The impact of the change was far-reaching. The push to concentration of ownership in each of the two markets was unleashed and, consequently, it fostered takeover bids by acquisitive entrepreneurs on more borrowed money. Critics railed that the government had given its media mates all they wanted.[86]

Days after the changes had been introduced, Rupert Murdoch made a successful bid for Herald and Weekly Times Pty Ltd and, in the process, came to dominate Australia's newsprint media with the long-term consequences discussed in chapter 11. In late 1986,

Murdoch sold the Herald and Weekly Times' stake in Channel 7 to Fairfax Ltd, but for an inflated price and only to see the ratings tumble. Enter Skase.

Skase showed his acumen for negotiation as it was widely acknowledged that he had struck a good deal in purchasing Channel 7 for $780 million. But more compellingly, the network was considered the one with the most potential for improvement.[87] Fairfax had let the station run down, especially in the Melbourne market.

Overnight, Skase had become one of Australia's largest television broadcasters. He was ready to take on Alan Bond, who had recently bought Channel 9 from Kerry Packer for $1 billion.

However, the Channel 7 deal had financial and psychological ramifications for Skase. Already feted for his supposed business acumen, Skase found that rescuing Channel 7 elevated him to near rock-star status. As one journalist recalled, Skase had made a triumphant return to Melbourne with his acquisition. When Skase pulled up in a limo outside the Seven studios for the first time, 'he was welcomed with a cheer'.[88] The trouble was, Skase began to believe this image was reality.

Derryn Hinch, Channel 7's then popular nightly current affairs host, recalled that once inside the station on his inaugural visit, Skase exuded all the confidence of an acclaimed movie star: 'He swept in, full of boyish charm, confidence and enthusiasm'. Hinch thought his new boss exuded an 'over-the-top, enthusiastic, charismatic, self-believing' demeanour that was, by now, his trademark.[89] He had big plans for the channel, he told staff, but quizzed later by journalists about how he intended to fund the purchase, he curtly replied 'from internal resources'. Of course, time would show that those 'internal resources' were, as John Beveridge writes, 'a merry-go-round of debt and paper shuffling that was always destined to collapse on itself if Skase ever stood still long enough for someone to add up the figures'.[90]

Hinch was struck by Skase's cavalier approach to debt. He recalled that one day in the Seven Network's inner sanctum in Sydney:

> Skase had just come from what must have been a cliff-edge meeting with some of his jittery bankers. Yet he was laughing and joking. I asked him how it had gone. Skase mimed a sort of Charlie Chaplin routine. In his clever suit and trick tie he danced and edged towards the door with his arms outspread. 'It's tight but we'll get out of it,' he said.[91]

Skase appeared to be losing touch with reality. He began to believe his own image, 'convinced that he could always manage to do the next deal and the next'.[92]

The Channel 7 deal left Qintex dangerously exposed to debt, and especially because the financial prospects for television networks in the late 1980s had darkened considerably; it was a time of diminished revenue and slashed profit margins.[93] In fact, just as Skase was putting the changes to Channel 7 in place, a prominent broker, James Capel, wrote a report entitled 'Qintex: Is it all Mirage?' Surely this should have given the National Companies and Securities Commission (NCSC) cause to act, but it had limited powers.

Capel had fundamentally summed up the problem with the company. For years Qintex had teetered on a mountain of borrowings. As it grew exponentially, so had its liabilities, and the cash flow needed to service its interest bill never looked like catching up.[94] Total debt across the group would eventually add up to $1.6 billion. A 2004 analysis of Qintex by Catherine Hoyte showed that the company never had a dependable cash flow.[95]

Behind the scenes, Skase's bravado over mounting debts gave way to panic. There was a frantic shuffling of shrinking funds from company to company within the group. The rule seemed to be 'when in doubt, borrow more and throw an even bigger party'.[96] True to form, it's just what Skase did. In 1987, the Qintex Christmas party was held at the Gold Coast Mirage resort. The ballroom air-conditioning was turned down to chill level, in line with the party theme of a white Christmas, allowing Skase to stride triumphantly onto centre stage to the sound of Bob Dylan's 'Quinn the Eskimo'. The party was a telling moment. Even though Qintex's debts were mounting, Skase still felt the need for the show to go on – filling the resort for the weekend with potential clients and investors along with journalists. Skase threw the biggest parties of all the eighties corporate cowboys.[97]

And the glossy image worked. The banks continued to be conned. Financial investment advisor and analyst Austin Donnelly argued that the financial experts 'were paying more attention to the highly promoted image of the company ... when anything other than a superficial analysis of the situation would have shown a far from promising future'.[98]

Manipulation of accounting practices was a key part in maintaining the illusion that Qintex was a profitable operation. Hoyte argues that Skase was involved in creative accounting, moving money between different parts of the group, and that he 'repeatedly stressed the value of the group's assets to distract attention from its debt burden'.[99] Accounting firm Wallace McMullin and Smail became Qintex's auditor in 1982–83, and its audits, 'consistently without qualification, legitimated the company's apparent financial status which allowed Qintex to flourish and helped create the group's mirage, until its collapse'.[100]

Inadequate corporate regulation exacerbated the problem of holding Skase and Qintex to account. The NCSC was unable to cope with the corporate excesses of the 1980s: 'It was under-funded, short staffed, and restricted by divided control'.[101] But the more serious claim about its failure was whether it was ever designed to be an effective watchdog. Seven of the eight commissioners were business people who maintained their contacts with the business sector.[102]

The beginning of the end

The purchase of Channel 7 undoubtedly satisfied Skase's ego, but it revealed the first chink in his debt-fuelled empire. When it came time to repay his escalating loans, Skase struggled to find the funds. But the setback didn't deter him. In fact, Skase was moving forward with his global ambitions, taking the Mirage resort concept to Hawaii and buying regional American television stations. The Skases bought an $11 million mansion in Beverly Hills that was renowned for sumptuous parties in the 1930s and '40s as their American base. Pixie was excited at the prospect of mixing it with Hollywood celebrities.[103]

Skase even managed to skate past the full impact of the catastrophic October 1987 stockmarket crash. 'Black Tuesday', 20 October, had loomed ominously in Australia after the overnight falls on Wall Street. 'When the trading started it was just a maelstrom', one young floor trader 'chalkie', frantically updating long chalk boards, recalled decades later.[104] The Qintex share price fell 20 per cent, but this was below the average fall of 25 per cent across the market. The sale of the Port Douglas resort condos was coming on stream and prices exceeded expectations, providing Qintex with much-needed cash flow.[105] However, as one fund manager summed up Skase's position after the purchase of Channel 7, 'He doesn't have much margin for error'.[106]

Somehow Skase compartmentalised his growing problems over debt. During 1987, he had spent $780 million buying Channel 7, $330 million on his Mirage resorts, $80 million on his Hawaiian resorts, and $250 million on American television stations, bringing Qintex's overall debt to $1.6 billion. But on paper, the Qintex empire was valued in excess of $2.2 billion.

The show could go on. In September 1988, Skase celebrated his fortieth birthday at a glittering party at Bromley. Guests included Queensland Premier Mike Ahern (who had replaced Sir Joh) and Opposition leader Wayne Goss. The free-wheeling wonderboy was feted by all.[107] The birthday bash reportedly cost $500 000.[108]

In the same month, Skase formally opened the Port Douglas resort. The five days of lavish entertainment featured a gaggle of international and national celebrities and officials flown in on private jets. Skase stood in the centre of celebrations surrounded by the glitterati of 1989:

'Greg Norman chatted with Pat Cash, Captain Mark Phillips rubbed shoulders with John Farnham and Formula One driver Nigel Mansell. An odd collection of pale, drunken stockbrokers, bankers and journalists tried in vain to blend in with the suntanned celebrities'.[109]

Skase invented his own golf tournament to coincide with the opening and used his Channel 7 network to promote the opening nationwide. Lawrence van der Plaat had a ringside seat at the festivities and recorded his observations. Once the effect of the alcohol really kicked in, 'many of the guests ended up in the lagoons, designer wear cast aside, while one company director was seen on a hotel balcony suite in a very compromising position behind a younger woman who was gripping the balustrade tightly'.[110]

Christopher and Pixie were ecstatic at the success of the event.

Not only was Skase able to con the banks, he also got saturation media coverage for free. Being seduced by the eighties powerful corporate leaders was an occupational hazard for the media, according to business reporter Ian Verrender. Most business reporters, he argues, began to believe they were part of the business world: 'that the reason they are being squired to upmarket restaurants, to corporate boxes and offered trips to exotic places is that they are part of the team'.[111]

By the late 1980s, Qintex was at increasing risk of folding. Rising interest rates created a breach in the dam wall, but the toll from years of mismanagement propelled the wall to collapse. Craig Pratt, one of Qintex's senior financial officers, states that the company had problems with cash flow from the time he began with the group in 1986 and that the situation got worse, exacerbated by 'head office overheads, which were substantial' – in other words, Skase's opulent lifestyle.[112]

Skase turned to the legendary CEO of the Hong Kong Bank of Australia, James Yonge. A polarising figure, Yonge was regarded as a brilliant financial mind by his supporters and an arrogant, reckless lender by his critics for backing so many of the eighties entrepreneurs, in quickly arranged deals. In addition to facilitating access to quick finance, Yonge had a tendency to overrate the abilities of entrepreneurs.[113] As a consequence of his dealings with Yonge, Skase sold off 49 per cent of his Mirage complexes to a Japanese consortium for $433 million. But, instead of consolidating, he went for broke, exposing the Hong Kong Bank to great risk.

The last deal

On 31 March 1989, Sir Leo Hielscher, the retired former head of the Queensland Treasury who had recently accepted an invitation to sit on the Qintex board, got a shock reading the paper over breakfast. Leaping off the page was the news that Skase had launched a $1.2 billion bid for MGM/United Artists in the United States. Placing such a respected financial luminary as Sir Leo on the board had been a calculated move by Skase to signal the investment community 'that Qintex was okay and worth backing'. However, Hielscher, who knew nothing of the plan before it appeared in the financial press, had every reason to be surprised. He had already been unnerved by the dysfunctional culture of the company, and the fact that the board had only met once in the previous nine months. After reading of the bid, Hielscher, citing 'personal reasons', resigned.[114]

Skase not only neglected to inform his board of the proposed move, he also hadn't bothered to arrange any firm finance for the eye-watering deal. Like a desperate gambler, Skase had reasoned that he needed a growth strategy to prevent Qintex from going under; the only alternative was a fire sale of ever more assets.

But what exactly was he trying to buy at MGM? Skase was focused on the studio's library of films, which could be rented to television and cable networks hungry for programming material. But some in the industry thought that the once proud studio was now living on its past glories.[115]

For Skase, though, it was the deal of a lifetime. He had fantasised for years about becoming an even bigger media mogul by taking Hollywood by storm. As van der Plaat learnt, ever since Skase's

1984 trip to Los Angeles, 'he had been determined to replicate his successful formula in America'.[116] But Skase was flying blind. After announcing the proposed deal, he arranged a meeting with one of his senior executives and, flashing a piece of paper documenting the deal, simply said: 'find a way to fund this'.[117]

Skase was being hopelessly outclassed by two of the most experienced and ruthless global corporate chiefs: Kirk Kerkorian, president and CEO of MGM, and Rupert Murdoch, chairman and CEO of News Ltd.

Kerkorian was the style of business tycoon Skase had long aspired to become. The son of Armenian immigrants, the self-made billionaire combined the instincts of an avid gambler with a calm, unruffled manner.[118] His career epitomised the skills and daring of both a corporate raider and a corporate builder. Known as 'the king of Las Vegas', he had had a leading role in developing the city's glitzy tourist strip through real estate, casino and hotel projects. In 1967, Kerkorian built the world's then largest hotel, the International, with Elvis Presley headlining the entertainment. Clearly, he outranked Skase by orders of magnitude.

And Murdoch was Skase's ideal of a global media tycoon. Murdoch became one of the world's media giants during the media revolution of the 1980s. By the late eighties, the relentlessly focused Murdoch was well on the way to cementing a global media empire that brought both great wealth and enormous power. But Skase was no match for Murdoch's cold, ruthless approach to business.

Once Skase had announced his bid, he thought he had Kerkorian's in-principle agreement when the two shook hands on the deal. But Murdoch came circling with a higher offer, and Kerkorian continued to negotiate behind Skase's back. Murdoch made a $400 million higher offer, forcing Skase to match and pushing him into a ludicrously over-stretched financial position. As Alan Kohler observed, Kerkorian was causing 'the ground to shift and sway beneath Christopher Skase's feet'.[119]

And when he failed to find the first monthly instalment of $50 million, it was basically over for Qintex.[120] The company's share price descended into junk status. Qintex went into receivership in November 1989 as Australia entered a recession under the impact of crippling interest rates. Skase's earnings never matched the scale of his debts.[121]

Pixie remembered the day the business collapsed as 'a whirlwind, just petrifying'; the company went down

> like a pack of cards … Christopher came home and locked himself in the library. He was very rattled and I knew something was wrong. He had finance people and bank people all around him – it was frenzied. He shielded me from a lot of it, but it was like being in freefall.[122]

While the drama of the collapse was unfolding, Skase's fate had also been sealed from within the company. Sir Lenox had recently resigned from the board, and Skase had to find another person in Australia who would join Qintex and be prepared to sign the cheques that siphoned money to his private companies. He believed that the former Ampol CEO Ted Harris would be the sort of person he needed. But, as Gottliebsen wrote, 'It was a horrendous error. Harris was not that sort of person'. When the day came for Ted Harris to sign his first cheque he refused to do so. Harris had discovered the $40 million that had been siphoned off for 'management fees', an amount he regarded as excessive and unjustified. Harris informed the NCSC of his concerns and it began investigations. Skase saw the writing on the wall.[123] Lawrence van der Plaat added to Skase's woes. He turned informer for the Australian Securities Commission, delivering them a bundle of incriminating documents; he later wrote a tell-all book. There was no suggestion that he was ever involved in any of Skase's wrong-doings.

Doing a runner

Once he realised he was under investigation, Skase began executing plans for an escape route overseas. In late 1989, he enlisted various family members to set up bank accounts into which he deposited millions of dollars, which were then transferred into accounts in the Cayman Islands and Austria. Financial auditor Max Donnelly, who by then had been appointed Skase's bankruptcy trustee, and who spent years trying to chase down Skase's assets, explained: 'I found a money trail of about $10 million running through Austria and [the] Cayman Islands. But it's what I haven't found that is of more concern. I wouldn't be surprised if it was more like $50 million'.[124] On Majorca, Skase boasted that he had $100 million to funnel to the island.[125] Either way he had stolen a fortune. Not surprisingly, Skase had an uncooperative attitude towards Donnelly, which made it almost impossible for the auditor to sort out Skase's estate. And the problem for the Australian Securities Commission, which had recently replaced the NCSC, was the hangover investigations they had from the collapse of several of the eighties cowboys' companies; the agency was overwhelmed.[126]

At the time of Donnelly's initial investigations, Skase was still free to travel, and it was while he was working around Europe as a consultant to Russian exile Zooab Tchokotoa that Skase came across a property owned by his business colleague – the $3 million walled Majorcan estate La Noria, which he bought.

Some time in early 1990 as well, Skase loaded into two shipping containers a pair of Rolls-Royces, a BMW, fifteen Bang & Olufsen stereos, televisions, and enough beds, marble furniture and antiques to spread through the nine-bedroom estate.[127] The containers were shipped to London where they were warehoused for a year so that investigators would lose the trail. According to Max Donnelly, the two Rolls-Royces were subsequently sold and the money deposited into an Austrian bank account.

With loads of cash, furniture and personal effects, Skase just had to await his opportunity. Due to appear back in court in Australia, Skase hadn't worked out the final details of his exit. On Thursday, 13 June 1991, he made the bold move to help facilitate his bankruptcy. Exploiting loopholes in the bankruptcy laws, Skase gathered together twenty-two Brisbane-based friends who were owed money, including restaurateurs and florists, and persuaded them to petition the Federal Court in Brisbane to have him declared a bankrupt. The friends were owed just short of $80 000. One, a doctor, was owed just $25. The loophole in the bankruptcy laws meant that by sheer weight of numbers, they could outvote the handful of banks owed millions of dollars. It was a master stroke that successfully blocked his major creditors from moving against him in the New South Wales Supreme Court. More importantly, it allowed Skase to take control of his own affairs. Anyone dealing with Skase now had to act through his trustee. He chose a Brisbane accountant, Neville Pocock.

By law, Pocock was required to take possession of Skase's passport, which he did. But Pocock made a fatal miscalculation when he returned the passport twenty-four hours later because, he reasoned, Skase had met all conditions, that he had to return to Spain for work and that he had agreed to return when instructed to. Pocock was then dumped by an angry banking syndicate, which replaced him with Max Donnelly. But it was too late, Skase was gone within twenty-four hours.

Final plans for a possible escape had been executed in the weeks leading up to Pocock's appointment. A hideaway was secured to stay the night before Skase could seize an opportunity to extricate himself from Brisbane. With the return of his passport, this turned out to be 3 July 1991. Skase's long-time head of security, Bill Jones, revealed this part of the plan after his boss's death. Jones, a former British and Australian SAS commando, rented two apartments as hideouts. One was in a nursing home on Brisbane's northside where Skase stayed the night before he left; the other was a backup home on the Gold Coast: 'we simply rented the units for a month, stocked them with Jack Daniels and Grange Hermitage and waited for instructions'.[128]

On the appointed night, Jones commandeered two vehicles to take Skase to Brisbane airport from his hideaway; one carrying the about-to-be fugitive and one driven by Jones with Skase's luggage. Once inside the airport, Skase boarded a Malaysian Airlines flight to Kuala Lumpur, where he then boarded another flight to Europe. La Noria – and ignominy – awaited.

The wash-up

The dangerous excesses of the 1980s entrepreneurs cast a long shadow over Australian society. During the early to mid-1990s, Skase kept up his highly publicised fight against extradition; Bond was in and out of court and jail and the WA Inc Royal Commission kept issuing sordid revelations about government–business dealings involving state and national corporate leaders. And the collective mismanagement of the risks associated with deregulation contributed to an economy reeling from high interest rates and a crippling level of overseas debt, with the latter fuelling the former. Most of the debt had been accrued by the corporate cowboys and most of it had been consumed in unproductive takeovers. The costs were being borne by all Australians.[129] Amid the clamour of this continuing fallout, voices were raised about the flaws in the design and implementation of deregulation. In 1990 alone, criticism and calls for reform penetrated all corners of the mainstream media.

Liquidation expert David Crawford took aim at banks for their poor lending practices; at CEOs for their lack of underlying morality; and at governments for a lack of regulation. Some of the practices indulged in by CEOs 'were so bad as to call into question our regulatory systems'.[130]

The *Canberra Times* focused on the decline in corporate morality over the previous decade and argued that while it didn't begin in the era of deregulation, 'it certainly spread', and that bankers, lawyers, politicians and accountants were all to blame.[131]

University of Canberra academic and corporate researcher Professor Roman Tomasic laid the blame for the string of corporate collapses squarely at the feet of government. There was a lack of preparedness by the Hawke government, he argued, 'to lay down strict ground rules'. Warming to his critique, Tomasic said that governments and banks 'were heedless of any long term view' and that, as a society, 'we haven't been concerned anywhere near with the ethical base of business in this country'. Regulatory agencies, he concluded, needed to 'clean up their act'.[132]

But as Henry Bosch, the retiring chair of the NCSC lamented, there were clear reasons why his agency had failed to bring the corporate cowboys to justice. Too few had gone to jail, he said. But his belief in co-regulation between the business community and the government, within a system of cooperation between the states and the Commonwealth, had proved unequal to the task of controlling bad corporate behaviour. However, Bosch was on solid ground in his attack on the lack of federal funding; the 'chicken feed' of funds to tackle the corporate gunslingers and their takeover mania. In 1990, his agency received only half the funding of the National Crime Authority.[133]

These informed voices all pointed to three things: corporations willingly abrogated responsibility for any commitment to social obligations; governments were, at best, lukewarm about effective corporate regulation; and a wide-ranging reform program was needed to protect society from the excesses of rogue corporations.

But as the dust settled on the decade of Australia's wild west economy, the Hawke government set about on a new approach to regulation – one which centralised its activities in Canberra. How would this work?

The Skase saga petered out when Christopher died of stomach

cancer in 2001, having successfully avoided extradition to Australia. Pixie remained in exile until she slipped quietly back into the country in 2008 and has maintained a low profile ever since.

4

'THE SHAMBOLIC JOURNEY INTO OBLIVION': HIH INSURANCE

A distressed Marilyn Reidy only discovered that Australia's second largest insurance company had collapsed when it was too late. It came like a bolt of lightning. After all, HIH Insurance seemed impregnable. Headed by Ray Williams, HIH comprised more than 240 companies in sixteen countries, accumulated in record time, a feat cementing Williams' reputation as a strong leader and a legend of the industry. But none of this counted when, on 15 March 2001, Reidy tried to make a claim. She and her husband, who was incapacitated by a brain tumour, depended on his HIH cheques to survive. But when Reidy tried to cash her cheque from HIH it bounced. Later that day came the official announcement that the company had crashed, owing $5.3 billion – at the time, the largest corporate collapse ever unleashed on the country.[1] The Reidys were without an income for at least the next three months.[2]

Just hours before the Reidys' HIH cheque bounced, there had been a feeding frenzy inside the company. Aware their cash cow was bleeding to death, HIH executives and their mates began desperately trying to cash cheques and grab bonuses. HIH lawyers and tax advisors were paid out hundreds of thousands of dollars. In total, $3 million disappeared in the last twenty-four hours before HIH went into liquidation.[3]

The implosion of HIH is still regarded by some as Australia's most significant corporate collapse.[4] It was as if a bomb had blasted a giant hole in the country's economy: the insurance industry was left paralysed with one million worthless insurance policies; tens of thousands of shareholders fretted over their worthless equity; and about one thousand employees lost their jobs, literally overnight. But these were just the immediate impacts. A cloud hung over everyday commercial activity. The $2 billion building industry descended into turmoil, as did the work of professional groups like lawyers and engineers who had to turn away clients for lack of cover against negligence. Disabled people could no longer receive their regular payments; car accident victims insured with HIH were left waiting for operations and other medical procedures, and countless professional indemnity, public liability, home warranty and travel insurance holders found themselves uninsured for outstanding claims. Premiums across the industry skyrocketed.

Without public liability cover, councils and not-for-profit organisations cancelled community and sporting events. As one observer commented, the HIH collapse 'left a trail of broken marriages, bankruptcies and shattered dreams'.[5] And confidence evaporated in the insurance industry and the system of regulation. The public even questioned the integrity of the free-market system itself.[6] It's no wonder that, after the collapse, Williams lamented that he had become 'the most hated man in Australia'.[7] His was a mighty fall from grace.

Like Edelsten, Bond and Skase, Williams had cultivated a high public profile. He was a recipient of the Order of Australia for his extensive charitable donations on behalf of HIH. He was the epitome of the savvy CEO but without the brashness and flashiness of the eighties corporate cowboys. The white-haired, square-jawed sixty-eight-year-old was lean and fit, with chiselled facial features, trademark neatly pressed dark blue suits, double-cuffed shirts replete with gold cufflinks, perfectly knotted ties, and a firm, sincere, double-handed handshake. Add stylish, rimless glasses through which he looked upon the world with an intense but sincere-looking gaze and Williams conveyed an air of impeccable manners and 'old boy' establishment authority.

But appearances were deceptive. Williams had slipped into a by-now familiar pattern of corporate leadership infused by grandiosity, self-delusion and risk-taking. Like former failed entrepreneurs, Williams' disastrous management style was facilitated by a compliant board and regulators who averted their gaze. HIH was a slow-moving train wreck.

Insurance is one of the most profitable industries on the planet, but it's also one of the riskiest. In the United States, a thousand insurance companies failed between 1969 and 2015.[8] In an attempt to stay profitable, insurance companies have long used statistical analysis to calculate the cost of premiums for their clients and what their future liabilities will be. Successful companies try to balance out profitable 'short tail' products – such as car and home insurance – which can be settled quickly, with 'long tail' products – such as death, disability and income protection – which carry future, but indeterminate, timelines. 'Long tail' insurance is like looking into the future with a crystal ball.

The HIH collapse happened in the shadow of changes to Australia's system of financial regulation. In 1996, the Howard government had appointed the Wallis Inquiry, headed by AMP's head, Stan Wallis, to examine the issue. As journalist Adele Ferguson has written, Wallis was a 'corporate blue blood': 'He was never going to rock the boat'.[9] And the five committee members on the inquiry were all market-orientated individuals from within the financial services industry and academia. Not surprisingly, it was criticised by some for not being a fully independent review.[10]

The inquiry recommended consolidating the separate regulators for banking, insurance and securities into the one centralised agency. This became the Australian Securities and Investment Commission (ASIC), which in 1998 took over the role of regulator from the Australian Securities Commission to be a 'corporate law watchdog'. But Wallis recommended that regulatory intervention be kept to a minimum and proposed a system of voluntary codes overseen by ASIC. As the chair of ASIC, Greg Medcraft, later explained, Australia's financial regulation 'is based on self-execution and relies on people doing the right thing'. There would be no restrictions imposed on the type of financial products that could be sold to everyday people, no matter the risk.

The inquiry took the view that in a capitalist economy financial corporations had to be allowed to fail.[11] At the same time, it recognised the importance of treating customers honestly and fairly.[12] The Wallis committee never resolved these competing aims.

Who knew?

In one of the worst kept secrets in Australian business circles, HIH was widely known to be in financial difficulties prior to its collapse. Mark Westfield, business writer for *The Australian*, was one of several journalists who investigated HIH's financial difficulties from 1997 onwards. In fact, Westfield had suspected that the company was little more than a giant Ponzi scheme – relying on revenue growth to pay for its discounted rates for insurance cover and its rising payouts.[13] The problems at HIH were deemed so serious by HIH's majority shareholder, Swiss insurer Winterthur, that it sold its holding in 1998 after only three years of a business partnership. And in March 2000 the group's principal actuary warned that HIH faced dire consequences unless it changed its accounting policies.[14]

Senior operatives inside HIH knew about the scale of mismanagement within the company. In mid-2000, Jeff Simpson, who had resigned as deputy general manager finance at HIH Insurance a year earlier, was wrestling with his conscience about some of the dodgy financial practices at his old firm. He was considering alerting the insurance regulator, the Australian Prudential Regulation Authority (APRA), about his concerns. The agency had been established only the year before to act as Commonwealth licensing agency and supervisory regulator to banks, and to insurance and superannuation companies with the power to intervene if it suspected mismanagement.

Some of Simpson's contacts in the insurance industry warned him against such action: 'Be careful, Simmo, are you sure you know what you are doing?', they advised.[15] And why wouldn't they be concerned for a colleague? HIH was an industry juggernaut, and whistleblowers always seem to come off badly.

However, Simpson knew that HIH had been involved in sharp accounting practices and he surmised that the latest annual report that Williams had signed off in June 2000 was probably a lie. He was right. Williams had told a big lie in claiming that the company was 'rock solid, sound and dependable' when it was sinking in a sea of debt.

Despite the significant risks, Simpson found the nerve to contact APRA. In mid-2000 he attended a meeting at the agency and subsequently sent it a twenty-one-page document outlining HIH's problems, concluding that the company was in breach of minimum solvency provisions. APRA officers later admitted that Simpson was treated as 'a disgruntled former employee' and his report was therefore not acted upon.[16] As Simpson found out, it was strangely disinterested in investigating the company. In fact, APRA warned that Simpson would be opening himself up to legal action.[17]

In September 2000, the Queensland government raised its concerns about the problems at HIH with APRA.[18] As one journalist noted in *The Australian,* the agency had 'sat on their hands while HIH went into a tailspin'.[19] The Howard government's federal Finance Services Minister, Joe Hockey, was concerned enough about the information floating around openly about the company's troubles prior to the collapse that he approached the company. However, he chose to accept its assurances that it had the situation in hand.[20]

The immediate fallout

In the corridors of power, the collapse had presented the federal government with a number of sticky political problems. It had cut across Howard's boast that Australian business rules didn't need tightening because corporations followed the spirit of the law.[21] How wrong he was. Hockey had to set about devising a rescue package for the thousands of affected victims. By the end of May 2001, and in response to rising public anger, Howard backflipped on his opposition to appointing an inquiry into the collapse and established a royal commission.

The royal commission was headed by Justice Neville Owen, an insolvency expert who sat on the Supreme Court of Western Australia. After he had waded through the evidence of 122 witnesses and 18 700 pages of transcripts he prised open HIH's rotten corporate culture: a Pandora's box of shonky practices, greed and ineptitude at the heart of one of the country's largest companies. The company was, he said, on 'a shambolic journey into oblivion'.[22]

In hindsight, the collapse of HIH was inevitable. But how did such a flawed operation stay afloat for so long? And how did it stumble over the edge so suddenly? Like the demise of Edelsten, Bond and Skase, the roots of HIH's collapse lay with its charismatic leader.

The rise of Ray Williams

Ray Williams had a stellar rise to corporate heavy-weight. Like Bond and Skase, Williams came from a humble background. He was born in the Sydney suburb of Epping, and his mother worked as a psychiatric nurse, his father as a truck driver and part-time bookmaker. After leaving school at fifteen, Williams found employment with Sydney's Metropolitan Water and Sewerage Board where he moved quickly into the medical branch dealing with workers' compensation claims. Here he discovered his paternal side. Often the victims of accidents were lonely migrants who spoke no English. Williams started giving them budgerigars and was delighted to find that having a pet aided their recovery.[23] And thus began Williams' career-long paternalistic attachment to gift-giving.

With little more than restless ambition, Williams got his start running his own business purely by chance. In 1964, he met Michael Payne, a highly successful English insurance underwriter who worked for Lloyd's. Payne was on one of his regular visits to Australia and took a shine to the eager young man. Together they set up MW Payne Liability Agencies in 1986.[24] Payne, who was more like a patron than a boss, saw Australia as an insurance gold mine and left Williams in charge of operations, 'a lone rider on a more or less lawless frontier'.[25]

Under Williams, MW Payne grew quickly, and the company was floated in 1992 as CE Health Holdings with nearly $40 million in assets. The company was later named HIH Insurance. In an early sign of Williams' unshakable confidence in his company and himself, he managed to convince the sceptics that he and his colleagues had the expertise to out-perform in an extremely complex market. Like every successful salesman, Williams conveyed infectious optimism – to some he was known as 'Blue Sky Ray'. It was this optimism that enabled him to negotiate a bonus of nearly $5 million on completion of the 1992 float.[26]

However, the float nearly didn't go ahead at all. Some investors raised concerns over a critical report compiled by funds manager Nick Selvaratnam from BMZ Australia which highlighted that the company had focused on the 'long tail' end of the market and that it had grown 'at such an aggressive rate it was hard to assess its profitability'.[27] Williams responded by placing a ban on staff interacting with Selvaratnam, a policy he maintained with any critics of the company.[28]

Selvaratnam had, in fact, pinpointed the flaw in HIH's business model – its reliance on the risky 'long tail' end of the insurance market. Little did he know that the flaws weren't just in the business model but also in the company's dysfunctional culture, which had been shaped by Williams' personality. However, these flaws were papered over for a time when, in 1995, CE Health merged with Swiss insurer Winterthur Insurance to form HIH Winterthur.

Williams was 'the mercurial epicentre of all things HIH' and 'a God-like chief'.[29] He was also, however, an enigma. Both by temperament and design, he fashioned an opaque public persona, other than his well-known fanaticism for fitness and his interest in philanthropy. In an age of increasingly celebrity CEOs, Williams balanced being the public face of a high-profile corporation with an intensely private life. A frequent traveller to London, he is said to have liked to sit at the very front of first class, often booking the seat next to him to avoid company.[30]

However, the public/private split wasn't the only fault line in Williams' personality. Those who had watched his career noticed other contradictions. Williams' paternalistic and caring side coexisted with streaks of arrogance and egotism. On the caring side, he was always asking after the welfare of the wives and children of his executive team (to which women were never appointed). But he was also 'a control freak'[31] who channelled his humble beginnings into a 'lust for money'.[32]

Journalist Andrew Main, who wrote extensively about the HIH collapse, saw in Williams' personality 'the insecurity-driven relentless drive to succeed'.[33] And somewhere early in his career Williams had discovered that he didn't like having a boss and became determined to strike out on his own. Lurking behind this desire was Williams' aversion to criticism and his strong need to exercise control in all aspects of his life.

Williams fashioned a business empire that was an extension of these contradictions. The two dominant sides to his personality – authoritarian and paternalistic – fused in his running of HIH.

The leadership style permeated all aspects of the company, down to staff appearance. Williams decreed that female staffers could not wear long pants at work; 'Ladies', he thought, 'should wear a skirt'.[34] For men, he outlawed beards and moustaches.[35] It was as if he thought of HIH not just as a private company but also as a family in which he sat as the patriarchal head.

Williams' autocratic nature was bolstered by his fundamentalist

Christian beliefs. The HIH boss was a Christadelphian,[36] a member of a small, cult-like sect whose believers wished to reconnect with the literal word of the Bible and the culture of Christianity as it arose in the first century AD. Christadelphians, like those of other fundamentalist religions, propagated the view that there is one right way of thinking, which is found in the Bible. They take a hard line on the subordinate role of women, forbidding them to preach or pray at their meetings.[37] And they adopt a mantle of superiority when it comes to being 'saved'; on Christ's return only they will become immortal – non-Christadelphians will be destroyed. Williams had total devotion to the Christadelphian Church; he even built a chapel in the grounds of his mansion at Lake Macquarie, north of Sydney.[38]

The likely impact of religious fundamentalism on a leader of a large, complex organisation such as a corporation can't escape consideration. Psychological studies reveal that 'fundamentalism discourages any logical reasoning or scientific evidence that challenges its scripture, making it inherently maladaptive'.[39] In other words, his dogmatic, autocratic style was likely forged, at least in part, in his faith. After his departure from HIH, Williams was reported to have 'thrown himself at the mercy of God'.[40] But fundamentalist religion also gave Williams a belief in his own special gifts – a feeling of omnipotence. He would lay his hands on members of his HIH family as if healing them with divine powers he thought he possessed.[41]

Combining authoritarianism and paternalism, Williams thus found a way to be both a popular and an unaccountable leader – a benevolent autocrat. In the short term it looked to be an inspired model as HIH grew exponentially through acquisitions, but in the long term it proved disastrous.

Inside Williams' corporate fiefdom

Patronage in return for loyalty was the thread connecting HIH operations in the decade before it collapsed. Loyalty meant everything to Williams. As one observer noted, Williams expected blind loyalty from staff: 'When he got it, he judged that you were one of "Ray's people" [and] he would be extremely generous ... If you weren't one of Ray's people, the career track went nowhere'.[42]

An insider knew as much too. Suellen Henry was a one-time analyst in the HIH audit team at Arthur Andersen. In 2004, she offered her observations on Williams to the ABC's *7.30 Report*: 'In my mind, he surrounded himself with people who said, "Yes, Ray. Whatever you think, Ray, we'll do".'[43]

Finance director and board member Dominic Fodera was a beneficiary of Williams' leadership style of patronage in return for loyalty. Fodera had been enticed from his position as a partner at Arthur Andersen, where he had overseen the HIH account, with a 'golden hello' offer from Williams of $1.2 million, which, critics maintained, transformed him into 'Ray's labrador'.[44]

No one in senior management dared question Williams. All quickly learned that their success 'depended on modelling yourself on Ray and telling him what he wanted to hear'.[45] As Suellen Henry recalled: 'unpleasant information was hidden, filtered or sanitised' because Williams, 'didn't like to hear any criticism of his strategies or the way he was running HIH ... he could be very aggressive if you asked any difficult questions'. When she did ask some, as part of her job in the Arthur Andersen audit team, she found herself banned from talking to HIH.[46]

Fodera was later forced to defend his broader role at HIH overseeing a system of accounting that manufactured profits when there should have been losses.[47] He was later jailed for 'failing to act honestly in the discharge of the duties of his office'.[48] Of course, every person has agency over their own actions, but Fodera can also be seen as one of the victims of the corporate culture Williams developed at HIH. At his trial, character witness Baptist minister Martin Duffy spoke on behalf of Fodera, insisting that he was a person 'of real integrity'. He said that Fodera had been 'overly loyal to Williams', describing their relationship as 'very unusual and paternal'. Duffy noted Fodera was susceptible to such a deferential relationship because his own father had been away for most of his childhood, spending time in jail for violence.[49] For this reason, the prospect of prison was, for Fodera, a 'nightmare', fearing that his children would be forced to replicate his own childhood experience.[50]

But Fodera was not alone among the senior people at HIH who may have felt the pressure arising from special payments made by Williams. Such payments were also made to managing director Terry Cassidy and to executive director George Sturesteps. Several others were made to 'loyal lieutenants' and 'old friends' who had worked for Williams for years.[51] HIH is an example, as was Bond Corporation, of the rise of excessive remuneration adversely impacting on corporate culture; it produced a warped sense of entitlement that accompanied the glorification of corporations in society.[52]

HIH's managing director, Terry Cassidy, was jailed for, among other offences, lying to APRA and signing back-dated documents. He committed these offences even though the judge at his trial concluded that he was not the architect of the offences and neither did he obtain any benefits from them.[53] Somehow, he rationalised that his actions were to the benefit of HIH.

In addition to receiving a special one-off payment from Williams, Sturesteps was showered with financial benefits by Williams, including round-the-world first-class travel and accommodation for himself and his wife, Beryl, platinum American Express cards and loans from HIH to purchase two apartments in San Francisco.[54]

Sturesteps was disqualified by APRA from being a company director in relation to the collapse. In something of an understatement, the agency found he had 'demonstrated a lack of knowledge, competence or diligence' in carrying out his duties at HIH. He was the twentieth person APRA disqualified in relation to the demise of the company.[55]

While the individual circumstances in each of these cases differ, and can't all be discussed here, what connects them is the warped corporate culture of HIH. Williams was so consumed by being a benevolent autocrat that no one in the senior echelons of the organisation appeared to be bothered with ethical standards. Everyone was bowing to the founder and chief, who was consumed by every autocrat's desire: to create a lifestyle commensurate with his perceived status.

And there was more than a hint of authoritarianism about Williams; he could lash out when he felt his control was being undermined. He would get angry if he got even a sniff of discussions about the company taking place without his presence. Board member Neville Head told the royal commission about Williams' displeasure over a luncheon meeting arranged between himself and two other non-executive directors. When Williams found out about the meeting, he was not only angry, he slipped into paranoia: 'There appear to be people working against me', he let fly at Head.[56]

The high life

Ambition for wealth and empire building went hand-in-hand in Williams' view of the world. He built a palatial mansion on Lake Macquarie, called Gwandalan Manor, a Mediterranean-style, six-bedroom house, set in a 25-hectare, high-security compound. Williams and his wife, Rita, owned two houses in Sydney's Mosman, a holiday unit in Surfers Paradise, and an apartment in Perisher Valley. From the 1980s, Williams progressively put these properties in his wife's name.[57] Rounding out the opulent lifestyle, the couple owned a BMW and a Rolls-Royce. And Williams' office was decked out in a style befitting a king, including a marble bathroom with a spa and gold taps.

It's clear that Williams shared in the culture of ostentatious excess that, by the 1990s, had become characteristic of many CEOs. This culture dictated that the benchmarks by which a person's worth was gauged were lavishly styled properties, yachts, and multiple expensive cars. In turn, social scientists argued that such ostentation, evident globally, was leading to a rise of 'cultural narcissism', characterised by illusionary expectations, inflated self-concepts, along with a demand for a perfect image.[58] It was also having a corrosive impact on business ethics.

To buttress his vanity, Williams used HIH funds to buy himself the status of a respected philanthropist. Of course, it was not unusual for businesses to engage in philanthropy. However, in HIH's case, Williams acted unilaterally, with neither a dedicated budget, nor the explicit approval of the board; the items were approved after they had been allocated by Williams.[59]

In the last decade of HIH's existence, Williams donated millions of the company's funds to charity. The accolades followed: an honorary doctor of law from Monash University; a medical institute named after him; and the Order of Australia. Behind the persona of the benevolent autocrat lay an insecure man whose vanity needed to be constantly stoked.[60]

Philanthropic largesse was only part of the soft power Williams wielded through HIH. The company was a generous supporter of the Liberal Party's 500 Club, founded in the early 1980s to channel business funds into the party to ensure that it supported a pro-business agenda. Williams donated nearly half a million dollars of HIH's funds between 1994 and 2000, making it one of the party's biggest donors and entitling him to 500 Club membership.[61] Was Williams buying influence in the increasingly murky world of political donations? 'It seems likely', wrote Howard Spender, research director of the Australasian Centre for Corporate Responsibility. Ray Williams, he argued, 'anticipated his generosity would result in a political predisposition towards lighter scrutiny by regulatory authorities of HIH in particular, as well as of insurance in general'. Shareholders and the public paid the price.[62]

Patronage spread around like confetti

At times, Williams used HIH as a personal piggy bank to dispense favours – and not just to his executive team. Frank Holland, an old friend of Williams, was given an interest-free unsecured loan of $486 000 that was not repaid for seven years – an omission that did not prevent him being presented with a $1600 box of Alfred Dunhill cigars by Williams.[63]

Favoured HIH employee Stuart Korchinski received a range of special benefits. In 2000 the accountant was granted a bonus of $158 000 and a $17 000 trip back to Canada when his father died. When Korchinski left HIH at the end of 2000, Williams increased his payout by $75 000 to $910 000, sold him his company car (a Saab convertible) for $1000 and wrote off a $250 000 housing loan.[64]

And there was a generous gift to Colin Richardson, a merchant banker and advisor to Williams, who had arranged a loan of $10 million for him to purchase a controlling interest in the company at the time of the public float. He was given round-the-world air tickets for himself, his wife, his four children and their nanny to compensate him for an 'awful' Christmas when he had to work.

Williams' secretary, Rita Young, was showered with favourable treatment. Her salary of $105 000 was thought to be the highest then paid in Australia for such a position. However, after she moved to the Gold Coast two years before the collapse, she was flown to Sydney each week and put up at the five-star Hotel Intercontinental. Williams valued her so much that he gave her a Millennium Ball, a large spherical object costing over $3000.[65]

There's no suggestion that either Young, Richardson, Korchinski or Holland engaged in any wrong-doing by being in receipt of Williams' generosity.

HIH staff were granted access to the gravy train through extravagant annual Christmas parties. These started in the early 1990s and evolved into legendary corporate events, held in each of the six state capitals. The Sydney head office party was always the most lavishly organised. Large venues such as the Powerhouse Museum, the Intercontinental Hotel or the Australian Jockey Club were hired for the 800 invitees. Each year the party was themed – 'gangster', 'South American', 'Alcatraz' or 'Vegas', and as the decade wore on, these corporate parties came to have 'the dark rendering of pre-war Berlin cabaret' – gaudy, bawdy and wild – 'overlain with the shadow of impending disaster'.[66]

Staff were ferried to and from venues in taxis and mini buses, with Williams typically arriving in a chauffeured limousine. Somewhere in the wee hours of the morning, as the last of the French champagne was being drained, guests sat back and marvelled as Williams handed out $8000-apiece watches to staff who had served fifteen years with the company or to lucky clients.[67]

The HIH party culture reached its apogee of extravagance in 1999, the year that the company officially posted its first loss. Costing $1.67 million, the New Year's Eve bash was billed as the world's best ever party, the blurb for the event explaining that: 'On arrival, invitees entered the party through a time tunnel to discover an exotic space experience which transported guests into a new millennium'.[68] Williams had no limits placed on the budget for his extravaganzas; they were 'blank cheque parties'. The events seemed both to feed his ego and to cement staff loyalty.

When public knowledge of the party culture oozed out of the royal commission hearings, the tabloid press went to town in condemnation: 'HIH sailed to ruin on a sea of champagne', screamed a headline in the *Daily Telegraph*.[69] However, Williams' unrestrained gifts and parties were merely rounding errors in the $5.3 billion debt. Their purpose was to enhance his power. In doing so, the largesse Williams doled out reflected a broader cultural problem: the lack of robust internal control mechanisms throughout the company. HIH was like a boat without a rudder.

By the late 1990s, Williams had been sitting atop HIH for nearly a decade as the benevolent autocrat, convinced of his own infallibility. Consequently, he was unable to see the arrival of two financial sharks circling the rotting carcass of HIH and who, in rapid time, stripped it to its bare bones. Rodney Adler and Brad Cooper were financially tied at the hip when they came into Williams' orbit; his dealings with them revealed the depth of his incompetence.

Rodney Adler: Sydney's A-list opportunist

In the late 1990s, Rodney Adler, the flashy eastern suburbs Sydney businessman with impeccable social connections, had a problem. He needed to off-load his insurance company FAI (Fire and All Risk Insurance) before it sank without trace. Just how Ray Williams came to his rescue seems like a plot from a bad movie, which is how Adler himself came to think of his dealings with HIH.

Adler inherited FAI at the age of twenty-nine after the untimely death of his father, Larry, who had built the company from scratch after arriving in Australia from his native Hungary after World War II. During the war he had foraged for food and paid smugglers to help him escape to Vienna when he was still in his teens.[70] Larry was a wheeler-dealer more interested in high-risk investment than mundane insurance. In fact, FAI was dubbed 'Fuck All Insurance' by its more canny detractors.[71] A stellar dealmaker, Larry was a private banker to some of Australia's most notorious entrepreneurs. He relished his jack-blunt nature. 'I have nothing to do with my competitors,' Larry said in 1967. 'What's the point? If I lunched with those people we could only tell lies to one another.'[72] Larry bulldozed his way to wealth and a millionaire's lifestyle in Sydney's glitzy and cliquey eastern suburbs where children of the wealthy connect with each other from birth.[73]

Larry's son, Rodney, was born with the proverbial silver spoon in his mouth, but very much in the shadow of his legendary business father. Educated at the elite Cranbrook School with the likes of James Packer, Jodee Rich and Warwick Fairfax, Adler was known as a cocky and disruptive student more given to high jinks than serious study.[74] He never quite shed his 'spoilt brat' image,[75] nor could he hide his ambition to be a billionaire like his friend James Packer.[76]

When he took over FAI from his father, Adler found a troubled company burdened by long-tail claims. Icarus-like, he rebuilt the company, flying high on the wings of venture capital. A lender of last resort, he made a pile of money being the man stockbrokers flocked to for risk capital. A mansion in ritzy Point Piper followed. Adler revelled in his celebrity status as a hot-shot deal-maker and, living as if unconstrained by any rules, liked to hang out with colourful characters, including several underworld figures. During the HIH royal commission, it was revealed that Adler was a friend of the New York mafioso Jeffrey Pokross, an FBI informant. In one conversation taped in 2000, Pokross told a friend that 'when you go out with Adler, when you go out with Rodney, you're going out as an equal … and here's a guy who you're not kissing his ass, because he's a f---ing lunatic'.[77]

But Adler had a well-honed opportunistic eye for a business deal. In 1995, he became a founding investor in his friend Jodee Rich's ill-fated telco company, One.Tel. The company's bust in 2001 was yet another tale of a son of a rich father driven to prove himself by thinking big. With One.Tel, the smooth-talking and charming Rich, who exuded 'hard talking business hyperbole',[78] wanted to take on the big telecommunications companies. Adler helped him bring James Packer – son of Kerry – and Lachlan Murdoch – son of Rupert – on board as investors. Both were trainee tycoons in their respective fathers' media empires and were now cutting their teeth in the business world in their own right.

One.Tel had a meteoric rise, becoming the fourth largest telco in the country before it imploded in 2001, brought down to earth by poor management; Rich's reputation as a guru businessman took a dive. As one commentator noted: 'At One.Tel you never had to dig far to find trouble'.[79] But critics argued that One.Tel was never designed to be a sustainable operation. According to this view, the business plan of aggressive marketing and ridiculously cheap pricing was designed to force the big telcos to buy out One.Tel, and so make a tidy profit for its backers; 'the big companies are happy, and the customers and workers get screwed'.[80]

Whether or not a buyout was the end game, One.Tel was based on a risky business model of trying to gouge market share. The company had set out to be a maverick in the industry. And its accounting practices were unusual. According to the liquidator's inquiry into One.Tel, multimillion-dollar bonuses paid to the founders 'were effectively hidden from public scrutiny by questionable accounting practices'.[81]

But Adler eventually outsmarted his old mates. He sold his ten million shares before One.Tel went up in smoke. Packer and Murdoch lost a combined $950 million in the collapse.[82] It was a rare occasion when the old school tie turned out to be a liability rather than an asset. One.Tel couldn't fail, it was widely assumed, due to the business luminaries who backed it. But it did, and Kerry Packer was furious, insisting, in his typically belligerent manner, that Rich's right testicle be delivered to him.[83] ASIC came circling, trying to determine who was to blame for the crash, and froze Rich's assets. However, after a gruelling eight-year legal battle, the agency lost the case they brought against Rich for allegedly failing to act with due diligence as an executive of the company. For young James Packer especially, the collapse of One.Tel ushered in an 'excruciating period of social embarrassment, of cancelled dinner parties and friendships lost'.[84]

Before his canny exit from One.Tel, Adler was informed, in 1997, of a shortfall in FAI's reserves but failed to make reference to the rapidly declining health of the company in his reports to the board.[85] His next move was to engage the help of high-profile merchant banker (and later prime minister) Malcolm Turnbull, the newly appointed head of investment firm Goldman Sachs Australia. Turnbull, who was friendly with Adler, was under pressure from New York to produce some 'rainmaker deals'.[86] Dropping by one day on Adler, the smart and confident Turnbull proposed a joint venture privatisation deal, but this fell through when Turnbull estimated FAI's value at only $20 million.

After Turnbull had pulled out of a deal with FAI, Adler started courting HIH. It was a natural course of action for him to explore. Williams had made an offer to take over FAI after Adler's father died. At the time, Williams had hankered to mentor Rodney, but was rebuffed.[87] When it was Adler's turn to make the overture, Williams' fondness for the company and its owner was undimmed. Williams made Adler a deal so generous in its terms it appeared to have been conjured in financial heaven: a $300 million takeover bid, a personal payout for Adler of $3.7 million, a $40 000-a-month consultancy at HIH and a seat on the board.[88] Adler cemented his stake in the company by becoming a major shareholder.

However, as Justice Owen later detailed, Williams had struck the deal out of thin air: Williams had undertaken no due diligence and the proposal was rushed through the board when only five of the twelve board members were present. Those participating did not have access to all relevant documentation, including a report prepared by HIH's financial advisors. It was passed with 'scant consideration' which, in any event was always likely to have been the outcome, given Williams' domination of the board.[89]

In effect, HIH had bought a dud. Senior FAI actuary Peter McCarthy told Justice Owen that FAI was at that stage insolvent, that it had knowingly published false accounts, and that if HIH had not bought it, the group would have collapsed.[90] Instead of being worth the $300 million Williams had paid, FAI blasted a $250 million dollar hole in HIH's worsening financial position.[91]

But more trouble followed in the wake of Williams' decision to take over FAI and to offer Adler a seat on the board. FAI had a stake in a struggling burglar alarm company, Home Security International (HSI), which was transferred to HIH in the takeover. Williams' lack of due diligence on the FAI deal in general meant that he had paid no attention to the financial ticking time bomb that was HSI and its founder, the 'cash-hungry' 'young hustler', Brad Cooper.[92]

Adler had first taken a shine to Cooper, a school drop-out and jack-of-all trades, in 1990 when, through FAI, Adler backed him with venture capital to start a burglar alarm business. They struck a deal to provide the equipment as part of a reduced premium package to FAI insurance customers. Brash, boisterous, with an irrepressible determination to pursue wealth and fame, Cooper was, by the late 1990s, at the height of his success – selling alarms in the domestic market, riding high as a motivational speaker, and on the board of the Collingwood Football Club where he was mates with high-profile club president Eddie McGuire. A larger-than-life character, he peppered conversations with phrases like 'on a scale of one to 10, this is 150' and 'this is unbelievable'.[93] Rodney Adler was among many who succumbed to the wily ways of 'Brad the Talker'.

Through sheer force of personality, Cooper had barged his way into the fast money set. He loved his exotic toys. He is said to have hired a security guard to watch over his Ferrari when it was parked in the street.[94] To his friends, Cooper, with his peroxide-blond hair, infectious charm and bonhomie, was the quintessential Aussie larrikin made good. But, like Adler, he had a dark side.

With Adler's help, HSI was floated on the American stockmarket in 1997, but Cooper's attempts to expand internationally stretched resources to breaking point.[95] And he seized his chance to talk his way into making the failing HSI a project for Williams to fund.

Just why Williams decided to spend tens of millions of dollars on a shonky businessman with an ailing company taxed the understanding of Justice Owen. It seems to have been a combination of Williams' fixation with growth opportunities, his gross incompetence and Cooper's legendary ability to sell himself.

In fact, Cooper was a star public speaker, charging $70 000 for a one-hour talk on the business speaking circuit. According to one property tycoon, nobody in the country came close to Cooper's ability to sell a concept and to inspire people.[96] Indeed, his Magic Moments six-pack of inspirational cassettes garnered $5 million in international sales. Cooper was, in fact, selling little more than his rags-to-riches story laced with business homilies. However, like circus acts of old, he was an entertainer first and foremost.[97]

In the end, HSI cost HIH $45 million and, as Justice Owen explained, while it represented a small amount of HIH's overall losses it highlighted Williams' gross ineptitude. Instead of dumping Cooper and selling down his assets, Williams doubled down on investing in HSI without devising any strategy or making sound judgments about Cooper and acting accordingly.[98]

While Cooper was trying to raid HIH for all he could get, his mate Adler was conjuring his own scam. Not content with his personal windfall out of the takeover, Adler, as newly installed board member, moved to extract further funds from HIH as if it were his private bank. And again, Williams proved an easy target.

Adler was planning a scam on financial markets. He had formed a company, Pacific Eagle Equities (PEE), which he used as a cover for a scheme to artificially boost HIH's share price, which had begun to fall, threatening the value of his holdings. He convinced Williams to withdraw $10 million from HIH and to channel the funds through PEE, from which he purchased 2.5 million HIH shares. At the same time, he used his connections in the financial world to spread the message that HIH shares were undervalued and presented an opportunity for a quick profit.[99]

The deception would later become the subject of legal action against Adler but in the meantime it failed to halt HIH's slide into the abyss. As the situation grew more dire after Williams had been forced to vacate his position in October 2000, Adler fought a bitter power struggle with Geoffrey Cohen for control of the board. Adler was desperate to absolve himself of responsibility for HIH's dire financial position.[100] However, his disruptive tactics failed and in February

2001, Cohen pressured Adler to resign as a director. In his typically brash manner, Adler wrote to all FAI directors foreshadowing the likely legal drama that awaited them all:

> Everyone would love the litigation to commence, it is topical, it is HIH – the demise of a great company – it is FAI – an Australia-wide brand name – it is Rodney Adler, it is Arthur Andersen, it is Goldman Sachs. It has the makings of a great movie.[101]

What can explain Adler's descent into criminal behaviour? Interviewed after his release from prison in 2007, Adler appeared to indicate that he had developed a few, grudging insights. Journalist Ruth Ostrow reported that Adler bravely let her run through the possible psychological conditions that precipitated his downfall:

> Narcissism? 'Possibly.' Charming? Manipulative? 'I hope so,' he laughs, 'in business you have to be.' Grandiose? Unlikeable? 'Let's say I have a certain "sense of humour". I shouldn't have been so flippant at the trial.'[102]

The road to ruin

'Where did the money go?' Justice Owen rhetorically asked in his HIH findings. It didn't go anywhere. He found that, '[I]n the main, the money was never there'. That led to a shortage of a couple of billion dollars in the coffers to pay policyholders' claims. The royal commissioner highlighted that Williams had never developed a viable business model for HIH. He concluded that the company had grossly underestimated its liabilities, overestimated its assets, charged premiums that were too low and lacked sufficient reserves for future claims, especially 'long-term' claims.[103]

The mask had fallen. Williams was never the industry guru that he had projected himself to be. From the time HIH was floated as a public company in 1992, Williams developed the business as a high-risk-oriented company, underpinned by his own extraordinary ineptitude. He lacked the necessary skills to manage such a complex business. His 'success' was in developing a corporate culture that covered this up through his creepy, intimidating and self-serving 'benevolent-autocrat' style of leadership. But, as Justice Owen crisply stated, 'blind faith' was placed in a leader who was 'ill-equipped for the task'.[104] Williams' decision-making was little more than 'optimistic guesswork'.[105]

The culture at HIH made a mockery of the concept of corporate governance. 'HIH had a corporate governance model. The directors said so in the annual reports,' Owen said with barely disguised sarcasm. It had guidelines for corporate governance, underwriting practices and investment. They just weren't adhered to very often. Owen lamented that the HIH case showed that the very concept of corporate governance was at risk of being reduced to 'a mantra without regard to its real import'.[106]

The self-serving evidence that Ray Williams dished up to Owen had, predictably, evaporated more quickly than a tropical downpour. Williams had sought to throw Adler under the proverbial bus; to make out that the purchase of FAI was a 'contaminant or pollutant', which had 'tainted' his group with its 'poisonous impact'. Such was the 'deception' that no amount of caution would have saved HIH from the FAI catastrophe, Williams vented.[107]

Williams, ever out of his depth, and deluded into believing in his own narrative, couldn't face the reality behind HIH's long-term structural problems. The common reasons why insurance companies fail are threefold: insufficient reserves, inadequate pricing of products and/or growth that was too rapid.[108] HIH suffered from all three problems, but it wasn't until the late 1990s that they could no longer be covered up by turning a blind eye.[109] During the 1990s, there was enough in HIH's coffers for extravagance, largesse, and paying too much for businesses acquired and completely dud acquisitions.

Eventually the company's coffers were emptied, ironically on the same day that payment was made on the last of Williams' purchases of glitzy watches to give out to staff. It was a final act of folly.

Both Williams and the board share the responsibility for the collapse. For his part, Williams scoffed at industry best standards which stipulated that reserves should be at around 70 per cent probability. He thought that this would be an excuse for his claims officers 'to put their feet up on the desk'; that they wouldn't hustle for more business.[110] In fact, Williams continually lobbied against government setting minimum targets for reserves.

Williams' other problem revolved around his badly executed push for growth, his 'unbridled craving for international expansion at any cost'.[111] His entry into the UK and US insurance markets was a disaster as both slowly bled tens of millions of dollars from the mid-1990s. As Suellen Henry explained: 'I thought they were acquiring things all over the world and I just didn't think they understood what they were acquiring and I didn't think they had the management depth to integrate those businesses'.[112] HIH's British manager wrote to Williams in 1995 warning of the extent of the losses, yet the company's public reports continued to paint a rosy picture. It was in response to these losses that HIH pursued the domestic market even more vigorously, undercutting the competition.[113]

The growth of HIH, albeit on shaky foundations, convinced Williams that he was the indispensable industry guru, a self-confidence that he projected to the wider world. He was occasionally spotted in the early morning in Centennial Park wearing a car tyre around his waist, which was attached to the bumper bar of his Rolls-Royce with a rope. With the chauffeur inside holding the wheel, the fitness fanatic slowly pulled the 2-tonne Roller around the park.[114] Williams indulged in expensive meals on the corporate expense account. In one three-week period, he spent $9000, including $2000 in tips, on three dinners at restaurants in Port Douglas and Sydney.[115]

The compliant board

Given Williams' breathtaking incompetence in running HIH, it is surprising that the company didn't crash much sooner than it did. Crucially, Williams was propped up by the company board. He controlled all appointments, as benefitted his autocratic personality, and mostly he selected old friends and, critically, three former partners from auditors Arthur Andersen. As mentioned, several board members were treated with exceptional generosity. In these ways Williams engineered a compliant board.

Day after day in testimony to the royal commission came accounts of the board's failings because no one in the boardroom was prepared to challenge Williams. 'It was the abrogation of boardroom responsibility', wrote Matthew Horan in the *Sunday Telegraph*, that indulged not only Williams' self-belief but his ability to 'get away with "papering over the cracks".'[116]

'Directors were unduly deferential to Williams, rarely questioned or rejected a recommendation from management', commented journalist Michael Sexton. Compounding their shortcomings, he noted, board members 'failed to challenge or endorse company strategy and had little understanding of conflicts of interest'. Therefore, 'not coming to grips with the serious problems of under provisioning in the accounts, the board was never able to deal with the looming crisis'.[117]

The disconnect between board members and the operation of the company under Williams was revealed in a small, but insightful, exchange between board member Bob Stitt and Wayne Martin QC, counsel assisting the royal commissioner, during which Stitt admitted that he had been unaware of Williams' expenditure on lavish parties and gifts and 'that if he had known, he would have asked some questions'.[118]

Problems with the board started at the top; chair Geoffrey Cohen, who had been appointed to his position at the time of the public float in 1992, was assessed by Justice Owen as being 'ineffective'.[119] As chair, of course, Cohen had ticked off on all the bad decisions made by Williams and failed to rein in the company's expenditure. As discussed below, he was in charge of the annual audit conducted by Arthur Andersen.

As well, Cohen failed to provide leadership for the rest of the board. Owen found that collectively board members did very little of a serious nature: 'At board level, there was little, if any analysis of the future strategy of the company'. However, as Owen noted, strategy should have been the role of management. But it didn't develop one. It was as if the entire company was wandering through fog.

Owen recognised that however passive the board chose to be, they were duped by management on a number of occasions and they had to contend with Williams' high-handed manner. This was revealed in one exchange between Fodera and Wayne Martin. The QC asked the board member and director of finance whether he was aware that the company was flying Williams' secretary, Rita Young, from the Gold Coast each week and putting her up in the Intercontinental Hotel:

> Fodera: 'Yes … I believe Mr Cassidy [another board member] and I just queried it with Mr Williams.'
>
> Martin: 'What did he say?'
>
> Fodera: 'I think, none of your business.'[120]

Cohen eventually had all charges against him dropped. In defence of his actions at HIH he told the press: 'Maybe I am a bit stupid in the reliance I placed on the executive directors, but I took them to be honest people'.[121]

HIH showed again how easily boards can be captured by an autocratic company head such as Williams. The royal commission systematically exposed the flaws of the board. That had never happened before in the cloistered history of company boards in Australia.

Arthur Andersen's crooked audits

Few aspects of HIH operations were as systematically crooked as the external audits provided by the big US-based firm of Arthur Andersen. An audit is meant to give a full and fair picture of a company's financial position and underpins corporate integrity and the interests of shareholders. At HIH this unglamorous, but vital function, was poisoned by unethical behaviour. Indeed, Arthur Andersen's audits papered over the cracks of William's ineptitude.

Arthur Andersen, which had audited HIH for decades, brought to the task a business model based on an inbuilt conflict of interest; that is, from its beginnings in 1913, it sold consulting services to its clients while undertaking its auditing work, thereby diminishing its independence. The firm came to be led by corporate egoists bent on profit maximisation. The tone had been set in 1989 when the US-based general manager of global operations, Jim Edwards, went on stage at the company's annual conference with a tiger on a leash to the booming sound of the song, 'Eye of the Tiger': 'His message was that it was a jungle out there, and that every partner had to double his fee income in three years'.[122]

Thereafter, Arthur Andersen's culture of conflict of interest went into overdrive: 'Accountants who failed to toe the line with the firm's new direction were shifted aside and replaced by those who could turn moderately profitable auditing assignments into money-spinners'.[123] The separation between the auditing and consulting functions of the company gave way to the chase for profits.

HIH paid Arthur Andersen $1.6 million in non-auditing work in 2000, along with $1.7 million for the actual audit. But the payment for consultancy work was one strand in a high-pressure relationship between the two companies.

As previously mentioned, the presence of three former Arthur Andersen partners on the board of HIH – arranged by Williams – helped promote a symbiotic relationship between the two companies. Cohen, himself a former Arthur Andersen partner, and as chair of HIH's own audit committee, cemented these ties. Williams was the only person in the company who could have facilitated such an arrangement. We cannot be sure, but it seems likely that Williams always planned to have a compliant auditor prepare the company's books.

Symptomatic of this cosy relationship was the fact that Arthur Andersen paid Cohen consultancy fees for nearly a decade while he was also on the board of HIH. However, the payments were not disclosed.[124] Such blurring of the relationship between Cohen and Arthur Andersen led Justice Owen to state that the chair had no understanding of conflict of interest.

The end result of the symbiotic relationship between HIH and Arthur Andersen was catastrophic for both the company, its shareholders and the broader Australian public. Andersen was all too willing to sign off on HIH's aggressive accounting practices. As the royal commission heard, Arthur Andersen continually yielded to management when it knew it should not be doing so.[125] Such duplicity is simply staggering.

Arthur Andersen came to an inglorious end months after the scandal that erupted around its role in the implosion of HIH and which had been teased out in evidence to the royal commission. The company had also overseen the fraudulent accounting that led to giant US energy company Enron collapsing like a house of cards. When Arthur Andersen was indicted for obstructing justice over the Enron collapse, thousands of staff lost their jobs overnight and, in a short time, the Chicago headquarters, which once employed 27 000 staff, resembled a ghost town.[126]

ASIC gets its man

The rottenness eating away at HIH put the spotlight on ASIC's role. Why didn't it prevent the collapse? In 2006, Jeremy Cooper, then the deputy chair of ASIC, offered a *mea culpa* of sorts. He told a conference that the agency was 'less well informed about HIH than it should have been'.[127] But how could they be ill-informed when HIH's troubles had been so widely canvassed in financial and political circles?

Stung by the criticism of its failure to act as a watchdog, ASIC activated its investigative arm and began a probe of the entrails of the company. In March 2003, while Royal Commissioner Justice Owen was still grinding his way through the reams of damning evidence of the company's collapse, ASIC homed in on the banking transactions of Bill Howard, HIH general manager of finance. In December 2000, Howard had opened a safety deposit box. ASIC had reason to believe that it had been stuffed with ill-gotten gains. As the regulator established, Howard had, for several years, been bribed by Brad Cooper. Ever the grifter, Cooper believed that he was owed substantial amounts of money from HIH and promised to look after Howard if he helped retrieve his funds.[128]

Howard seemed an unlikely character to become involved in graft. He was an unpretentious, sports-loving, beer-drinking, blokey accountant. But colleagues later recalled that behind Howard's mild-mannered exterior lay a weakness that 'Brad the Talker' zeroed in on. Howard, colleagues said, 'took a swaggering pride' in his own importance within HIH; he was 'a big name-dropper', a 'big noter' and he fancied himself as a 'wheeler-dealer'.[129] And, in the dystopian world of HIH management, Howard could sign cheques and have no one to answer to.[130]

When he agreed to secretly meet with Cooper in February 2001, Cooper made him an alluring offer. 'What you need is something to blow a bit of wind through your hair', he said to Howard. 'With all the trouble at HIH, it would do you the world of good.' Within weeks

Howard was driving around in a green BMW convertible, paid for by Cooper.[131]

Thus began Howard's secret world. In all, he received $124 000 from Cooper over multiple meetings in the following year, moneys that Howard slipped into his deposit box. In return, Howard shovelled millions to Cooper.

When ASIC came circling, Howard decided to turn HIH supergrass, suppling ASIC with every skerrick of information about the inner workings of HIH which it used to bring charges against Williams, Adler, Fodera and Cooper. In return for his cooperation, Howard negotiated a plea bargain with ASIC that saw him plead guilty to two counts of receiving bribes from Cooper and using his position dishonestly, in return for a suspended three-year sentence.

Williams was eventually charged with issuing misleading financial statements and breaching his duties as a director. He was sentenced to four and a half years (with parole). The price paid for corporate rogue behaviour continued to be small, relative to the harm inflicted. Both Williams and Adler returned to the high life after only several years in jail, both having legally squirrelled away their assets in their wives' names.

In fact, in 2008 when Williams was released from Silverwater Jail in Sydney, community anger over his conduct was still burning bright. Channelling this anger, journalist Janet Fife-Yeomans, writing for News.com.au, commented that Williams was

> treading the sickening and well-worn path of corporate crooks – straight from life as a common criminal in a barren jail cell back to life as a king and a cushy retirement. It is proof again, if it was needed, that there really is one law for the rich and another for the poor.[132]

Adler at least fessed up to the long-term consequences of being a white-collar criminal. He told journalist Ruth Ostrow in 2016 that he was recently used as a case study at a university lecture on corporate crime. His daughter, studying to be a lawyer, was in that class.

In all, seventeen people were charged over the HIH collapse.[133]

The political fix

The collapse of HIH forced the Howard government to temporarily backtrack on its small-government, free-market ideological mantra. In addition to the establishment of the royal commission into HIH, Cabinet agreed to back Hockey's proposal of an assistance scheme to alleviate genuine hardship cases. As Hockey later reflected: 'We [the government] basically took over the running of the second biggest insurance company in the country – and we did it in six weeks'.[134]

But tackling the structural weaknesses in Australia's legal framework of corporate law was not on the government's agenda. In 2002, John Howard backed away from demands for enhanced corporate legislation. Self-regulation coupled with appropriate 'but not excessive' levels of government involvement was what Australia needed, Howard explained.[135] It was too big a step for the Prime Minister to reckon with the fundamental ideological ideas that had driven his entire career.

Consequently, corporations continued to pose periodic big risks to ordinary Australians. Firstly, as Nick James, senior lecturer at University of Queensland Law School, pointed out in the wash-up of the HIH scandal, it had become difficult if not impossible to talk about corporations and their governance 'other than in terms of profit and loss, deregulation and investor protection. Nearly all of the literature on Australian corporate law theory, for example, is framed within a neo-liberal worldview'.[136] In other words, minimal government intervention, inadequate regulation and market freedom would continue to reign in Australia. And, as the career of Ray Williams had shown, CEOs could be rewarded not just with stratospheric wealth but with an Order of Australia for operating and manipulating this system.

The second big risk posed by corporations embodied the very essence of the neo-liberal worldview: that directors and executives continued to privilege themselves in setting their own level of remuneration, reinforcing the idea that risks were justified if they were in the pursuit of ever larger profits and shareholder wealth. In the wake of the HIH scandal, executive remuneration spiralled upwards. Disconnected from the reality of performance, and with no checks on the eye-watering packages on offer, investors and the public were at the mercy of a new gilded elite. 'For every big pay packet', commented journalist and shareholder activist Stephen Mayne, 'there seems to be one for bad performance'.[137] And some of the rising remuneration was based around secret deals. In October 2002, as the HIH scandal was still raging, the *Daily Telegraph* led with a front-page story that exposed deals that delivered a combined $42 million to six executives without shareholders' knowledge.[138]

These were ominous warnings.

5
A PLOT FROM MACHIAVELLI: JAMES HARDIE INDUSTRIES

Many Australians have a lasting impression of Bernie Banton, the gravel-voiced, fist-pumping campaigner for asbestos victims, of which he was one. Between 2000 and his death in 2007, images of him tied to an oxygen tank issuing statements laced with his quick temper and flashes of lively humour regularly featured on television news bulletins as he tenaciously took on James Hardie Industries, the largest manufacturer of deadly asbestos products in Australia. For decades, Hardie had played legal hardball with victims. Banton became the public face of a community campaign to force the company to live up to its moral obligations to compensate victims. When a furore erupted in 2004 over Hardie's inadequate provision for a medical compensation fund it had established to aid victims, amid allegations that it had lied about the level of funding, a fired-up Banton was in the forefront in exposing the company's callousness.[1]

Banton was one of society's unsung battlers. He'd been a jack-of-all trades before getting a job in 1968 at Hardie's western Sydney factory, not far from where he grew up. Little did he realise at the time that he, and his fellow workers, were risking their lives working for the company. The company was knowingly killing its workers, who were covered each day in deadly asbestos dust. Not only that, it wanted to be rid of the compensation claims that were putting a drag on company profits.

The problem for Hardie was not just the extent of their liabilities but the nature of the two diseases associated with exposure to asbestos products: asbestosis, a scarring of the lungs; and mesothelioma, a deadly cancer of the lungs. The onset of both diseases is unpredictable; in some victims onset can occur decades after exposure. As the biggest producer of asbestos products in Australia, Hardie was facing a decades-long drain on its resources from claimants. It set out to plot its way out of the dark side of its history.

In 1999, senior management began to carefully plan a company restructure to achieve the goal of ridding itself of asbestos victims. The aim was set out in board papers: 'a complete end to asbestos litigation'.[2] The company planned to skimp on the Medical Research and Compensation Foundation it established in 2001 and relocate to the Netherlands where it would be legally free from any further claims from victims. Two subsidiary companies would be left in Australia to handle claims from the underfunded Foundation.

The restructuring plan continued to wind its way through the planning process. Then, on 16 February 2001, Hardie directors signed off on a press release to the Australian Stock Exchange that they thought would solve the problem. The press release said that the Foundation was fully funded. It was a lie. But it wasn't just a casual mistake. Australia's oldest manufacturers of building products had engaged in a 'brazen corporate scam'.[3] The appalling saga illustrates how an unethical and unscrupulous culture can overwhelm a company as it chases shareholder value. But in Hardie's case this problem was greatly magnified by its history.

Hardie may well have got away with the plan to leave victims in the lurch had it not lied to the stock exchange about the level of funding for the Foundation. Only extraordinary circumstances involving a company whistleblower led to the plan unravelling three years later, whereupon a commission of inquiry was set up in early 2004, headed by senior New South Wales lawyer David Jackson QC. With an eye for forensic detail, Jackson laid bare the planning among senior Hardie executives and the compliance of its directors.

Once his report was released in September 2004, the Australian Securities and Investment Commission (ASIC), the timid regulator, was forced to act. In an unprecedented action, it brought civil charges against the entire senior management of the company. The case became known as 'the Hardie 10'. In 2008–09 it gripped media attention; all those changes were slapped with penalties.

The Hardie scandal is a pivotal case in the nation's business history. But it is a perplexing scandal to unravel. Everyone involved was described as decent; none was accused of seeking monetary advantage; and the CEO, Peter Macdonald, did not appear to possess obvious narcissistic qualities. In other words, most of the obvious causes of bad corporate behaviour were absent. But appearances were deceptive at Hardie.

The rise of a deadly industry

Asbestos has been mined since ancient times, valued as a highly versatile, strong, cheap, non-flammable and malleable substance for use in building, textiles and construction. However, a 2000-year-old warning from the Roman naturalist, Pliny the Elder, proved prescient. In the first century AD he observed that slaves wearing asbestos cloth grew ill and died. His warning went unheeded. During the industrial revolution asbestos was mined on a large scale. During the twentieth century, it became a highly valued, globally traded product. The full extent of its lethal nature was only slowly prised open by medical science.

Before this awareness became public in the 1940s and '50s, asbestos had become a ubiquitous building material in Australia. James Hardie began manufacturing in 1917, the company having been founded as a trading business in 1892 by two Scottish businessmen, James Hardie and Andrew Reid, the former partner selling out to Reid, who became the sole proprietor.[4] The surge in post-World War

II immigration created a heightened demand for cheap housing and associated infrastructure. Asbestos filled the bill: Australia became the highest per capita user of the product in the world.

For decades, as many Australians can only too well recall, the country's urban landscape was dotted with modest fibro homes made from asbestos-reinforced cement sheeting. Entire working-class suburbs were built with the material, along with schools and other buildings. Asbestos had other uses: fences, piping and the linings of car brakes, for example. It was also used as filler in cement.

James Hardie imported much of the material from overseas but developed a partnership with Colonial Sugar Refinery in its Western Australian Wittenoom mine, which operated until 1966. Hardie also operated its own mine – the Baryulgil asbestos mine – near Grafton in northern New South Wales. It had an equally tragic history as Wittenoom. Employing nearly all its workforce from the local Bundjalung Aboriginal community, the mine had the reputation of being one of the filthiest in Australia and, over time, it devastated the Bundjalung people. Dust permeated their houses, their children played in the tailings dam and tailings were spread around the grounds. Many members of the community died prematurely from their catastrophic contact with asbestos.[5] Hardie also imported asbestos at a rate of 1000 tonnes a year until the company ceased all production in 1987.[6]

With the highest per capita usage in the world, Australia, not surprisingly, has had the highest per capita incidence of asbestos-related diseases. Hardie was on the front line of liability. Sufferers were not just the workers in mines and factories but in the many places where the company's products were used: power stations, shipyards and railways. But it was largely a disease imposed on working-class people across a variety of trades. Later on, home renovators were caught up in the asbestos epidemic.

As early as the 1920s asbestosis was identified as a disease in both workers and users of asbestos products. But it was not known to be fatal. However, this changed in the 1940s when Hardie's medical officer began diagnosing cases of mesothelioma. In a move that came to define Hardie's management of asbestos-related diseases for decades to come, the company adopted a policy of keeping workers ignorant of their condition while allowing them to continue in their roles. Workers were loyal to the company, whose patriarchal business culture deluded management into thinking that they had the best interests of workers at heart.[7] The reality is much uglier; workers were sacrificial lambs for Hardie's profits.

In 1957, the full extent of the dangers of exposure to asbestos dust was confirmed in a study published in the *Medical Journal of Australia*. Dr DL Gordon Thomas wrote that asbestos disease, once established, was 'a grave threat to life and health'. Thomas pointed out that it was not only people handling asbestos in its raw state who were at risk but also anyone 'sawing, cutting and finishing any product containing asbestos – for example brake linings, asbestos sheeting and various insulating materials'. The article went to Jock Reid, a Hardie director, with a note from a company officer: 'I do not think there is anything in this which we do not already know'.[8]

But there was no government follow-up to the study; health authorities didn't consider asbestos an urgent issue. As a consequence, Hardie went about business as usual – ignoring the need for safety standards, denying the seriousness of asbestos-related diseases and adopting a position of resisting all claims for compensation. Management was simply indifferent.[9]

And the level of indifference was shocking. Hardie factory workers were known as 'the snowmen': 'At the end of each shift they would emerge coated with asbestos powder, their eyes the only thing visible through the white dust'.[10] Many of the young men hired to work at the company's Camellia asbestos plant near Parramatta were post-war European migrants and others were recruited from the Burnside orphans' home at Parramatta – they were called 'Reid boys'.[11]

During the 1960s, Hardie safety officer Peter Russell said the company was well aware of the dangers of asbestos. Russell repeatedly urged the company to improve working conditions and to put warnings on its products, advising that the company could, in future, become 'a sitting duck for claims'. But his warnings were brushed off: 'The prime concern of James Hardie during this period was its bottom line'.[12]

In the 1970s, Hardie came under more pressure from the media, unions and the World Health Organization to cease using asbestos in its products. Government should have shut the industry down, but didn't. The reason involves the complex dynamics that exist between powerful corporations and the state. Hardie became an early example of state capture by a corporation. This occurs when a corporation uses its political influence to shape or control the decision-making processes of government, shifting outcomes away from the public good towards their own narrow interests. The process is mostly unseen by the public because it happens through political donations, lobbying, exchanging personnel between company and government, or because of real or implied threats by a company.[13] The fossil fuel industry is a notorious example of how a company can use its power to exercise influence on government decision making. And, as we will see later, there are other examples of the same phenomenon, notably in the gambling industry.

James Hardie and state capture

By the time the dangers of asbestos had percolated from the medical profession to wider society, James Hardie was an established fixture not just among the business community but in Australian society generally. It was an icon – as much a part of Australia's identity as BHP. From the time it commenced manufacturing operations during World War I, Hardie's main product – the cement sheeting Fibrolite – became synonymous with the nation's progress. The reasons are straightforward – the company was a pioneer of Australian manufacturing, employing thousands of workers and using local materials. And Fibrolite was seen as a genuinely innovative product: light, sturdy, fire resistant and cheap to transport. By the 1930s, Hardie was regularly trumpeted in the press as 'A Great Australian Industry' with a chain of factories in Sydney, Melbourne, Brisbane and Perth.[14] In the 1940s, it was hailed as essential to Australia's war effort – allowing rapid completion of huge building complexes essential to the operations of the army and air force. And by the 1950s, James Hardie was seen as part of the development of Australia itself'.[15] The company was depicted as the very epitome of modernity and efficiency.

By the 1960s, Hardie had become a post-war industrial powerhouse run by a family dynasty whose interests were threaded into elite circles of government and society. Between the 1930s and mid-1970s, it was headed by Sir John Thyne Reid, known as Jock, the son of one of the original founders. Sir John was a deeply religious man. Joining him in the 1950s was his son, also John. The Reids became an immensely wealthy establishment family, the epitome of 'old money'.[16] Enjoying continuously rapid growth, the company became 'an old favourite' among investors.[17] Sir John was a one-time Commissioner of the ABC and sat on numerous establishment-type committees, including that of the Victorian Symphony Orchestra.

Hardie partnered with government instrumentalities and other businesses to provide products like concrete asbestos pipes to large development projects, allowing the company to boast in its advertising that it was working 'to meet the special requirements of Australia's public authorities and industries'. And Sir John was a domineering type, used to getting his own way.[18] When son John took over in the mid-1970s, he became a director of ten other companies, including BHP, Qantas and Avis. Reid was seen as the personification of corporate power in Australia.[19] And James Hardie fostered its public image by sponsoring, for more than two decades, a high-profile motor-racing event, the James Hardie 1000.

The Reids, of course, had personal knowledge of the dangers of asbestos: 'They were intimately involved in the business. Employees knew their faces – they used to walk around the factory floors'.[20] Yet they appeared to have wilfully ignored the reality that the company was injuring and killing its workers. Instead, Hardie controlled the way governments minimised concerns about asbestos. In New South Wales, the Mines Inspectorate relied on the company's knowledge regarding monitoring and controlling asbestos fibre in the workplace; Hardie had representatives on that committee. In Victoria, new regulations for asbestos exposure were developed in 1956 but were not enacted until 1978. And when the first compensation cases were settled in court, Hardie insisted on confidential clauses.[21] And all the while, it denied the truth. Writing in the company's 1979 annual report, for example, management stated that '[a]uthorities are agreed that there is no known hazard to health in using our products'.[22] The company narrative, therefore, continued to be built on lies and denial cheered on by society's elites. It just beggars belief.

When Hardie ceased production of asbestos products in Australia in 1987, it turned its attention to the development of new building products, especially its cellulose-based ferro-cement products, which took off in America. By the late 1990s, the organisation had transformed itself into an international success story with most of its business, along with its company headquarters, located in the United States.

But the legacy of Hardie's image and reputation lingered in the Australian imagination. Even by the late 1980s, the *Canberra Times* lamented the 'enormous political and social inertia' about the dangers of asbestos. Earlier in the decade, it was discovered that the National Library of Australia (built 1961) had been constructed with sprayed asbestos in the roof, and the new Parliament House (built 1981) had asbestos-filled fire doors. The asbestos in both structures had to be removed at great expense.[23]

Hardie's multi-layered corporate culture

Hardie had been rotting away for decades with its toxic culture of lies and denial when, in the late 1990s, management actively began to plan its way out of responsibility for asbestos victims. Yet just how a collection of respected corporate managers and directors could deliberately plan such a callous strategy defies easy explanation.

At the heart of the scandal was the participation of the key individuals in 'Machiavellian behaviour' – a personality typology appropriated from the writings of Nicolò Machiavelli, the 16th-century diplomat and political theorist who was a close observer of power. Inside corporations, people acting in a Machiavellian manner are 'scheming, unscrupulous or cunning' in the pursuit of a goal; they try to avoid attracting undue attention to themselves.[24] Researchers have found a strong link between Machiavellianism and unethical behaviour.[25] Hardie's is an unusual case of this form of corporate behaviour – key senior management contrived among themselves to act in a Machiavellian way. Their concern was not to arouse any suspicion about their motives outside the company. What seems obvious, too, is that Hardie's history propelled management into this moral vacuum.

But individual personality traits also played a part in the decision to lie about the funding for the Medical Research and Compensation Foundation. Put through the wringer at an official inquiry and a Supreme Court case, directors and executives garnered plenty of testimonials as to their decent characters. But evidence presented also showed a constellation of very human flaws: executives who were overzealous, dogmatic, ambitious and with a propensity for self-deception – to bend the rules while being convinced of the higher purpose of pursuing shareholder return. Some of the directors shared similar qualities, while others were prepared to turn a blind eye, or at least not to ask hard questions.

The resort to denial stuck with the company; victims were transformed into 'the other'. They were looked upon by management with disdain.[26] As Commissioner Jackson himself found, as time went by, Hardie regarded asbestos liabilities as 'legacy issues' or part of the 'rump' and as a source of 'management distraction', which it would be 'desirable to separate'.[27]

The deputy head of communications at Hardie during the scandal, Steve Ashe, admitted in an internal memo that the company's reputation was widely known. He acknowledged that it 'has a history of not disclosing the truth – for its own gain'.[28] By the 1990s, the 'price' of becoming a successful global corporation appears to have been some level of cognitive dissonance from its asbestos past. The push was on for greater shareholder value.

Striving for maximum shareholder value is, of course, the essence of corporate existence. But Hardie is an example of the moral shallowness of this theory of economics. As the company's history showed, maximising shareholder value is a slippery slope, easily morphed by some corporations, like Hardie, into 'advancing the interests of shareholders at all costs'.[29] Backed by powerful interests, shareholder value can overwhelm the public interest, as the victims of James Hardie – and their families – know only too well.

In the lead-up to the scandal, maximising shareholder value intensified with the appointment of two key directorships. The first was Alan McGregor, who joined the Hardie board in 1989 and became its chair in 1995. A product of Geelong Grammar, and Adelaide and Cambridge universities, McGregor was an experienced, valued and trusted director. He had sat on and chaired the boards of numerous large companies. Regarded as a highly ethical person, he had received the Order of Australia in 1987. Yet those who have closely studied Hardie as a company note that, under his tenure as chair, there was a significant shift 'to a more aggressive shareholder value focussed style'.[30] He was a key backer of Macdonald, with the two forming 'a tight unit'.[31] As a long-standing chair McGregor could have put an end to the restructure, but didn't. He was also a substantial investor in Hardie.[32]

The second crucial board appointment in the 1990s was, literally, eye-catching. High-flying corporate identity Meredith Hellicar joined the board in 1992. A trained lawyer, she was a rarity in corporate Australia at the time – a prominent female executive in the male-dominated culture of boardrooms. Before she joined Hardie, she had earned a reputation as a tough, hands-on executive in 'hard businesses' such as law, logistics and the coal industry.[33] The product of an elite Sydney private school, Hellicar was singled out at a young age for being bright and demanding and destined for success. After studying law, she came to the attention of major power players during her stint heading the New South Wales Coal Association where she had dealt with some of the fiercest unions in the country. In her rise to the top, Hellicar cut a striking figure, with her helmet-styled, platinum-blonde hair and pastel-coloured power suits.

Relishing her senior roles in male-dominated industries, Hellicar became a role model for corporate women.[34] The media loved her. A straight shooter, Hellicar had a headmistress-like manner and didn't suffer fools. No one doubted her integrity. Before her involvement in Hardie's restructure, her career had been untainted by scandal. But some of those who dealt with her during the height of the scandal were struck by a seeming contradiction in her personality. Behind the polite façade, Hellicar seemed to lack empathy. Bernie Banton observed that she was a 'cold and dispassionate person'.[35] ACTU leader and prominent asbestos campaigner Greg Combet was equally suspicious of Hellicar: 'She was very keen for us to know that, really, she was a good person'.[36]

Hellicar certainly kept a distance from victims of asbestos diseases. Until she assumed the chair at Hardie in 2003, Hellicar had not met a victim. According to critics, she was mainly concerned with 'hobnobbing with those who've profited from asbestos's suitability as an ingredient in building products: the shareholders, lawyers, company directors like herself'.[37] By disposition and background, Hellicar was an instinctive advocate for maximising shareholder value.[38] Hellicar couldn't escape her own role; as a long-standing director and lawyer, she 'was in on every key decision that led to the crisis'.[39]

A trio of senior executives, also recruited in the 1990s, reflected and reinforced the key planks of Hardie's culture: aggressive growth, maximum shareholder value and fencing off asbestos-related liabilities. Peter Macdonald became CEO in 1999, having overseen the heady growth in the company's US operations. Ambitious and hard-working, he led the restructure.[40] His overall aim was to 'wow' US investors with Hardie's aggressive growth strategy.[41] The strategy matched Macdonald's own personality: sharp, driven and disciplined. He was always formidably well briefed.[42] But he harboured a more dubious side. In his company history of Hardie, Gideon Haigh depicts Macdonald as a binary thinker – issues were couched in black and white terms. And he was 'temperamentally drawn to total solutions'.[43] Commissioner Jackson also wrote critically of Macdonald, saying that the evidence he gave about his role in the restructure 'tended to be self-serving'.[44]

Peter Shafron became the chief in-house lawyer in 1997. A prize-winning honours graduate from Sydney University, he had written a 'lively' textbook on complying with trade practices law in which he noted that a 'veritable Dante's inferno awaits those found in breach of the Trade Practices Act'. Yet he, too, crossed the ethical line. Promotion, a million-dollar annual salary plus bonuses was the reward for 'pulling off a tough assignment' at Hardie.[45] He also had a spymaster's flair for secrecy and intrigue.[46]

Phillip Morley came from an atypical background for a Hardie executive – or any big company executive. He had grown up in a fibro house in a working-class family in Sydney's western suburbs – a stone's throw from the James Hardie factory at Camelia. Retaining elements of his working-class roots, Morley mixed easily with company employees. Quick to share a laugh or listen to an company concerns, he used to keep in touch with his old schoolmates and attended his high school's fortieth annual reunion. His connection to asbestos was deeply personal, as a former school friend told a journalist: 'A lot of the guys had fathers who had worked at James Hardie and contracted asbestos diseases'.[47] As chief financial officer, he signed off on the funding for the Foundation.

This trio of executives were the principal architects for change. They worked out of the company's US headquarters in the town of Mission Viejo in southern California, a series of gated communities, whose immaculately landscaped gardens were lovingly tended by Mexican workers.[48] The Hardie executives were in a fast lane to success overseeing the stellar growth of the company in America. Together they 'ruled James Hardie Industries ... like colonial masters'. Caught up in the exuberance and ego of the rapid expansion, the trio enjoyed the fruits of success: 'Macdonald at various times drove a Porsche, a Mercedes four-wheel drive and an Eddie Bauer Ford truck. Shafron had a gold Mercedes'.[49] Isolated in their sterile gated communities, and cut off for large periods of time from the mounting legal challenges from asbestos claimants, the young Hardie executives focused their energies on statistics, models and capital returns.[50]

As Gideon Haigh perceptively noted, these recent arrivals had little time, patience or tolerance for hearing anything about asbestos-related illness.[51]

Planning the way out

By the late 1990s, Hardie faced three major impediments in its quest to be a major global player in the manufacture of building products. The first was tax. Eighty-five per cent of the company's profits were earned in America and the company was required to pay tax on those profits. The problem arose when it sent dividends to the company's Australian shareholders; America applied a 15 per cent tax on those dividends. In proposing to shift to the Netherlands, Hardie wanted to take advantage of the tax treaty the country had with America which cut dividend tax from 15 per cent to 5 per cent. In addition, the company saw major new growth opportunities in Europe.[52]

Hardie's second, and more pressing, impediment to growth was perceived to be its asbestos-related liabilities. The idea was to make the cheapest provision for victims thought 'marketable' so that the company could go off and focus on its more lucrative interests.[53]

Lastly, Hardie had experienced difficulties in raising loans in the United States because of the company's links to asbestos claimants.[54]

The enticing advantage of relocating to the Netherlands lay in the legal ring-fencing the country offered to protect Hardie from any future claims by victims. Victims' capacity to gain access to the company's Netherlands-based assets was thought to be unlikely because there was no reciprocal agreement between Australia and the Netherlands on money matters. This requirement for a reciprocal agreement had been made explicit in the Commonwealth *Foreign Judgments Act 1991*.[55]

But those planning the restructure realised from the outset that it was a delicate balancing act to pull off, and especially the creation of the Foundation. What level of funding for it would be thought credible? How would such a figure be determined and how could their plan be sold to the public? Macdonald got to work on a policy position paper addressing these issues, known as the 'Green Project'.

The first task was to obtain legal advice about corporation law. The advice confirmed that, while it was allowable to split the company and leave the subsidiaries underfunded to meet asbestos claims, it wasn't mandated under law either.[56]

The same flexible interpretation of corporate law was applied to deciding on the level of funding for the proposed Foundation. Hardie directors were advised by external lawyers that the level of funding must be guided by what was of benefit to shareholders. But trying to apply such a vague requirement did not provide clear guidance on social norms and expectations.[57] That was left to the management and directors to decide.

Shafron and Macdonald understood that the level of funding allocated to the proposed Foundation was the most sensitive issue in the whole exercise. In March 2000, Shafron asked Hardie's actuarial firm, Trowbridge, for an updated assessment of liabilities. Hardie management brought to this task their own agenda. They wanted the revised figure to be as low as possible but one which avoided adverse criticism that could jeopardise the restructure going ahead.

Trowbridge had undertaken actuarial reports for Hardie since 1996, so receiving a request for an update was not unexpected. Peter Shafron had overall responsibility to liaise with Trowbridge. Not surprisingly, it was a fraught exercise from the start, with Machiavellian undertones. Commissioner Jackson examined in detail the process by which Trowbridge arrived at a figure of $294 million for the Foundation. He found Shafron continually interfered, leaning on Trowbridge to keep the figure as low as possible. He wrote that Shafron had 'sought to exercise a great deal of influence over the contents of the Trowbridge Report'.[58] Trowbridge director David Minty later claimed that Hardie had denied access to its latest data with the excuse that the computer programmer was on leave; Shafron insisted that the actuaries told him that they didn't need the latest figures.[59]

Trowbridge responded to these pressures by couching their findings with qualifications and expressions of uncertainty while trying to maintain a credible methodology. Trowbridge was just one of a cast of professional advisors whose reputations came under scrutiny through their relationship with Hardie. There was a question mark about whether 'some advisers became too close to Hardie and lost their ability to give fearless and frank counsel'.[60]

Like a spider's web, rogue corporations are a trap for the unwary. David Minty learned just how fraught working for Hardie could be. When he appeared before the Jackson Commission, he maintained that the company had misused the report he had compiled; Jackson queried this assumption. The press reported the following exchange:

> Mr Jackson said that as soon as James Hardie told the stock exchange it had set up 'a fully funded foundation [providing] certainty for both claimants and shareholders', it must have been obvious to Trowbridge that the statement was wrong.
>
> 'Why didn't Trowbridge stand up and say "that's not correct"?' Mr Jackson asked. 'The press release said … that in arriving at that conclusion [James Hardie] had relied on what Trowbridge had said.'
>
> Mr Robertson [counsel for Trowbridge] replied: 'If the question is, "Was there a legal duty under the general law or the Trade Practices Act for Trowbridge in those circumstances to act as a policeman", we would say the answer is no.[61]

Minty was later disciplined by the Institute of Actuaries because he had 'proceeded on a serious misunderstanding of the nature, purpose and completeness of his work'. In their press statement about the action, the Institute's spokesperson said that the disciplinary measure would 'be a reminder to all actuaries of their continuing professional and ethical obligations'.[62]

Questions were raised about the final figure for the Foundation as soon as the draft report was completed, including from Hardie's lawyers. Shafron, keen to test out what might be defended in a potentially hotly contested public debate, asked Steve Ashe from Hardie's Corporate Affairs team to review the Trowbridge figure from a PR perspective. He was scathing about the proposed $294 million for the Foundation. It 'does not leave the reader with confidence that the amount of $294 million is sufficient. In fact, one could easily be left with the impression that the amount is insufficient'. Trowbridge, the review highlighted, 'seems to be warning against the use of their assessment for anything other than internal matters – certainly not as the basis for calculating separation costs'.[63]

What followed next defies belief. Hardie decided to reject the warnings it received about the questionable figure, to not release the Trowbridge report publicly and to embark on a public relations campaign to sell the $294 million figure to the stock exchange and the wider public.

The build-up to the 15 February board meeting

Towards the end of 2000, Macdonald's focus shifted to the upcoming board meeting to be held on 15 February 2001. Early that month, papers relating to the restructure and the proposed Foundation were sent to board members. The company's solicitors prepared draft minutes of the meeting which were signed off as a correct record at the subsequent April board meeting.[64]

Included in the board papers for the February meeting was one prepared by Macdonald recommending the restructure and urging directors to 'act now'. The reason Macdonald gave for the urgency was the impending introduction of new accounting standards which would adversely affect the company's accounts by requiring provision for present and future asbestos liabilities.

Also included in the board papers were two other documents: the infamous press release for its approval, and a proposed communications strategy to ensure that the restructure was favourably received by government and the media.

The press release, which carried Macdonald's signature, read, in part, that:

> The Medical Research and Compensation Foundation ... has sufficient funds to meet all legitimate compensation claims ... [it] provided certainty for both claimants and shareholders ... Its establishment has effectively resolved James Hardie's asbestos liability and this will allow management to focus entirely on growing the company for the benefit of all shareholders.

Clearly this claim was false and Macdonald and Shafron knew it to be so. But the press release made another false claim: that Hardie had obtained expert advice from PricewaterhouseCoopers (PwC) and Access Economics which 'had determined the level of funding'.[65] However, it emerged that neither company had provided such endorsement; in fact, they had each urged directors to satisfy themselves that the assumptions in the Trowbridge report were reasonable. But management never entertained any intention to listen to their advice; it was merely a stunt. In evidence before the Jackson Inquiry, Phillip Morley admitted that the review that Access and PwC were asked to do was an 'arid and pointless' exercise.[66]

Commissioner Jackson was incredulous at finding that no director had actually read the Trowbridge report; nor had they read any of the previous reports prepared by the firm. Jackson seemed to have a sharp intake of breath when he wrote: 'This seems extraordinary', adding that the board 'did not condescend to matters of detail'. He said that he found it difficult to accept that management believed there were sufficient funds in the Foundation.[67]

McGregor later admitted that board members had relied on management to 'interpret' the advice from experts. He further enumerated that a full report 'would have been available if we had asked for it'.[68] But were directors just being lazy, or were they disinclined to engage with the ugly truths behind the proposed restructure? Directors later claimed that they had been misinformed by management about the funding for the Foundation.

But these revelations did not emerge until the Jackson Inquiry. Meanwhile, directors attending the 15 February meeting had the added task of endorsing the communications strategy that had been prepared in association with prominent public relations firm Hawker Britton. By this time, 'corporate spin' had become the cutting edge of corporate power – a multimillion dollar industry aimed at outwitting and out-thinking pesky journalists. And Hardie faced 'a giant PR problem' in selling its restructure, including the

Foundation.[69] The management team settled on a simple but blunt approach:

> [u]se business media as the entry point into the news cycle, confine the issue to its financial implications, sell the story as great news for shareholders and, crucially, limit the opportunity for other media to report the really negative aspect of the restructure.[70]

The strategy made clear its central aim: 'Our strategy … is to "divide and conquer" the individual risks'.[71] Hardie had hoped to spin its way to their imagined grand future.

One of the risks identified in the communications strategy was the possibility that the New South Wales Carr government might appoint a government inquiry if the PR assault failed. Every effort was made to nullify this prospect. Hardie's communications chief, Greg Baxter, hired a TV crew and journalist to undertake a mock exercise of the key lines to be given to journalists.

To sell its case to the government, the strategy paper foreshadowed that the company planned to consult the former Labor powerbroker and senator, Stephen Loosley, then a partner at PwC, and the former national Labor national secretary, Gary Gray. Loosley, operating as a business lobbyist, was subsequently paid $50 000 to arrange meetings in 2001 between Hardie executives and several of Carr's senior staff. According to *The Guardian*, the object of the meeting was to ensure that 'the Carr Government did not put any "legislative impediment" in the way of its setting up its totally inadequate fund'.[72] Lobbying for big corporations lacks transparency and it remains unclear what exactly transpired at these meetings, but Jackson did find that Loosley had urged Hardie to strengthen the adequacy of the Foundation's funding.[73]

However, there was an unexpected last minute hitch. Hawker Britton got cold feet and pulled out, warned off by Greg Combet,

Secretary of the Australian Council of Trade Unions, who had told principal David Britton: 'keep an eye on those Hardie bastards! If they try to wriggle out of their asbestos liabilities [I'll] come down on them like a ton of bricks'.[74] But even their last-minute departure didn't stop the charade from going ahead.

Did the Carr government give the issue the consideration it deserved? Some thought not. As *The Age* commented: 'There have also been the obvious questions in Parliament about why the Government did not run some checks over Hardie's mathematics when Carr's Health Minister, John Della Bosca, vocally welcomed the establishment of the trust in February 2001'.[75] Carr would later explain that there wasn't much he could have done in any event because corporate law had, by then, become a federal matter.

But the politics surrounding the establishment of the Foundation lacked transparency. Over the years, Hardie had been a significant donor to both sides of politics;[76] only once the scandal erupted did each party undertake to ban donations from the company. As always, such donations raise disturbing questions about whether Hardie had, over the years, facilitated a compliant political response to the rising tide of scientific opinion that asbestos should have been banned.

The executive didn't have it all their own way. Several of the board members harboured sceptical views about the restructure and the funding of the Foundation. But as they hadn't fully engaged with the Trowbridge report, there was limited robust discussion at the board meeting. The dominant view was that, as directors, they couldn't fund the Foundation in any way that disadvantaged shareholders. But this stipulation was the legal equivalent of asking how long was a piece of string. And the board was under pressure from Macdonald to act with urgency to avoid coming under greater scrutiny from the proposed new accounting standards.

The grand plan unravels

Would Hardie's Machiavellian plan ever have succeeded? The truth is, the company very nearly pulled off their audacious restructure. Initial media reception was largely positive; the PR strategy seemed to have worked. But the spin didn't last long. The seeds of a backlash appeared within a matter of weeks when it dawned on the board appointed to run the Foundation that there was a serious shortfall of available funds. The fact that the board acted in such a proactive manner was likely not anticipated by Hardie management. Key appointees to the board were former Hardie insiders. Sir Llew Edwards, a former deputy premier of Queensland, had been a Hardie director since 1988 and only resigned to take on the role as head of the Foundation.

Edwards' decision to head the board is curious. He'd been on the inside while the Green Project was being developed. Surely he was aware of the company's aims for the Foundation? As a former medical doctor, he needed no briefing on the seriousness of asbestos-related diseases. And the matter was a personal one for him. Both his grandfathers had contracted dust-related lung disease working in the coal mines around his home town of Ipswich.[77]

As Liberal leader in Queensland during the 1980s, Sir Llew had a reputation as both 'a Queensland giant' and a bit of a political lightweight. He was junior partner to the right-wing, populist government led by Sir Joh Bjelke-Petersen, during which time he 'bristled at persistent criticism that he was a compliant junior partner [and] lampooned in the media holding onto Bjelke-Petersen's coat-tails'.[78] Was Sir Llew a loyal and compliant Hardie insider? From this distance, it's impossible to know. But he claimed to have higher motives. He said that, for years, he had advocated the need for the company to do the right thing by asbestos victims. But he'd also worked closely with Shafron and Macdonald.

Weeks into his new role, Edwards was contacted by Trowbridge partner David Minty with the grim news that claims were already running 40 per cent above expectations and that, as a consequence, total liabilities were $574 million. In other words, the Foundation was going to run out of money. The directors were shocked. Whether justified or not, they felt they had been deceived.

However, the directors now owned the problem and they appealed directly to Macdonald for additional funds. He repeatedly turned them down. So, in October 2003, Sir Llew blew the whistle on Hardie.

The jig was up. An outraged Carr set up the Jackson Inquiry. In addition to teasing out Hardie's scam in excruciating detail, Jackson exposed the limitations of the law's ability to control those corporations which, like Hardie, chose to ignore their social and ethical responsibilities. Hardie became the poster child for rogue corporations.

The Jackson Inquiry established that the cost of asbestos-related claims was $1.5 billion, or more than five times what Hardie had allocated. Ironically, the very success the company had achieved in America gave it plenty of capacity to be generous to asbestos victims.

Tackling corporate power

The publication of the Jackson Report in September 2004 had Hardie on the defensive. On the back of the sustained community campaign, the company negotiated a settlement with the New South Wales government in which it agreed to pay $185 million into the Asbestos Injuries Compensation Fund with further regular payments to be made over the minimum forty-year life of the agreement.

But Hardie directors and executives were not out of the woods. Although damning of the company's management, Jackson made no recommendations that charges be laid. He said that was the responsibility of the Commonwealth. Federal Treasurer Peter Costello gave additional funding to ASIC to explore mounting a legal case, which took several years to compile. By this stage ASIC had shifted from criminal to civil cases in its efforts to prosecute breaches of the *Corporations Act*. By shifting away from the use of criminal law, with its higher legal standards, it was hoped that ASIC could be more effective in punishing corporate misbehaviour.[79] But the risk inherent in that approach was the imposition of penalties that failed to send a message to corporate Australia.

In the meantime, the fallout from the report's revelations spurred the most intense public debate ever seen – then or now – about the role of corporations in Australian society. By the time the Foundation scandal erupted Hardie was seen as a company bereft of corporate ethics. Of course, plenty of companies engage in operations regarded by many as harmful to society. But it was the fact that Hardie had so deliberately set out to lie about its responsibilities that brought about the undoing of its directors and executives.

The Hardie case focused attention on corporate social responsibility (CSR), a concept that had been floating around in the academic business literature since the 1960s. As interest in CSR grew worldwide during the 1990s, it came to be seen as a set of voluntary measures by companies to integrate social and environmental concerns into their business operations; in other words, that businesses were responsible for their actions to a group wider than just shareholders.[80] However, as companies responded to the CSR 'industry', questions were raised as to whether companies were 'investing more energy in giving the impression that they care than actually changing the world'.[81]

In fact, it was easy for corporations, like Hardie, to ignore their wider responsibilities because they were not required to report on the broader impact of their operations. Mandatory reporting of a company's economic, social and environmental impacts – the so-called triple bottom line – was a logical extension of this gap.

The public outrage over the Hardie scandal led to calls for greater action on CSR. New South Wales Attorney-General Bob Debus weighed into the debate about the need for tougher laws on corporate social responsibility. 'I cannot understand', he told the *Sydney Morning Herald*, 'that directors and managers should assume it's appropriate for a company to behave in a profoundly anti-social way in order that they maximise profits to shareholders.' But because some corporations did interpret the law in this way, he argued governments should consider recasting the corporations law. He received support from Rob Hulls, his Victorian counterpart.[82]

That outrage was further fanned by the release, in 2005, of the Canadian documentary *The Corporation*, based on Joel Bakan's book of the same name. Reviews of the award-winning film were widely published in the Australian media. Its central theme was designed to be provocative: if the typical global corporation were a human being, it would be a psychopath, given that it fitted all the accepted diagnostic definitions. The timing of the documentary's release was prescient, in light of the rampaging destruction unleashed by the 1980s entrepreneurs and, more recently by HIH. And now there was the Hardie scandal. It seemed that Australia was fertile ground for Bakan's critique.

At the same time *The Corporation* was released, John Clarke, a former profiler with the New South Wales police, released his book, *Working with Monsters: How to Identify and Protect Yourself from the Workplace Psychopath.* While Clarke was at pains to show that people with a psychopathic profile could be found in a range of organisations, corporations were among them. In fact, Clarke was a consultant to companies that suspected such people inhabited their ranks. 'For the psychopath', Clarke wrote, 'vaulting their way up the ranks ... is paramount and simple'.[83]

Thus, at the time of the Hardie scandal, debate about the potential for destructive tendencies among corporations had preoccupied public debate. There was pressure for action. Two inquiries were established to consider CSR. The Howard government instructed the Corporations and Markets Advisory Committee, a Sydney-based group of industry practitioners, to review CSR requirements, and the parliamentary Joint Committee on Corporations and Financial Services established an inquiry into the issue.

Both sets of findings rejected a more enforceable approach to CSR and were heavily influenced by opposition from the Business Council of Australia and ASIC. And critics were able to take advantage of the ambiguity around CSR. It proved easy to muddy the waters around the challenges of making corporations more accountable to society in the interests of protecting corporate profits.

The rejection of enhancing measures for CSR represented a 'final blow'[84] for changes to the *Corporations Act 2001*, introduced by Howard government just as Hardie management was devising its plan.

The trial

As the death knell sounded on regulating for CSR, ASIC continued to work up the case for charging Hardie senior management and directors. By 2009, 9000 Australians had died from asbestos-related diseases and another 9000 were expected to die in the next thirteen years.[85]

It was surprising that ASIC decided to get tough with both Hardie executives and directors. Although Commissioner Jackson had exposed the deceptions of Hardie executives – Macdonald (also a director), Shafron and Morley – it was going to be a difficult challenge to find that directors had failed in their duties. The *Corporations Act* is a complex and ambiguous piece of legislation. Although it provides for criminal penalties for directors who recklessly or dishonestly breach their directors' duties, who are dishonest in regard to financial and audit obligations, and who knowingly provide defective documents or statements, it contains a 'get out' clause that allows breaches of directors' duties to be exonerated if 'the person has acted honestly; and having regard to all the circumstances in the case.'[86] Critics might say that the 'old boys club' of directors had to be protected.

In the wider sense, the *Corporations Act* wasn't framed for a company like Hardie with its long history of killing its workers. ASIC could not deliver retrospective justice. But the case was, nonetheless, set to test the resolve of ASIC in bringing the current management group to account.

The trial was set to revolve around the 16 February press release in which the three executives had allegedly lied about the level of funding for the Foundation and failed to advise the board about the true situation. Thus, the case against the three was, on paper at least, more straightforward.

But ASIC claimed that directors were also liable because they did not exercise sufficient care and diligence in questioning the executives about the adequacy of funding. However, the *Corporations Act* again muddied the waters on any potential action against them because of the provision that says that it is 'reasonable' for directors to rely on information or advice provided by management and external advisors of a sub-committee of the board.

Effectively, under the *Corporations Act*, directors were given plenty of protection to collect big fees and remain largely unaccountable. Prosecution lawyers had their work cut out. As journalist Elizabeth Sexton wrote at the start of the trial, the challenge for Justice Ian Gzell was deciding exactly what happened in the 15 February meeting: 'Who said what? Who withheld what? Who was too complacent? Who was too naïve?' And if fault was found, did all directors and executives bear equal responsibility?[87] By the time the case came before the New South Wales Supreme Court in late September 2008, former chair Alan McGregor had died and Llew Edwards had managed a lucky escape because he had resigned an hour into the meeting to take up a directorship with the Foundation.

When the trial started, twenty asbestos victims and family members gathered to claim a seat in the court room. Attending was Karen Banton, wife of Bernie Banton, who had succumbed the previous November to mesothelioma. He'd been granted an Order of Australia for his tireless work representing victims, and he was granted a state funeral in further recognition of his activism. Inside, the court room was packed with a small army of lawyers working for ASIC and the defendants, whose corporate reputations were on the line.

On the first day of the trial, some of the lawyers for the defendants believed that ASIC did not have enough evidence 'to get to first base'.[88] ASIC's barrister, Tony Bannon, was relying on the 15 February minutes but, within days, it became clear that the defendants were going to challenge the accuracy of those minutes. Bannon tried to point out the obvious: 'We didn't understand that the public company directors were going to assert that their own minutes, which they confirmed, are incorrect'.[89]

However, Justice Gzell did not believe the directors' 'chorus of non-recollection', which proved to be a damning finding. Greg Baxter, head of PR at Hardie, gave evidence from the witness box that he recalled taking a draft of the press release with him to the board meeting. Two other directors – Michael Brown and Martin Koffell – indicated that the press release was discussed.[90]

Meredith Hellicar attempted to hold out but was shown up by the evidence. Bannon produced email evidence to show that directors held a phone hook-up five days after the meeting to discuss the reaction to the media release. Her attempts to deny the existence of this meeting, citing that she was at a seminar in Queensland on that day, were undone by telephone records. Thereafter Hellicar abandoned her stance.[91] However, in the process she was on the receiving end of a scathing character assessment from Gzell, who said that 'there was a dogmatism in her testimony that I do not accept' and, more seriously, that Hellicar 'proved to be inaccurate on a number of occasions. I found Ms Hellicar to be a most unsatisfactory witness'.[92]

In his judgment, Gzell found that the seven non-executive directors, including Hellicar, had engaged in a 'flagrant' abuse of their duties when they knew, or ought to have known, that the press release was misleading and constituted a 'deliberate attempt' to influence the sharemarket into accepting the restructure.[93] The three executives were found to have breached their duties by failing to advise the board of the limitations of the advice from PwC and Access Economics and, in Macdonald's case, of having known (or ought to have known) that the press release was misleading. Macdonald, as the driver of the Green Project, was disqualified from senior management for fifteen years and fined $350 000; Shafron was disqualified for seven years and fined $75 000; and Phillip Morley was fined $35 000 and banned for five years. The non-executive directors were disqualified for five years and fined $30 000. All but Macdonald appealed and, in a surprise ruling, had the charges overturned in the New South Wales Supreme Court, only to have them reinstated with reduced penalties in the High Court.

However, the very meaning of penalties was called into question when it was revealed that Macdonald walked away from Hardie with a $8.83 million payout; Shafron with $1.17 million; and Hellicar with $1 million.

The significance of the judgment in the Hardie trial can be seen in two different ways. On the one hand, never before had a boardroom been blitzed with charges against its senior executives and directors for the decisions they had made. A clear message was sent to corporations around the country that knowingly issuing false statements would not pass a benign interpretation of the *Corporations Act* and that directors, especially, must be certain of the details around board decisions.

But the core of the Hardie case brings into sharp relief the dark side of the pull exerted on corporations by shareholder value. Most of the companies covered in this book were dragged into scandal one way or another because they failed to balance this goal with the public interest.

6
THE CULT: STORM FINANCIAL

The co-founder of financial planning firm Storm Financial, Emmanuel 'Manny' Cassimatis, looked pale and sickly as he prepared to address the 500-odd company faithful who packed out Townsville's Riverway Arts Centre in early November 2008. And well he might. Cassimatis knew that his company was in deep trouble and those who had come to be reassured by him were anxious about the continuing slide in the Australian share market.

Townsville was the home base for the once plucky company. It was where Emmanuel and his co-director wife, Julie, established their business in 1994, providing financial advice and arranging financial products for clients seeking to build their retirement income. Storm made them one of Queensland's wealthiest couples and a national player in the booming financial planning industry. The company went on to open offices throughout the eastern states, amassing $6 billion in funds. Now, the city's power couple were facing worried folks with whom they shared deep roots. The corporate culture of Storm had proved to be a mirage: instead of providing safe investments, the Cassimatises had lured clients into borrowing over their heads. The deregulated financial market had encouraged them to put ordinary people at grave risk. The Howard government had remained committed to the view that the financial system was a competitive market that should be free of interference.[1] And the regulators were again nowhere in sight. The combination had propelled Storm over the cliff.

Storm Financial had ridden the seventeen-year bull market. The Cassimatises had cashed in on the good times by persuading ordinary people to surf the wave of the rising stock market. The couple had continually reassured such investors that mortgaging their houses and taking out loans from one of the big banks to invest in stocks was a strategy that would never crash, let alone financially drown them.

As he took to the podium, Emmanuel had lost his usual confident, arrogant swagger. He'd always looked more like an aging wrestler with his stocky frame, large, bald-domed head and jowly cheeks, than a financial guru. The faithful were shocked at the changed demeanour of their hero. As one later explained: 'He's one of the great salesmen, he could sell ice to Eskimos, and when he came into this meeting I thought, "This bloke doesn't appear to be his old self"'.[2]

Indeed, Emmanuel couldn't hide the gut-wrenching truth that the share market was in freefall, having lost 40 per cent from its peak less than a year before. The Global Financial Crisis (GFC) was wreaking havoc on global share markets and Storm's strategy of risking all on this financial strategy, as if the stock market were a casino where the punters never lost, was imploding. 'The enormity of the risk finally sank in for the first time for many of those assembled', one journalist noted.[3]

At the end of the tense meeting questions were invited. A seventy-year-old woman stood up and cut to the chase: 'Manny, those of us who have mortgages, can the banks take our houses?' For the first time, Cassimatis responded candidly: 'Yes they can, and be afraid'. It was the beginning of the end. Cassimatis knew that the Commonwealth Bank (CBA) was closing in on their clients' loans. So concerned was he that, after the meeting, he flew down to Sydney to plead with CBA officials, who were the biggest providers of bank loans to Storm clients, to extend a $60 million lifeline to bail them out. His plea fell on deaf ears. Worried about the interests of its own shareholders, the bank panicked and called in the loans to Storm clients. With the flick of a switch, and after years of shovelling money into Storm, the CBA consigned the Cassimatises to the financial dust bin. But what was the CBA doing in the first place, backing such a flaky, high-risk operation as Storm Financial?

A few days later, Storm collapsed and within a few weeks the livelihoods of 3000 of its 14 000 clients were destroyed almost overnight.[4] Storm went bankrupt owing $3.6 billion to its investors.[5] The company has been described as Australia's worst corporate collapse in terms of its impact on ordinary Australians.[6] However, the collapse of Storm was merely one of a series of scandals that engulfed the financial services sector at the time, totalling more than $9 billion in losses to clients.[7] A joint parliamentary inquiry was established in 2009 into the financial services sector to examine the collapse of Storm, among others.

The rise of Emmanuel Cassimatis

To the Storm faithful, Emmanuel possessed almost movie-star charisma. This was reflected in the near cult-like following he and Julie had developed in Townsville, making clients feel part of a big family of 'Stormers'. The seductive approach had been perfected over the several decades Emmanuel had spent in the financial services industry.

The rise of the Cassimatises mirrored the boom in the financial services industry that accompanied the introduction of federal Labor's compulsory superannuation in 1991 and with it a pool of hundreds of billions of dollars of investment funds – a veritable pot of gold for the industry. A landmark reform championed by Prime Minister Paul Keating, compulsory 'super' improved the lives of ordinary Australians. But it had unintended consequences. It spurred a financial services industry imbued with a ruthless culture: one that charged high fees for advice and exploited clients by taking commissions to direct them into designated financial products. In other words, financial advisers didn't always act in the best interests of their clients.[8] Large sections of the industry had become 'the sales force for financial product manufacturers'.[9]

Keating's successor, Liberal Prime Minister John Howard, became a champion of the self-funded retirement industry upon his election in

1996. His government highlighted the rising number of baby boomers heading into retirement and warned that the Commonwealth pension system may not keep pace. For that reason, the government encouraged people to take responsibility for funding their own retirement by creating their own managed superannuation funds.[10] Many who did so sought advice from financial advisors. But who were the advisors? The simple answer was – anybody. Few who called themselves advisors at the time the industry expanded had any formal qualifications. As one advisor told the press in 1989: 'You can come in from selling cars. Just get yourself a licence and you're out there'.[11]

As a consequence of these changes, increasing numbers of people were drawn into a lightly regulated and rapacious financial services industry. And Emmanuel and Julie Cassimatis were masters at creating an appealing corporate image to target unsuspecting and vulnerable clients. They understood their client base because in the distant past both came from similar backgrounds.

'We grew up piss-poor,' explained Atherton-born Emmanuel in the typically unvarnished north Queensland vernacular. He was the son of Greek parents who migrated to Australia from the island of Kythera after enduring the hardships of World War II and the Greek civil war (1946–49), and went on to run a corner store. Julie Cassimatis was also from a family of battlers, raised in Townsville as one of nine children. Her mother was a homemaker and her father was a jockey and later worked as a scaffolder.

As Emmanuel was fond of telling the press: 'We learned the importance of values and ethics. Don't make promises lightly and when you do make a promise, die before you break it'.[12] If that wasn't wholesome enough, Emmanuel liked to spruik the company's core philosophy: 'I know it sounds really cliched but success comes from having a client focus,' he said. 'Client focus is not the key, it's everything.'[13] But the reality was very different. Inside the financial planning industry, Emmanuel Cassimatis had long been known as a risk taker.[14]

Emmanuel started as a financial planner in 1972 when he joined the MLC group. It was there that he met Julie, who was working as a secretary at the company. Concerns about his preference for risk-taking advice emerged in the late 1980s when he was still at MLC. He came to blows with auditors on a number of occasions, as one journalist later found: 'What is known was that while he was with MLC he geared his clients at a much higher rate than the "acceptable level"'.[15]

After leaving MLC, the Cassimatises created Ozdaq Securities and began selling a model of highly gearing clients with loans, which produced a number of close shaves for clients.[16] However, throughout the 1990s, Ozdaq Securities grew steadily, although largely under the public radar. Its headquarters remained in Townsville, but it began to attract clients from around the country via the Cassimatises' former MLC agents, who they had continued to cultivate. Other customers were referred by existing clients, while some came to the business through the takeover of smaller financial planning firms. The couple continued to hone their aggressive pitch to clients, 'often advising people to go further into debt, even re-mortgaging their homes, to fund more investment'.[17] They justified the soundness of this approach by only investing in the best performing and most solid stocks. Theirs was not a Ponzi-style scheme, but this didn't mitigate its inherent riskiness.[18]

Increasingly, the Cassimatis business model came to rely on margin lending, which drove the rivers of gold that later flowed into their personal accounts. When they took out a margin loan on the advice of financial planners such as the Cassimatises, most Australian investors had no idea of the consequent high level of risk involved. This was because the facility allowed them to borrow from banks to purchase shares in excess of the value of their properties; the bank carried the exposed part of the loan. However, if the margin loan turned sour because of market volatility, the client was supposed to receive a 'margin call' to top it up with either more funds or by selling off a portion of the shares. If they didn't adjust the margin loan, the assets in their portfolio could be sold off without prior warning.

Margin loans were one of the financial products that came onto the market in the early 2000s that proved a boon to banks and financial advisors. By 2008, margin loans was a $38 billion dollar industry. Like fool's gold, margin lending was an attractive but deceptive product. In the bull market, which had reigned for the previous decade, the facility offered the opportunity to borrow more and, hence, make more money. But the industry was the equivalent of the financial Wild West. It was 'unwatched and unregulated',[19] another failure of government. But by pushing margin loans on less affluent clients, the banks and Storm were effectively gouging vulnerable people. To the Cassimatises, margin loans buffed up their returns. The greater the level of the loans, the greater the fees and commissions earned by the couple. Each 'step' cost clients an additional fee of about 7 per cent on the capital.[20]

The pair boosted their business strategy in 2000 at the same time they built the most opulent house in Townsville, a five-storey mansion directly behind the CBD, looking out to Magnetic Island. They began to promote their own success story as a key marketing tool, continuing a tradition begun by Alan Bond. In 2006, the company had changed its name to Storm Financial and embarked on a $5 million expansion of its Townsville headquarters, signifying its status as one of the country's leading financial services firms.[21]

However, the company failed in its effort to list on the Australian stock market in late 2007 because it could not get the major financial institutions on board; the float was ultimately pulled. Nevertheless, the Cassimatises' confidence remained undented. At the time of the failed float, three non-executive directors were appointed to the board of the company. A judge later found that they had had limited understanding of the Storm model and were passive directors. Board meetings were little more than information sessions run by the Cassimatises, who spun their well-oiled upbeat tale.[22]

Everything about the couple – at least as they presented themselves in public – showed a strong desire for wealth and status. In an industry noted for the ability of greedy operators to gouge high fees and lucrative commissions, the Cassimatises 'charged high' – a 7–8 per cent fee leveraged on the total amount invested in the market (estimated to be the highest fees in the marketplace),[23] as well as a 1 per cent annual fee, along with fees from fund managers.[24] The Cassimatises amassed an estimated personal fortune of $450 million by 2008.

And the couple loved to flaunt their extravagant lifestyle. 'We're people who have an excess of everything,' an unashamed Julie Cassimatis told Brisbane's *Sunday Mail* when the couple featured at number 22 in Queensland's Top 100 Rich List.[25]

However, the couple appeared to exist in a parallel world. Despite their fixation on excess, they believed they existed for a higher purpose. This was to bring the benefits of capitalism to ordinary people. 'Part of our vision', Emmanuel explained 'is to put within reach of the average Australian the wealth creation instruments within our capitalist system that is traditionally the domain of the rich'.[26] They were their own best ambassadors for selling a profligate lifestyle.

The Cassimatises' rags to riches story, and their mission to spread wealth, proved an inspiration to many.[27] The local press fawned over their opulent lifestyle. The *Townsville Bulletin* gushed when treated to 'an exclusive tour' of their Townsville mansion, the city's 'most desirable residence'. Designed around a tiered Waterford crystal chandelier, the eight-bedroom, five-level residence featured uninterrupted views of the harbour, Cleveland Bay, Ross River, Magnetic Island and Townsville city, accessed through multiple entertaining decks.[28] Some likened the building to a wedding cake.[29]

The couple also owned a mansion in Brisbane that featured a helipad, a ballroom and a driving range, and they commuted between the two residences by Learjet.

Exactly how did the Cassimatises build a business based on putting ordinary Australians at extraordinary risk, and how did they fly under the radar for so long?

The Big Mac approach to financial planning

Storm lured thousands of their clients who were on modest incomes to invest like they had money to burn.

Tracey Richards, a newly divorced mother of three, was thirty-eight when she contacted Storm in 2001 to discuss her plans for the future. By 2005, Ms Richards wasn't happy with her investments and wanted out. However, she was allegedly convinced by Storm to increase her investment, including proceeds from the sale of her unit. On Storm's advice she borrowed through Macquarie Bank, which lent her $2 million without assessing her ability to service the margin loan on her $24 000 salary.[30] Ms Richards, and others like her, were lured into such risky loan arrangements because the banking sector itself had gone rogue, overtaken by a culture of greed. Banks simply inflated the assets and incomes of people like Ms Richards in order to increase the amount of their borrowings.[31]

Jack and Frances Dale were recently retired self-funded retirees from North Queensland when they were lured to Storm from MLC where they had $350 000 in superannuation. They were advised to apply for a $260 000 margin loan, which Storm would arrange, from Colonial First State, a subsidiary of the CBA. The reason given for the margin loan, the Dales were told, 'was to "apply the muscle"'. This was Storm lingo to get the investment 'off to a kick start' – in the Dales' case, a $600 000 initial investment into Storm-badged funds with Colonial First State. Their portfolio went well until the GFC and the sudden cessation of their margin loan on a simple instruction from the CBA. They lost their home in the collapse of Storm.[32]

Another couple, the Doyles, arrived at Storm's Townsville headquarters in March 2006 already owning a $450 000 home and with $640 000 in superannuation. Two-and-a-half years later, their super had evaporated, their share portfolio had been sold and they had racked up a debt of $456 000 on their home: 'In return for this disastrous advice, which saw them increase their borrowings or exposure to the stock market no fewer than 11 times in 25 months, the Doyles paid Storm $152 000 in fees'.[33]

These three cases were replicated many times over. In fact, about 90 per cent of Storm clients were advised to take out loans against their houses and margin loans.[34]

Were these people financially naïve or just plain greedy? Some thought the financial temptations offered by the Cassimatises were just too great, as a Townsville competitor to Storm Financial explained: 'Everyone wants to make fast money and when you put a sensible approach in front of them and they compare it to a "Stormified" approach, the greedy always want to be "Stormified"'.[35] 'Stormified' was the couple's in-group term for the firm's model of encouraging clients to be 'double geared' with both margin and home loans to invest the maximum amount of funds in the stock market.

However, Storm's clients rejected the claim of greed. Many told the parliamentary inquiry into the financial services sector that their aim in taking Storm's advice 'was simply to generate an independent income during retirement'; to be independent and 'never have to claim a pension off the government'.[36] In the words of a former Storm employee, the clients were 'not your usual high-flying bankers and entrepreneurs revelling in risk'[37] but 'decent, hard-working Aussies', 'unsophisticated mums and dads' – plumbers, electricians, retirees and defence personnel.[38] Most were located in Queensland and Victoria with a sprinkling in New South Wales; a high proportion were from Italian and Greek backgrounds. Most were from lower socio-economic backgrounds and naïve about the world of high finance.[39]

Initially, everything centred around introducing prospective clients to what many referred to as 'the product': Storm's one-size-fits-all approach of leveraging assets into the stock market aided with access to mortgages and margin loans provided by banks. Rather than tailoring advice to the particular needs of clients as required under the *Corporations Act 2001*, potential clients were lured into over-leveraging on the stock market.

As Emmanuel Cassimatis candidly told the parliamentary inquiry, Storm was a 'production line' with separate 'cells' in its various offices, each of which carried out its function as part of the production process, so that everyone received the same advice. Only five of Storm's staff were certified financial planners, the rest were salespeople trained by the Cassimatises.[40] Poorly trained staff seemed part of the company's business model. As one Storm investor told the *Townsville Bulletin*, staff pushed and bullied clients to increase margin loans and house mortgages.[41]

Eagerly waiting at the end of this assembly line of advice was Emmanuel, who signed off on all investment proposals.[42]

Explaining his approach to the parliamentary inquiry, Emmanuel proudly drew upon the example of McDonald's as if it had provided the inspiration for Storm Financial: 'McDonald's would be the classic [example] – they [have] the burgers and that's what they have, and if you don't want it you go elsewhere'.[43] Not surprisingly, one commentator described Storm as a 'financial advice factory'.[44]

'The family'

The Cassimatises sold the image of their business as a 'family' of loyal clients. One former staff member, who lost her job in the company's crash, told the *Townsville Bulletin* that Storm was like a cult and that 'clients were brainwashed'. Preferring to speak anonymously, she added: 'senior financial advisors were made to think they were invincible'.[45] Storm investors Jo-Anne and Alan Harding were also critical of Storm's educational sessions: 'A high degree of importance was placed on "educating" prospective clients but in hind sight this only "educated" (or should I say indoctrinated) us on the aspects they were trying to sell us on'.[46]

One Storm client explained that 'at the seminars ... Emmanuel Cassimatis would say, "you are perfectly safe with us. If we were to give you the wrong advice you could sue us, because we have insurance to cover that"'.[47] Another said: 'We were assured that our home was safe'.[48] Clients heard these repeated assurances as gilt-edged guarantees.

Allen Myers QC, a lawyer acting for ASIC, described Storm's initial education sessions for its investors as being similar to 'Scientology and other systems of odd belief': 'The education experience was compulsory. One had to be a believer before one entered the family'.[49]

And Emmanuel dressed for the part of cult hero. When not in a business suit he preferred to dress in a large black T-shirt adorned with a large crucifix, making him look like an archbishop.[50]

Storm was able to exploit the culture it had forged around being a loyal, friendly, family-centred company. Renewed pitches were made to clients to lift their level of exposure to the stock market and margin loans, and Storm clients 'did exactly as they were told'.[51] As one devastated client explained to the parliamentary inquiry, 'we were told/warned not to question their advice "as the people who do well are the ones who follow our advice"'.[52]

And the 'family' was rewarded with extravagant parties and holidays. Like the culture Ray Williams and Christopher Skase created around extravagance, 'Storm's excesses were legendary in the finance world', one commentator noted.[53] Themed Christmas parties complete with fire twirlers and dancers were put on for the faithful clients and hundreds were taken on lavish foreign holidays. The holidays were designed to show customers how to enjoy their wealth.[54] Several Storm clients who compiled a confidential submission to the parliamentary inquiry regarded the group holidays as part of the company's cult-like approach, designed to convey 'special secrets to life happiness delivered with a smile and a cappuccino. Thus, the overseas trips with lots of glitz and glamour … to make you feel they were friends and we were with special business people'.[55]

A trip to the company's Townsville head office was intended to be a positive emotional experience, beginning as soon as clients walked in the door. They were shown to an open-plan kitchen where they could sit and chat, have a coffee or a cool drink and cakes and treats. Behind the table was a wall of glass that stretched for much of the length of the building, providing attractive views over the city and surrounds. Below the floor-to-ceiling glass was a reflection pool, which ran along the edge of the building outside. 'We are constantly looking for the wow factor,' Julie Cassimatis explained. 'We want to make people feel instantly comfortable ... and the kitchen is the hub of the home. Customers say it's lovely to be here. We don't want it to be a chore to come and see your financial planner. We are constantly lifting the game with customer service.'[56] Even the toilets had a wow factor, reflecting the couple's fetish that 'If the toilets are spectacular then the rest of it [the business] must be on par'. Yet the whole purpose of the experience was 'to woo clients in style'.[57]

However, style only went so far. To complement the corporate culture created around the idea of the 'trusted family friendly' business model, Storm developed a highly visible and aggressive marketing campaign with television advertisements, weekly seminars and enthusiastic endorsement from prominent sports figures.[58] There were few scruples underlying the business model. The 'financial hamburger advice' was offered as holy writ to anyone signing up with Storm and, as a former Storm staff member testified, 'almost no applications were turned away'.[59]

The sales pitch had one additional dimension: an appeal to fear and uncertainty. 'Storm whispered in everyone's ear [that] you will not have enough money to fund your retirement; the government is going to cut the pension,' one investor recalled.[60] The company doubled down on preying on clients' uncertainty by regularly including on its statements the words: 'We have identified that your current asset base is not large enough to fund the lifestyle you desire now or in the future'.[61] Such fears tapped into the political zeitgeist.

The Cassimatises' 'hard sell' papered over the cracks in their model. As the parliamentary inquiry found, there was a:

> lack of clarity around this critical facet of the Storm model. The leveraged investment strategy was sold to clients on the basis that there were sufficient buffers and triggers in place, as well as cash reserve funds, to ensure that any margin call situation could be appropriately managed. It seems remarkably careless, from Storm's point of view, to leave any room for doubt around this process.[62]

The CBA ... just another bunch of spivs?

On 28 October 2008, as the global financial markets were in meltdown, one hundred of the CBA's top financial planners flew to Auckland for their annual three-day bash, the highlight being a 1980s-themed fancy-dress party at the city's five-star Sky City Grand Hotel. Champagne flowed freely; the costumes featured big hairdos and plenty of bling jewellery; and the dancing continued into the early hours. Trophies were handed out to the best (that is, the most lucrative) twelve of the planners. Days later, Storm collapsed. The excess of the occasion – reminiscent of a latter-day extravaganza from the court of Louis XIV – says much about the culture driving the CBA and why it had hitched itself to Storm. Fat bonuses had created a desperate quest to drive sales at CBA and across the sector generally. In fact, insiders at CBA told investigative journalists Adele Ferguson and Chris Vedelago from *The Age* that 'planners were indoctrinated to focus on sales and fees at any cost'.[63]

The Cassimatises would not have been able to build their empire of pain without the active support of the banks, and the bank that provided the largest source of funds was the CBA. The Bank of Queensland and Macquarie Group were among the others. Some observers believe that the CBA was the driving force in the transformation of Storm Financial 'from a two-bit provincial outfit to a large-scale "get rich quick" enterprise'.[64] Indeed, clients of Storm spoke of the 'umbilical connection' with the CBA.[65] But why would the bank, with its historically forged iconic brand, develop a close business relationship with such a flaky, risky and regionally based operation such as Storm Financial? The answer, of course, is money.

As we saw with the case of James Hardie, one of the consequences of the rise of free-market ideology during the 1980s and the embrace of deregulation during the reforms of the 1980s and '90s, was the fixation within big corporations on shareholder value. It became a mantra. Getting value for shareholders, explained Monash Professor of Finance Kevin Davis, became equated with an attitude within corporations that their objective was to maximise profits at all costs: 'How much can we get out of this deal?' As opposed to saying, 'any transaction we're engaged in, both parties should benefit'.[66] Australian banks, in particular, fell into this moral vacuum just as HIH had done.

Under the Howard government, the financial planning industry had been allowed to flourish in an unregulated environment. This reflected the ideological bias of the government along with the political reality that the party had had a long history of looking after the banks and financial planners, who, in turn, had been big donors to both sides of politics, but especially to the Liberal Party.[67]

The elevated ideological faith in the free market encouraged the big four banks and AMP to establish subsidiary companies to enter the lucrative field of financial planning. Together they spent billions of dollars buying up wealth management businesses, ending up controlling 80 per cent of financial planners, whose job it was 'to flog their products'.[68] But it was difficult for prospective clients to know whether any suburban financial planner was ultimately connected to the big boys of Sydney and Melbourne.[69] The industry became riddled with conflicts of interest, a situation the banks were determined to preserve: they were against anything that might curb their reach into the pockets of Australians and their retirement savings.[70]

The CBA first developed a relationship with Storm in 1994 and upped its involvement in the early 2000s when the Cassimatises began their aggressive marketing approach to clients.[71] From this time, the bank 'fuelled the fantasies of Storm', throwing every available facility at their clients: mortgages, margin loans and index funds (a bundle of stocks and bonds designed to reflect the share market). No other bank involved with Storm offered such a range.[72] By the time of the GFC, the CBA had $3 billion tied up with Storm.[73]

According to Ron Jelich, the former business manager at Storm, 'Clients became nameless cogs in a giant money-making machine ... as a resource that could be tapped for more and more money'. The best interests of the clients, he said, 'were subjugated to the best interests of Storm and the banks'.[74] And these interests included commissions on margin loans.

While it's not clear the precise role that commissions, or kickbacks, played in the business operations of Storm and the CBA, they were standard practice in the industry and, by the early 2000s, were attracting increasing public concern. *The Age* reported in 2004 that ASIC was 'failing to prosecute financial planners who received "soft-dollar commissions" without disclosing them'.[75] The paper returned to the issue two years later, again complaining that mum-and-dad investors were 'generally kept in the dark about complex, secretive kickbacks their planner receives from investment managers for putting people into a particular investment'.[76] Over the next few years, commissions became a goldmine for financial planners who, according to ASIC, relied on them for more than 60 per cent of revenue. In 2008, despite the financial crisis, financial planners received $1.4 billion in commissions.[77]

Whether or not commissions played a significant role in the relationship between Storm and the CBA, the kickbacks would have just been the icing on the cake because the CBA had engineered Storm to be a cash cow for the bank. In 2007, CBA initiated a secret deal with the Cassimatises to offer Storm clients the highest risk profile of all the 7000 financial planners linked to the bank.[78] The relationship was even further solidified when the CBA opened an office in the Townsville headquarters of Storm to process loan applications.

But like the gauche retailers on TV shopping channels, the CBA was offering *even more*. Part of the deal offered to Storm also included generous property evaluations so that clients could borrow additional funds. As Duncan Hughes reported for the *Australian Financial Review* in 2008, there was a frenzied atmosphere in the Townsville headquarters as the end of the financial year loomed. Representatives from both companies worked through Townsville Show Day signing up $25 million of loan applications from investors to meet the end-of-financial-year deadline.[79]

This process of rapid-fire approval, initiated by the CBA, extended to the automatic revaluation of Storm clients' properties using a computerised method. The updated values were then forwarded to Storm, which activated the Cassimatises to encourage clients into further borrowing.[80] It looked like Storm and the CBA had been intent on plundering their clients.

Denise Brailey, a respected consumer advocate who ran the Banking and Finance Consumers Support Association, alleged in her submission to the parliamentary inquiry that banks deliberately set out to grow margin loan lending by targeting low-income families with mortgages; people the industry saw as 'asset rich and income poor'. They were offered the facility without an adequate vetting process. Brailey had dealt with hundreds of such distressed victims. In 2005, she alerted federal authorities, including ASIC, that loan application forms 'were grossly altered after signatures obtained, without the knowledge of the clients and without authority. Income details were exaggerated and employment details tampered with'.

Brailey argued that providing marginal loans to poorer people highlighted the flawed culture of banking in Australia; that is:

> bank shareholders want perpetual profit growth and the executives are paid big bonuses to grow earnings. There are two main ways to achieve it – sell more product or make bigger profit margins from existing product. The big four banks have been doing both, and both are bad for customers.[81]

Additionally, Brailey argued, the margin loan market had 'all the hallmarks of wide-spread looting of people's assets, similar to the American "Savings and Loans Scandal"'.[82] This scandal, which raged during the 1980s and '90s, saw the collapse of over a thousand mortgage providers in what has been seen as the greatest disaster of American banking since the Great Depression.[83]

Brailey's criticism was supported by experts in the banking field. According to Joseph Healy, who had had an international banking career, the business practices in the CBA were underpinned by a US-based sales framework , 'which was implemented to increase product sales and cross-selling of products', which 'fuelled "animal spirits" in banking'.[84] Healy argued that the failure to rein in the culture of high-risk banking was not just the responsibility of senior management, but also of boards. Boards are supposed to take corporate risk seriously. Yet this was not the case at the CBA.

How this key function slipped from the board's focus is difficult to explain. The bank had become embroiled in a series of scandals, prompting a report into its culture in 2018. Compiled by the Australian Prudential Regulatory Authority, the report was scathing of the bank's culture and the failings of its board:

> The Board, together with its Risk, Audit and Remuneration Committees, demonstrated significant shortcomings in the governance of nonfinancial risks. For much of the period under review, the Board did not demonstrate rigour of oversight and challenge to CBA management.[85]

It's not surprising, therefore, that the CBA's relationship with Storm was riddled with unaddressed risks.

How were ordinary clients supposed to be aware of the avaricious culture of banks? Even if prospective clients fully grasped the potential risks of margin loans, few appreciated how margin calls operated. How clients were informed of potential problems was an entirely grey area: was it the responsibility of Storm or the banks, or both? The problem was that margin lending was part of the prevailing fetish for unregulated free markets. Not surprisingly, the boom in margin lending began to elicit ever more strident warnings from financial experts. In 2000, ASIC 'fired out a missive to investors alerting them to the dangers of the margin lending market'.[86] When the bubble inevitably burst, the carnage was guaranteed to be terrible. Storm clients were the financial equivalent of sitting ducks.

The Cassismatises thought differently. They had an unshakeable faith that their approach could survive any financial downturn. They based this on developing an intensely loyal client base and forging what they thought was a solid relationship with major banks, and especially with the CBA. Emmanuel believed Storm was 'the financial equivalent of an unsinkable ship'.[87] This sense of invincibility radiated out to clients. One recalled his advisor saying 'not to worry about going into margin call because Storm would not allow it to happen because it had a central "dam" of money'. Such a reassurance was taken to mean that Storm had developed a protective relationship with the banks, especially the CBA and Macquarie.[88]

But what agreement did the Cassimatises really have with the CBA? Was the bank just stringing the couple along for its own commercial benefit? As banking had become a dog-eat-dog world of competition for shareholder value, the couple were playing out of their league. This, at least, was the opinion of their accountants and auditors, the high-profile firm PricewaterhouseCoopers (PwC). In a risk review report conducted in February 2008, PwC wrote that the Cassimatises were a risk 'because they were naive, entrepreneurial and did not listen to advice'. And, 'they may not have the broad judgment to run a large listed company or deal with capital market players'.[89]

The Cassimatises, of course, believed they were smart operators, smart enough at least, to quieten the deepest fears among their clients that they could lose their homes in a downturn. Class action lawyer Stewart Levitt, who represented Storm clients following the collapse of the company, described Emmanuel as 'extremely shrewd and self-focused; a born survivor'.[90]

Finger pointing

Once the company crashed, the Cassimatises blamed the CBA for the entire fiasco; they felt they had been 'sold down the river' by the bank's swift action on margin loans.[91] However, this overlooks the role the couple played in setting and monitoring the margin rates. The indicator at which a margin call was to be invoked was set abnormally high by the couple[92] and, as Julie explained when she appeared before the Federal Court in November 2009, 'Storm had no obligation to monitor the state of its clients' margin loans to ensure they weren't reaching risky levels' and admitted that the company's software 'didn't allow for easy monitoring'.[93]

However, the CBA continued to deflect responsibility for the carnage created by the margin loan recalls. A CBA official told the parliamentary committee that the bank had been in 'constant communication' with Storm about which of their clients should receive margin calls but, apparently, didn't see it as their responsibility to follow through directly with Storm's clients. In the wake of the Storm margin call fiasco, the CBA announced that it would henceforth notify both financial intermediaries and clients of any impending margin calls, rather than communicating through a client's financial advisor as it had in the past.[94]

Macquarie Bank had a different view of the responsibility for issuing margin calls. Its chief executive at the time, Richard Sheppard, blamed the failure on either incompetence or wilful negligence on the part of the Cassimatises. He told the press that 'the system of relying on financial planners' to contact its margin loan customers had failed in the case of its Storm Financial customers. Macquarie, he said, became aware its Storm Financial clients were not receiving margin calls from the financial planner in mid-October 2008. It sent three executives to Storm's Townsville head office for two days on 23 and 24 October and, from 29 October, decided to send margin calls to 359 customers in November. But throughout September and October, Macquarie had sent about a thousand margin calls to Storm Financial, most of which were never received by the borrowers.

The issue of margin calls and who was responsible bounced back and forth without resolution.

Sheppard at least indicated that Macquarie had the problem in its sights and tried to find a solution. The CBA, critics claim, just pulled the plug on Storm clients. The bank's cut-throat response may have been linked to the fallout from the GFC.

In the aftermath of the global financial disaster, the CBA eyed off the opportunity to purchase Bankwest, an old established Western Australian institution which was part-owned by a British bank, HBOS. When HBOS went under in the GFC it sought to unload Bankwest. In early October 2008, CBA purchased the bank for $2.1 billion only to find Bankwest's books were full of bad debts.[95] The behaviour of the CBA towards its Bankwest customers aroused heated controversy; it's alleged that in order to deal with Bankwest's bad loans the CBA pursued a policy of clawing back its arrangements with Bankwest customers – upping their interest rates, demanding full payment of loans and refusing to refinance. Real distress was caused to many of these customers, whose complaints were aired during the 2019 royal commission into the banks.

How were Storm clients linked to these wider financial stresses? It's possible that the CBA, in angling to move on Bankwest, at the very time that Storm was imploding, wanted to put itself in the best possible financial position to go ahead with the purchase. This, at least, is the view held by Stewart Levitt view, who dealt with CBA on behalf of Storm clients throughout this period. He said the CBA changed its tune on margin calls at the very same time it moved on Bankwest.[96]

For investors, Storm and the CBA's evasion on margin calls helped seal their fate. As one Storm investor told the parliamentary inquiry: 'If we had been sold down early enough then there would have been enough cash in that accelerator cash account to cover the margin loan and there would have been enough money for us to live on – to pay our bills and petrol; the lot – while the market was doing its thing'.[97] Still, some Storm clients continued to blame the CBA and other banks for calling in their loans. However, while it's clear that both Storm and the banks acted shabbily, their actions were enabled by the federal government not enforcing proper regulation on margin loans.

Even by the time Storm collapsed, the CBA knew that its financial planning division had been cited for serious misconduct by ASIC. In a letter written in February 2008 to the bank's then general manager of wealth management, the regulator stated that 'we are concerned that your data suggests your compliance framework is not adequately detecting serious misconduct'. The misconduct being unaddressed by the bank included 'fraud and dishonest conduct', 'deliberate or reckless failure to disclose fees, costs, charges, relationship and warnings' and 'no evidence of appropriate advice'.[98] ASIC failed to follow up with an investigation, depriving Storm clients of critical information that may have saved them from disaster.

ASIC failed a second time to take seriously warnings that the CBA's financial planning arm was operating with questionable ethics. This time, information was given to it by a whistleblower inside the bank. By October 2008, Jeff Morris, who had joined Commonwealth Financial Planning earlier that year, had become concerned about the severe losses and emotional distress being suffered by many elderly and vulnerable clients due to the poor advice they received. He contacted ASIC alleging misconduct and a bank cover-up but was ignored.

Morris became a campaigner for banking reform. He later told a 2014 Senate inquiry into the performance of ASIC that, for a long time, the agency had

> propagated the myth, even to Parliament, that all was fine with the major players in the advice industry. Since the major players were the bulk of the industry, by implication all was well; except at the fringes, which ASIC would of course need far more resources to police. In reality, I think, ASIC believed everything was fine with the big players because that was what the major players were telling them.[99]

Shocked Storm investors began calling on ASIC to explain why it had not taken action earlier to prevent, or soften, the collapse.[100] But ASIC had always been a lame-duck regulator, as was revealed in a Senate inquiry into the agency in 2013. Anne Lampe, a journalist and former employee of ASIC's media unit, told the inquiry that investment clients often had a misleading impression of the role of the agency. She stated that because advisors are licensed, investors believe that they have passed some kind of integrity and competence screening process and that ASIC has provided a stamp of approval. But as Lampe stated: 'They couldn't be more wrong. The licensing process is simply a tick all boxes procedure and regulation of financial advisors and fund managers who invest the money appears to be ineffective'.[101]

Timid as ASIC might have been, at the time Storm collapsed the agency was still grappling with a ghost of its past: One.Tel. In November 2008, an eight-year-long campaign to bring Jodee Rich and director Mark Silbermann to account had ended in a Supreme Court judgment by Justice Robert Austin. ASIC had sought to fine the pair $92 million and have them banned from running companies. The corporate watchdog claimed the men misled the One.Tel board, including James Packer and Lachlan Murdoch, about the financial state of the company. But, in a 3000-page judgment, Austin found

ASIC had failed to prove any aspect of its case. With tens of millions in costs awarded against the agency, it was a brutal lesson in the difficulty of taking on the big end of town.[102]

The ineffectiveness of ASIC was, in turn, a reflection of the 'light touch' regulation that continued to flow from the Howard-era policy of deregulation. As the parliamentary inquiry into the financial services sector argued: 'These principles were based on "efficient markets theory"', or minimum government. These ideas had shaped ASIC's role and powers.[103] In 2014, a Senate inquiry into ASIC produced damning findings on the agency's lack of effectiveness. The inquiry described the regulator as a 'toothless tiger' or 'gummy shark' when it comes to enforcement. It was too slow to act, lacked transparency and was too trusting of the big end of town. This timidity resulted from the reluctance of ASIC to take on complex court cases and its lack of resources to match well-resourced firms.[104]

In other words, Storm clients had been duped by government as well. The case of Storm Financial raised the same problem that had existed since the bankruptcies of the eighties corporate cowboys and was again revisited with the collapse of HIH. Was it reasonable to expect regulators to prevent corporate collapse? If not, what was their purpose? But if they were intended to protect the public, how should they be resourced and administered? Ordinary Australians could be forgiven for thinking that successive governments didn't have straight answers to these questions.

The struggle for justice

Meanwhile, devastated Storm clients had to fight tooth and nail to obtain some form of compensation. Because the collapse occurred as a consequence of the GFC, the Rudd Labor government was preoccupied with the challenge of staving off a recession. There were potential victims everywhere. But in January 2009, a small group of former Storm clients formed the Storm Investor Consumer Action

Group (SICAG) to press for a settlement with the CBA and other banks. Most probably they couldn't have imagined the legal minefield they had entered.

The wheels of justice turned agonisingly slowly. In May 2010, nearly a year and a half after the collapse, journalist Stuart Washington, who had extensively covered the collapse, reported in the *Sydney Morning Herald* that the plight of these investors was 'slipping from the public gaze as the caravan moves on'. A petition to Prime Minister Rudd hadn't altered their circumstances; the CBA had agreed to a resolution process which yet hadn't produced a result while the other banks involved in Storm – notably the Bank of Queensland and Macquarie Group – had made no public concessions about their treatment of Storm investors. As Washington concluded, Storm investors had been given precious little assurance that their post-collapse interests were being looked after.[105]

Still, SICAG pressed on. They were fortunate to enlist the services of Nationals Senator John Williams to assist Storm victims he brought with him empathy and determination, qualities that had been forged in his own family's brush with the bastardry of banks. He was instrumental in persuading the Senate to hold a joint parliamentary inquiry into the collapse while also attending SICAG meetings where he saw 'looks of fear, confusion and despair' among those attending. Speaking at the meetings he told Storm investors not to be daunted by the prospect of fighting the banks. In the process he watched SICAG develop into a highly effective 'people power' organisation, one that gained the respect of politicians, lawyers, regulators and the media.[106]

As a consequence of the pressure and publicity SICAG managed to build, Storm victims eventually managed to settle with the banks involved. Here is not the place to examine the details of the complex and long-running series of class actions involving the banks tied up with Storm. As a process, class actions have been described as a 'long and drawn-out procedural Stalingrad'.[107] It must have seemed this way to Storm victims. In 2012, the CBA agreed to compensation of

$136 million on top of the $132 million that the bank had earlier negotiated. However, this amount meant that most had settled for about 10 per cent of their equity and paid about $70 000 each in legal fees.[108] The Bank of Queensland agreed to pay $17 million in compensation; Macquarie settled for $82 million. The basis of these claims rested on the failure of the banks to issue margin calls, 'which would have triggered their exit from the deals and limited their exposure to loss'.[109]

Not all Storm investors were happy with the deal handed to them by the CBA. A separate group mounted another class action against the CBA, Macquarie Bank and the Bank of Queensland. According to lawyer Stewart Levitt, who acted for these Storm clients, they 'didn't want to let the banks off the hook'. Levitt's firm produced a fifty-minute documentary, called *Piggy Banks*, detailing the impact of Storm's collapse on victims, the funding for which was raised by the victims themselves. The low-budget film was completed in six months. However, these class actions took three years to resolve, only to result in pretty much the same deal offered to the other CBA clients. Nonetheless, most still felt satisfied that they had the opportunity to air their concerns in court.[110]

Storm victims were angry not only over being dudded by the banks but also by ASIC. A separate class action was mounted by Stewart Levitt against the agency. When the action was announced in 2013, Levitt argued that it was based on the grounds that:

> ASIC allowed all this to happen. They watched it for 10 years and approved it and even endorsed it. We have many instances of people who tell us that, before they invested in Storm, they contacted ASIC and said, 'should we?' And ASIC said yes. And this was to self-funded retirees.[111]

It was the first legal case of its kind against ASIC, testing the boundaries of how far a regulator could be held accountable for its actions.

Three years later, Justice Jacqueline Gleeson of the Federal Court dismissed the claim, finding that it did not identify how ASIC's conduct was responsible for the clients' losses and what it should have done to prevent Storm's collapse. In criticising the decision, Levitt surely had a point when he said that the decision effectively handed ASIC not only 'a licence to fail, but also, condoned the agency for having given the Storm model a pass when it should have been marked as fail'.[112] If, indeed, ASIC had failed, and couldn't be held accountable, it appeared to have no useful purpose.

ASIC was finally dragged into mounting a case against the Cassimatises, commencing in late 2010 on the grounds that the couple had breached their duties as directors. The Federal Court, which did not hand down its decision until 2016, found against the Cassimatises. Justice Edelman criticised their lack of remorse and fined them $70 000 each and barred them from holding directorships for seven years.[113] The couple appealed this decision but it was upheld in 2018. Victims slammed the verdict.[114] They were unlikely to have been assuaged even if the maximum penalty of $200 000 had been imposed. White-collar crime continued to be dealt with by a slap on the wrist. The impression was reinforced when no action was taken against the three non-executive directors, raising another round of questioning about whether such directors should be held liable for catastrophic compliance failures in a company.[115]

Apart from being the proverbial lawyers' picnic, the legal stoushes over Storm highlighted limitations in the legal system in protecting ordinary people from financial sharks. Taking years to resolve and returning a bare minimum of clients' losses, the legal system had effectively sent a message to the financial industry that it could only ever expect a rap over the knuckles for trying to rip off ordinary people. The slap on the wrist handed out to the Cassimatises only served to reinforce this message.

Following the collapse of their company, the Cassimatises sold their Townsville mansion, but they continued to domicile in opulent style in their slightly less grand Brisbane home, originally bought through a family trust. A decade after the crash of their company, Emmanuel was reported to be retired, while Julie worked as a receptionist at a veterinary clinic.[116]

A decade on and life wasn't in any way happy for Storm's victims. Many had been left with nothing but a toll of emotional scars.[117]

In the wake of the collapse of Storm the Rudd Labor government established the aforementioned parliamentary inquiry into the financial services industry, which found that the sector was riddled with conflicts of interest that had driven the exploitation of clients. It recommended government introduce far-reaching reform: establish a clear legal requirement for advisors to act in the best interests of their clients; abolish commissions; improve transparency around fees; and strengthen the powers of ASIC.[118]

The Rudd government introduced legislation to reflect the recommendations against a blizzard of lobbying from the sector, which argued that it could be wiped out with the loss of tens of thousands of jobs. The banks were in the forefront of opposition to the legislation. Consequently, the government deferred the reforms. In 2010, the incoming Liberal government led by Tony Abbott dropped support for the legislation. University of New South Wales academic Linda Edwards writes in her study of the fraught financial services reform process: 'The Coalition's embrace of the banks' policy preferences was stunning in its brashness, and their imperviousness to the political cost'. The banks, she writes, had a strong grip on the centres of power in the Liberal Party.

What was behind the Abbott government's embrace of the banks? Did powerful bankers simply convince the government of the merits of their case or were there deeper forces at work? We will never know conclusively. But we do know that the big four banks, together with the broader finance sector, continued to be among the biggest political donors, the vast bulk of which went to the Liberal and National parties.[119] Such largesse leaves the impression that governments can be bought by powerful vested interests, whether or not this is the case.

Hence, a once-in-a-generation opportunity for wholesale reform of the financial services sector resulted in only modest reforms.[120] Not only was there a winding back in the legal requirement for advisors to act in their clients' best interests but also commissions were reinstated, allowing financial incentives for bank tellers and associated call centres to flog superannuation products. Banks, in particular, wanted to expand the reach and range of their wealth management businesses.[121]

In hindsight, there were multiple layers of complexity involved in Storm's collapse. It shared similarities with other cases in this book – Bond Corporation, Qintex and HIH – in that it was subject to the ambition and self-intertest of a single, charismatic, domineering leader bent on acquiring power and extreme wealth. Studies show that companies with a celebrity-orientated and autocratic organisational culture have a high chance of sinking.[122] But Julie and Emmanuel Cassimatis were egged on by a dangerously deregulated financial sector that had captured the decision-making processes of government. The 2007–08 global financial crisis had exposed the broader problem of the pursuit of excessive risk and greed by banking and other financial institutions such that corporate regulation was thrust from the pages of academic journals to the front of media outlets. Significant changes should have occurred to the way corporations operated but, as this didn't happen, more pain for ordinary Australians followed.

7
FRANCHISING EXPLOITATION: 7-ELEVEN

On 24 September 2015, a little-known billionaire, Russell Withers, and his company, 7-Eleven Holdings, which he co-owned with his sister Beverley Barlow, was in the midst of a media firestorm. Criticism was coming from all quarters about revelations that the company was involved in a huge scam of underpaying the wages of its workers. And, on that day, Withers was due to give evidence to a Senate inquiry concerning the allegations. The reclusive billionaire was about to become a household name.

The inquiry had been generated by a joint investigation aired a few weeks earlier by ABC's *Four Corners* and the Fairfax media, headed by Adele Ferguson, that had put the company to the sword over its alleged cover-up of systemic underpayment of wages across its 626 stores around Australia through the falsification of records. According to one estimate, 7-Eleven was involved in the 'largest wage fraud in Australian history'.[1]

Claims of a business model little better than slavery had blanketed the media following the *Four Corners* revelations.[2] Withers was in damage control. But before giving his evidence to the Senate, he was widely seen to have stuffed up the company's initial response to the allegations. Instead of a quick, thought-through response to limit the damage, 7-Eleven had opted for denial. The company blamed its franchisees for having acted unlawfully.[3] But franchisees hit back, putting the blame on the franchise model operated by 7-Eleven.

Thus, when Withers faced the Senate, his franchise model was at risk of imploding; angry franchisees were on the cusp of revolt.[4] Withers had decided that a change of tack was necessary. This likely didn't come easily. With his heavy build, fleshy face and imperious air, he doesn't look like a man who'd quickly change his mind. Nevertheless, in his evidence he struck a more apologetic, humble tone, taking responsibility for the disaster. 7-Eleven, Withers told senators, was 'blindsided' by the revelations. The company was not only embarrassed but 'horrified'. As chair, he apologised on behalf of the company, but he stopped short of accepting blame for a cover-up; there wasn't one, he assured the parliamentarians. He promised to quickly fix the problem. But Withers' appearance failed to stem further haemorrhaging of the company's brand. The suggestion of a cover-up lingered, or at least the inference that the company had turned a blind eye to wage fraud.

The distinction is an important one. To borrow a famous old line: What did Withers and 7-Eleven executives know, and when did they know it? Unlike other scandals in this book, 7-Eleven was not subjected to a judicial inquiry, so there's been no definitive answer to that question. This raises another question: Why do some corporations involved in egregious conduct get a blowtorch turned on them and others don't? Inquiries are the only mechanism society has to fully prise open the inner workings of powerful corporations, especially those whose activities are the subject of community concerns. In the absence of an official finding, Withers' claim that he and the executives knew nothing about the wage fraud stands, but it hasn't gone unchallenged.

In the wake of his Senate appearance, the reclusive Withers suddenly found himself publicly scrutinised. A journalist from the *Herald Sun* visited his $10 million dollar rural retreat in the Yarra Valley and reported that 'the fairytale home', which was set back from the road and surrounded by manicured gardens, had a team of workers on-site. The headline to the story said it all: 'No skimping at home'.[5]

His sister, Bev Barlow, had a media stake-out outside her mansion in Melbourne's Brighton. Even more reclusive than her brother, Bev was reported to be furious with Russell because she couldn't leave the house during the scandal.[6] But what had propelled the Withers family into the cauldron of a corporate scandal? In retrospect it appears to have been inevitable, as the company's culture embodied multiple drivers indicating the potential for scandal: a deregulated labour market, 7-Eleven's excessively profit-driven corporate culture, a franchise industry that had the ear of government, and the regulator – ASIC – which didn't involve itself in the scandal.

Exploitation and the franchise model

Over the past fifty years, the franchise industry has grown into a major sector of the economy. Starting off in the early 1970s with American chains such as KFC, Pizza Hut and McDonald's, the industry rapidly expanded into a sector that in Australia today comprises approximately 79 000 operating franchises employing 470 000 direct employees.[7] The sector represents nearly 10 per cent of Australia's GDP.[8]

While not all owners of franchise operations run their businesses unethically, the model contains flaws. Jenny Buchan, Professor of Business at the University New South Wales, argues that where franchises have a committed franchisor (that is, the owner), a proven and evolving brand, and franchisees that are well supported, the model works well. However, if any of these components is missing, 'franchisees can quickly become unprofitable and things can turn ugly'.[9] Indeed, a range of corporations were alleged to have been involved in underpayment of wages, including the Retail Food Group, the country's largest food franchise retailer with iconic brands such as Donut King, Brumby's, Gloria Jeans, Domino's Pizza, United Petroleum and Caltex. Exploitation of vulnerable franchisees and workers had become a business model.[10]

Franchising is an industry with a powerful voice. Advocating for its business model is the Franchise Council of Australia (FCA), the peak body for the sector. Formed in the early 1980s, it grew to become highly influential across all aspects of franchising. Despite its claims to work for the interests of all parties in the industry – franchisors, franchisees and salaried staff – in reality, it has been a spokesperson for the corporate interests running the industry. As a parliamentary select committee noted, the FCA

> does not appear to provide a balanced representation of franchisor and franchisee views, and this is likely because of its membership composition. There are almost no franchisee members of the FCA, and membership of the FCA is dominated by franchisors. In effect, the FCA is captive to the interests of franchisors.[11]

This situation created a power imbalance in the franchise industry that allowed greed to run rampant.[12]

The rise of 7-Eleven Australia

Sometimes cheekily described as 'a third-generation grocer',[13] Russell Withers has a family connection to food retailing dating back to 1912 when his grandfather George established a grocery business in Melbourne's South Yarra. Russell's father Reg Withers, joined the family company at the end of World War I, when the business had two retail grocery stores in Melbourne (South Yarra and Richmond). The family then branched out into grocery bulk-buying and wholesaling and distribution.[14]

From such inauspicious beginnings, the Withers family built an empire. In the late 1970s, Russell spotted a trend in retailing and capitalised on his instincts. Withers saw that Melbourne's corner shops and grocery stores were dying and that his third-generation wholesale grocery company was likely to die with them. He travelled to the

United States and negotiated the purchase of the Australian rights to 7–Eleven convenience stores. A business that originated in Dallas in 1927, the name 7-Eleven was coined as a brand in 1947 to reflect its opening hours, and stores already sported its trademark red, yellow and green stripes against an over-sized number 7. Withers opened his first store in Melbourne in 1977 and ran the first six himself to see how it would go in Australia.[15]

By the time the wages scandal erupted in 2015, 7-Eleven Australia was the country's second largest private company (after Anthony Pratt's Visy). It boasted an impressive $4 billion in annual sales.[16] Its board was mostly kept to a close family affair: Russell's wife, his sister and her husband and, for a time, father Reginald. The two non-family members were both experienced and respected company directors.

Core business: Worker exploitation at 7-Eleven

The rapid expansion of the 7-Eleven chain occurred in the wake of some of the most profound changes to the Australian labour market – and to the wider society – seen since World War II. From the mid-1990s, government policy shifted from a widely regulated labour market to a partly deregulated one. Unions suffered a long-term erosion of membership. In addition, the labour market came to rely on a surge in temporary, rather than permanent, migration. Constituting 11 per cent of the Australian workforce (over one million workers), such temporary arrivals were placed on a long conveyor belt to citizenship rendering them vulnerable non-citizens.[17]

In 1996, the Coalition government led by John Howard hastened this transformation with the introduction of the 475 visa program, which, together with the explosive growth of international students on temporary work visas, produced a largely invisible workforce outside the security of collective labour market agreements. Employer groups had championed these changes in order to create a flexible supply of workers to augment their business models. While both groups found employment at 7-Eleven stores, international students formed the bulk of employees.[18] Exploitation was inevitable.

A few years before the scandal broke in Australian, the company's US operation was exposed for the poor treatment of its workforce. Federal agents raided forty stores across eight states, arresting nine managers for exploiting workers. Employees were found to be working up to a hundred hours per week, forced to live in houses owned by the franchisees, and weren't paid for all their work time. Some employees had been working under those conditions for more than a decade. It was described as a 'modern plantation system'. The exploitation went unnoticed by the parent company 'because 7-Eleven's corporate overseers simply didn't have a system in place to prevent it'.[19] The raid on stores was not the only indicator that 7-Eleven's US culture was plagued with ethical problems, which were widely aired on an 'Unhappy Franchisees' website.[20]

Like its American counterpart, 7-Eleven's business model in Australia morphed into a culture of exploitation, based around taking advantage of both international students and recent migrants. The former were employed as general workers and the latter as lease-holders of stores – franchisees. Each group needs to be examined separately.

International students

Mohamed Rashid Ullat Thodi became part of 7-Eleven's exploited labour force. He arrived in Geelong from India in 2007 to study architecture and construction management. Unsuccessful after applying for forty positions, and facing high living expenses and university fees, he sought a position at a 7-Eleven store. After two months working as an unpaid trainee, cleaning toilets, windows and air-conditioning vents, stacking shelves and mopping floors he eventually began to earn $10 per hour, working approximately fifty hours each week, although his payslip recorded only twenty hours at the award wage rate. His employer had a ready-made answer for this discrepancy: it was an arrangement designed to benefit him by disguising the fact that he was exceeding the forty-hours-per-fortnight work restriction on his student visa. When, a year later, he requested a pay rise to $11 per hour, he was summarily dismissed.

Ullat Thodi later recalled to a Senate inquiry into exploitation of temporary migrant workers that 7-Eleven workers came under heavy pressure from franchisees, who told them:

> 'We are like a family. We'll give you a job and help you out. Work more hours than the 20-hour limit.' … I have been told, 'Don't go and speak about your pay to anybody, because if you do you'll be in trouble because they will find out you are working more than 20 hours, then you will be deported.'

International students, Thodi further explained, were trapped by the combination of the high fees they had to pay for their university course and the visa condition restricting them to twenty hours work per week during their periods of study.[21]

Throughout the 7-Eleven chain, underpayment was a well-oiled practice. It was widely referred to as the 'half pay scam', whereby an employee worked forty hours in a week, but was only paid for twenty hours.[22] In other cases, workers were forced into 'cashbacks', where managers would pay workers the correct amount on their books but compel them to withdraw money and return a portion of their wages.[23]

In these ways, franchisees obtained cheap labour, and temporary visa holders were offered a fictitious way to keep within their maximum allowable hours. At the time, the legal minimum wage was $17.70 per hour but, with entitlements, a twenty-one-year-old fast food employee could earn $24.30 per hour.[24]

How did such a practice seep into the company's stores in different states? As one critic noted: 'How do 400+ franchisees from China, India and Pakistan, owning 620+ stores in four states, all learn how to manipulate the books in the exact same fashion …?'[25]

After the scandal broke over 7-Eleven, two inquiries were undertaken by the Senate Education and Employment Committee to document the problem, the first in 2016 and the second a year later. The one conducted in 2017 found serious worker exploitation among well-known companies, including 7-Eleven, Pizza Hut, Domino's Pizza, Caltex and United Petroleum.[26] Agricultural workers on the 457 program were in a similarly vulnerable position.

The inquiry in 2017 heard evidence from the Fair Work Ombudsman, whose task was to enforce minimum standards and regulations for employment, that it lacked the tools to deal with 'the systematic exploitation of workers'.[27] As a consequence of their investigation, the committee concluded that some franchisees and labour hiring firms had built a business model based on underpaying workers.

The legal system discouraged underpaid workers from taking action. Workers had only twenty-one days in which to make a complaint – which rarely occurred – and they were subjected to a $69.60 application fee, a significant barrier when most were already struggling financially. Adding to the high legal bar was the drip-fed hysteria around deportation conveyed by friends and co-workers.[28]

Workers on late-night or Sunday-night shifts were especially exploited. Payments for working alone on these shifts differed, but some workers were on $10 an hour when they should have been paid $37.05.[29] For this paltry sum, 7-Eleven night workers faced the unnerving prospect of encountering junkies, drunks and psychotics, any one of whom could pull a knife on an employee in an instant. In the 1990s, hundreds of Melbourne's late-night outlets were held up with weapons each year. Both crims and police considered 7-Elevens 'soft targets'.[30]

One Indian 7-Eleven employee working the night shift explained that he 'felt strange' working all night, struggling to keep his eyes open: 'I can't sleep. If I fall asleep I'll be killed. It's not easy to work behind there. There's danger. But you learn about people. How to face them, how to talk'.[31] And, if a customer drove off without paying for petrol, the franchisee made the employee responsible for the loss. One employee paid the owner a total of $200 for petrol that had been stolen on four or five occasions when he had been rostered on duty.[32]

Migrant franchisees

Sydney class-action lawyer Stewart Levitt was visiting the United States in 2013 when he read about the raids on American 7-Eleven stores. Returning to Australia, he was drawn into the wage fraud scandal by representing the exploited franchisees: Asian migrants eager to develop their own businesses in Australia. Many were set up to fail by the 7-Eleven business model.

Levitt alleges that 7-Eleven practised a form of 'de facto ethnic selection of franchisees' in order to choose store owners less likely to blow the whistle on company practices. Franchisees, he claims, were overwhelmingly migrants from the Indian subcontinent, which has weak labour laws: 'Having addressed rallies of around 100 franchisees at a time ... it is rare to see a white face, it is counter-intuitive to believe that this was not a deliberate policy'.[33]

Once selected, 7-Eleven arranged finance for the prospective franchisees. Levitt argues that the company formed a close relationship with the ANZ bank to facilitate the loans: 'New migrants couldn't get loans for a business because they had no track record in the country; they had no real borrowing capacity'. Levitt argues that both 7-Eleven and ANZ (which had 70 per cent of the market for the funding of the company's franchisees) lured franchisees into unsustainable loan agreements. With the backing of 7-Eleven, ANZ arranged favourable loans of up to 70 per cent of the cost of leases in a tripartite agreement. Often with poor English skills and little or no business experience or understanding of Australian commerce or law, franchisees didn't always realise that the profit margins on stores were not as rosy as they were told by the company. The projected profits of their businesses were, according to Levitt, 'based on an understatement of wages';

indeed, franchisees were lured into the business of becoming a 7-Eleven franchisee on inflated financial statements because few if any stores were paying award wages.[34]

But migrants were attracted to becoming a 7-Eleven franchisee because they were willing to work hard and because the 7-Eleven system was suited to people who were still coming to terms with how the country worked.[35] Consequently, there was a steady stream of new franchisees waiting to take over a store somewhere.[36] Withers and his family became billionaires selling such dreams.

It was these loan agreements that propelled franchisees into underpaying wages and which left them high and dry without a capacity to repay their loans if their lease agreements were terminated, or not renewed, by 7-Eleven. 'They were basically buying their way into their own bondage,' argues Levitt.[37]

7-Eleven builds its empire

7-Eleven was part of a revolution in Australian and global retailing around the rise of convenience stores. In Australia these stores sold tobacco, beverages and common everyday grocery items, along with junk food and, later, petrol; they replaced the traditional milk bar and the corner store.[38] The sector has been dominated by 7-Eleven, Coles Express and Woolworths, with the Withers family being the market leader.

With a pool of vulnerable workers and aspiring migrants to draw upon, 7-Eleven's business model came to revolve around three key elements: extracting maximum profit by exploiting workers and franchisees; centralising control operations; and eliminating key quality controls. This quest for maximum profit through poor management practices seems to have become the defining feature of 7-Eleven's culture. Indeed, the Fair Work Ombudsman, in its 2016 inquiry into the company, referred to 'a culture of acceptance that working at 7-Eleven means a lower rate of pay' along with excessive work hours for visa holders 'without it being reported because it will be disguised by the franchisee'.[39] Underpayment was common knowledge throughout the company, according to several franchisees: 'Listen, we all underpay. It is essentially what we signed up to. We bought into the model. We all knew what we were getting into. That is the 7-Eleven model'.[40]

If such allegations are correct, the 7-Eleven business model doomed both franchisees and workers.[41] In the first instance, Withers departed from the American 7-Eleven model of a 50/50 split of gross profits between head office and franchisees. Up until 2015, head office in Australia was taking a 57 per cent cut of gross profits, leaving franchisees with 43 per cent, from which they had to pay wages.[42] Virtually all other franchise systems in Australia operated on a smaller profit take from the owners.[43] Consequently, there was little room for the payment of award salaries.[44] The Fair Work Ombudsman estimated that many stores would have registered a net loss had they not underpaid wages.[45] In fact, it was widely known in the sector that, to be viable, convenience stores required labour costs to be held to 7 per cent of total costs, but to comply with legal minimum wages, labour costs should be lifted to 13 per cent, whereupon franchisees lost money.[46]

The 7-Eleven model was also based around strong control exercised by head office. In the US parent company, 7-Eleven was considered more like an employee–employer model than one based around the independence offered in a franchise model. All individual store receipts were deposited into the head office account, from which franchisees' obligations, notably wages, were deducted.[47]

Throughout its Australian operations, 7-Eleven maintained the same dominance over its franchisees. The Fair Work Ombudsman found that franchisees had a low level of control over their businesses. Their operations were closely managed in relation to stock levels, promotions and management of the foods associated with the brand.[48] District managers visited stores fortnightly, issuing detailed instructions on managing the business, covering topics including store image, occupational health and safety, and payroll.[49]

As part of its business model, 7-Eleven maintained a centralised payroll system for workers employed by franchisees. However, the system had built-in flexibility. Indeed, the payroll system at 7-Eleven, it was alleged, 'allowed franchisees to pay whatever rate they liked, even if it was below the legal minimum'.[50] It was this flexible, loosely administered payroll system that allowed 7-Eleven to deny responsibility for the underpayment scandal.

However, loose management of the payroll system was not the only administrative loophole allowing the underpayment of wages to flourish. 7-Eleven also had a system of manual timesheets operated by the franchisee, but with no verifiable clock-in system.[51] According to Emmaline McKenna, a payroll officer at 7-Eleven head office, management was disinterested in changing the system despite the gross anomalies it created. She was told by the company that they were 'a processing department and not to question what we were given'.[52] Nevertheless, McKenna informed her supervisor and HR manager about her concerns: 'I sent emails every week and then it got to the point where I was asked not to deal with the HR manager, because I continued to put pressure on to get responses'. She described the culture at 7-Eleven as 'care-free'; she and her co-workers knew that they weren't being listened to so they performed the daily job 'just to get across the line'.[53]

The widespread underpayment of wages enhanced the profitability of 7-Eleven and its stores. A key part of the business model was a continual expansion in the number of stores, especially after 7-Eleven went into direct competition with Caltex and Shell in the 'petrol wars'. The increased competition centred around the co-location of convenience stores with the sale of petrol. However, the policy of expansion depended on stores showing artificial profitability.

In fact, before the wage fraud scandal erupted, unprofitable stores didn't appear to be an issue for 7-Eleven head office. Stores were opened in close proximity to existing stores, boosting the company's profit with little regard for the viability of franchisees.[54] Failed franchisees were just another source of increased profit in a process referred to as 'churning'; new fees could be garnered from incoming franchisees. 7-Eleven in the United States faced accusations of deliberately engineering churning and the same appeared to be part of the Australian operation, given the company's cavalier approach to the location of its stores.

7-Eleven maintained a system of internal audits of stores undertaken by trained company auditors. Yet, these audits focused far more attention on the condition of the Slurpee machine and the cleanliness of the store than on payroll compliance.[55] And, up until 2015, the audits appeared to deliberately side-step discovering possible wage fraud because, according to the Fair Work Ombudsman, they 'did not appear to involve reconciliation of the time records with the wage records'.[56] This was despite the fact that, as mentioned, 7-Eleven head office had very high levels of control across their network, more than typically was the case with other franchise arrangements.[57]

Consequently, most 7-Eleven workers had next to no documentation to substantiate the hours they worked and how much they had actually been paid. This system of unaddressed loopholes allowed a fraudulent recording system to be created on a system-wide basis.[58] This 'anything goes' system made it very difficult for the Fair Work Ombudsman to prosecute 7-Eleven franchisees. As Natalie James, the Fair Work Ombudsman, told the Senate inquiry on temporary workers: 'I cannot emphasise enough how difficult it is to get evidence acceptable in a court of law when the records have been fabricated'.[59]

For all the grey areas of the laws governing franchising, which allowed the company to claim plausible deniability, 7-Eleven was seen to have a moral responsibility to rectify the abuse. The Senate committee inquiring into the exploitation of temporary workers thought so: 'the ultimate responsibility had to lie with 7-Eleven because their business model underpinned the systemic abuse of workplace law'.[60]

Investigating 7-Eleven

The 2016 Senate committee put it to the company's CEO, Warren Wilmot, that 7-Eleven head office had used the franchise structure to insulate itself from any knowledge of underpayment: 'I think it has been described as a very thin veil between your organisation, at the head office level, and the actual franchise structure, which has provided you with a degree of plausible deniability of knowledge'. Wilmot rejected the assertion.[61]

But someone in 7-Eleven management knew that government officials had been raising concerns about underpayment of wages, because the company first came onto the radar of the Fair Work Commission in 2008. The agency had received regular reports alleging underpayment of wages. After conducting dozens of audits, Fair Work had facilitated the return of $112 000 to eighty-eight employees.[62] Audits into the company continued in 2009 and 2011 negotiating the return of $140 000 in underpaid wages to 182 7-Eleven employees. One prosecution also resulted from these audits. Adele Ferguson covered the case for the *Australian Financial Review*, revealing that it was discussed by some of the company's directors:

> The case, relating to employee Mohamed Thodi, who was grossly underpaid by the franchisee, resulted in the judge saying '7-Eleven management admitted to the court that non-compliance with workplace laws was relatively common amongst 7-Eleven franchises'.[63]

When giving evidence to the Senate inquiry into temporary workers' visas, Fair Work Ombudsman Natalie James stated: 'We had hoped that these activities [between 2009 and 2011] had resulted in the franchise cleaning up its act'.[64] No such change occurred.

In 2014, Fair Work again became concerned about underpayment in the 7-Eleven network. As James explained, the agency commenced a broader inquiry, 'a piece of work that does not merely respond to complaints but involves proactive compliance work. Our aim here is to assess the root cause of the non-compliance that we have been hearing about'.[65]

Raids on 7-Eleven stores commenced. Between 7 and 11 am on 13 September 2014 a team of fair work inspectors, in a military-style operation, simultaneously made unannounced visits to twenty stores in Melbourne, Sydney and Brisbane. They interviewed staff, took photos of rosters, collected time sheets and obtained CCTV footage of staff movements. They even examined the logs of when staff had inspected freezers as required under health laws. The upshot of the investigation was that 'significant underpayment of wages was identified'.[66] Tellingly, the 2014 raid found 60 per cent of the twenty stores raided had payroll issues. This was double the findings of a previous Fair Work raid in 2011.[67]

Fair Work then sought a meeting with 7-Eleven management. As Michael Campbell, Deputy Fair Work Ombudsman, told the 2016 Senate inquiry:

> there was no doubt that the agency explained to 7-Eleven management the range and seriousness of the company's compliance issues around underpayment of wages. 'It would', he said, 'be unlikely that they would have left that meeting without some appreciation that franchisees were in the gun'.[68]

But why hadn't the Fair Work Ombudsman managed to crack open the case of exploitation and put an end to the practice of underpayment of wages? Some of the members of the 2016 Senate inquiry expressed their frustration that there seemed no easy answer to this question. New South Wales Labor Senator Deborah O'Neill poured out her frustration to Natalie James:

> We go through all this process with an employer that is proven to be untrustworthy, proven to be exploiting workers, and then another three or four years later … we are going back over the same territory. Surely there is something wrong with this process. Is the problem with the law? Is the law inadequate or is the current regulatory structure, of which you are a part, inadequate?[69]

In defending her organisation, James blamed the franchise model itself: too much could be hidden from view by lack of transparency. Perhaps the question was too political for a bureaucrat like James to answer fully. Others thought that Fair Work had been deliberately under-resourced so that it did not pose a threat to business models.[70]

Apparently, all this official activity didn't reach Withers and the executive.

An unlikely consumer advocate gets involved

If 7-Eleven believed that it could fob off a government agency, then presumably directors were little troubled by the arrival of a private sleuth poking his nose in the company's business. But it hadn't reckoned on the determination and zealousness of Michael Fraser. Describing himself as a consumer advocate, Fraser had been a critic of Australian banks and caused a national stir when, in 2013, his name was splashed across the front pages of the *Sydney Morning Herald* and *The Age* when the Commonwealth Bank of Australia got caught red handed in a spying scandal. Senior politicians were spied on and photographed by private detectives at a political fund-raiser for Nationals Senator John Williams, who had spearheaded a Senate inquiry into the bank's financial planning scandal. CBA had hired global security firm G4S to conduct 'Operation Lantern', directed at Fraser, who was to speak at the fund-raiser.[71]

When he found out about the undercover surveillance operation, an irate Senator Williams demanded to know: 'What the hell is going on here? Am I being monitored by some mob employed by the Commonwealth Bank?'[72] He demanded and received an apology from the bank, but the facts don't alter this disturbing incident: the CBA showed disdain for democratic rights by deploying undercover operatives to spy on a party political meeting because a key critic – in this case Fraser – was attending the meeting.

Fraser's involvement with 7-Eleven began almost by accident. In 2012, he had moved directly next door to a 7-Eleven store on the Gold Coast which he regularly frequented and where he formed a close friendship with an employee, Narasimha Rao Pendem (known as Sam), who was originally from India. Even though he had three degrees, he worked in the 7-Eleven store on what Fraser observed as looking like a 'never ending shift'. The two became friends, whereupon Fraser said to Sam one day that he must be very wealthy due to all the hours that he worked. He was surprised by Sam's response; he told him that he was getting a flat rate of $12 per hour: 'At the time, I didn't know how much he should be getting and nor did Sam, however, he was pretty sure he was being paid about half of what he was entitled to'.[73]

Sam told Fraser that this was 7-Eleven practice and that underpayment of workers was happening in every 7-Eleven store. Disbelieving his friend's claim, Fraser began visiting other stores between Brisbane and the Gold Coast. He liaised with many of the workers in their homes to avoid the extensive electronic surveillance in 7-Eleven stores.[74] Although it took a while to build trust, one by one the workers told Fraser that they were being underpaid and that it was well known by the workers, the franchisees, and 7-Eleven that this was the norm in stores around Australia.

In evidence he gave to the Senate inquiry into the exploitation of temporary workers, Fraser stated that he had contacted Warren Wilmot, with evidence that the wage scam was systemic at 7-Eleven and that the problem could only be solved by 7-Eleven head office. In several emails, he told Wilmot that underpayment was widespread:

> So I said to him: 'If this going is on, it is systemic and it's not something that can be fixed with a Fair Work complaint or by reporting the franchisee; it is something that must come from head office. They must fix it there, because it's systemic.'[75]

In fact, Fraser told ABC radio that between 2012 and 2015 he had repeatedly written to Wilmot, who never responded to his emails.[76] And he'd also phoned 7-Eleven head office: 'they were quite dismissive on the phone. I said, "Well, I've got evidence here of people being underpaid in a store. Might you want to know about that? I would like to give you the evidence." And they told me on the phone, "We're not interested".'[77] However, it's not clear from Fraser's evidence how far up the management chain he was communicating with. And Wilmot denied any knowledge of the underpayment scam.

Fraser also reported his discovery that franchisees around the country told him that prior to taking ownership of their store, they had expressed their concern to head office during their training about having to underpay staff to make a profit: 'On all accounts, they were asked to change the topic or all of their questions were dismissed'.[78]

However, Fraser didn't give up on his quest to expose the exploitation at 7-Eleven. When Adele Ferguson contacted him in 2015 in the course of her research, he became a critical link in the exposé that finally brought 7-Eleven to account.

The *Four Corners* exposé

Adele Ferguson, of ABC's *Four Corners*, has explained that she first heard about the wage scandal at 7-Eleven when Michael Fraser contacted her explaining that he had just finished visiting sixty stores around the country with the disturbing discovery that all the stores he had visited were underpaying staff. The people he spoke to were miserable and frightened because they were students on visas. She said she was shocked by Fraser's account given that 7-Eleven was such a big, familiar brand. Fraser then put Ferguson in touch with students who had been victims of wage fraud and whose stories needed to be told. 'I realised it really was systemic,' she explained. She began looking into the company's business model 'to see why so many franchisees were part of the scam. Was it greed or out of necessity?'[79]

When approached by *Four Corners*, Withers and his fellow directors declined to be interviewed. The decision allowed the program, watched by one million viewers, to develop its critique without the company's viewpoint. Deciding whether or not to be involved was more likely to have been the moment when Withers became blind-sided. What would he say in defence of his company?

On 31 August 2015, the *Four Corners* program screened '7-Eleven: The Price of Convenience'. Upholding the program's reputation for fearless investigative journalism, the program also featured a whistleblower – a company insider – who added to the claims that underpayment was widespread, with staff paid as little as $10 per hour, and that the company was aware of the issue across the network. Elaborating further, the whistleblower said that:

> Head office is not just turning a blind eye, it's a fundamental part of their business. They can't run 7-Eleven as profitably as they have without letting this happen, so the business is very proud of itself and the achievements and the money it's made and the success it's had, but the reality is it's built on something not much different from slavery.[80]

However, as Ferguson noted: '7-Eleven is the tip of the iceberg and Australia has a dark side to its labour market that is spiralling out of control'.[81]

Ferguson, Sarah Danckert and Klaus Toft together won a Walkley Award for business journalism for the program.

An independent panel appointed

As part of its strategy to fix the problem of underpayment, 7-Eleven announced, on 3 September 2015, the details of the independent panel it had promised in the immediate aftermath of the *Four Corners* program. Professor Allan Fels, the highly respected former chair of the Australian Competition and Consumer Commission, was appointed to a two-person independent panel, along with Dr David Cousins, a consumer policy advocate. Known as the Fels Wage Fairness Panel, it was charged with developing a process of identifying and rectifying underpayment claims.

By May 2016, the panel had already processed about 400 claims, worth about $14 million, and had about 2000 under way – implying a total cost of about $84 million. The process appeared to be going smoothly until, out of the blue, 7-Eleven sacked the panel. Fels was told of the decision over the phone.

In announcing the dismissal of the panel, 7-Eleven claimed that Professor Fels had agreed to hand the cases over to 7-Eleven. This was not the case; the company had invented their own reason to sack the panel. Within hours Fels went on various media outlets and directly contradicted the company's claim that he and Cousins had, in the words of 7-Eleven 'agreed to transition the claims process'.[82] 'That's not correct', he explained, 'we didn't agree to this at all'. 7-Eleven had another self-inflicted public relations disaster on its hands. Social media went into overdrive; the company was castigated for once again selling out its workers. The media aimed their barbs directly at the Withers family. As Ferguson wrote, it was these very exploited workers who have 'enabled them [the Withers family] to purchase private jets, mansions and a property empire that looks like a game of Monopoly'.[83]

Fels fanned the public relations disaster by lashing the company not just for inventing the reason for the sacking, but by pinpointing the reason behind the company's decision: 'It's the bills, the payments, that's behind this – it's to save money', he said.[84]

Newly appointed 7-Eleven chair Michael Smith justified moving the process in-house because it would drive faster results, with more people getting paid.[85] However, others thought that 7-Eleven underestimated the scale and complexity of the repayments and decided it would be best to fire the panel and, presumably, take a more conservative approach to future calculations.[86]

The wash-up

The 7-Eleven wages scandal should have been a pivotal moment in the nation's history, a chance to rekindle the national ethos of 'a fair go', but it was let slip.

Reform to the sector has been continually stymied. In 2017, in the wake of the 7-Eleven scandal, the Turnbull Coalition government brought a bill to Parliament to better hold franchisors to account. In what was described as 'potentially game changing laws',[87] franchisors were to be made liable for the underpayment of workers by their franchisees, breaches of which would incur fines of up to $540 000.[88] But the bill came under fire from both the Australian Industry Group (AIG) and the FCA and was quickly withdrawn. The AIG warned that the changes would deter investment in the franchise industry, a claim which seemed to acknowledge that underpayment of wages was built into the industry's business models.

The FCA mounted a fierce lobbying campaign led by a former Liberal minister, Bruce Billson. Billson's effort was described as 'an intense behind-the-scenes lobbying campaign' with visits, calls and texts to MPs that reached into the heart of the government and the party room.[89]

Several years later, Turnbull's replacement as prime minister, Scott Morrison, finally made it clear that the government didn't have the stomach to take on franchise reform.[90] It was yet another example of the capacity of corporate interests to capture government decision-making. The consequences of inaction were disastrous. In December

2021, a study entitled *Lives in Limbo*, undertaken by the Migrant Workers' Centre, found that 65 per cent of the workers interviewed had experienced wage theft and other labour market abuses. The situation had become so entrenched, argued the authors of the report, that Australia could now be classified as 'a guest worker state'. Young, temporary visa holders were being exploited, while the goal posts on attaining permanent residency was 'kept just out of reach'.[91]

No action was taken against anyone from 7-Eleven management. Exploiting workers on a systematic scale apparently didn't contravene the 'due diligence' requirement in the *Corporations Act*. Perhaps ASIC believed that Withers' claim of not knowing about the exploitation would stand up in court. Or maybe the agency thought that Withers' pockets were too deep to take him on. Whatever the reasoning, an opportunity was lost to rein in bad corporate behaviour.

By 2020, 7-Eleven had paid back a total of $173 million to 4043 past and present employees, but otherwise the company incurred no other penalty. Allan Fels claimed that amount represented only a fraction of the chain's unpaid wages.[92] Russell Withers remains high on the list of Australia's most wealthy individuals. Sister Beverley passed away in 2017.

The franchisees who mounted a class action against 7-Eleven and ANZ faced a similarly drawn-out process of redress. In September 2021, 7-Eleven paid out $98 million in compensation. A year earlier, action against ANZ was dropped until the outcome of the 7-Eleven case and hasn't been resumed. As Stewart Levitt explained, class actions, by their nature, represent only partial justice. Taking on the 'top end of town' is a formidable challenge: 'You don't get much from the legal system. You get more from trying to identify the problem and creating an opportunity – through use of the media and politics – to apply sanctions on the wrong-doer which may act as a deterrent'.[93]

The 7-Eleven case highlights the destructive forces driving some corporations: profits are everything and people are expendable. The fact that numerous corporations sought and continue to exploit vulnerable workers via underhanded means underlines the dearth of ethics in many of the nation's companies.

8

DARK MONEY: THE FEDERAL GROUP

On 12 December 2017, Rebecca White, the recently appointed leader of Tasmania's Labor Opposition, fronted a media conference to announce one of the boldest policy shifts in the state's recent history. Breaking with half a century of bipartisan support for the state's gambling laws, the youthful and untested leader, who claimed New Zealand Prime Minister Jacinda Ardern as a role model, shocked the assembled media by committing her party to phasing out poker machines in clubs and pubs by 2023 should they win government at the forthcoming election. No party in Australia had ever made such a commitment.

White announced the policy in the full knowledge of the political risks it posed. The Federal Group, owner of Federal Hotels, held a lucrative monopoly over the licensing of pokies and casinos in the state. Running the privately owned Sydney-based company, established in the 1940s as Federal Hotels by Greg Farrell senior, eventually fell to Greg junior and, under his leadership, the Farrell family became among the richest people in the country. Both father and son acquired reputations as ruthless and secretive power-brokers. In 1989, Greg junior changed the company's name to the Federal Group, although it was also known by its original. As one observer noted, 'White picked a fight with the biggest opponent she could have found in Tasmania'.[1] Others agreed. According to Wayne Crawford, one of the state's most respected political analysts, White's policy shift was 'an unthinkable challenge to vested interests'.[2] In effect, a political lamb had ventured into a corporate lion's den in a state with a history of both crony capitalism and corruption scandals. Small, remote and bucolic Tasmania – for years affectionately known as the Apple Isle – had a rotten core.

The response from the Federal Group to Labor's announcement was swift and brutal. It embarked on the most expensive campaign advertising blitz – and the most blatantly partisan – in the state's history to try to stop Labor attaining government. The intervention incensed many observers, who claimed that the 2018 election – which saw the Liberals retain power – had been bought.[3]

Debate over the influence of corporate donations to political parties is nothing new, nor is the accompanying concern about the erosion of democracy this entails. In the 2018 Tasmanian state election, the Federal Group played by the existing electoral laws – but these laws, as they have operated in Tasmania especially, show how the public interest can be sidelined in favour of corporate business models. Gambling is a legitimate business, but it's also a controversial one, with public interest debates over the extent and forms allowable so as to minimise harm to the community from problem gambling. The public record shows that Federal has wielded enormous power in Tasmania for decades and that when its business model of reliance on poker machines was challenged by Labor's change of policy it did all it could to protect its interests. This made the 2018 election one of the most controversial in the state's history. And, as the election was keenly watched by gambling interests across the nation, it had broader implications. Those implications were crystal clear: the gambling industry across Australia wanted to protect the rivers of gold they derive from poker machines. White's anti-pokies policy was probably the greatest threat to these ambitions in decades.

Labor's new brand?

What was White thinking when she made Labor such a large target? Holding a degree in journalism and commerce, the novice leader had a reputation for being smart and hard-working.[4] She firmly believed that Labor had a compelling case; that banning pokies was not only the right decision, it was popular. Polls conducted over several years showed that the vast majority of Tasmanians opposed the insidious infiltration of pokies into clubs and pubs.[5] And a vibrant network of community and welfare groups had emerged to politicise the damaging socio-economic costs of gambling – robbing many vulnerable Tasmanians of their livelihoods and mental health and diverting funds away from productive areas of the economy.

And White bought a deeply personal interest to the issue. Her steely determination to ban pokies arose from a stint she spent as a younger woman working at Wrest Point Casino in Hobart. By the 1990s, the once elegant tourist drawcard had slowly descended into the Federal Group's 'faded jewel in their crown'.[6] As a young adult, White found the experience confronting. She witnessed first-hand the desperate, the lonely and the addicted: 'I saw people who were so exhausted from sitting at the machine for so long without taking a break that they fell off their chair and had to be taken to hospital'.[7]

Lastly, circumstances had forced White's hand to deal with the issue. As the existing monopoly agreement over pokies was set to expire in a few years' time, all political parties – Labor, Greens and Liberals – had to enter the 2018 election with a policy on the future arrangements for the gaming industry. Labor decided to go for broke.

Despite the risks, White had reason to feel buoyant at her press conference. Sporting long blonde hair and a beaming smile, she had the makings of a political winner. At the time of the announcement, she was more popular than Premier Will Hodgman and Labor was level-pegging with the government in opinion polls.

The Hodgman government was spooked.[8] And more so because Labor's anti-pokies policy assumed more significance than merely sharpening the differences between the two major parties on a crucial issue; it symbolised a broader cultural shift in the state. In taking head-on the state's gaming industry and its most powerful corporate player, White signalled that Labor had remodelled its brand away from the old style of Tasmanian politics marked by deference to greedy corporate interests, based around secret deals, that had long dominated the state. The 'new' Tasmania required more transparency and accountability. It proved to be a fatal mistake.

Crony capitalism and the rise of the Federal Group

In no other Australian state was government favouritism towards corporations more systematically developed than in Tasmania. Over the decades, the state's model of crony capitalism fostered rogue behaviour by a number of corporations, which were allowed to develop tentacle-like control over key sectors of the economy: forestry, fish farming and gambling. In turn, servicing this favouritism has, since the 1940s, frayed the state's shallow democratic culture. Tasmania's small size meant that its political system was vulnerable to the influence wielded by the same handful of powerful business interests.[9] The cementing of these close relationships created the Tasmanian model of crony capitalism.[10]

Both Labor and Liberal leveraged the benefits of close ties to big business and learned through hard political lessons not to threaten these relationships. The model demanded the sidestepping of government accountability. Successive governments signed on. In return for lucrative monopolistic licensing arrangements, governments believed they could sell the benefits of economic development, which were perceived to be otherwise difficult to secure given the state's isolation. And politicians could garner largely unaccountable political donations and access to post-political careers in the corporate world. But crony capitalism inevitably bred corruption scandals that regularly bubbled to the surface of public discourse, leading to persistent calls for reform.[11]

In these ways, a few powerful corporations were given seemingly limitless power. The controversial Tasmanian woodchip company Gunns Ltd was a notorious example of this unaccountable power. So was Tasmania's burgeoning salmon industry led by Tassal corporation, which has been allowed to put continual growth of the multi-billion dollar industry ahead of the health of the Tasmanian environment. Tasmanian-born and internationally acclaimed novelist Richard Flanagan has documented the power of the salmon industry in his 2021 book, *Toxic: The Rotting Underbelly of the Tasmanian Salmon Industry.* And, as Tasmanian federal independent member Andrew Wilke has said of the Federal Group: 'They seem to still be able to call the shots and that has always been the case in Tasmania. What the Farrell family want, they get'.[12]

The rise of a juggernaut

The rise of the Federal Group is inseparable from Tasmania's post-war model of crony capitalism. Greg Farrell senior established the company when he bought Wrest Point Riviera Hotel in 1948, a new development on the picturesque Derwent River waterfront. Twenty years later, the complex was transformed into Australia's first legal casino in circumstances so controversial that the legacy lingers to this day.

In the late 1960s there was widespread opposition to a casino in the normally conservative state. However, Farrell senior unleashed a promotional campaign reassuring locals that the development would 'be more hotel than gambling den' and that it would put Tasmania 'on the map'.[13] The government promised there would be no poker machines, which had been legalised in New South Wales a decade earlier.

Nevertheless, opposition festered and the project only came to fruition when Farrell enlisted powerful backers in Eric Reece's Labor government who, together, pressured Parliament to pass the legislation in haste without proper scrutiny. In what was described by some parliamentarians as an exercise in 'political trickery', the establishment of the Wrest Point Casino in 1968 marked the beginning of Federal Hotels' reputation for controversial dealings with Tasmanian governments.[14]

Those dealings became even murkier. The following year a full-blown corruption scandal erupted over an attempt to hand a competitor of Federal Hotels the right to develop a second casino in Launceston. Initiating the move was the incoming Liberal government led by Angus Bethune which had defeated, by the slenderest of margins, the tired Reece government. In the same year approval for the second casino was rammed through Parliament. Bethune hated the very idea of monopolies.

The actual details of the scandal don't need re-telling here; they are set out in convincing detail in historian James Boyce's *Losing Streak: How Tasmania was Gamed by the Gambling Industry*. The point for the purpose of this chapter is straightforward. Federal Hotels was alleged to have been one of the prime movers behind the claim that a bribe was offered to an independent member of parliament, Kevin Lyons, son of former Australian prime minister Joe Lyons, to resign in order to bring down the Bethune government. Such a move would kill off a potential rival to Federal Hotels. In the subsequent election, the company campaigned for the return of a Labor government. As Boyce writes, the 'perception of corruption and cover-up surrounding this affair has continued to fester because all the circumstances of Kevin Lyons' resignation … were not adequately investigated'.[15]

The episode established Federal Group's hardball approach to politics. As events transpired, a second casino licence was granted to Launceston and it was awarded to Federal, cementing its monopoly status in Tasmania's casino market. Bigger deals were to follow. In 1985, Greg Farrell senior persuaded the Liberal government led by Robin Gray to introduce poker machines into Federal's casinos. Again the company mounted a publicity campaign to quell community concerns. Introduction of the machines was 'no big deal', the company claimed, in fact they were akin to a social service: 'the machines are designed for people who are shy, lack confidence or do not understand the rules of a game and wish to gamble away from the scrutiny of others'.[16] Only Bob Brown, leader of the newly formed Greens, and then a state member of Parliament, voted against their introduction.

To begin with, only fifty poker machines were introduced at Wrest Point, but their numbers quickly escalated and the once-touted entertainment hub was slowly transformed into a dreary 'pokies barn'. But real wealth started flowing to the Farrell family, allowing Greg Farrell junior, on the death of his father in 1989, to purchase all the shares in the company and rename it as the Federal Group, to reflect the company's diversified tourist operations. He assumed the position of chair and CEO, with his four siblings becoming directors. Federal and the Farrells became one and the same entity.

Next came 'the deal of the century', when Federal was given an exclusive licence in 1993 to expand poker machines into clubs and pubs at no cost in terms of its licence fee. Not surprisingly, the Farrell family's wealth grew exponentially; in a little over a decade they were lifted onto Australia's rich list.

But how was such a deal struck? Timing had something to do with the generosity extended to the company. By the early 1990s, Tasmania had been hit by a debt crisis, one that was not helped by having one of the highest per head rates of gambling in the nation, coupled with the lowest gambling taxes.[17] The Liberal government led by Ray Groom was searching for more ways to raise revenue. He responded to pressure from the licensed clubs lobby, which argued that introducing pokies to regional RSL and football clubs would allow them to survive the economic downturn.

The Farrells were outraged at the potential loss of their monopoly over pokies. In an outburst that would reverberate on the company, Greg Farrell claimed that extending pokies into the community would 'grant access to those who could least afford to gamble'.[18] So too did then Opposition gambling spokesperson, Paul Lennon, who campaigned to have the plan scrapped, insisting the machines would inflict misery on Tasmanian families.[19]

Then suddenly, as the debate was deadlocked due to opposition from across the community,[20] the Federal Group was granted the exclusive licence at a very favourable tax rate for fifteen years. Farrell and Lennon quickly jettisoned their opposition to pokies outside the casinos based on concerns for ordinary punters. Incredibly, the state had given away one of its most valuable licences for free. No one really knows how it happened. Liberal MP, Bob Cheek smelt a rat. He later wrote that behind closed doors, Groom caved in to a threat made by Farrell to downsize his operations if he wasn't granted the monopoly licence.[21] But this was little more than speculation, however informed it might have been. Others believe that it was just one of those terrible Tasmanian stories involving crony capitalism.[22] Groom may well have seen the political advantage of getting the Federal Group politically onside, and the government believed that it had prised from Farrell an agreement to undertake $25 million of investment in the state. However, this part of the agreement was so lacking in detail that Federal could have spent nothing and still complied.[23]

The Farrell family had proved adept at managing the politics of Tasmania's sleazy political system, but it now had a huge incentive to protect its rivers of gold and the opulent lifestyle enjoyed by the family.

In 2003, with five years still left on the agreement, Farrell sought to extend the deal. Labor was back in power. Jim Bacon, a charismatic, former radical student and Builders Labourers Federation official, had been Premier since 1999, with Paul Lennon, also a former union official, as his deputy.

Farrell approached the government on the pretext that the company's bankers wanted more long-term security on the licence. Bacon and Lennon were more than happy to lock in a deal, this time a twenty-year extension and without alteration to the licence being granted free of charge. There was no consultation with the public, the Parliament or even the Cabinet.[24]

Outrage erupted when the deal become known, and none more so than from a newly elected Liberal member of Parliament, Peter Gutwein. He was shocked at the trampling of the democratic process, telling his fellow parliamentarians that: 'I thought politics was about democracy. But it is not about democracy; it is about stealth, secrecy and a government not wanting to be accountable'.[25] In a few barbed sentences, Gutwein had called out Tasmanian's model of crony capitalism.

Gutwein had an unusual background for a Liberal politician. Describing himself as a 'migrant son of a migrant', his grandfather had migrated to Britain from central Europe and, later, his mother and father migrated to Tasmania when he was a boy. A self-made man, Gutwein has been described as a Liberal moderate with a social conscience.[26] Eventually becoming Treasurer and then Premier, Gutwein would come face-to-face with the reality of Tasmanian politics.

In the meantime, Labor struck a favourable new deal with the Federal Group. Bacon and Lennon were a perfect fit to run the crony model of governance. Lennon's attributes are discussed below but, for his part, Bacon, the chain-smoking and gravel-voiced Premier, was a master Machiavellian politician: sunny and optimistic in public with a grand vision to turn Tasmania into a tiger economy while keeping one foot solidly planted in the 'old' crony model. An authoritarian at heart, he had a love of intrigue and media manipulation. For example, he and Lennon cemented the controversial monopolistic forestry arrangements for Gunns Ltd.[27] CEO John Gay was propelled into key economic advisory positions in the state government.

With Lennon acting as both deputy premier and Minister for Gaming, a deal with the Federal Group was never in doubt. Together they fended off claims from Citibank that the monopolistic licence renewed for Federal would fetch $130 million if it had been put out to tender. But Bacon and Lennon 'loved big dinners down at Wrest Point with the bosses'; Bacon even met his second wife at the venue where she had been one of the company's star croupiers.[28]

Federal Group's business model

Despite Federal's reputation for constructing some high-class tourist accommodation on the island, gambling remained the company's money-spinner. Its business model was to install the highest possible number of poker machines in low-income areas and keep the taxation and regulatory regime as low as possible while maintaining the exclusive monopoly in the company's hands. No gaming operator in any other state had managed to achieve such a lucrative outcome.

But there was no disguising one reality. Eighty per cent of Federal's revenue was estimated to be derived from the rapacious poker machines.[29] Even if this estimate was over the mark, the pokies' arm of the business was the real profit centre.[30] And, with experts claiming that the machines are designed to maximise the potential for gambling addiction, they are, according to critics, a licence to print money. But the business had an even darker side: about half the money flowing into pokies is thought to come from people with a gambling problem.[31] Pokies function like a reverse system of taxation – transferring money from the poor to the rich. And the social toll caused by problem gambling in the state was confirmed by an Anglicare report published in 2015. It found people reporting high levels of relationship stress and breakdown, food shortages, general ill-health, extreme levels of debt and, in a few instances, attempted suicide, due to escalating problems with gambling.[32]

With Tasmanians losing over $100 million a year on pokies, the Farrell family became seriously wealthy, amassing a fortune of nearly half a billion dollars by the time it entered the Rich List in 2006. To cement these profits the company had, over the years, purchased twelve large pubs, which were stacked with poker machines. Over ninety other venues leased machines owned by the company. In total, the Federal Group owned 3500 poker machines across the state.[33]

Not surprisingly, Greg Farrell has a different view of the ethics of pokies and hence his business model. He maintains that gambling is a legitimate business; that people have a right to choose to entertain themselves in this way; and that the company has had effective measures in place to deal with problem gambling.[34]

But the reality on the ground has, for years, contradicted these comfortable assertions. Tony Foster, the Mayor of Brighton, a predominantly low-income outer suburb of Hobart, explained that the unique arrangements surrounding Federal's monopoly included granting the company the sole right to decide where to locate the machines:

> The more disadvantaged a local government area, the more likely it is to have many pokies … This monopoly system has allowed operators to cherry pick the market and concentrate the location of poker machines in lower socio-economic areas to maximise profits. In doing so it has continued to cause preventable harm to tens of thousands of vulnerable Tasmanians every year, while lining the pockets of a few.[35]

In addition to Brighton, Glenorchy is another mainly lower socio-economic suburb of Hobart infiltrated with pokies. It's known as the 'pokies golden mile' where it's almost impossible to enter a supermarket without passing a pokies venue.[36]

Capturing the state

The Farrell family has been able to take full advantage of Tasmania's weak democratic culture to develop a 'risk management' model of government–corporate relations to protect their monopoly. For decades, the Farrells have had all bases covered to ensure political compliance. And the company executed the strategy without breaking any laws or raising any suggestion that they had engaged in personal corruption of Tasmanian politics.

At the forefront of Federal's corporate strategy has been the creation of an image: the Farrells were passionate about Tasmania. This benevolent image belied the fact that they lived in Sydney and most of the profits from their pokies and casinos left the state and were used to generate their opulent lifestyle. However, part of this lifestyle was built in Tasmania when the family purchased an old colonial-era property outside Launceston. It was here that Farrell could project his Tasmanian roots. As one journalist found when visiting the property, Farrell would be found 'seated in a deep antique chair with a priceless pastoral scene by [Tasmanian] painter John Glover on the wall behind him, Greg Farrell seems very much the picture of a Tasmanian patriarch'.[37]

The Tasmanian-generated image was a powerful one. 'The Farrells, portrayed themselves', noted one observer, as 'driven to help develop the island state they love, to foster investment and employment'.[38] But this self-styled narrative of the beneficent businessman sits uneasily with the dark side of gambling. Those claiming to know Farrell acknowledge that he has a blind spot about the social impact of the industry.[39]

As head of the company, Greg Farrell has actively cultivated relationships with politicians from both the major parties – frequently dining with them and attending fund-raising events. As Tasmania's weak electoral law allows any corporation to donate to individual candidates without having to disclose such donations, there was a built-in incentive for politicians to curry his favour. Andrew Wilkie has expressed deep concern about the contributions from gambling interests to individual politicians: 'I, for one, find it no better than brown paper bags of cash being handed over in other countries'.[40]

Naturally, the Federal Group has donated generously to both sides of politics.[41] Again, Tasmania's electoral law, credited with being the most lax of any state electoral law, facilitated his efforts.[42] Donors to Tasmania's major parties have enjoyed the highest non-disclosure caps in the country and are not required to disclose donations until the end of the financial year. In addition, donations to non-party political entities have not been covered in the legislation. Such weak laws are a breeding ground for 'dark money': money flowing to political parties that is unaccounted for in official declarations of political donations. But 'dark money', while conjuring a sinister undermining of democracy, is not necessarily illegal. Corporations, or other wealthy interests, are able to exploit loopholes in existing electoral laws across Australia in ways that make it hard for the public to trace the source of the money that ends up in the coffers of political parties. It has become a normalised part of the political system.

A recent Australian study by the Centre for Public Integrity calculated that over $90 million dollars that found its way to political parties was hidden from public view in the period 2021–2.[43] No laws were broken in the process. The issue is what does such money buy? If Federal could be described as being engaged in the 'dark money' side of politics, it's nothing more than other corporations were engaged in as well.

The potential for Federal's generosity to buy political influence operated as a shadowy presence over the political system. Indeed, Farrell was given access to the corridors of power with membership of peak bodies including the Tourism Industry Council of Tasmania, the Chamber of Commerce and Industry, the Tasmanian Hospitality Association and the Property Council of Tasmania.[44] Such high-level networking paid off for the Federal Group. As James Boyce writes, all the peak bodies that have the company as a member 'have played a role in defending [its] exclusive poker machine licence'.[45]

Incredibly, the political reach of the Federal Group extended to research on problem gambling. In 1998, the company funded a research project undertaken by Anglicare. Taking a hands-on approach, Greg Farrell turned up to meetings of the researchers 'insisting on the right of veto over their recommendations'.[46] But then Farrell had strong links to the Anglican Church as well.[47]

Farrell also adopted the tactic of currying favour with the community through regular donations to sporting clubs, arts and community organisations. For local groups that needed a little help, the Farrells were 'only a phone call away'.[48] The company claims to spend nearly $1 million a year on the community.[49]

Boyce argues that the influence of the extensive networks built by the Farrells cannot be overestimated. People in Tasmania, he explained, 'fear all these networks. They rely on government jobs and powerful interests. People are afraid to speak out'.[50]

Additionally, Federal had developed a highly strategic approach to its licence renewal. According to Boyce, Farrell would wait for 'trigger points' before initiating confidential negotiations with the government. Such trigger points occurred when the government needed something from Federal, and at a time of low political risk, many years out from an election. Such an approach circumvented public discussion. 'All negotiations would occur behind closed doors. The results were presented as fait accompli signed contracts – even when these deals required legislative approval'.[51]

Another tactic deployed by the Federal Group was to quash any dissenting political voices. In 2008, for example, Will Hodgman, then newly installed as Opposition Liberal leader, asked a question in Parliament about the delays and downgrading of Federal's promised East Coast tourist development that was part of securing the license extension in 2003. The state Liberals were reassessing their gaming policy and deciding whether to support reducing the number of machines in Tasmania. Hodgman acknowledged that the 'party faithful' were pressuring the Liberals to reduce the number of pokies.[52]

The response from the Federal Group was startling, to say the least. Full-page advertisements, in the form of a personal letter from Greg Farrell attacking the Liberals, were taken out in all three of the state's daily newspapers. The company's manager of corporate affairs continued the pile-on, declaring that the 'irresponsible actions of the State Liberals seriously called into question their capacity to be genuinely considered capable of governing Tasmania'. Hodgman's leadership was placed 'under siege' by Farrell's intervention.[53] He never again publicly criticised the company, showing, according to critics, 'that he [had] learnt his lesson'.[54]

Employing high-powered lobbyists has become a standard tactic of corporations to foster favourable relations with governments. Often such lobbyists are former politicians, and Federal has continually deployed this approach. In 2016, for example, it added former premier Paul Lennon to its public relations arsenal. Lennon's career has been marinated in Tasmania's model of crony capitalism. To him it was about delivering jobs to the state. He was deputy premier when Federal Hotels 'stitched up' (as some thought) the 2003 secret licence extension with Jim Bacon's Labor government. A bare-knuckle politician with a fondness for profanities and expensive silk ties, Lennon had spent his career in state politics as Parliament's 'most resolute defender of the ruling model of corporate government'.[55] Succeeding Jim Bacon upon the latter's death from cancer in 2004, Lennon resigned from the premiership in 2008 amid unsubstantiated, but widely publicised, allegations that he was the beneficiary of a house renovation arranged courtesy of Gunns Ltd.[56]

With no official inquiry held into the allegations, Lennon escaped any potentially adverse finding about his conduct as a politician, but he has remained a colourful public figure with an ongoing, post-political career fondness for visiting casinos.

When this controversial figure was appointed to the Federal Group as a lobbyist, a predictable chorus of criticism followed. Andrew Wilkie said the company's engagement of Lennon demonstrated the symbiotic relationship between the poker machine industry and Tasmanian politicians: 'Hiring Mr Lennon is also testimony to the increasing community pressure for poker machine reform and the fact that the industry feels it needs to wheel out the big guns'.[57] Farrell had his eye on the next round of licence extension negotiations ahead of the 2018 state election.

When lobbyists proved too subtle a tool, a resort to political intimidation was also in Federal's playbook of tactics to keep its monopoly. On several occasions it is thought to have threatened to review its investments in Tasmania should it lose its exclusive pokies licence. Speculation about such threats had circulated in the past but were confined to the corridors of power and their veracity remained unclear. However, a few days after Rebecca White announced Labor's policy to phase out pokies, Greg Farrell went on the offensive in public. At a media conference flanked by some of the company's 2000 staff, an angry-looking Farrell pulled the political lever of job losses and then issued a threat to review the company's presence in Tasmania: 'This will have a huge impact, directly, on the people we employ, on the suppliers who support our businesses and on our ability to execute our strategies of future growth', he said.[58] Farrell's tone was unmistakably belligerent. But perhaps, in his mind, Farrell was stating the obvious: pokies were the rivers of gold that made possible for all the other benefits the company brought to Tasmania. That's the problem with crony capitalism; without proper political transparency and accountability, the public can't know where the truth lies.

But the resort to the 'nuclear option' – attempting to influence the course of an election – had not been deployed by the Federal Group since the murky 1969 election. Like his father, Greg junior could sense when the power of the company was under serious question.

But what personality did Greg Farrell bring to managing his company's relationship with governments in such a varied and successful way?

A different type of CEO?

On the surface, Greg Farrell differed markedly from the high-profile, ego-driven, publicity-obsessed CEOs whose capacities and destructive failings litter the pages of this book. He was one of the most bland CEOs of a major corporation in the country. He was typically described by those who casually met him as genial, reserved, softly spoken, with a love of the finer things in life. Photographs of him capture a face as friendly as a local restaurateur. He would 'rather talk about the John Glover paintings on his walls than poker machines', observed one journalist.[59] In fact, Farrell's reclusiveness earned him a place on the ABC's 2020 list of 'the 10 most powerful Australians you've likely never heard of'.[60]

Much of Farrell's mild-mannered nature appears genuine. He shies away from unnecessary conflict. In 2002, for example, a journalist from the *Sunday Tasmanian* described him, provocatively, as 'the J. R. Ewing of Tasmania',[61] after the fictional egocentric, amoral American oilman played by Larry Hagman in the popular TV show *Dallas*. A senior executive with the newspaper worried that, when Farrell phoned on the day the article appeared, trouble might be in the offing. But Farrell simply wanted to pass on that he was 'a bit disappointed with the characterisation'. He accepted a personal apology from the executive but was otherwise happy to move on and talk about his charitable interests.[62]

Farrell is a puzzle. It is hard to reconcile the image of the amiable country squire with the ruthlessly successful businessman. Was Farrell deliberately elusive? Some think he has had a strategy to keep a low profile in the state.[63] After all, who would want to attract too much attention when your privately owned company is the beneficiary of a fortune made from exclusive rights to gaming renewed in dubious circumstances?

Maybe the key to Farrell is his capacity for compartmentalisation. On the one hand, he is naturally, or willingly, the media-shy, retiring, genial person in ordinary dealings with people, but when in business mode, critics allege, he switches to a secretive, strategic, ruthless operator. Psychologists remind us that 'people who have compartmentalized minds have diversified personalities which enable them to behave differently and appropriately in a variety of situations'.[64] And such minds appear untroubled by a lack of integration between their disparate, duelling sides.

Glimpses of Farrell's capacity to switch modes occasionally surfaced. In his dealings with Farrell, James Boyce, who worked for a time as head of research at Anglicare, encountered the head of Federal as 'softly spoken and friendly', but when his interests appeared to be under threat, he turned red in the face and began shouting.[65]

Labor's fatal confrontation with Federal Hotels

The confrontation between the state Labor Party and the gaming industry at the 2018 election was several years in the making. In 2015, David Walsh, the founder of MONA (Museum of New and Old Art), the wildly popular avant-garde art gallery carved into a sandstone cliff face on the Derwent River waterfront a short drive from the Hobart CBD, wanted to explore the possibility of opening a small high-end casino without poker machines. He needed to help offset the costs of running his gallery, which had helped boost tourism to the state from around Australia and overseas. His unique art gallery has become so popular that the term 'the MONA effect' was coined to describe its contribution to the Tasmanian economy from the legions of tourists who flock to visit the complex.[66] But Walsh, himself a highly successful gambler, seemed to underestimate the resolve of the Federal Group.

Walsh is an unconventional character. A battler who grew up in the same working-class areas of Hobart where the Federal Group planted their business model, Walsh had a genius for mathematics. He took on gaming houses around the world, earning a fortune as a professional gambler, the proceeds from which he ploughed into to his idiosyncratic art collection, which became the basis of MONA. Much admired in the state for pouring his own money and art collection into such a valued tourist asset, he has defied the prevailing model of power. As journalist Sally Glaezter noted in her profile of him, it has taken politicians some time to work out Walsh because he tends not to play by their rules.[67] He has been known to tell politicians seeking donations to 'fuck off'. He also avoids conversations with politicians not directly related to the matter at hand. But politicians nonetheless feel indebted to Walsh because of the contribution he has made to the state.

Walsh knew that his proposal would step on the toes of the Federal Group and therefore he would need the government to negotiate with the company. In fact, he publicly flagged that his proposed casino would require 'some goodwill' on the part of the Federal Group.[68] Farrell, however, knew that he had the upper hand and years of experience to any such dealings with potential competitors.

Negotiations between the parties, facilitated by Treasurer Peter Gutwein, quickly went pear-shaped. Walsh learned Farrell would only acquiesce to his high-end, no-pokies model if Federal Group was granted another monopoly pokies deal. In early September 2015, Walsh withdrew his application for a casino licence, but not before lighting a fuse under simmering community disquiet about the gaming industry.[69]

Walsh hated poker machines and he didn't want to be implicated in any sordid pokies deal. In the blog he wrote after withdrawing from the talks, Walsh made his opposition to poker machines clear – describing them as a 'moral outrage' – and that he could not do a deal that promoted them through supporting the existing monopoly. He later told the media: 'So Federal may have played their cards very well indeed. And since I could not support an extension of their poker machine monopoly, it looks like I have played my hand like a novice'.[70]

The falling out between Walsh and the Federal Group had an immediate impact. He opened up a Pandora's box of community disquiet and put pressure on the Hodgman government to end the secret deals with the Farrell family's company.[71] The Group was on the political backfoot for the first time in decades.

The pressure only increased when the government announced it had established a parliamentary inquiry into the gaming industry – largely in response to the community disquiet stirred by Walsh. It had a brief to examine taxation and licensing arrangements, along with community attitudes towards gambling. In another twist to the plot enveloping the Federal Group, a key member of this committee was Scott Bacon, the Opposition Treasurer and son of the former Premier, Jim Bacon. Scott was well known around Tasmania 'as a bloke not afraid of a flutter of his own' and 'no enemy of the gaming industry'.[72] Yet something strange happened to Scott in the course of the inquiry. He heard experts explain how machines manipulated players' perceptions of their odds; that pokies generated little employment; and how they sucked money out of communities.[73]

And so White and Bacon began to discuss potential policies in response to the inquiry's findings. According to observers, some nervous nellies in Labor wanted to adopt a moderate stance based around boosting harm minimisation, but evidence presented to the parliamentary inquiry suggested none of these measures would make much difference. Eventually White and Bacon decided to go all-in; pokies would be phased out. Representatives of the Farrell Group were summoned to a meeting before the public announcement was made. One of them was so shocked he began to 'twitch', one observer recounted.[74] Bacon later told the media that Labor's policy was 'the right thing to do'.[75]

The Federal Group realised it would now have to cede some ground. Political support was fracturing. The company had already handed a submission to the parliamentary inquiry in which it proposed a system for its monopoly to be broken up in return for the owners of pubs and clubs taking over the licences for the machines installed in their venues. This was a particularly generous scheme for the family because it had already bought the twelve most lucrative pokies pubs in the state.[76] It became the policy that the Liberals took to the election and which reversed a commitment the party had recently made to an open tender process for the gaming industry.[77] It was now 'game on' as the election neared.

The dirty tricks campaign

During the March 2018 state election, the political skies opened up and rained down a torrent of advertising – the vast bulk of it directed at stopping Labor winning the election. Television ads were 'wall to wall'; newspapers were filled with double-page spreads and wrap-around banners; radio fizzed with thirty-second rants; some billboards were so large they contravened the electoral law; and banners draped across the face of old Victorian pubs sagged under their weight.[78] Behind this tsunami of advertising was a consortium of gaming money led by the Federal Group.

While the state's weak election laws prevent an accurate assessment of the total funding Federal directed towards defeating Labor, all commentators were struck with how awash the election campaign was with money. The Liberal Party alone was estimated to have spent $5 million on advertising – much of it supplied by Federal. This was an unprecedented advertising blitz in the small state, and it is thought the Liberals outspent Labor by a factor of 10 to 1.[79]

This level of spending enabled the Federal Group to make gaming – and Labor's policy – the central issue of the campaign. 'This was a referendum on gaming', a spokesperson for the company crowed to the press.[80]

And, there was more at stake in the election than just the fate of poker machine policy in Tasmania. The policy articulated by White's Labor Party was the first attempt by either of the two major parties in any state in the country to commit to withdrawing pokies from pubs and clubs.[81] The Tasmanian electoral contest was the first real opportunity in Australia 'to roll back the pokies juggernaut'.[82] Consequently, the gambling industry across mainland states kept a close eye on the result, with some speculating that they had skin in the game in the effort mounted to derail Labor.[83]

What made the campaign so successful?

Principally, the pro-pokies campaign turned the socio-economic harm of gaming into a pro-jobs issue. The supposed threat to jobs united Federal Group and several peak pro-gambling and hospitality lobby groups to mount a grassroots campaign around two slogans: 'Save Our Jobs' and 'Love Your Local'. Television advertising featured employees from clubs and pubs expressing concern about the potential loss of their jobs.

Greg Farrell said the eleven Federal staff featured in the advertisements all stuck up their hands to help fight the Labor policy, within days of it being announced: 'They gave up their holidays to film content for the campaign, providing unscripted responses to questions on their feelings about Tasmania, Federal Group and the future', he said.[84]

The jobs issue – always a sensitive one in a state with a history of high unemployment – took on a life of its own. The figure of 5100 job losses stemming from Labor's phase-out pokie policy was widely publicised during the campaign and was endorsed by the pro-pokies campaign organisers and by senior Liberals, including Peter Gutwein.[85] The fact that the figure was preposterously inflated hardly cut through the campaign blitzkrieg of advertising.

The origins of the claim of over 5000 job losses lay in a survey conducted by the gaming industry in response to Labor's policy announcement. Yet the industry refused to release its methodology, claiming commercial-in-confidence. Even its total of 5100 job losses was broken down into two parts – 1086 full-time jobs would be lost immediately, with the remaining 4014 'affected' by reduced hours and 'changed duties'– whatever that meant.

The survey was so flimsy as to be meaningless, a fact supported by a 2017 Tasmanian Department of Treasury and Finance report. The report found that there were 1086 full-time jobs involved in the delivery of gaming services across the state and only 371 in pubs and clubs.[86] Indeed, other studies had shown that employment in pubs and clubs had fallen by 14 per cent since the introduction of pokies in the late 1990s.[87]

Tasmanian-based economist Saul Eslake summed up the dishonesty about the pitch on job losses: 'What ever impact on employment is, if there is one, it is much less than what is claimed. It assumes that every job associated with pubs and clubs is under threat. That is just nonsense'.[88]

Allied with the exaggerated claim of job losses was the implied appeal to identity politics. Banners reading, 'Labor and the Greens think you're stupid … Don't let them tell you what to do', was a less than subtle delve into anti-elitist sentiment directed at the residents of working-class suburbs and towns where pubs and clubs housed pokies and held meat raffles. It was designed to 'wedge' Labor from this core constituency. As one of the employees featured in the advertising campaign declared: 'As a young man, before I was old enough to vote, my dad told me that Labor looked after the working man … that's clearly not the case anymore. I don't think I could ever in good conscience vote for them again'.[89]

The thrust of the 'Love Your Local' campaign also touched a deep nerve about the traditional role of local pubs in the community. No doubt local pubs and clubs with poker machines still performed this role, but they had also been transformed by the Federal Group's business model of locating pokies in pubs and clubs, which had all but obliterated their community role in some venues.

The Elwick Hotel in the heart of largely working-class Glenorchy was a case in point. Owned by Federal, the elegant Edwardian establishment topped the list of annual losses from pokies by its players at $4.5 million. Described as the company's 'jewel in the crown', it had been transformed by poker machines. By the time of the 2018 election, the hotel rooms were long gone, as was the kitchen, and the front bar shut by 10 pm on a Saturday, earlier on most other nights. The bulk of its floorspace was given over to a gaming room, which was open from 8 am to 4 am.[90] According to the Salvation Army, on one occasion, the hotel management allowed a woman with an obvious and severe cognitive disability to 'put her food money' into a poker machine.[91] Nevertheless, during the campaign, the hotel carried a prominent banner, strung across its front, 'Save Our Jobs. Vote Liberal'. All ninety-two hotels with poker machines joined in the push for the Liberal government to be returned.

The campaign degenerated into lies and excess. The Love Your Local Campaign was forced to delete one advertisement suggesting that Anzac Day would have to be cancelled.[92] And an organised social media trolling campaign targeted publicans who didn't have poker machines on their premises. One Hobart publican, Doug O'Neil, explained to the press that his establishment was attacked on its Facebook page:

> There are a few trolls out there that'll jump on any single post and have a go, or knock down restaurants or pubs that say anything against pokies. [There are] false reviews, saying they came in and the food was terrible, and we know they've never been here. I've had people say they were here when we were shut.[93]

The Labor Party maintained that the troll campaign was organised by the gaming industry.[94]

When pressed on the campaign tactics organised by the pro-pokies lobby, Premier Will Hodgman fell back on the argument of free choice in defence of the gaming industry, and professed a 'disinterest in campaign funding details'.[95] Not surprisingly, critics allege that the party had 'sold itself to the gaming and hotels industry'.[96] And Farrell declined to specify the total amount of funding his company directed at the campaign.

Although the 2018 Tasmanian election was fought on three major issues – gambling, gun control and health – it was the first of these issues that proved to be the most controversial and arguably the most influential. It was credited with blunting the swing to Labor, allowing the incumbent Liberal government to hold onto office.[97]

The 2018 election wasn't just a big win for the Federal Group, it was also a victory for crony capitalism and the elites, like the Farrell family, who are its principal beneficiaries. Following the Liberals' re-election, Peter Gutwein, who became Premier following Hodgman's resignation in January 2020, abandoned a promise to reform the election laws. By doing so, he perpetuated, at least for the foreseeable future, one of the drivers of the state's model of crony capitalism.[98]

Scared from Labor's bruising election loss, Rebecca White announced that Labor would ditch its anti-pokies policy. And the Federal Group's profits continued to rise off the back of gaming, particularly as Tasmania remained largely immune to Covid-caused lockdowns. In fact, some experts argued that increased Covid payments, including through JobSeeker and JobKeeper, underpinned the company's rise in profits because some punters had more cash to pour into machines.[99]

Premier Gutwein, the man outraged by the Federal Group's trampling of democracy in Tasmania twenty years previously, had overseen the enactment of Federal Group's preferred changes to the gaming industry. Politicians, of course, are entitled to change their minds on issues, and often do. But critics argued that Gutwein had caved in to the gambling industry with the introduction of the Gaming Control Amendment Bill, later enacted, which would strip Federal Hotels of its monopoly, allowing venues to own or lease their own poker machines. Estimates indicate that under this regime, returns from pokies could rise to more than $14 million a year.[100] And the Federal Group is poised to leverage the new opportunities presented in the legislation. In return for the termination of its monopoly, the government has slashed the taxes the company pays on its poker machines at its two casinos. This is estimated to lead to a loss of $250 million to state coffers over the next two decades, while being a correspondingly handy boost to Federal's bottom line. The legislation contained no significant harm minimisation measures and locked in the contractual arrangements for the industry until 2043.

Bitterly opposed by the Greens and a handful of independents, who claimed that it was 'a prize for the gambling industry', Labor sided with the government to pass the legislation. Gutwein claimed that 'his conscience is clear'[101] over the passage of the legislation. After all, he explained, he took it to the 2018 election.

9

'HORROR STORIES': BUPA AGED CARE

In May 2010, the *Sunday Telegraph* conducted an undercover investigation into nursing homes. In Sydney, journalist Rosie Squires posed as a volunteer to work in two of the country's biggest privately owned aged care corporations – the Domain Principal Group and Bupa Aged Care. No such systematic investigation had ever been carried out into the sector to try to better understand why there had been a continual string of stories about the abuse occurring in nursing homes.

Squires kept a detailed diary of what she witnessed which she summed up as: 'gut-wrenching'. Under-resourced nurses and aged care workers battled away in a business model that was designed to put profit before caring. Squires' brave investigation documented abuse on a horrific level: residents left lying in wet incontinence pads for hours on end; others left staring blankly at television sets for equally long periods of time; residents who were under-fed; and instances of physical and mental abuse. And almost all residents suffered from severe loneliness; many simply wanted to die.[1]

Squires' article brought into sharp focus the shocking deficiencies in sections of the private aged care system that were part of broad-reaching social experiment in the sector: could big corporations provide better care using the competitive ethos of the free market? Squires' answer seemed to be a definite 'no'. Profits were driving greed and a drastic lowering of service.

The Domain Principal Group was owned by AMP-backed Principal Health Care, which, in 2006, had bought out the Ramsay Health Care nursing home group. And British-based Bupa Aged Care had set up in Australia in 2007. It was part of the Bupa Healthcare Group, a major provider of private health insurance. Both companies responded to the opportunities opened up after the Howard government passed the *Aged Care Act 1997*, the purpose of which was to facilitate the entry of corporations into aged care as part of a deregulation of the sector after decades of underfunding by governments. Previously the sector had been run by a mix of not-for-profit charities, government-run institutions, small for-profit private companies and only one large for-profit provider – the Moran Health Care Group.

The entry of the big players had far-reaching implications for aged care and human services generally. Squires saw clear evidence of systemic problems associated with failings of federal government policy for the aged. The shortage of nurses in each facility stemmed from the poor wages aged care workers received and the lack of enforcement of standards which flowed from Howard's 1997 aged care reforms. The nursing homes Squires worked in had never failed an inspection: 'They have a clean record from the national accreditation body, overseen by the Federal Government'. Here was clear evidence that the corporate-backed aged care sector had captured government decision-making. Such capture was often a driver of scandal.

Within a few years Bupa overtook Domain (which had twenty facilities)[2] to become the largest aged care provider in the country with seventy-eight homes and over 7400 residents in its care. It also gained a reputation as among the worst, if not the worst, corporation involved in aged care. Bupa became one of the most ruthless cost-cutters in the sector. It lived up to its reputation in Britain of pursuing profit before care.[3] In fact, Michael Wynne, a retired doctor, academic and persistent critic of the free market approach to aged care wrote at the time of Bupa's entry into Australia that its suitability to set up operations here should have been called into question, given that 'it was so commercially aggressive that it was prepared to under-fund and so compromise care'.[4] Tragically, Wynne's assessment proved to be correct.

By 2019, more than half of Bupa's nursing homes in Australia were failing basic standards of care; 30 per cent were putting the health and safety of the elderly at 'serious risk' and thirteen had been 'sanctioned' leading to a withdrawal of government funds.[5] In fact, following Squires' article, concerned relatives gradually came forward with 'horror stories' about Bupa homes, including maggot-infested wounds, malnourishment, neglect, medication mismanagement, assault and sexual abuse.[6] One horrific example of an elderly resident in a Bupa facility being bashed by a worker was filmed and became part of the pressure that built on the Morrison Coalition government to establish the 2018 royal commission into the sector.[7] Bupa was accused of contributing to the deaths of several residents who had been left untreated with serious medical conditions.[8]

It's an understatement to say that Bupa Aged Care went rogue. But the company built its excessively profit-driven culture on the back of a deregulated model for aged care.

The rise of the Moran empire

'The greying of Australia means big business', noted the *Sydney Morning Herald* in 1988.[9] The paper was noting a trend that was only just become apparent under the Labor government led by Bob Hawke (1983–91). The proportion of people aged over sixty-five in the total population was starting to appreciably grow. In fact, it rose from 9 per cent in 1977 to 15 per cent twenty years later. As a consequence, federal funding to aged care was growing exponentially. Sydney entrepreneur Doug Moran spotted this trend before most, and built Australia's first nursing home empire, becoming the single most powerful force in the industry.

Doug Moran's life was a classic rags-to-riches story: from a deprived childhood living in a tent to domiciling in the lap of luxury at Swifts, the Sydney Gothic Revival mansion in Darling Point.

The determination of the nursing home mogul to build wealth was forged during the Depression. Moran's father, Michael, a coal miner, was a victim of the great Newcastle lock-out of 1929. Forced to move on, the family of five children relocated to the Mary Valley, near Gympie, where Michael cut railway sleepers and grew bananas and pineapples. They lived in tents for six years, eating little more than damper and dripping. Doug, the eldest, left school at eleven to work in a timber mill.[10]

Deep scars were seared into Moran's personality: 'Anyone with a bit of intelligence could see the tragedy of that place [the Mary Valley]', he said, 'that complete hole of a place'. At twelve, and with no more than a smattering of education, Moran ran away to live a Tom Sawyer-like existence making his own way in an uncertain world: bellboy, cabin boy at fourteen on an American tanker, and serving in the British merchant navy on a troop and supply ship during World War II. After the war, he worked as a storeman in Sydney's Rocks district when, catching up on his education, he experienced an epiphany: 'I ... read about the fortunes that had been made from American real estate by the Vanderbilts and Morgans in the 19th century. I thought I would have a go myself at Kings Cross'.[11]

Moran liked to tell the story of his meteoric rise to the press. It helped buff his image as a high achiever and satisfied his urge to promulgate the enduring life lessons of his improbable journey. Like other brilliant but flawed entrepreneurs, the short, straight-backed, barrel-chested Moran, who was blind in one eye from an accident, was relentlessly self-promoting. He could turn on the charm when needed and capture the limelight when it suited him. He built deep connections to the Liberal Party and became an influential force. Highly controlling, he expected to get his own way and was convinced he was always right.[12]

In his private life, Moran was a domineering and intimidating patriarch. He and his wife, Greta, expected their seven children to succeed and join the company: 'failure to perform was not tolerated and there were bitter sibling rivalries'.[13]

Moran's daughter, Kerry Jones, said her father was always looking to be on the attack: 'My father is used to just saying "Get stuffed", and whoever it is just goes away. He's done it to hundreds of people. My father just does what he wants'.[14] In fact, observers of Moran claimed that it was 'dicey' to be too close to him because when a person fell out of favour, 'the end is swift'.[15] However, while Moran's charm and ruthlessness help explain his rise to wealth and power, his company avoided a catastrophic demise as happened to other, turbo-charged CEOs. Doug's early life had also taught him the value of discipline. He saw life as a Darwinian struggle for survival.

Moran and the privatisation of aged care

With his newly acquired aspiration for US gilded-age era wealth, Moran established himself in real estate convinced he was destined for success.[16] But another epiphany struck him from an unexpected quarter. When his grandmother became frail, he was distressed at the poor standard of facilities for the aged. Taking out a ten-year lease on a property in Sydney's McMahons Point in 1954, he opened his first nursing home with sixteen beds. His involvement in the sector deepened when FAI founder Larry Adler paid Moran to run nursing homes Adler had purchased from his insurance business. In 1987, Adler sold his eight nursing homes and five private hospitals to Moran.[17]

During the 1980s and '90s, Moran built his nursing home empire by targeting the wealthy who could afford to splash out on five-star facilities. The Moran Health Care Group charged clients for silver service, twenty-four-hour nursing care and other add-ons. A two-tiered aged care system began to take shape: resort-like accommodation for the rich – pioneered by Moran – and Dickensian-style facilities run by government and small, for-profit operators for the less well off.

By 1997, Moran owned fifty nursing homes, employed 7000 staff and had amassed $250 million in personal wealth.[18] Moran achieved something of a rare feat in aged care – the lowest cost structure in the industry, but maintaining a reputation for providing quality.[19]

And, as the population aged, Moran could see even richer pickings for aged care, all underpinned by increased government funding. A passionate right-wing ideologue with ready-made pro-market solutions to the challenges of aged care, Moran became a powerful presence in the Liberal Party at state and federal level to push for further deregulation and privatisation, the centrepiece of which was authorisation from government to charge the aged upfront in the form of uncapped bonds to enter facilities. This, he thought, would inject much-needed capital to expand the sector. But these controversial ideas needed government backing. As journalist Margot Saville commented: 'Moran needs to have good links with politicians because he is the dominant operator in an industry that he himself admits is "underwritten and guaranteed" by the government'.[20]

In addition to generous donations to the Liberal Party, Moran made a habit of befriending health ministers and individual politicians.[21] He became 'a formidable lobbying machine'[22] through a strategy of recruiting Liberal politicians and backing them financially.[23] Those who studied his business operation noted that Moran's success in becoming Australia's largest operator of nursing homes was 'a combination of hard work and exquisitely arranged political patronage'.

Moran became a skilled political insider. He relentlessly courted the conservative side of politics, pushing for bolder private sector involvement: his Darlinghurst headquarters operated virtually as an extension of the Liberal Party, with phones running hot with talk of candidates and preselections.[24] Interestingly, Moran seemed to believe that backing individual candidates rather than general donations to the party organisation gave him greater influence.

When John Howard came to power in March 1996, the problems

festering in aged care had escalated, with serious implications for the federal budget. There was a lack of supply of nursing home beds, the quality of many homes was poor and services across the country were unequally distributed. New strategic thinking was required.

Moran had the answer to the challenges of the aged sector: a stronger role for the private sector. He'd spent years lobbying for such a direction from government. Moran had a direct line of influence to the office of the incoming Health Minister, Michael Wooldridge. Wooldridge was advised on aged care by Bob Woods, who had been a consultant to the Doug Moran nursing home empire.[25]

Moran was able to enlist other powerful corporate players in aged care. Andrew Turner, the charismatic founder of US corporation Sun Healthcare, reinforced the ideologically driven pro-market fix for aged care. Turner had built a national aged care chain, which collapsed in America in 2000 amid a series of allegations involving fraud and poor standards of care in its nursing home. However, before the collapse, Turner set up the company in Australia and spoke with politicians and corporations, pushing his idea that there were efficiencies to be made in the aged care system that the free market could implement.[26]

The influence of Moran and Turner was soon evident in the statements made by senior Liberal politicians. Bronwyn Bishop was on record when she took over the portfolio of aged care as saying that to staff nursing homes 'you only needed middle-aged women with kind hearts to give tender, loving care'.[27]

Howard's deregulation revolution

John Howard pitched himself to the electorate at the 1996 election as a reassuring leader, not a transformative one. Yet he had formulated a radical plan for aged care that was released on an unsuspecting public twelve months after the election.

Before the passage of the government's *Aged Care Act 1997*, the federal government regulated the nursing home industry, mandating minimum staffing numbers and qualifications. These mandates restricted profitability.[28]

Such regulation was not sufficient, however, to prevent abuses occurring. In 1996, for example, *The Age* reported that nearly all of Victoria's nursing homes inspected by the federal government did not meet the minimum standards of care – and at least seventy former state-run nursing homes had never been monitored. A *Sunday Age* investigation found that breaches in the basic health care, dignity, safety and security of elderly residents occurred in most nursing homes.[29]

Howard's reforms represented the most significant change to aged care in at least a generation. In fact, Doug Moran boasted about the influence he had had on Howard's legislation. Even allowing for hyperbole, he was not far off the mark. On the other hand, the push for privatisation was not simply an outcome of political lobbying; it resonated with Howard's well-known ideological commitment to privatisation and the free market.

The *Aged Care Act* embodied all that Moran had been seeking: a greater shift to privatisation, deregulation, increased fees for residents and the provision for an uncapped nursing home bond. The latter reform met a storm of public protest when people realised that their frail aged relatives would have to sell their family home to be able to gain entry to a nursing home. It was dropped as a consequence. But otherwise, Moran had got all he wanted: the Act created a deregulated, for-profit framework for the expansion of the aged care industry. Nonetheless, Moran had a very public falling out with Howard over the Prime Minister's dumping of the proposal for the aged care bond. True to form, Moran turned on those who stood up to him.

But Howard, together with Moran, had left a ticking time bomb in the aged care sector. In the quest for privatisation, the Act changed several fundamental principles that had underpinned residential care for the elderly. The legislation cut out the requirement for set staffing numbers and qualifications. It stated that providers were required to employ 'adequate numbers of appropriately skilled and trained staff'. It was up to the providers to determine what constituted 'adequate numbers' and 'appropriately skilled'.[30]

The Act also freed nursing home operators from having to allocate a set proportion of government subsidies to patient care, which previously they had been required to do. Journalist Adele Horin put it this way: 'Proprietors hated this time-consuming system of accounting for nursing care expenditure, and successfully lobbied the Howard Government to give them a pot of money to be spent as they saw fit'. They wanted to be judged on outcomes alone.[31]

Lastly, the Act provided 'light touch' regulation.[32]

The Howard government failed to assess the appropriateness of its ideological framework. Aged care experts criticised the government's approach. They warned that profit and caring for the aged were incompatible policy objectives and that neo-liberal ideas about the benefits of free markets were inappropriate. This was inevitably the case when the client group was vulnerable and unable to make informed choices and where competition might force down, rather than improve, standards. As one observer noted:

> Once you replace 'quality care' as the imperative with 'pursuit of profit' as the imperative, of course, an aged-care operator is going to cut corners … Worse, once the operator gets costs down in whatever grisly way, other operators have to follow suit to stay competitive.[33]

The director of the Catholic Health Care Association, Francis Sullivan, questioned the shift towards private sector homes, describing it as 'a very worrying trend'. He drew a fundamental distinction between the private and non-profit sectors: 'Any surplus we make is poured back into the home. It doesn't go to the shareholders'.[34]

Doug Moran was a multi-million-dollar winner from the Howard government's shift to private ownership of nursing homes. In 1999, two years after the introduction of the *Aged Care Act*, estimates showed that the Moran Health Care Group had won bed licences worth almost $10 million in New South Wales during that time. The beds made up about 12 per cent of Australia's new nursing home places, well above the Moran Group's 3.5 per cent share of the national nursing home market. In 2000, 55 per cent of national aged care licences allocated went to the private sector, which had traditionally had only 27 per cent of the market.[35]

Howard's reforms were like a magnet to large corporations. 'Once you are in [the nursing home] business you have a guaranteed government income,' explained Kevin Moss, the managing director of Omega Australia Health Care. 'It's a very good business. It's been a cottage industry in Australia ... and some have milked the cow. But we are trying to get it more corporatised and professional'. AMP Life Ltd took a similar view. It bought nursing homes to lease back to operators. Between 1998 and 2000, it bought forty properties, including thirty formerly owned by Doug Moran. It made its money from the rent, with the lessee running the business and bearing the legal responsibilities.[36] Macquarie Bank found the sector 'sexy', with its listed cashbox Macquarie Capital Alliance Group paying about $125 million to the Salvation Army for fourteen homes, comprising 1400 aged care beds and 800 independent living units.[37] Privatisation was on in earnest.

Corporations wasted no time in reaping the benefits of the Howard reforms. And standards rapidly declined. In 1998, twelve months after the passage of the *Aged Care Act*, a survey of 700 aged care nurses obtained by *The Age* showed that an overwhelming majority believed that standards of care had dropped in the previous twelve months and there had been a dramatic reduction in the number of qualified staff. Shortages of basic equipment such as gloves, lifting machines and linen were common, nurses claimed.[38]

The origins of the aged care crisis

In March 2000, a scandal erupted in aged care that was so shocking it rocked the nation's conscience and its confidence in Howard's radical free-market model.

In mid-January staff of the Riverside Nursing Home, in the outer Melbourne suburb of Patterson Lakes, had been asked to bathe the elderly residents in diluted kerosene to deal with a scabies outbreak in the facility. It was a 'remedy' straight out of a dust-covered 19th-century medical textbook, grasped, it was speculated, as a cheaper alternative to buying bottles of lotion.[39] It was completely in keeping with the cost-cutting mantra driving the home's operation. However, it was a task that the night staff were, understandably, reluctant to perform, as they later told their union – the Australian Nursing Federation.

Riverside had had a troubled history. It had been owned between 1985 to 1998 by two companies, Riverside Nursing Care Pty Ltd and Illawong Retirement Living Pty Ltd.

Throughout the 1990s, residents and staff were trapped in a grim struggle away from the public eye. The home was indebted and badly managed, resources were scarce and management was indifferent or too distracted to address the problems this created. The consequences for residents were devastating. Wounds went untreated while old dressings were left leaking fluids. Some residents were left in wet incontinence pads. The food was fly-blown and sometimes infested with maggots. There was a lack of basic materials like bed linen and latex gloves. Curtains and blinds were missing from some windows, leaving elderly people exposed to the hot sun. And, disturbingly, medication was either often not administered or left in unlocked cabinets.[40]

Staff at Riverside described the home in almost Dickensian terms: 'old, damp and dirty' and run by a culture of fear.[41] And governments had been turning a blind eye to the abuses in the home. Complaints to management about the atrocious treatment in the sixty-bed facility fell on deaf ears.

Just as Howard was finalising his government's aged care reforms, the federal government withdrew funds from the home and a liquidator, Greg Andrews, was sent in to wind up Riverside. He issued the alarming finding that it was not the worst aged care home he had inspected and, 'as far as government regulations were concerned, it [Riverside] was a total failure across the board'.[42] But no one was listening.

A report undertaken by the federal Department of Aged Care in 2000 identified that standards in Riverside were not being met. Then came the kerosene bath incident. How it unfolded and the responses to it should have led government to take a deep look at the flawed free-market model.

When the instruction came for the baths to be put into operation, nurses were deeply unsettled. One nurse was dispatched to a local hospital for advice on the resurrected procedure and another phoned a drugs and poison information hotline. Their fears were confirmed: kerosene baths were inappropriate under any circumstances. Tensions then erupted in the home over the order; the night staff refused to comply with it. However, the next morning, other staff were given the order and – 'whether through ignorance … or through fear of the consequences if they refused – they complied'.[43] It took a long while to 'treat' all the fifty-seven residents – most were weak, slow, frail or sick; a few suffered from dementia. The senior nurse authorising the procedure later explained that she had confidence in the treatment because it had been used to treat head lice in the 'olden days'.[44]

Each resident was bathed in the hazardous solution for seven minutes, the fumes from which were 'so strong that the bathroom door was left open, fans were positioned to blow the smell away and staff were advised to take constant breaks'.[45]

But the ramifications were not limited to residents with skin conditions. Because the baths were not effectively cleaned or decontaminated between each treatment, other residents unaffected by the condition were adversely impacted, including those who had open wounds, catheters and feeding tubes into their abdomens. These residents 'were likely to have had the toxic kerosene solution tracking down into their bodies'.[46] Eight residents received blisters and burns. One elderly woman died two days later; the peg-tube inserted into her stomach to assist feeding was not closed when she was given the bath.[47]

On the day of the procedure, seven staff and members of the union independently contacted the complaints resolution section of the Department of Aged Care. In the following days, there was a mass walk-out of staff, and the home descended into chaos. Dumbfounded, management appeared incapable of taking decisions: 'they simply did not have the knowledge or the understanding needed to do anything about the situation'.[48]

The staff later explained that they deeply regretted their decision to bathe the residents; they would not have gone ahead if they hadn't been overworked. Nevertheless, the supervising nurse was sacked.[49]

However, it took four weeks for federal officials to visit the home. The reasons for such a lack of urgency are mystifying. It was as if the Howard government, or the Department of Aged Care, was fearful of lifting the lid on the prized free-market reforms and exposing the dark presence of its powerful backers. Eventually, the Aged Care Standards and Accreditation Agency (ACSAA), established as the aged care regulator by the Howard government as part of its 1997 reform package, conducted an audit of Riverside and released its findings in March 2000, which documented the full horror of the episode.

The Riverside scandal has lodged in the memory of many Australians as a tragic symptom of government failure in aged care. It was the catalyst that exposed the wider collapse of standards. Twenty years after the incident, the *Courier-Mail* commented that the incident so sickened Australians 'that the shame still looms large over the aged-care sector'.[50] But what was really learned from the tragedy?

Despite years of complaints about the home, and the appointment of an audit team, federal Aged Care Minister Bronwyn Bishop, known for her quick tongue and relentless ambition, was accused of evading her responsibility in dealing with the scandal. On 16 February 2000, she had announced in Parliament that a home was under inspection, but she declined to name which one and said that she'd only heard about the problems a few days before.[51] Bishop's aspirations to succeed John Howard to become the nation's first female prime minister now hung in the balance: could the political fallout be contained?

What Bishop actually knew, and when, came to dog the minister. The entire Riverside scandal blew up on the government like a fireworks display – sparks went off in all directions. It exposed flaws in the government's new reforms and it raised questions about Bishop's competence as a minister. The Labor Opposition bayed for her resignation, claiming that she had not acted swiftly enough on the problems at Riverside, but Bishop held firm. In her defence, aged care had bedevilled all recent federal governments, and Bishop was Howard's third minister in the portfolio. But the shift to corporate involvement in the sector added additional pressure on the government to hold the sector to account.

Critics argued that Bishop failed to adequately monitor aged care facilities across the sector. On becoming minister she had promised to initiate surprise visits but had not done so, and the department she oversaw was criticised for being slow to clamp down on negligence in nursing homes.[52] But this was not just a failure of a single minister, it was a failing of the government's policy of light-touch regulation. Nonetheless, it was Bishop who bore the brunt of the political attack for the Riverside scandal.

She had had access to the bad reports issued on the home under the previous Labor government, yet appeared to have taken little or no action.[53] Journalist Michael Gordon observed about the Riverside crisis: 'why didn't she [Bishop] order spot checks after problems were identified in the middle of last year?'[54]

But much of the responsibility for the debacle in aged care – and by implication in Riverside – fell on Prime Minister Howard. He didn't help Bishop's cause by claiming that there was no broader crisis in aged care: 'I don't accept it's a crisis', he told ABC TV at the height of the scandal: 'that is just a ridiculous exaggeration. It is a very sad and regrettable incident concerning one nursing home'.[55] Yet Howard should have known about persistent problems in the sector. In 1998, *The Age* had published the findings of an investigation showing that the federal government had a secret list of homes that it regarded as facilities of concern, forty-one of which were Victorian homes accommodating about 1700 people.[56] Howard also failed to disclose that the Department of Aged Care had received 4000 complaints sector-wide over the two and a half years prior to the Riverside atrocity.[57]

The press grabbed hold of the Riverside story like a dog at a bone, sensing a systemic crisis in aged care spurred by the government's 1997 reforms. Journalist Adele Horin expressed the public's indignation at the turn of events at Riverside and its wider implications for aged care. The government's reforms had, she argued, 'given proprietors the kind of freedom to spend taxpayers' money they have dreamed about for more than a decade'.[58]

In the wake of the scandal, Bishop did introduce some notable reforms. A system of accreditation was introduced whereby nursing homes were assessed against forty-four standards with funding tied to accreditation. But problems remained deeply entrenched: lack of beds, lack of funding, over-worked and underpaid aged care workers, and an accreditation system that failed to crack down on unscrupulous providers. Riverside was not an aberration; scandals became commonplace.[59] And, it must be acknowledged, Bishop was far from the only aged care minister to have been seen to have failed the sector.

In the midst of a slowly unfolding crisis in aged care, Bupa's rise came to symbolise the new rapacious corporate culture that would dominate the sector.

Bupa's corporate culture

Bupa developed a business model driven by profits above any other measure. One of Bupa's managers told the Royal Commission into Aged Care Quality and Safety that 'there had been too much emphasis at Bupa on the financial drivers of the business'.[60] The manager also stated that 'it was clear that there was a need for greater governance at the aged care board level. There may have been a lack of robust discussion at board level about the problems which the executives were aware of as a result of their roles'.[61]

In fact, the 2018 royal commission found that residents' rights and needs were continually sacrificed in favour of growth targets. However, in Bupa's idealisation of its business practices, it believed it was committed to 'provide a person-centred approach' which prioritised the residents' rights and needs.

This discrepancy between the real and the imagined is a telling insight into how poor organisational culture drove Bupa headlong into a series of outrages that the company preferred to ignore. As experts have long agreed, culture is a critical ingredient in the performance of a company, and poor culture leads to poor outcomes and, in extreme cases, can destroy an organisation. Yet, as the case studies in this book show, it is a requirement that is easily sidelined in the single-minded pursuit of profit.

Organisational culture can be a difficult issue for a corporation to address. It's usually defined as the shared norms of an organisation: 'a consensus about what things mean and how things get done'.[62] Because it is intangible and therefore hard to measure, management can dismiss its relevance and double-down on profit, which is easy to calculate. It can also fall through the cracks between the roles of management and board. Whose responsibility is it to focus on the culture of a corporation? The short answer is that both senior management and the board have a role, with the former setting the tone and the latter overseeing the compliance.[63]

Both arms of management at Bupa failed to develop a culture that balanced profits with people. But a succession of CEOs at the company both in Britain and Australia had created the fixation on the ruthless pursuit of profits. Their approach went unchallenged because, until 2019, positions on the board were given exclusively to executive directors; that is, to people invested in the existing values.

Group think has been found to be a common problem on boards where corporations have got into trouble. Boards select members who share a common corporate background. Diversity is lacking. Board members think alike and are lulled into complacency, and fail to challenge the hubris of CEOs.[64] This risk increases manifold times if the board lacks independent members. But it's not clear why Bupa would have chosen a sub-optimal governance model. Did it not want its decisions challenged?

In examining Bupa's corporate culture, the royal commission undertook an intensive case study of Bupa's South Hobart Nursing Home. During the hearings, witnesses stripped away the hollowness of Bupa's claims of providing quality care.

As part of its idealised commitment to quality care, Bupa instituted yearly audits to monitor compliance with accreditation standards. The royal commission found that in the first audit undertaken in 2014, the Bupa audit team found that the facility did not comply with six of the fourteen expected outcomes, including clinical care, medication management, pain management, nutrition and hydration. In its next audit, undertaken in 2016, the audit team found little or no improvement in standards of care. In her appearance before the royal commission, Bupa regional director Stephanie Hechenberger admitted that the 2016 audit 'demonstrated Bupa South Hobart had a record of historical non-compliance'.[65] Her honest admission showed how managers in a ruthless corporation could be forced into acting in ways that they might not have thought appropriate.

In fact, clinical staff employed at the home had tried to inform management about the poor standard of care. Dr Elizabeth Monks, contracted at the home in 2014 as a general practitioner, informed management about the 'extremely worrying' standards of care at Bupa South Hobart. But nothing changed. Dr Monks said her complaints were ignored. There was one further internal audit, in 2018, and the results were even worse than those in 2016.

While standards continued to slide at the home, the royal commission found that head office set in place a destructive mission: an edict across the company to make further cuts to staff and materials. On 9 May 2017, the director of operations of Bupa Aged Care Australia (BACA) sent an email to all Bupa general managers, regional support managers and regional directors in which he highlighted the 'need to move with urgency to improve BACA's commercial position'. While professing to maintain the quality of care, the director wanted to 'double our current monthly profit' by cutting staff and materials. He included the following exhortation to all the managers: 'If you're an 81–120 bed home, we ask you to save the equivalent of at least 2 shifts'. The culture at Bupa with regard to cost-cutting was straightforward: there 'were no sacred cows and anything's possible'.[66] The effort to further drive staff costs down was given a corporate name: Project James.[67]

Peter Rozen, counsel assisting the commission, argued that '[T]hese cost-cutting strategies were devised and driven by the finance operation at Bupa's head office, in part to respond to funding reforms introduced by the Commonwealth ... [They were] implemented enthusiastically across the Bupa Aged Care business'.[68] Some have argued that the mandate for the additional cuts to staff for under-performing came from the company's UK headquarters, even though Australia and New Zealand accounted for 40 per cent of Bupa's global revenue of $22.38 billion in 2017.[69]

The staffing cuts had a further deleterious impact on quality of care at Bupa homes, including South Hobart where Dr Monks continued to speak out. She warned superiors that the cuts were leading to 'premature deaths and hugely increased morbidity'. She was ostracised for her candidness.[70]

An anonymous former Bupa manager told *The Guardian* that 'managers of homes were under pressure to cut costs – including by restricting overtime, curbing the food bill and deploying fewer level-four trained carers on the floor because they are more expensive than inexperienced staff'.[71] Another former staff member told the paper that any sanctions imposed on Bupa had no long-term impact: 'as soon as they get their accreditation back all the things they put in place, to prevent further incidents ... they ditch them and it goes back to how it was'.[72]

Bupa's toxic culture of greed was not just based on collapsed standards and denial but also on manipulation of the true situation. Additional confirmation of their warped culture emerged through evidence to the royal commission into aged care. Bethia Wilson and Dr Penny Webster told the commission that their consultancy firm had been engaged by Bupa to provide advice after the South Hobart facility had been sanctioned in 2018. They examined eight of Bupa's facilities across the country. But upon providing their report, Bupa management asked Wilson and Webster to remove the word 'systemic' from their report relating to the South Hobart facility and replace it with 'emerging themes'. As Dr Webster told the commission: 'There was a general comment that we considered most of the failures we were seeing were systemic. Bupa didn't want people collectively to know how bad things were'. She said that they received very little feedback from Bupa on their report and came to the conclusion that their recommendations hadn't been actioned. 'Our overarching view', Webster told the commission, 'is that we would prefer euthanasia than to go and live in one of those places [that is, Bupa's aged care facilities]'.[73]

Bupa's profit-at-all costs model

Just how lucrative the aged care industry had become for corporate operators isn't easy to assess. But in 2014, the annual survey of the industry conducted by Bentley Chartered Accountants was given to the online newspaper *Crikey*. The survey covered 179 nursing homes around the country and found that net profits jumped 159 per cent in the previous year alone – from $4.14 to $10.72 per resident per day.[74]

Bupa was in the forefront of this profits bonanza. Low wages were a key component of the company's business plan, as it was across the sector. A Bupa-registered nurse with at least seven years' experience earned in 2017 $5.04 an hour less than public health sector nurses, who received $45.45 an hour. Poor pay and understaffing created further opportunities to maximise profit while continuing to undermine the quality of care.[75] Bupa's personal care workers were among the lowest paid in the sector. And understaffing was an entrenched practice at the company. Night staff at Bupa's Ballarat nursing home, for example, rostered one nurse and four carers for 144 residents. One Bupa worker explained that 'Bupa are terrible with staffing. If someone is sick, they just don't replace them'.[76] Exacerbating the problem of low wages was Bupa's underpayment of wages. Between 2014 and 2020 Bupa underpaid about 18 000 workers about $75 million, money which it did later reimburse.

Signifying its culture of profit maximisation, Bupa was also engaged in tax minimisation. In 2015–16 and across all of its operations, Bupa made $7.5 billion in revenue and yet paid only $105 million in tax, a rate of 1.4 per cent. According to a report compiled by the Tax Justice Network, Bupa's corporate structure in Australia is highly complex and such complexities comprising 'extensive related party transactions are a hallmark of aggressive tax avoidance. Related party transactions are frequently used to shift profits to jurisdictions or entities with lower tax rates or other tax benefits'.[77]

Poor pay, staff cuts and a culture of profit maximisation had a range of serious impacts on the residents of Bupa's South Hobart nursing home. Malnutrition was among the most serious. A dietitian was appalled to find more than half of the residents at the facility were malnourished or at risk of malnourishment when she was called in as a consultant in late 2018. Ngaire Hobbins said staff were in 'panic mode' when she visited the site over three days in November of that year. The malnourishment rates were 'appalling' and she found 'no evidence of a dietitian having visited the site for at least the previous year'. But the main problem was not just the quality of the food, it was lack of staff to help residents eat, as Hobbins explained:

> I went to visit one lady who was wheelchair bound, with a tray in front of her in her room which had the remains of breakfast and supper from the night before on it. Lunch was on its way from the kitchen.[78]

Slowly starving residents hadn't awakened Bupa's management to the deleterious impacts of the squeeze on staffing, at least until forced to do so. The company's focus on profit maximisation was revealed in another of its schemes: it gouged money from its elderly clients for services that it didn't provide. The Australian Competition and Consumer Commission (ACCC) conducted an investigation into the matter and found that from April 2013 to June 2018, residents at twenty of Bupa's aged care homes in New South Wales, Victoria, Queensland and Tasmania paid for a package of extra services, including hot breakfasts, dementia smart rooms, covered outdoor exercise areas, large book libraries and travel escorts for outside appointments, that it failed to supply or only partially supplied. Nonetheless, residents were charged $100 a day for the phantom extras. ACCC chair Rod Sims said that the scam 'smacks of amazing indifference'. Sims launched legal action against Bupa which resulted in the Federal Court ordering Bupa to repay $6 million to residents of the twenty nursing care homes.[79]

Why wasn't Bupa's licence revoked for these serious and repeated transgressions? The first reason was the sheer size of its operations. With over 7400 residents at its seventy-eight homes, it is questionable whether the government could revoke Bupa's accreditation without catastrophic consequences for the residents. 'They have a terrible record, but I just think that Bupa is too big to fail,' maintained Lynda Saltarelli, from advocacy group Aged Care Crisis Inc.[80] Others shared this blunt view. Paul Versteege, from the Combined Pensioner and Superannuation Association, believed that the compliance system, including sanctions and threats to revoke operating licences, was 'an absolute joke'. 'Every time the regulator slaps a notice on Bupa, it just laughs, because it knows it's too big to fail,' he said.[81]

Bupa had developed close connections to the top echelons of power. Between 2010 and 2020 the company had donated nearly half a million dollars to both the federal Liberal and Labor parties. As with other cases of corporate donations, it appeared that the company was attempting to buy favouritism. It seems extraordinary that, instead of revoking its licence as scandals engulfed the company, the Morrison government handed Bupa two new lucrative contracts: to provide health services to the more than 80 000 defence personnel, and health examinations to people applying for visas.[82]

As the case of Bupa shows, the big corporates had come to control the aged care 'industry' in their own interests. Like every major industry group, aged care had a powerful lobby group: the National Aged Care Alliance, representing the for-profit sector. Non-government aged care groups maintain that, since its formation in 2000, the Alliance has been an influential body on policy development in the sector. But the influence of corporate interests went further still. As Aged Care Crisis Inc., a lobby group critical of the for-profit model, has highlighted, 'There is a long list of industry leaders and bureaucrats that have been part of a revolving door between government and industry. Past politicians have enjoyed lucrative careers as industry leaders and managers'.[83]

Such a self-interested symbiotic relationship shaped the toxic culture in aged care. 'Talk to enough people in the system', wrote Michael Bachelard in *The Age* in 2017, 'and you repeatedly hear this comment: "It's all about the money. Operators have become a powerful lobby that fiercely resists any reduction in government subsidies or any increase in oversight"'.[84] Others agreed about the power exerted by lobby groups on behalf of the for-profit aged care sector which, according to the Australasian Centre for Corporate Responsibility, has resulted in 'the regulatory capture of our politicians, regulators and health department bureaucrats'.[85]

Successive governments were largely prepared to comply with the industry. The royal commission highlighted the twenty-year failure behind the Howard government's aged care reforms. Letting the market take care of itself, the commission argued,

> has allowed the network of providers to become more concentrated over the last decade, with a significant expansion in very large providers. There has also been a rapid expansion in home care providers, with limited scrutiny applied to their suitability.[86]

A culture of greed morphed into a toxic culture at Bupa which filtered down to all levels of the company's aged care business. Dr Elizabeth Monks highlighted this aspect of Bupa's culture to the royal commission:

> I am 100% sure there is a culture amongst [General managers] not to report problems so that they look good to the powers that be, they don't want to be red flagged … red flag means to stand out among the 72 facilities because something is wrong.[87]

The crisis in aged care – from the Riverside scandal to Bupa's serial abuses of the elderly – reveals the dearth of governance and corporate ethics in Australian business. The problems were systemic across time and across companies. Successive federal governments had a role to play in this crisis. For decades, they had failed to rein in the greed and deficient management driving a large section of the private aged care sector. Then, from 1997, the Howard government unleashed a free-market reform agenda on the public with a green light to corporate pursuit of profits. The elderly were simply sitting ducks.

The royal commission into aged care delivered a scathing report into the sector, but the royal commissioners didn't make any recommendations specifically relating to Bupa's operations or that of any other provider. But this left unaddressed whether any of the executives at Bupa or any other aged care provider should have been held directly accountable for the failures at their facilities. Companies were sanctioned, but was that enough? Should the *Corporations Act* have been invoked? As stated many times in this book, it is a requirement under the Act for corporations to act with due diligence. Was this requirement somehow inappropriate in these circumstances? Should ASIC have considered the matter?

If banking royal commissioner Kenneth Haynes could castigate ASIC for its lack of action on holding the banks to account, the same criticism applies to the regulator's failure to investigate the business models operating in corporate-run nursing homes before they caused so much damage. And the government could have changed the *Corporations Act* to make it crystal clear that corporations have responsibility to their stakeholders, in this case vulnerable people in their care. The only conclusion that can be reached is that the chase for profits is acceptable so long as specific laws aren't broken. What does that say about modern capitalism?

10
'FREE PASS TO PAEDOPHILES': WESTPAC

On 19 November 2019, on the twentieth floor of the Westpac building in Kent Street, Sydney, Lindsay Maxsted, chair of Westpac and a corporate blue-blood, was scanning a recently released document from AUSTRAC, the little-known financial regulator. It alleged the company had been involved in widespread contravention of its anti-money laundering responsibilities under the *Anti-Money Laundering and Counter-Terrorism Act 2006*. Maxsted was, he later told *The Australian,* casting an eagle eye over the details of the bank's alleged 23 million contraventions of the Act. It would be a confronting experience.

Reading through the document, Maxsted initially thought that there was no need for panic – the bank could handle AUSTRAC's call for civil penalties to be imposed. It was only when Maxsted reached page thirty-eight of the document that he said his stomach started to churn. He had come across excruciating details of twelve bank customers who had made payments that AUSTRAC linked to child trafficking, live streaming of child sexual shows and child prostitution. Maxsted said he was 'sickened' by the revelations. But he offered the further comment that they had come 'out of the blue; there was no preparation for it in my mind'.[1] Maxsted's follow-up reaction became highly contested. Had Westpac management simply wandered innocently into a scandal that quickly engulfed the company and shook the community's trust in the bank?

But, firstly, some technicalities. Created in the early 1980s, AUSTRAC (Australian Transaction Reports and Analysis Centre) is the Australian government agency responsible for detecting, deterring and disrupting criminal abuse of the financial system to protect the community from serious and organised crime. As part of a bank's licence to operate, it is required to work with AUSTRAC to help prevent criminals laundering money, financing terrorism or other criminal activity, notably child sexual abuse. Each time money goes in and out of the country, any business covered under the Act must lodge an International Funds Transfer Instruction (IFTI) report to AUSTRAC covering key details about the sender and receiver and information about what the payment is for. It's a costly and time-consuming exercise, but a vital one. Efficient management of such data is central to the task – having a centralised system that holds and tracks information built into algorithms from which 'red flags' can be raised to alert businesses about suspicious patterns of spending.[2] Banks, of course, are a key link in the detection and stopping of the nefarious activities surrounding international transfers of money.

The consequences of Westpac's dereliction of its legal obligations was graphically illustrated in the AUSTRAC court statement. One of the examples it highlighted was 'Customer 1', who transferred money to a person located in the Philippines, and who was later arrested in November 2015 for child trafficking and child exploitation involving the live streaming of child sex shows and offering children for sex. And Westpac did nothing.

In later settling the court case, Westpac admitted that it had failed to properly report more than 19.5 million IFTIs (some were regarded as too old) involving more than A$11 billion in total. The bank also did not pass on information regarding the origins of some of the IFTIs and did not communicate the source of funds to other banks in the transfer chain. Furthermore, Westpac admitted it did not keep records relating to the origin of some of these international fund transfers. It also accepted that it did not properly assess and monitor risks associated with money movements in and out of Australia, including transactions involving jurisdictions that were known to be high risk. The bank also said it had failed to carry out appropriate customer due diligence in relation to suspicious transactions associated with possible child exploitation. It was the last of these failings that understandably caused an uproar. In its statement, AUSTRAC claimed that, since at least 2013, Westpac failed to identify, mitigate and manage the risks associated with money laundering and at no stage did it introduce appropriate risk-based systems.[3]

AUSTRAC's senior management had a deep commitment to stopping the abuse of children. It was a top priority.[4] The agency was alert to Australians using money transfers to both child sex tourism and online streaming. They had identified and assisted in charging exploiters. Yet, they depended upon Australian banks, along with other institutions, reporting their international money transfers. Operating on the dark web, child porn sites are difficult to infiltrate unless the money trail can be accessed.[5]

Westpac was in a deep hole – failing to comply with its money laundering obligations, which led to it being caught out bankrolling paedophiles. Of course, it never consciously set out on such a course. Nevertheless, the company found itself in a firestorm of reputational damage. In an alarming indictment of Westpac's senior leadership, AUSTRAC had called out systemic failures in the bank's governance systems. Westpac had surpassed all the banking scandals of the past decade to become, 'the main banking horror story'.[6]

But how had the reputation of such a venerable institution been felled by a tiny regulator that most people had never even heard of? The short answer lies in Westpac's corporate culture.

At the heart of the scandal were two contradictory views – that of AUSTRAC, which alleged a major failure of governance had occurred at the bank, and that of Westpac's senior management, whose chair and CEO, Brian Hartzer, said he had never encountered the issue until he'd read their report. But as investigative journalist Adele Ferguson, who had written extensively on the failings of the big four banks,[7] pointed out: 'How the bank thought it could get away with peddling the argument that they didn't know beggars belief. The fact is they should have known'.[8]

But herein lies a familiar conundrum about corporate scandals: they are sometimes clouded in conflicting assertions from powerful people about who knew what when, and whether or not too little was done to prevent a company sinking into the quicksand of scandal. The same problem was embedded in the case of 7-Eleven (see chapter 7). At face value, AUSTRAC's assertion of governance failures at the bank is not necessarily inconsistent with claims by Hartzer and Maxsted that they knew nothing of the impending disaster contained in AUSTRAC's report. And there are reasons discussed below suggesting this might have been the case, even though it reflects poorly on the bank's culture. But, with no definitive answer to this question of what Hartzer and Maxsted knew, the focus has to be on Westpac's culture and its leadership style, which together created a scandal of the bank's own making.

The scale of Westpac's failings

It's hard to overstate the impact of AUSTRAC's forty-seven-page court statement. The mostly dry, legally worded document was laced with explosive accusations about Westpac's failings. As journalist Pamela Williams noted, it 'blew up Westpac's image as a pillar of anything'.[9] Such a challenge to the bank's standing came somewhat as a surprise. Among the big four banks, Westpac had emerged from the recently completed Royal Commission into Misconduct in the Banking, Superannuation and Financial Services Industry with a relatively clean bill of health. Established in 2017, the royal commission delivered its final report in February 2019. Revelations of fraud and cover-ups led to heads rolling at the Commonwealth Bank, the National Bank and AMP.

However, Hartzer had only been required to put in a brief appearance at the royal commission and was seen to have acquitted himself well. For someone known for his feisty character, Hartzer struck 'a surprisingly agreeable and conciliatory tone'.[10] And Maxsted wasn't required to appear at all. Consequently, Westpac missed most of the fallout from the banking royal commission. But any confidence the bank took from its light brush with the commission was horribly misplaced; it failed to see the public's loss of trust in banks and big business in general that had accompanied the commission's findings.[11]

Central to AUSTRAC's claims against Westpac was the company's choice of inferior technology to monitor international financial transactions. It had uncovered evidence about the link between Westpac's customers using its LitePay financial transaction service and child sexual abuse in several developing countries. Westpac adopted LitePay in 2016, after Brian Hartzer took over. It was a cheap way for customers to send up to $3000 to twenty-two countries around the world for low fees of between $5 and $8.[12] It chose this system over the more expensive, but more effective, SWIFT system, which had higher standards of customer identification and, therefore, had become the global gold standard for preventing financial crime via cross-border money transfers.

Westpac wanted a low-priced, efficient means of sending low-value, large-volume payments. At a time when the bank racked up over $6 billion in profits, it had opted for a cheap option to fulfil one of its crucial legal and social obligations. Its decision to adopt its LitePay platform, as opposed to the more expensive SWIFT technology, is a perfect example of the culture of focusing on short-term profits while ignoring the longer-term risks. Here was Westpac's culture in stark relief: a strong focus on profits as the overriding objective with risk and compliance as secondary issues.

In their statement, AUSTRAC said senior management at Westpac were specifically briefed on the risks relating to LitePay in June 2016. Inexplicably, Westpac continued with the same ineffective system. It acted slowly in rectifying the problems. As a consequence, AUSTRAC maintained, Westpac failed to detect activity on its customers' accounts indicative of child exploitation.[13] In fact, each name, described by AUSTRAC as Customers 1, 2, 3, 4, 5 and so on up to 12, represented the likelihood that a child had been abused, filmed and assaulted for between $80 and $200, with the payments running through Westpac accounts. And the bank had failed, allegedly, to monitor these customers until it was too late.[14]

'Customer 12', for example, had had a prior conviction for child exploitation and had been a customer of Westpac since 2016. On 3 June 2019, the customer transferred more money to the Philippines in a manner that should have aroused suspicion. However, the bank did not become aware of the conviction until three days later, on 7 June. Over the next two months, the convicted sex offender made another ten transfers, totalling $2612, to the Philippines.[15]

The Philippines was well known as a country frequented by travelling child sex offenders. And it was also well known that, over recent years, technological advances had turned the country into a global hub for live-streaming child sexual abuse.[16]

In all, the twelve customers transferred $500 000 to the Philippines alone in more than 3000 separate transfers. AUSTRAC said if Westpac had properly monitored these accounts, it could have figured out what was going on as early as 2014, arguing that the bank had ignored the red flags in its international transfer system. These involved customers with no apparent ties to the Philippines making small but regular transactions to multiple beneficiaries. Such a pattern of transactions can indicate the purchase of live-streaming child exploitation material.

After AUSTRAC launched its legal action against Westpac, a subsequent review uncovered a further 250 customers who made suspicious transactions to the Philippines, other parts of South-East Asia and Mexico. In other words, 262 customers exhibited tell-tale signs of engaging in overseas child exploitation.[17] Thus, Westpac's lax approach was exploited by paedophiles, but it could also have allowed other criminals and terrorists to transfer money out of Australia without detection.[18]

Compounding Westpac's reputational damage was the charge of hypocrisy. In the years leading up to its 'outing' over its links to child sexual abuse, the bank had tried to boost its corporate image by promoting its commitment to stop human trafficking. In 2016, the bank hosted a lavish business luncheon that promised to expose 'the truth about human trafficking'. US-based reporter and globally recognised human trafficking expert Christine Dolan was the guest speaker at the event. Since the lunch, the bank had released an annual Slavery and Human Trafficking statement touting its 'zero tolerance' for the criminal practice.[19] And Hartzer was a former chair of the charity Save The Children, which works in areas like the Philippines with the victims of child exploitation. No one could accuse Westpac of not being informed about the issue or of failing to demonstrate concern. But such displays didn't matter. Westpac championed human rights at the very same time it was ignoring them.

The scandal took a deep toll on Westpac's 33 000 staff, especially those in the financial crime prevention unit in western Sydney. After the scandal broke, Hartzer visited the unit to talk to them and later reporting that they 'were devastated because they thought they were doing what they needed to do'. Staff were left to fret over whether they had missed something; had something fallen between the cracks?[20] The big corporate machine of which they were a part had badly let them down.

Cultural failings at Westpac

Who was responsible for Westpac's failure to uphold anti-money laundering responsibilities? Lindsay Maxsted had a definite view. In July 2019, just months before the scandal broke, he expounded upon his management philosophy in an interview with the *Weekend Australian*. The chair of a board, he said, has to have a reason to be there – to have a 'a broader view of the company'. And, he argued, the overall responsibility for systemic issues sits with the board: 'systemic issues and non-financial risk areas are where people ask, "where was the board?"'[21]

In addition, Hartzer claimed that improving the bank's culture was a key priority. In 2017, he told federal Parliament's economics committee that 'the most important area of focus for us is culture – enabling a strong service ethos and behaving in ways that earn and retain trust'.[22] He also emphasised the bank's commitment to strong risk management. The reality was so very different that it appeared that Westpac had morphed into a Janus-faced institution – projecting a positive image to the world while practising a very different set of standards inside the organisation.

Amanda Wood, Westpac's former anti-money laundering reporting officer, claimed that a very different culture did exist inside the company from that of its carefully crafted corporate image. In an interview she gave after the scandal broke, she said that the upper echelons of the bank weren't initially worried about the missing millions of money transfers because they believed it was a technical breach that wouldn't attract a big fine. 'The initial response was not really about "how do we fix this?"' she said, adding: 'The response was at least partially about: "how do we get ourselves out of this? How do we deflect attention from it?"' Wood said her advice about the seriousness of the breaches wasn't well received inside the organisation, contradicting the assurances made by Hartzer that Westpac was developing a culture that encouraged openness. In a July 2018 address to the American Chamber of Commerce he gave a glowing description of the bank as a place 'where people challenge decisions or processes that don't seem right, and are empowered to fix them on the spot'.[23] Wood, however, had a different experience:

> I don't think I was blamed for what happened but I don't think they liked the fact that if they asked me I said that a civil penalty action would be likely. They were trying to tell themselves that that's not what the outcome would be. The talk around the executive table was that it was small-value, low-risk transactions.[24]

Wood portrayed the bank's culture as focused on obeying compliance laws without being committed to their underlying objectives. In others words, she said, the bank fell short of having an ethical culture.

After she raised her concerns to Westpac's senior management, Wood was told that the bank wanted a person in her position with more international experience. She knocked back a different job on the same pay with less responsibility, instead accepting a redundancy and starting up an anti-money laundering consultancy business. Her treatment looks shabby to say the least; another case of a whistleblower paying the penalty for speaking out. But that's not how Maxsted saw the issue. This was not an incident of a whistleblower being treated poorly, he told the media. Rather, the bank was 'trying to strengthen the organisation in terms of capability'.[25]

Deeper concerns about Westpac's culture

Westpac's defence of its mistaken involvement in child sexual abuse rested on two grounds. Firstly, that senior management was not aware of the bank's involvement until the release of the AUSTRAC report, and secondly, that systems failures were responsible for the oversights in detecting potential paedophiles.[26] Both claims have been challenged. As mentioned, AUSTRAC had briefed the bank about its potential failures in 2016 and, as detailed in its statement of filing, the bank had detected paedophile traffic on its LitePay system but either failed to act, or failed to act quickly.

Was Westpac simply uncaring about its wider social responsibilities? Hetty Johnston, founder of child protection advocacy group Bravehearts, thought so. She castigated the bank for showing 'an unbelievable and inhuman disinterest'.[27]

How could such a rotten culture fester in such an iconic institution? The simple answer is that the culture of Australian banking had been rotten for a long time. Hence, the shocking revelations that emanated from the banking royal commission: fees for no service; life insurance for the dead; and fee gouging on superannuation accounts. In his final report Commissioner Kenneth Hayne decried a 'sales culture', which 'measured sales and profit, but not compliance with the law and proper standards'. Too often, he wrote, banks were driven by greed – 'the pursuit of short term profit at the expense of basic standards of honesty'.[28]

A rotten banking culture had for decades produced one scandal after another. How had such egregious behaviour gone on for so long?

ASIC, the nation's corporate watchdog, continued its poor track record of reining in bad corporate behaviour. The agency admitted as much. In 2014, the agency's chair, Greg Medcraft, publicly lamented that Australia was too soft in punishing corporate offenders. Warming to his theme, Medcraft went on to explain that the nation 'was a bit of a paradise for white-collar criminals'. The answer, he said, was 'to lift the fear and suppress the greed ... the only thing that scares white-collar criminals is going to jail'. ASIC, he further explained, had discovered its crime-busting mojo and would not 'be captive to the big end of town'.[29] But commentators on economic matters doubted Medcralf's new-found determination to hold corporations to account. Economist and conservative newspaper columnist Judith Sloan argued that it wasn't overstating the case 'to claim that the regulators have been captured by the [finance] industry – or at least by the big firms ... they are supposed to control'.[30] Nonetheless, Medcraft did muscle up and won a few court judgments against the big four banks.

The banks continued to play dare-devil over their risk management processes. Macquarie University researcher Professor Elizabeth Sheedy co-authored a series of papers on how the banks managed risk culture. She and her co-authors compared three major Australian and four major Canadian banks. Sheedy wouldn't reveal whether Westpac was part of the Australian group, but her studies highlighted a statistically significant difference between the risk culture of the Canadian and Australian banks. In particular, the Australian banks showed a higher degree of 'avoidance' – indicating 'a culture where issues are ignored, swept under the carpet, downplayed'.[31]

Inside Westpac, the focus on a profit-at-all cost culture was reinforced by its troubled past. In the early 1990s, the bank was plagued by two unrelated events that helped shape its culture. One involved the bank's attempts to cover up letters showing its mishandling of foreign currency loans that left borrowers millions of dollars worse off. Journalist Max Walsh termed the scandal 'Westpac's Watergate' and said that it showed 'a culture of arrogance and an inability to acknowledge wrongdoing'.[32] Evan Jones, economist and long-time campaigner against the banks' abuse of power, argued that Westpac learned one lesson from the foreign loans affair – 'the banking sector could act with impunity'.[33]

At much the same time, Westpac was plunged into a 'near-death' experience when corporate credit losses pushed the bank to the brink of insolvency and saw it slip from being Australia's largest bank to third largest. A review team was appointed in 2018 at the request of the Australian Prudential Regulation Authority (APRA) to investigate Westpac's organisational culture. The team highlighted this fall as one of the defining features of the bank's current struggle to develop all aspects of a positive culture. The near-death experience, the review team wrote, still loomed large in the company's corporate memory. It was a 'trauma' that galvanised a comprehensive rebuilding effort.[34]

The origins of the review need noting. APRA, whose responsibility is to promote stability in financial institutions, has had a history of being a weak, secretive regulator that is too close to the industry.

Leading into the establishment of the banking royal commission, as revelations piled up about misconduct in the banks, APRA was described as a 'hear no evil, see no evil' regulator, with an 'embarrassing' record over the past decade.[35] The agency was part of the culture of light-touch financial regulation established decades ago in the Wallis report, instigated by Prime Minister John Howard. Largely funded by the finance industry it was, as Adele Ferguson has written, put in a compromising position 'as the policeman being paid by those who policed it'.[36]

In his 2018 report, Commissioner Hayne depicted APRA as a toothless tiger that had never taken any financial institution under its remit to court for misconduct.[37] In the wake of this stinging criticism, APRA requested all the major banks conduct self-assessment reviews.

Westpac's self-assessment review was undertaken by staff from the bank working with outside consultants and was completed a year before the child sex scandal erupted. It's difficult to judge just how independent the review was, especially because it didn't identify Westpac's compliance failures. Nonetheless, the review contains useful insights into how these failures occurred. Key to these insights was that, because of its organisational history, Westpac's management of non-financial risks was less 'mature' than its management of financial risks. In other words, prioritising financial risks over non-financial ones – and failing to see the connection between the two – was hardwired into the bank's culture. Vulnerable children paid the price.

Other factors played a role in Westpac's failure to sufficiently tackle non-financial risks such as child sexual abuse. The review team highlighted 'an excessive focus' on a 'good news culture' within Westpac. Directors interviewed by the review team noted 'a tendency for reporting of issues to be accompanied by "comforting" messages regarding actions underway to address issues and messages weighted towards "good news"'.[38]

This tendency towards the superficial was, in turn, exacerbated by an excessive concern about career repercussions for delivering bad news. Despite the bank's stated encouragement to staff to 'speak up', critics claimed that this goal wasn't embedded in the company's organisational culture. It's possible, therefore, that managers lower down the chain concealed information to keep their jobs. Maxsted said that AUSTRAC's meetings with the bank were only with low-level Westpac executives,[39] but he failed to explain why these executives didn't deliver the information to Hartzer, or why the board didn't ask for updates on the issue, especially after it became clear that banks faced a tougher enforcement policy from AUSTRAC.

But the failure of Westpac's leadership to monitor its anti-money laundering obligations was exacerbated by another factor. It was overburdened by a dysfunctional bureaucratic management process that focused on meetings and information, which clogged up effective analysis.[40] This is how Hartzer and Maxsted claimed that they knew nothing about the anti-money laundering breaches; they were bottled up in the bank's bureaucracy.

It was Hartzer's job as CEO to address these governance failings. But Hartzer appears not to have given a clear signal to the board to focus on its risk culture, let alone specifically on its anti-money laundering responsibilities. And the board, weighed down by paperwork, didn't bring the issue into clear focus either. Board advisory specialist Tim Boyle says there may have been an added reason why the board did not bring the issue into clear focus. Most boards, he said, in the context of the Westpac scandal, want to spend time on strategy and culture but 'have too few tools to understand the operating culture beyond what management says or the application of generic surveys'.[41] But obfuscation doesn't exonerate boards. Their job is to ask the hard questions.

Arrogance also played a part in the indifferent attitude at Westpac and the other big banks towards taking organisational risk seriously. For years the big four banks regarded AUSTRAC as 'an ignorant and toothless tiger'.[42] It's not hard to understand why. For close to a decade after its establishment in 2007, the agency adopted a softly,

softly approach, largely working with the banks to do the right thing. For their part, the big four banks had 'comprehensively ignored' their individual responsibility to monitor and report on international financial transactions.[43]

Journalist and shareholder activist Stephen Mayne believes that the arrogance of the banks led to a string of money-laundering compliance failures. Banks instinctively thought that 'the long-standing history of regulators not being tough on banks would continue'. They simply came to believe they occupied an unassailable position in Australian society. 'When you've got an oligopoly', Mayne notes, 'making $400 billion a year pre-tax, from time to time they're all going to get lazy and greedy'.[44] Westpac fell into this trap. It completely failed to recognise that it had a problem.

Westpac was one of the big four banks that failed to take notice that AUSTRAC had shifted gear from an educational to an enforcement agency with the appointment in 2014 of CEO Paul Jevtovic, who told the media: 'I will be merciless for those who recklessly or through indifference don't meet their obligations'. He held good to his word. In 2017, AUSTRAC successfully prosecuted gambling and entertainment group Tabcorp for failing to comply with its monitoring obligations, winning a then-record $45 million fine. Jevtovic used the case to issue a warning to companies that boards and senior management across all industries 'should take note' to ensure that they are fully compliant with their anti-money laundering obligations.[45]

Jevtovic's tough approach was continued by his successor, Nicole Rose, who, upon her appointment in 2017, made it clear that she was going to further ramp up surveillance across the 14 000 organisations reporting their information to AUSTRAC. Rose had an extensive background working in criminal intelligence and, along with her team, completed the overhaul of the agency into a determined crime-busting outfit. They inherited from Jevtovic a court case mounted against the Commonwealth Bank (CBA) for its 54 000 breaches of the anti-money laundering legislation which, in June 2018, had resulted in a then-record $700 million fine. It was the first time AUSTRAC had moved against a bank, and it sent 'shockwaves through the financial services sector'.[46]

During the time it took to conclude the CBA case, Rose made two things clear: firstly, that she and her team were shocked at the extent of money laundering involving organised crime, child exploitation and drug importation, and secondly, that all banks were now aware of the risks associated with money laundering.[47] Westpac either ignored or dismissed the implications of these clear signals of a tougher regulatory environment. As Amanda Wood revealed, Westpac's senior management weren't that worried about being fined.

Up until AUSTRAC moved against Westpac, the company was a merry-go-round of incompetence, arrogance and indifference about its anti-money laundering obligations and the implications this had for vulnerable children in countries like the Philippines. Maxsted, the board and Hartzer had collectively underestimated the expertise and determination of AUSTRAC. Only by finally dragging Westpac into court could it get the necessary action to protect children.

A desperate bid to hang on

On the day AUSTRAC filed its court action in November 2019, all eyes turned to Westpac's senior management. According to close associates, Hartzer was never going to give up the top job at Westpac without a fight.[48] However, his attempts to hang on only served to escalate the story. And the board, too, dug in. Consequently, the public's outrage was fanned for an entire week. Between Tuesday, 19 November, when AUSTRAC filed its court action, and Tuesday, 26 November, when the board finally announced a clean-out, Westpac consumed the news cycle. In the process, the company became a textbook example of how not to handle a corporate crisis.

In the first instance, Hartzer declined to make himself fully available to answer media questions. On the afternoon of the 19th, he held only a limited teleconference with the media. It looked to some that Hartzer was hiding behind the advice of Westpac spin doctors.[49] While adopting a contrite demeanour in the face of the crisis, he declared himself disgusted with AUSTRAC's revelations and said he would get to the bottom of them. But he denied any knowledge of the dozen of its customers specifically identified by AUSTRAC as potentially involved in child sexual abuse. 'The first time I saw them was this morning and I was like everyone else … utterly horrified,' he told the media. And while he fully endorsed the veracity of AUSTRAC's findings, he did object to the claims that senior executives and the board had been indifferent to the crime of child sexual abuse: 'We have not been indifferent', he insisted.[50]

American-born Brian Hartzer had arrived in Australia in the mid-1970s as a graduate of Princeton University where he studied European history. The articulate, well-presented young American caught the attention of ANZ's CEO, John McFarlane, who recruited Hartzer, making him head of credit cards, then elevating him to run ANZ's retail banking operations. All went swimmingly; Hartzer loved the Australian lifestyle and he was popular at the bank, where he was seen as personable and genuinely good with people.[51] But behind the affable appearance was a driven man. By his own admission, he'd spent years living on adrenaline and caffeine; 'on a bit of a roller coaster'.[52] Overlooked when the top job at ANZ fell vacant, Hartzer packed his bags and spent a few years at the Royal Bank of Scotland before returning to Australia where Westpac was keen to enlist his services, giving him the top job on the retirement of Gail Kelly in 2014. He had achieved his ambition of becoming the boss of one of the country's big four banks.[53]

Hartzer had ascended to the top of Australia's financial world without any apparent missteps or shortcomings. He had entered the rarefied world of an executive banker – a multimillion-dollar salary, generous bonuses and the trappings of wealth. Hartzer moved into a $12.75 million mansion in Sydney's exclusive Vaucluse and later added to his real estate portfolio with the purchase of a $6.8 million sandstone weekender at Pittwater.[54]

Hartzer brought into sharp focus one of the dilemmas of modern corporations. What happens to an organisation when it hands out stratospheric salaries to CEOs generated by its own relentless determination to chase profits? Amanda Wood had seen this problem up close: 'The thing that drives Westpac and the problem at the bank is the people at the top are driven by status, power and money and they don't understand that the obligations have a social purpose'.[55]

One of Hartzer's traits was clear: he had a long history of fighting back against regulators.[56] Hartzer was in the front line of the banking 'culture wars', which, in the lead-up to the appointment of the royal commission, had seen banking executives trying to fight off calls for increased regulation to improve bank culture.[57]

Despite the perilous position Hartzer was in on the afternoon of 19 November 2019, chair Lindsay Maxsted had his back. Maxsted, acknowledged as one of the most powerful boardroom operators in the country,[58] had already announced his retirement from the board, to take effect from the middle of 2020. But he was now in an invidious position: a moment he had spent his entire career trying to avoid. He was facing allegations that he had been involved in a company that had made bad decisions. Maxsted, an accountant by training, was known for his integrity, his command over company spreadsheets and a calm approach. By the time he became chair of Westpac in 2011, he was regarded as one of the most formidable corporate recovery specialists in the country. Dealing with bankruptcy and company turnarounds was his forte. He also sat on the board of BHP and chaired toll-road operator Transurban. But like other busy chairs in the cloistered world of company boards, was he overloaded?

Maxsted: The quintessential insider

Maxsted had had a stellar rise to the commanding view from Westpac's Sydney headquarters. Powering his journey from a state school in Geelong to the very top of boardroom Australia was his legendary attention to detail; 'numbers ran in Maxsted's veins'.[59] He had played a pivotal role as CEO of accountancy firm KPMG, a position he assumed in 2000. Maxsted steered the high-profile company through the most turbulent era for accountancy – when the very integrity of the accountancy industry had been exposed by the collapses of HIH and Arthur Andersen. His front-row seat at the summit of capitalism had honed some lessons on the causes of corporate collapses. In 2005, he opined that 'Very rarely do you see a business fail because of some external force. Most of the time, the person running the business at some point made very bad decisions'.[60]

As mentioned, Maxsted was well aware that risk management was a core function of the responsibilities of boards; in fact he sat on the board's risk management committee. Therefore, his reputation was also on the line. And he, too, had his own role in the banking culture wars lurking in his background. Stop bashing the banks, he cried in 2015, 'all the banks are good'.[61] 'There's no culture problem in banks,' Maxsted insisted in 2016.[62]

It wasn't surprising when, instead of showing Hartzer the door on 19 November 2019, and closely following him, as many shareholders believed he should have, Maxsted attempted to save Hartzer's career and his own reputation. Surely, as a chair with the most powerful connections at the top end of town,[63] he could calm the turbulent waters engulfing Westpac? And secure in his conviction that AUSTRAC's warning had never reached the CEO or the board, Maxsted believed that the swift removal of Hartzer would constitute 'an amazing piece of destabilisation' for the bank.[64] He was embarking on one of the highest-risk power-plays in modern Australian corporate history.

However, Maxsted's judgment was grossly misplaced. He hadn't counted on the extent of the outrage in the federal government, and in the top echelons of the industry superannuation funds. Usually the two groups were uneasy bedfellows because of the Liberal Party's dislike of the union-backed industry funds. But Maxsted had the backing of the board to hold the line. It had met in an emergency session on Thursday, 21 November, the meeting ending with the senior executive team and the board of directors intact. No heads needed to roll; the board appeared to have exonerated the company's entire senior management team.[65]

Maxsted spent Saturday, 23 November cobbling together a plan to save Hartzer and, potentially, every board member. After consulting the executive team, he signed off on an announcement to be released on Sunday setting out in more detail the bank's contrition and the plans they had developed to set things right. Although an insider familiar with the planning session told The Australian that the strategy was 'to use PR and spin to get out of this mess without doing anything to fix the problem',[66] we don't know what went on inside the meetings Maxsted arranged.

As Maxsted embarked on his survival plan, a political pile-on was mounted by the federal government, which was baying for blood at Westpac. The day after AUSTRAC's announcement, Prime Minister Scott Morrison called for Hartzer to consider his position. Home Affairs Minister Peter Dutton was cuttingly blunt. Westpac, he said, 'had given a free pass to paedophiles'. The bank's bosses had been negligent, he went on, 'and there is a price to pay for that and that price will be paid and we have been very clear about it'.[67]

Having defended the banks, unsuccessfully, against persistent calls for a royal commission, the Morrison government was in no mood to continue defending them against their ongoing bad behaviour. And smacking down Westpac helped deflect attention from the reality that the government itself had been fending off criticism that it wasn't taking anti-money laundering sufficiently seriously. For a decade,

Australia had been regarded as an outlier in enforcing regulations to prevent the country's financial system from being used for criminal activities. Under heavy lobbying from industry groups, the government had repeatedly failed to extend the law to include lawyers, accountants and real estate agents – all big players in the dark world of criminally-inspired international financial transactions.[68]

Instead of reading the political tea leaves, Maxsted stuck to his plan of getting out a more contrite Sunday statement and undertaking a round of visits on the following Monday with the big financial institutions which held large parcels of Westpac shares. His reputation as a 'peacemaker' had never faced a sterner test.[69] He went into a series of intense face-to-face meetings on 25 November in his home city of Melbourne while staying online to another Westpac board member who performed the same role in Sydney.

As Maxsted shuffled his way around meetings with AustralianSuper, UniSuper, the Australian Council of Superannuation Investors (ACSI), and Institutional Shareholder Services, some of the feedback he got was more forceful than others but, nonetheless, a glaring truth emerged: there was no coming back from 'an all compassing governance catastrophe.'[70]

The Australian Council of Superannuation Investors, a peak body for $2.2 trillion in local industry superannuation and offshore pension funds, played a critical role in forcing Westpac to take some accountability for the AUSTRAC scandal. At a meeting with chair Louise Davidson, and representatives of some of the member funds, the message was clear: unless heads rolled, Maxsted was told, the funds would use their votes to threaten the re-election of directors and even a potential second 'strike' against the remuneration report that would trigger a vote to spill the board. Davidson, in particular, played a crucial role in this meeting. She has been described as a corporate player with a social conscience who was 'leading an activist superannuation outfit with more muscle than ever before'.[71]

When Maxsted tried to put his case to Vas Kolesnikoff, executive director of Institutional Shareholder Services, that the bank had been caught unawares over the child sex allegations, he was told that such a claim was implausible. 'I find it hard to believe', Kolesnikoff said, 'someone down the chain did not report these serious issues to superiors'.[72]

The message was the same from all the finance industry executives: Hartzer's resignation would not be sufficient atonement for the failure of the bank's governance. Maxsted had to bring forward his retirement and director Ewen Crouch, the chair of the board's risk and compliance committee, would not be able to stand for re-election at Westpac's forthcoming annual general meeting (AGM).

It was a brutal message to a corporate blue-blood like Maxsted. Board membership continued to be drawn mostly from a small group of elite white males who were well networked across the big companies. Repeated calls for increased gender and ethnic diversity were only slowly being answered. But the presence of powerful industry superannuation funds meant that the clubby boardroom mentality didn't exist to the same extent in the 'super' industry.[73] 'They are not from the establishment,' explained Allan Fels, the former head of the Australian Competition and Consumer Commission, of the powerful industry-based funds. 'In the old days the directors of the big investors were from the top end of town. They were part of the club that ran companies. But the industry funds are their own people and they have room to throw their weight around.'[74]

In throwing their weight around, the major industry funds demonstrated that they took their corporate social responsibility far more seriously than did Westpac, whose instinct was just to ride out the scandal.

While Maxsted was immersed in meetings on Monday the 25th, Hartzer still seemed confident of retaining his position. Early that morning, he had gathered his senior staff in a 'top-secret meeting' where he offered an explosive insight – he didn't actually take the ethical failings of the bank all that seriously. Hartzer is alleged to have said to those present that, while they had all read about the scandal in the media, it 'was not playing out as a high street issue' because 'for people in mainstream Australia going about their daily lives, this is not a major issue'. This was not, he reassured staff, an Enron or Lehman Brothers moment: 'What I need you to do more than anything is keep this business going'. Hartzer might have thought he was simply rallying the troops and didn't think about the tone of his comments, but he then went on to say he was very 'very sorry' the bank would be forced to cancel Christmas parties because, 'unfortunately in the heightened media environment it will not look good if we have our staff whooping it up with alcohol'.

Hartzer's comments were leaked to Peter van Onselen from *The Australian* and appeared the following day – the 26th – the day after Maxsted's attempted rescue mission.[75] His comments went viral.[76] But Hartzer already knew that he would be gone by the end of the week; Maxsted had phoned him the night before. However, release of the announcement was to be held over until the following day.

As Hartzer's tone-deaf comments spilled across the pages of the national daily, he was unavailable for comment because he was in meetings with the Treasury secretaries of the New South Wales and ACT governments about the intention of their governments to remove their lucrative banking services from Westpac. It must have been an awkward meeting for Hartzer, knowing that as CEO he was about to publicly fall on his sword. But still, Hartzer pushed back, telling the Treasury officials that 'if state governments start withdrawing their deposits then this reputational crisis would turn into a full-blown banking crisis that would damage the economy'.[77] Hours later he was gone, left to ponder how his dream of heading up one of the big four banks went sour so badly. But to assuage his disappointment, he walked away with a $2.7 million payout.

Maxsted was left with the invidious task of facing shareholders at the 12 December AGM, before his scheduled early retirement was to take effect. Doubtless he anticipated an angry reaction. For several years the shareholders at the AGMs of the big four banks had vented their fury at each of the scandals engulfing the banks. And this meeting was held against a backdrop of moral outrage at the revelations of the links to child sexual abuse, and also the decline in the company's share price that accompanied the scandal: in the preceding weeks, Westpac shares had dropped 9 per cent, lopping a hefty $9 billion from the company's market capitalisation.[78]

Maxsted opened the long, torturous meeting with a twenty-three-minute apology. But it was never going to placate the majority of the 500 attendees at the meeting. When questions followed, most of which focused on AUSTRAC matters, tempers flared and verbal abuse directed at the chair spilled out over the following six hours.

Asked why the board only recently found out about the AUSTRAC failures, Maxsted 'did not or could not give a direct answer'. Matters worsened when he was asked why Brian Hartzer was able to leave with a $2.7 million payout. Maxsted tried to explain that this was part of the terms of Hartzer's contract. Those attending the meeting noted that: 'Shareholders were quite unconvinced at this explanation and continued to voice their anger. Several hecklers joined the fray to interrupt the Chair'.[79]

In fact, Maxsted was jeered relentlessly, with verbal barbs hurled like weapons:

'Asleep at the wheel!'

'Sack the board!'

'Just go, Maxsted. Just go!'[80]

One shareholder called the board 'at best incompetent and negligent, and at worst complicit and culpable'. And Westpac's culture came in for attack. At one point, Daniel Gocher from the Australasian Centre for Corporate Responsibility took the microphone and told Maxsted that Westpac's 'Speak Up' program should be renamed 'Shut Up'.

The atmosphere darkened further over opposition to the board's proposed modest cut to the short-term bonuses for executives. Nearly

65 per cent of attendees opposed the measure, potentially triggering a spill against the board. The spill was averted when Westpac managed to secure the backing of major investors. Most shareholders were satisfied that some blood had been spilled and opted for stability.

The AGM must have been a humiliating experience for Maxsted, but in his trademark unruffled manner, he took the insults on the chin and tried to stick to the script – 'Westpac is a good bank. This was a terrible mistake'. And, he too, departed to ponder his future.

In September 2020, Westpac paid a $1.3 billion civil penalty, the largest fine in Australian corporate history.[81] But as AUSTRAC only takes action against reporting entities, individual directors and managers are not named or pursued. However, the fine and the departure of Maxsted, Hartzer and Ewen Crouch ended the bloodletting – at least for the time being – in the financial services industry. The spate of decapitations of CEOs emanating from the royal commission and the Westpac scandal had sent a clear message to corporations that mainstream investors were increasingly concerned about social, governance and environmental issues; that is, they expected corporations to take their social licence seriously. Westpac – along with other corporations – had too readily dismissed such concerns as a distraction from the pursuit of profit.

In June 2020, APRA undertook an investigation into possible breaches of the *Banking Act 1959*. The investigation was mounted after APRA had pledged, in the wake of criticisms it received from the royal commission, to take a harder line when dealing with its enforcement responsibilities. Its long-standing chair, Wayne Byres, said his agency would become 'constructively tough', especially over the behavioural standards in financial institutions.[82]

On face value, an investigation was not unwarranted. Section 37C(a) of the *Banking Act* requires banks to 'conduct their business with honesty and integrity and with due skill, care, and diligence.' This section also stipulates that the bank and senior management must take steps to prevent serious matters from arising by having appropriate governance, control and risk management and appropriate procedures for identifying and mediating problems as they arise.

When closing its investigation, however, APRA's deputy chair, John Lonsdale, explained that no evidence of breaches of the *Banking Act* had been found. Pondering this conclusion, Niall Coburn from Bond University wondered: how could ASIC find that 'Westpac did not operate with due skill and care and diligence, given the 47 pages of serious misdemeanours that AUSTRAC has gone to great lengths to expose and Westpac accepted?'[83]

ASIC also declined to determine that Westpac directors had breached their duties under the *Corporations Act 2001*. In fact, it didn't take action against any of the banks following the royal commission despite Commissioner Haynes making it clear that when ASIC saw a law being broken its first response should be 'why not litigate'.[84] But ASIC maintained that this strategy had had its day.[85] ASIC was again accused of being a 'gun shy' regulator. As ABC business editor Ian Verrender commented:[86]

> Since its inception decades ago, ASIC has had the power to launch criminal and civil proceedings against big business. But for the past 15 years, it has deliberately chosen not to. Instead, it's opted for what's known as 'enforceable undertakings' – effectively a slap on the wrist and a hollow threat that it may take real action if it ever happens again.

This lack of action is not surprising. The long history of deregulation in Australia had been to prioritise the interests of business. Light-touch regulation was the presumed handmaiden of this philosophy. Ordinary Australians caught up in one of the many financial scandals that arose out of the greed that gripped the industry experienced first-hand the wilful timidity of ASIC. The 2013 Senate inquiry into ASIC's performance was inundated with both named and anonymous submissions expressing people's disgust with the organisation. One complained that the organisation protected 'their Bank Mates'. Another complained that ASIC had 'fobbed them off'. One called the agency 'unscrupulous', and another felt that company directors had no fear of it.[87]

In fact, James Wheeldon, a former lawyer at ASIC, publicly criticised the regulator during the royal commission hearings into the banks, stating that the agency had a culture of 'subservience and acquiescence' when it came to the big banks. According to him, ASIC deferred 'to the banks, lawyers and their lobbyists'. He left in disgust as a consequence.[88]

Nothing seemed to have changed.

And the lessons from the banking royal commission failed to register across sections of corporate Australia. Commissioner Haynes made it crystal clear that there were unacceptable risks associated with remuneration schemes that focused on profit and ignored a corporation's social licence to operate. He warned that excessive remuneration packages increase the likelihood that a corporation 'will engage in misconduct, or conduct that falls below what the community expects'. And corporate governance and culture were fundamental issues for business to address. Specifically, Haynes said that 'boards do not operate effectively if they do not challenge management'.[89]

Westpac itself had ignored these warnings. The community was offered a fig leaf of justice after expressing its outrage over the company's conduct. Most of the existing board members remained; the CEO walked away with a motza payout; and the bank paid a fine equivalent to about 12 per cent of its annual profit – using shareholders' money. And eventually the yapping dogs fell silent.

11

'THE CLIMATE CHANGE HOAX': NEWS CORP

At midday on 10 January 2020, an email sat in the draft email box of News Corp's commercial finance manager, Emily Townsend, like a ticking bomb. Townsend was about to detonate the company's reputation. For months as bushfires had raged with increasing ferocity across a 500-kilometre stretch of eastern Australia, Townsend had grown more worried. Each night after work she had scanned fire maps and watched the fires creep closer to her partner's much-loved property in the Hawkesbury region, north of Sydney. And each morning as she drove to work she encountered the eerie sight of the city's skyscrapers looming out of drifts of black smoke like a scene from an apocalyptic movie. As the cycle repeated itself, Townsend began to see her powerful employer with new eyes.

As a member of the finance team, Townsend had not had any say over news coverage. In fact, she was encouraged by management to keep her views to herself. But News Corp papers had been running stories claiming that the fires had not been caused by climate change. When she read one story claiming that arson was the cause of the fires, she reached a tipping point. Although Townsend had already decided to resign from News Corp, she could no longer stomach what she saw as the company's lies and denial about climate change.

From 7 January until the 10th, sleep eluded Townsend as she pondered calling out the company's misinformation on Australia's worst-ever bushfire crisis. Then, on the morning of the 10th, she typed her email in a flurry of anger and anxiety. Intending it to have maximum impact inside the company, she addressed it to everyone including the chair and every executive. As she pressed 'send' at the stroke of midday, it felt as if the bustling open-plan office around her fell silent. She sat back in her chair shaking.[1] Her email didn't hold back:

> I have been severely impacted by the coverage of News Corp publications in relation to the fires, in particular the misinformation campaign that has tried to divert attention away from the real issue, which is climate change, to rather focus on arson (including misrepresenting facts). I find it unconscionable to continue working for this company, knowing I am contributing to the spread of climate change denial and lies. The reporting I have witnessed in *The Australian, The Daily Telegraph* and *Herald Sun* is not only irresponsible, but dangerous and damaging to our communities and beautiful planet that needs us more than ever.[2]

Townsend thought she was taking a stand inside the confines of News Corp; that her email would cause a ripple throughout the company and that she'd be escorted from the building. But within minutes her email had been leaked and gone viral. In no time she was answering the phone from an excited reporter from a rival news outlet. Suddenly, Townsend was confronted by stunned looks from her colleagues; no one had ever ratted on the company as pointedly as she had just done. By the time she left the building, with bewildered colleagues looking on, her 'goodbye email' was reverberating around the globe.

News Corp's critics pounced immediately. Townsend had confirmed what many had been decrying for years: that the company had been in the vanguard of spreading climate denialism through its newspaper and television outlets and then onto social media. Although a range of powerful vested interests promulgated climate denialism, News Corps' efforts had been influential in fostering the paralysing 'climate wars', derailing Australian politics for nearly two decades.[3]

The reach of the company in Australia is breathtaking. It owns 70 per cent of the country's daily newspapers, its only pay TV network (Sky News), and the nation's most viewed website – news.com.au. Every month 16 million Australians consume news produced by News Corp.[4] It is one of the most powerful organisations in Australia, and consistently supports the Liberal Party, the fossil fuel industry and influential conservative think-tanks.[5]

How Rupert Murdoch exercises his power has generated endless speculation and fascination. He's a domineering, charismatic leader able to enforce a high level of conformity across a sprawling empire through a loyal board and an equally loyal executive group.[6] Murdoch biographer, Michael Wolff, noted in 2007 that News Corp 'has been, for most of its history, distinguished by its self-effacing, if not weak executives'.[7] In fact, in 2012, in the wake of the exposé of News Corp's involvement in the British phone hacking scandal, involving the invasion of privacy of high-profile citizens, the board gave its 'full confidence' to Murdoch. It offered this support after a parliamentary committee said that he was 'not a fit person' to head a major international company.[8]

In addition to a compliant executive, Murdoch is known to choose editors for their ability and willingness to anticipate his thinking.[9] Critics allege that Murdoch's tendency towards authoritarianism is key to understanding how he achieves broad conformity across his media empire. Specifically, Murdoch has had a tendency to phone executives at random moments – conversations driven by his brooding silences. The technique was said to generate fear, and those who rebelled against it were swiftly removed.[10] Of course, throwing their weight around had long been *de rigueur* in the playbook of press barons. In Murdoch's case, his use of charm and flattery sits alongside his capacity to intimidate.[11]

Consequently, Murdoch has been the very essence of News Corp; one biographer calling him 'the Sun King'.[12] As Rodney E Lever, a former News Corp Queensland general manager, explained: 'In offices it was all Rupert, Rupert, Rupert. Rupert said this, Rupert said that'.[13] At one level the reverence is not surprising given the boss's reputation as a deal-maker extraordinaire, but it has meant that News Corp has revolved around the personality and ideas of Murdoch.[14]

The reach of News Corp's power

The power News Corp wields in Australia is magnified still further by the global reach of the Murdoch family. Stephen Mayne, founder of the influential Australian online newspaper, *Crikey,* argues that the Murdochs have been the most powerful family in the world since at least 2001 when they helped deliver George Bush to the US presidency over Al Gore in the disputed presidential election. And their power has been built, he argues, on a particular style of right-wing commentary.[15]

Former Liberal Prime Minister Malcolm Turnbull has also offered some insight into the way in which News Corp's influence works. He knew personally how influential the views of News Corp opinion writers and Sky News presenters were on the conservative side of politics. He gave evidence to the Senate inquiry into media diversity in April 2021, established after a campaign waged by himself and former Labor Prime Minister Kevin Rudd, over their shared concerns about the power wielded by News Corp in Australia. Turnbull told the inquiry of a conversation he had had with a federal Queensland Liberal National Party MP who told him that it's 'as though my branch members are having a meeting with Alan Jones and Peta Credlin every night'. Such a heavy reliance on News Corp's outlets, Turnbull explained, 'becomes like an echo chamber and one is feeding and driving the other'.[16] Murdoch, as Turnbull put it, created 'a market for crazy.'[17]

Turnbull's view is supported by experts. Rodney Tiffen, Emeritus Professor of government and international relations at Sydney University, argues that in an increasingly fragmented and polarised media market, conservative-minded people are heavily plugged into Murdoch's 'echo chamber' where the views espoused by its stable of right-wing commentators are repeated and reinforced for its audience.[18] In turn, this audience forms a large part of the base of both the Liberal and National parties. So Murdoch's real power is to influence the right of Australian politics, which has then politicised culture wars fuelled by News Corp outlets.

So when Townsend unleashed her criticism, she ignited a long-smouldering controversy in Australian politics and society. But her critique was overshadowed just a few days later by an even more extraordinary development: the Murdoch family openly split on climate change and the company's coverage of the bushfires. In mid-January 2020, the younger of Rupert Murdoch's two sons, James, publicly attacked his own company's coverage of climate change. And the summer bushfires were a catalyst in his and his wife Kathryn's festering disagreement within the Murdoch family over the issue.[19]

In a joint statement issued in Britain, the couple slammed News Corp. They expressed frustration with the 'on-going denial' about climate change in the coverage of the bushfires 'given the obvious evidence to the contrary'.[20] Later that year, James decided to 'pull the rip cord' and resigned from the family empire because he believed that it was 'legitimising disinformation' across its news coverage.[21] The couple, known for their progressive views on many issues, had grown exasperated 'pissing inside the tent'.[22] They did so having amassed their own personal fortune out of the company's business model.

And words matter. James' choice of 'disinformation' to describe News Corp is noteworthy. Townsend had preferred 'misinformation', which refers to the use of false information, regardless of the motive. Disinformation, however, carries a more sinister sense, as it is a type of misinformation that is intentionally false and intended to deceive, usually for purposes of acquiring wealth or power.[23] In using it, James appeared to want to skewer the dynasty's reputation.

James' outburst brought to a head the rivalry between himself and his older brother, Lachlan, who is regarded as even more right wing than his father.[24] As one commentator noted, the feuding between the two – especially over climate change – was 'well known within the company but up until now it has been largely dealt with quietly, away from the public domain'.[25] James' sudden departure left Lachlan the undisputed heir apparent.

Back in Australia, the fall-out from both Townsend's and James Murdoch's verbal grenades put News Corp on the defensive, but, typically, the company held its ground. CEO Michael Miller defended the company's coverage of the bushfires

> Contrary to what some critics have argued, News Corp does not deny climate change or the gravity of its threat. However, we – as is the traditional role of a publisher – do report a variety of views and opinions on this issue and many others that are important in the public discourse on the fires.[26]

Miller had a point … of sorts. News Corp has always been able to claim plausible deniability against the charge of pushing climate denialism. Views endorsing human-caused climate change have been aired in News Corp outlets. But, as one commentator noted, while not everyone on the News Corp payroll denies climate change, it has been the preponderance of denialist voices that has mattered: 'the loudest voices, the well-paid who are put up in lights'.[27] These have carried News Corp's war on climate science. And their impact has been insidious, as climate scientist Joëlle Gergis has explained: 'Once you plant those seeds of doubt, it stops an important conversation from taking place'.[28]

And, the insidious nature of News Corp's denialism carries the appearance of a crusade. Its defence of denialist voices is meant to sound like the company's willingness to protect free speech – standing up for 'courageous dissent', as opposed to the orthodoxy of scientific knowledge. But, as experts have repeatedly pointed out, climate change is 'a matter of the physical world, that turns on science and not opinion'.[29]

The commercialisation of controversy

By the summer of 2019, climate change denial was baked into News Corp's culture. It had begun publishing sceptical editorials on the issue in 1997.[30] In the lead-up to the first global climate change summit in Kyoto that same year, a News Corp editorial revealed the basis of Murdoch's ideological fixation on the issue; that climate change cloaked the green movement's real desire 'to see capitalism stop succeeding'.[31]

In fact, as David McKnight, an expert News Corp analyst has noted, 1997 was a turning point for the coverage of climate change in Murdoch's flagship newspaper, *The Australian*: 'As the scientific evidence for climate change strengthened, the newspaper's attitude went in the opposite direction'.[32]

For News Corp, saving capitalism meant aligning itself with the fossil fuel industry. It developed extensive commercial arrangements with multinational oil and gas companies and mining peak bodies through lucrative advertising deals.[33] The fossil fuel industry spends $200 million a year in Australia,[34] making it an important market for News Corp to target.

The company hosted international conferences at which journalists and executives mixed with fossil fuel executives. News Corp has been a key part of a network of power linking mining oligarchs, peak mining bodies, conservative think-tanks, the big four banks and the Liberal Party.[35] And Murdoch had significant ownership of shares in Genie Energy, which had leaseholdings for oil and gas in the Middle East, and also sat on the company's Strategic Advisory Board.[36] Murdoch was both a media and a mining businessman.

These confluences of interests have, according to Stephen Mayne, fostered a default position for Murdoch: 'It's a straight position of the Murdoch oligarchy media enterprise to link up with other oligarchs and always back capital over regulation'. And, conversely, Mayne argues, Murdoch finds it 'impossible to ever agree with the Greens on anything'.[37]

Murdoch found ways to commercialise climate change denialism. It became an integral part of News Corp's 'Foxification' of news, a term used to define the transformative approach to cable news that occurred when News Corp created Fox News in America in 1996. Programmed around 'opinionated' and 'politicised' news commentary, objectivity in news is sacrificed for ideology, controversial opinions and heated debates. It was an adaption to cable television of the 'tabloid approach' to print news that Murdoch had also built his tabloid newspapers around. But on television, the format of partisanship, controversy and aggressive hosts was ground-breaking, making Fox News the most profitable news channel in the United States; it was a fusion of 'political mission with commercial success'.[38]

In Fox News, Murdoch found a highly successful business model based on right-wing populist approaches to 'hot button' issues such as immigration, nationalism, environmental protectionism, globalism and climate change that appealed to an older, white and conservative audience, who remain important to advertisers: 'Opinionated commentators preaching to the populist prejudices of the right, resonate with their target audience'.[39] Murdoch's temperament has been forged in tabloid journalism – both in print and screen – where, critics allege, facts come second to sensation.[40]

And Fox News highlighted this critique. Studies of its coverage of climate change from the early days of its operation have produced clear and disturbing findings. Fox News has painted a very different picture of climate change than rival cable news services CNN and MSNBC. The tone of Fox has been consistently dismissive; it has been more likely to challenge scientific consensus; and it has undermined the reality of climate change by questioning its human causes.[41] Honed by the Murdoch empire in the United States, denialist arguments and tactics were imported directly into Australia.[42]

Thus, from the mid-1990s, News Corp had politicised and commercialised its treatment of climate change around its global empire. In Australia, *The Australian* led the way, as David McKnight has argued.[43] Sky News, Fox News' Australian equivalent, would also play a crucial role.

In 2007, however, Murdoch appeared to change tack. He publicly announced that News Corp would become a carbon neutral company. 'Climate change poses clear, catastrophic threats', Murdoch declared in a speech announcing the company's new climate initiative. 'We may not agree on the extent, but we certainly can't afford the risk of inaction.' The shift is said to have been sparked by a briefing given to Murdoch executives by Al Gore, prominent climate change advocate and former US vice president. They watched his film, *An Inconvenient Truth.*[44]

Thereafter, the company basked in its achievements. It submitted yearly reports on its environmental progress to the Carbon Disclosure Project (CDP), often receiving A grades for its efforts from the organisation. Ateli Iyalla, North American managing director of the CDP, said News Corp's disclosures placed it among the world's more responsible media corporations. 'They have a strong understanding of climate issues and climate risk,' he told the media.[45]

News Corp was trying to play both sides of the climate change issue: taking steps towards being a good corporate citizen, playing its part to prevent a climate emergency it knows is getting worse, while still giving a massive media platform to people who say the emergency isn't real.[46] How is this contradiction explained? As one observer noted, it showed Murdoch at his opportunistic best as a businessman:

> Murdoch is saving tens of millions of dollars due to the green initiatives, and at the same time earning record profits by feeding his global audience rage-inducing content attacking 'out-of-control' liberals and downplaying the crisis.[47]

Moreover, by launching his climate initiative Murdoch attempted to attract progressive consumers, or at least assuage criticism from some advertisers about the company's stance on climate change. During his 2007 speech, Murdoch said the initiative was, in part, about 'how we develop relationships with advertisers', later adding: 'Our advertisers are asking us for ways to reach audiences on this issue'.[48] Some regarded News Corp's climate initiative as a brilliant strategic move.

But the double play didn't last long. Over the succeeding years, any positive public relations benefit Murdoch hoped to derive from his climate initiative was swamped by News Corp's promotion of climate denialism. According to its critics, the company went into the Australian summer bushfire season with an organisational culture steeped in climate change denialism and promoting policy inaction, as the *New York Times'* Australian correspondent found:

> a search for 'climate change' in the main Murdoch outlets mostly yields stories condemning climate protestors who demand more aggressive action from the government; editorials arguing against 'radical climate change policy'; and opinion columns emphasizing the need for more backburning to control fires – if only the left-wing greenies would allow it to happen.[49]

In fact, in 2014, Murdoch revealed that he was, after all, a climate change sceptic/denier: 'We should approach climate change with great scepticism. Climate change has been going on as long as the planet is here. There will always be a little bit of it. We can't stop it'.[50] Is this what he really believes, or was the statement just another attempt to stir the pot? As is always the case with Murdoch, clear answers are elusive.

Murdoch's prevarications on the issue of climate change didn't stop critics alleging that his news outlets were having a damaging impact on public debate on the issue. Melbourne University's Centre for Advancing Journalism, for example, argues that News Corp's coverage of climate change has, over many years, fomented 'public confusion and distrust in climate science, thereby delaying effective policy responses'. As such, the Centre has argued, this coverage 'must be considered one of the most damaging, indeed catastrophic, abuses of media power in Australian history'.[51] Stephen Mayne contends that, having relentlessly promoted climate denialism for so long, 'it's impossible for them to back track'.[52]

Responding to the summer fires

As the firefighters' version of Armageddon unfolded in Australia's 2019/2020 bushfire season, Murdoch's agenda on climate change was presented with a serious challenge. Unprecedented in duration and size, the summer fires were a continuous vision of an apocalypse from September 2019 to the end of February 2020. They were among the world's worst fires ever recorded, with over 21 per cent of the total forested area of eastern Australia burned, an area larger than Portugal. Urban areas were severely impacted. Dense, noxious smoke blanketed Sydney for days, with the air quality index more than twelve times the hazardous level in parts of the city. Parts of Canberra registered an air quality index of 4650, more than twenty-three times the hazardous level.[53] In fact, over 11 million people were affected by smoke, 3500 homes were lost and thirty-three tragically died in the fires. A further 405 deaths were due to smoke-related causes.[54]

The effects on wildlife were also catastrophic, with an estimated 1 billion animals killed and 3 billion more impacted.[55] Sixty thousand koalas were killed, injured or affected in some way by the fires, pushing the species closer to extinction.[56] In addition, the fires produced between 650 million and 1.2 billion tonnes of carbon dioxide emissions, constituting more than the total annual amount of the country's emissions.[57]

Such a calamity had long been predicted as a consequence of climate change. And according to scientists, the link in the 2019/2020 fires was indisputable. As climate scientists Barbara Norman, Peter Newman and Will Steffen have pointed out, Australia experienced its hottest year on record in 2019. The average maximum temperature was 2.09°Celsius above the baseline, breaking 2°C for the first time, and a full 0.5°Celsius higher than the previous record. They further point out that 2019 was also the driest year on record for Australia, with rainfall across the continent a 'staggering' 40 per cent below the long-term average, 'setting up the forests to burn'.[58]

In the face of the unfolding crisis, News Corp – and the fossil fuel industry generally – faced a steep challenge in holding the line on climate denialism. Public opinion in favour of action on climate change had already hardened. By the time of the bushfires, polls had consistently shown that Australians see climate change as a major threat requiring aggressive intervention.[59]

Critics claimed that News Corp framed the bulk of its coverage of the fires away from the impact of climate change. To do so, it redoubled its 'double speak' on the issue – claiming it accepted the reality of climate change while promoting voices who denied the link between the severity of the fires and climate change. Murdoch himself led the way. Just as the fires were slowly gathering their destructive strength, he stood up at the company's November 2019 annual general meeting and declared 'there are no climate deniers around' his company.[60] By now he'd zig-zagged on the issue for so many years it's as if he could devise his own reality and believe it.

The divide on the coverage of the bushfires between News Corp and the other major news media organisations was so sharp they may as well have been on different planets. The public broadcasters, the ABC and SBS, along with the non-Murdoch-owned newspapers – *The Age*, the *Sydney Morning Herald* and *The Guardian* – framed the unfolding disaster as caused by climate change.[61] So, too, did the non-Murdoch global media. The *Los Angeles Times* called the fires 'a climate change warning to its leaders – and ours', and Britain's *Independent* newspaper ran a front-page headline: 'This is what a climate crisis looks like'.[62]

However, News Corp's coverage conjured a different picture. Not only did the company downplay the link to climate change, it sought to obscure it by marginalising its coverage and promoting alternative causes. News Corp faced a blizzard of criticism for its efforts.

At the height of the bushfire crisis, Paul Barry, presenter of ABC's influential *Media Watch* program, exposed how the stable of highly paid News Corp commentators were on the climate denial warpath. He described the onslaught as 'ground hog day':

> PETA CREDLIN: So, let me deal with the issue head on. Does climate change cause these fires? No.
> – *Credlin*, Sky News, 20 January, 2020

> CHRIS KENNY: … So that's the key. The drought. And if the drought can't be blamed on climate change you can't blame the fires on climate change, especially when so many are deliberately lit.
> – *The Kenny Report*, Sky News, 11 December, 2019

> ALAN JONES: What's burning in Victoria are eucalypts … When are we going to wake up and stop using this as an excuse to justify the climate change hoax?
> – *Richo & Jones*, Sky News, 29 January, 2019[63]

Barry could have plucked any number of denialist statements from Sky News commentators. Just a few months before the fires started, presenter Rowan Dean ranted that 'Climate change is a fraudulent and dangerous cult, which has paralysed and bewitched the ruling elites, and is driven by unscrupulous and sinister interests including the power-hungry socialist mob at the UN'.[64]

And then there's Andrew Bolt, promoted by News Corp as its most widely read columnist, who also presents the *Bolt Report* on Sky

News. Bolt, who does not hold a university degree in any discipline, but who has high regard for his own opinions, has railed against climate scientists for more than a decade with all the certainty of a scientific expert. But he's little more than a clever partisan with a deadpan serious manner. According to a review of his articles, 'he regularly sources stories from climate denialist blogs and promotes the work of climate science deniers and cherry-picks data to suggest climate scientists are wrong'.[65] It's standard-fare tabloid journalism perfected in the Murdoch stable: the shift to opinionated, sensationalised, right-wing commentary designed to appeal to a designated conservative audience and masquerading as informed opinion. In the process, Murdoch's columnists and presenters were elevated to being experts in everything, and especially on critiquing climate science.

In other words, News Corp was just being consistent in its coverage of the summer bushfire disaster, which has been to 'deny, delay, deflect and create outrage'.[66] And, the views Sky News propagates on climate change are felt beyond Australia. A report published by a British think-tank, the Institute for Strategic Dialogue, found that the partisan views of its host floated around the globe with the speed of a virus: 'Despite Sky News' international brand as a credible, mainstream outlet, its Australian subsidiary has repeatedly ranked in our monitoring and is often used as a content hub for influencers, sceptics and outlets across the globe'.[67] The report noted that Sky News was having a disproportionate contribution to global climate misinformation.

Among the erroneous claims News Corp made in its coverage of the fires was that the country had seen bushfires on the scale of 2019/2020 on previous occasions. Indeed, *The Australian* repeatedly argued the summer fire disaster was no worse than those of the past.[68] Experts said otherwise. The Bureau of Meteorology noted in its *Annual Climate Statement 2019*, published on 9 January 2020, that 'The extensive and long-lived fires appear to be the largest in scale in the modern record in New South Wales, while the total area burnt appears to be the largest in a single recorded fire season for eastern Australia'.[69] And the fires still had months to burn.

The Australian took the lead in peddling another falsehood about the 2019/2020 fires. On 7 January 2020, a headline blared from the paper, 'Firebugs fuelling crisis as arson arrest toll hits 183'. It was part of a broader effort by News Corp, repeated by conservative politicians, that widespread arson, rather than climate change, was the cause of the bushfires. But the figure was grossly misleading as Fact Checker.org verified:

> The story said that 'police arrested 183 people for lighting bushfires across Queensland, NSW, Victoria, South Australia and Tasmania in the past few months.' But that total of 183 arson arrests occurred over various periods in 2019, including all of 2019 in the case of Victoria. The story also referenced statistics since Nov. 8, 2019, from only one state – New South Wales. Police there announced that they had taken 'legal action' against 183 people for bushfire-related offenses. Only 24 of those people were charged for 'alleged deliberately-lit bushfires,' according to the police; others were cautioned or charged with different offences.[70]

Without a hint of irony, the *Daily Telegraph* attacked the ABC for drawing out the link between climate change and the bushfire crisis. 'It is high time bureaucrats and politicians', the paper argued,

> stopped blaming climate change for a bushfire crisis that is very much of their own making and is putting lives at risk. The ABC were at it again last week, fawning over 23 former fire and emergency leaders who commented, outside their area of expertise, about an alleged relationship between bushfires and

> climate change. It is worth asking how the non-expert views of such people are even newsworthy.[71]

The ABC published an online article in mid-January 2020 claiming that about 1 per cent of the summer's bushfires in New South Wales were caused by arsonists, and less in Victoria. The information came from state rural fire services.[72]

However, News Corp's claim that the fires were the work of arsonists went global. It was picked up by Murdoch's London *Sun*, tweeted in America by Donald Trump Jr, repeated by Murdoch's Fox News star Sean Hannity on his website, and promoted on Fox as the real cause of the fires.[73]

And the falsehoods kept coming. News Corp columnists promoted the discredited proposition that the fires were so intense because environmentalists and the Greens had opposed hazard reduction burns where dry fuel is burned off outside bushfire season. This was an old News Corp line of attack; in 2009, columnist Miranda Devine wrote that 'it is not arsonists who should be hanging from lampposts but greenies'. The claim was repeated by the Nationals' Senator Barnaby Joyce. However, the proposition was wrong on both counts – hazard reduction hadn't decreased and the Greens fully supported the activity.[74] One commentator put paid to the claims:

> As a minor party at state and federal level, not only are the Greens not in a political position to enforce such policy, they don't hold it in the first place. As they assert in a statement via their website: 'The Australian Greens *support* hazard reduction burning (before bushfire season) to reduce the impact of bushfire when guided by the best scientific, ecological and emergency service expertise.'[75]

News Corp's bushfires coverage was picked up online. Denialist articles were fanned into social media by #ArsonEmergency, amplifying the polarisation around the issue. One study found that 'spikes in social media posts using the #ArsonEmergency hashtag ... corresponded to the publication dates of denialist opinion pieces published by News Corp'.[76] Furthermore, News Corp's particular focus on arson as a cause of the fires 'helped sustain social media disinformation by providing credibility to otherwise baseless statements and by casting doubt on official explanations'.[77]

News Corp's bushfire coverage has been extensively analysed in research studies undertaken in the wake of the fires. In their study of four News Corp publications over the summer fire season – *The Australian, Herald Sun, Daily Telegraph,* and *Courier-Mail* – Wendy Bacon and Arunn Jegan analysed 8612 items. Forty-five per cent of all items either rejected or cast doubt on consensus scientific findings on climate change. The study also separated opinion pieces and reportage and found that 65 per cent of opinion pieces promoted climate change scepticism.[78] Based on their findings the authors conclude that 'News Corp continues to produce a substantial amount of content that rejects or undermines the findings of climate science'. In fact, News Corp 'suppresses debate to the advantage of sceptics by not engaging with evidence of fact'.[79]

Another study came to broadly similar conclusions. A team led by Louis Brailsford found that nearly 60 per cent of all articles questioning the science of climate change were published by News Corp newspapers.[80] It also found that the company published the highest number of articles attributing the fires to either arson or the lack of hazard reduction burning. The research team also noted the readiness with which News Corp opinion writers attack opposing voices. Thus, Greg Mullins, a former Commissioner for Fire and Rescue New South Wales and prominent voice for action on climate change to combat bushfires, was repeatedly attacked by News Corp opinion writers, with some claiming that his involvement was improper and politically motivated; one of Murdoch's warriors said that Mullins had joined a cult and had been brainwashed.[81] Even New South Wales Coalition Environment Minister Matt Kean was attacked when he dared to say that climate change was behind the fires. The *Daily Telegraph* denigrated the legitimacy of his volunteer fire-fighting commitments with the headline 'Faux Fighter'.[82] Former Prime Minister Malcolm Turnbull described this attack as vicious, deliberate and calculated:

> It was designed to not just punish him [Kean] but also send the message – and this is how it [News Corp] operates like a Mafia gang – that, if you step out of line, you will cop some of this too. That's the threat. So other politicians look at that and they say, 'Oh, gosh, I don't want to go there.' That is the reality.[83]

Michael Mann has had experience of being a target of News Corp. The Distinguished Professor of Atmospheric Science at Penn State University was on sabbatical leave in Australia during the summer bushfire crisis. He explained to the 2021 Senate inquiry into media diversity in Australia that as horrifying as it was to watch the disaster unfold, it was 'equally horrifying to watch the pernicious efforts by the Murdoch media to sow disinformation about what is happening … to promote thoroughly discredited myths'.

The fires were, Mann said, 'the stark reification of the model predictions I have long studied'. And, for more than two decades, he explained, he had been at the centre of Murdoch-spread smear campaigns in the United States, that were 'aimed simply at discrediting me as an individual, in an effort to discredit my science and my message'.[84]

Through its coverage, News Corp was attempting to salvage its wider agenda to deny the need for change. In an editorial in *The Australian* on 9 January 2020, the paper argued as much: 'On a dry continent prone to deadly bushfires for centuries, fuel reduction through controlled burning is vital … Changes to climate change policy, however, would have no immediate impact on bushfires'.

But what was the impact of News Corp's coverage of the bushfires? Did it lessen community support for action on climate change? There's no evidence that it did. The real effect, however, is seen as continuing to stifle support for action on climate change among Liberal and National Party MPs.

In step with the Morrison government

The role that News Corp played in downplaying the link between climate change and the 2019/2020 bushfires was doubly powerful because it paralleled the Morrison government's own attempts to deflect attention from this very connection. News Corp had a strong presence inside the top echelons of the government. The Prime Minister's speechwriter at the time of the fires was a former editor and chief of staff of New Corp's *Courier-Mail*, and his press secretary was a former chief of staff of News Corp's *Daily Telegraph*.[85]

Just days before the fires started, the Prime Minister told a mining group that new laws were needed to crack down on climate activists and progressives who 'want to tell you where to live, what job you can have, what you can say and what you can think'.[86] After he returned from a holiday in Hawaii at the beginning of the crisis, for which he received a barrage of criticism, Morrison doubled down on rejecting climate change as a cause of the fires. He told Radio 2GB in February 2020 that he was 'disappointed' that the bushfires had even been linked to climate change and climate policy.[87] And the Prime Minister continued to parrot the News Corp-friendly position of resisting change: 'We don't want job-destroying, economic-destroying, economy wrecking targets and goals, which won't change the fact that there have been bushfires … in Australia'.[88]

Federal cabinet ministers queued up to reinforce the myth that the fires were a natural part of this continent's climate cycles. And, as the fires were still blazing in February 2020, the Resources Minister, Keith Pitt, promptly set about announcing that his vision for the nation was more investment in coal, gas and uranium to lift standards of living.[89] In fact, the Morrison government approved over $100 million of new coal-mining projects during the bushfire crisis. As David Ritter, CEO of Greenpeace Australia, lamented:

> As the fires reached their crescendo, records show that state MPs met with the fossil fuel industry lobbyists on a weekly basis. In Queensland, the meetings occurred on average every five days. The fossil fuel industry persisted with plans for new projects just as if nothing had happened.[90]

We can't be sure that News Corp intended its summer disinformation campaign to assist in the approval of a raft of new coal projects at the same time. But muddying the waters over the causes of the bushfires no doubt provided useful cover to the power network supporting such an expansion.

The Press Council: A toothless tiger?

How did Murdoch and News Corp get away with such a misleading campaign at the height of a national emergency and not be held to account? There are two answers to this question. Firstly, as Stephen Mayne points out, 'in Australia, the laws are very slack when it comes to inaccurate or misleading reporting'.[91] And secondly, as Malcolm Turnbull has explained, 'Murdoch is completely unaccountable'.[92] As mentioned, News Corp's concentration of media power enables it to intimidate scientists, firefighters and the occasional recalcitrant politician while the company simultaneously dominates the Press Council, a weak regulatory body based on the idea of a self-regulating media.

The idea that a near-monopolistic corporation such as News Corp could be self-regulating exposes the flaws in the concept: that the powerful can capture the regulators; that the process is neither transparent nor accountable; and that it is too soft an approach.[93]

For decades, News Corp's sensationalist tabloid business model has highlighted these weaknesses.

Not surprisingly, News Corp campaigned against regulation of the press when the idea was first raised in 1975 by the Whitlam Labor government. A comparison with Nazi Germany was made in an editorial in *The Australian*: 'Monitoring of the Press. What country are we living in? It sounds ... like Dr Goebbels' Nazi Germany'.[94] Other media players joined the pile-on. Here is not the place to examine the reluctance of much of the press to be subjected to regulation or the limitations of the model of self-regulation. Others have undertaken this task.[95]

However, one structural weakness in the operation of the Press Council must be dealt with. The Council is funded by the news media, but because News Corp owns most of the Australian news media, 60 per cent of the Press Council's funds come from News Corp. According to Matthew Ricketson, Professor of Communication at Deakin University, the Press Council 'remains vulnerable to being disproportionately influenced by its biggest funder ... News Corporation Australia'.[96] In fact, the Press Council has long been criticised as a 'toothless tiger', too beholden to its publisher members.[97]

Ricketson was a member of the 2012 Finkelstein inquiry into media regulation, which had been established on a call by Senator Bob Brown, leader of the Greens at the time, following the revelations in Britain of the phone hacking of unsuspecting high-profile identities by Murdoch's News Limited newspaper *News of the World* and which has been described as lethal in the way it destroyed people's lives.[98] In response, Brown sought a general inquiry into the newspaper industry in Australia, which was headed by Justice Ray Finkelstein. He found that the system of regulation was weak and fragmented. The inquiry's recommendation for a government-funded system of media regulation met furious opposition, led by News Corp newspapers. 'Stalinists' came the cry from the *Daily Telegraph*.[99]

Allegations that the media, and especially News Corp, received a soft gloves approach to complaints emerged in the course of the 2021 Senate inquiry into media diversity. Under questioning from Labor Senator Kim Carr, Neville Stevens, the chair of the Press Council, acknowledged that of the 540 complaints received in 2020–21 involving News Corp publications only 59 of those complaints were resolved through to a remedy.[100]

It's not surprising, therefore, that a complaint to the Press Council about News Corp's article claiming the existence of 183 arsonists during the bushfire season was not upheld by the Council: 'The council concluded that the publication took reasonable steps to ensure that the report was accurate and not misleading when reporting information from various authorities,' the adjudication stated. Yet, as Graham Readfern, environment writer at the *Guardian* reported, police in Victoria stated that there was no intelligence that suspicious activity had started two major fires there. The New South Wales Rural Fire Service also said at the time that most of the larger fires were caused by lightning.[101]

Murdoch's pivot?

In September 2021, as the nation was still grappling with the social, environmental and economic costs of its worst bushfires, Murdoch issued a statement that took his many detractors by surprise. He said that News Corp's stable of newspapers, together with Sky News, would undertake a combined two-week campaign promoting the benefits of a carbon-neutral economy in the lead-up to the COP26 climate conference in Glasgow.

On face value, it seemed that Murdoch was signalling the end to his company's decades-long toxic promotion of climate denialism. However, sceptics were quick to question the sincerity of his motives. Was the billionaire press baron just bowing to the inevitable – that his continuing promotion of denialism in the face of extreme climate events such as the 2019/2020 bushfire season was no longer tenable? There was speculation that the sheer scale of the disaster 'might be the push News Corp needs to renounce denialism and change its partisan coverage of climate change'.[102]

But if this was the case, no one in News Corp told Sky News CEO, Paul Whittaker, who, on the announcement of the carbon-neutral campaign said that 'he was not aware of any plan to limit the views of dissenting conservative commentators'.[103] As always, Murdoch could find a way to have a foot in both camps – climate denialism and climate enlightenment.

A second possible explanation exists for Murdoch's pivot: the need to clean up his company's act for advertisers worried that so many big corporations and business peak bodies had begun to embrace a net zero emissions target by 2050. After all, it's not the first time Murdoch has shifted company policy on climate change for advertisers.

While there's no evidence that advertising on Sky News came under direct threat as a consequence of News Corp's bushfire coverage, there was a recent precedent. In 2018, American Express pulled its advertising from the channel after the airing of an interview with a far-right extremist caused the sort of furore that is the lifeblood of Sky.[104] Over the next month, several prominent Sky News programs were devoid of advertising, leading Andrew Bolt to fulminate: 'This war against Sky News, this vicious campaign over the past week [is] to drive Sky News off your screens and out of business'.[105] However, the campaign petered out and big Australian corporations continued to advertise on Sky, despite some having their respective commitments for action on climate change effectively undermined by the channel.

And a third possibility existed for Murdoch's pivot – that he was trying to give cover to the Morrison government as it, too, came under pressure to adopt a net zero emissions target by 2050 in the lead-up to the conference in Glasgow. News Corp acknowledged that it briefed the Morrison government on its upcoming campaign, but both parties denied any collusion.[106] There's no way of telling, of course, whether one or a combination of these motives played into Murdoch's announcement.

But what of the campaign itself? Did it live up Murdoch's stated intention to change the company's course on its approach to climate change? Gabi Mocatta, a Research Fellow in Climate Change Communication at the University of Tasmania, has studied News Corp's two-week campaign. She found that it was infused with a dual message: the windfall opportunities to be gained from renewable energy, while simultaneously rolling out business-as-usual narratives; defending Australia's carbon emissions as small compared to other countries; promoting Australian coal as cleaner than that of other countries; promoting natural gas; and advocating carbon capture and storage.[107]

So, as some critics allege, Murdoch's so-called pivot was all a bit of a greenwash.[108] The company has continued to give licence to its stable of climate deniers and it no doubt realises that net zero by 2050 is almost meaningless if it's not enforced: gas and coal continue to be ripped out of the ground and neither of Australia's two main political parties present much of a threat to that position.

And in 2022, News Ltd was taken to task by another, ineffectual media regulator – the Australian Communications and Media Authority (ACMA). Created in 2005 by the Howard government, ACMA has as its stated aim the regulation of communications and media services in Australia so as to maximise their economic and social benefits which include content issues. Whatever this actually meant, ACMA was set up to be a 'co-regulator'; that is, it must deal with any criticisms of the media in cooperation with the broadcasting industry. In other words, like the Press Council, it was designed for industry capture, which has turned out to be the case. A 2008 Senate committee found that a common criticism of ACMA was that it didn't take effective action against broadcasters that breached industry codes of practice.[109]

So, in December 2022, when ACMA issued a report finding that Sky News had breached codes of conduct in its coverage of climate change, it caused barely a ripple of concern at Murdoch corporate headquarters. The report investigated an anonymous complainant who had detailed eighty breaches at two Sky News programs – *Outsiders Weather* and *Sceptics Ice-Age Watch*. It was later revealed that Kevin Rudd issued the complaints as part of his campaign against News Corp. Over a ten-week period in 2021, his office collated eighty suspected breaches of the Codes of Practice, which stipulates, among other things, the need for separation of fact from opinion in the operation of media outlets and accuracy in reporting. For reasons not disclosed, ACMA dismissed all but six of Rudd's complaints and found four instances of breaches.[110]

Despite the small sample, ACMA again confirmed the ideological and commercial agenda pursued by Sky News in its coverage of climate change. ACMA found that in its four breaches, Sky News had failed to separate fact from commentary; misrepresented scientific research; included experts of doubtful credibility; and engaged in inaccurate reporting. So much for Murdoch's green pivot. And the penalty for such egregious lapses on such a crucial issue? Sky was merely required to review its systems to ensure that they complied with ACMA's code, and undertake appropriate staff training.

In a statement, an unrepentant Sky News said: 'We would like to assure Sky News Australia viewers of our ongoing commitment to broad discussion and debate on the issues they care about. We will not shy away from exploring a wide range of viewpoints'.[111]

Even if News Corp moderates its coverage of future bushfire crises in Australia, few will forget what happened in the summer of 2019/2020. A news corporation with great reach and influence pursued its own commercial and ideological agenda while the country burned. Then it sought to obscure the role it had played with a faux public relations campaign and continued to issue misinformation about climate change. The fact that its coverage didn't have any demonstrable impact on overall public opinion on climate change doesn't diminish the rogue nature of the campaign. News Corp was alone among the major media outlets in its coverage and, in giving voice to extreme denialists, laid itself open to the charge that it failed to uphold the best standards of journalism. But that claim remains merely opinion; the Press Council failed to find against News Corp coverage.

And what might Murdoch have learned from the experience? Likely nothing. According to Michael Wolff, who spent nine months off and on with the man and his inner circle to write his biography, *The Man Who Owns the News: Inside the Secret World of Rupert Murdoch,* Murdoch has no interest in the past: 'He cuts himself off from it … he has no use for memory. That's a distraction'.[112]

But the past is catching up with News Corp. It increasingly appears that the influence of the company's news outlets is waning in Australia. Recent election results highlight the company's diminishing power to influence election results. Despite waging aggressive campaigns against the Anthony Albanese-led Labor Party at the May 2022 federal election and Dan Andrews' Labor government at the subsequent Victorian state election, both were triumphant at the polls. And climate action figured prominently in the federal election campaign.

Nevertheless, the company's commentators will still howl at the moon when they are moved to do so. We are all left to ponder the legacy of that constant howling.

12
INFILTRATED BY CRIMINALS: CROWN RESORTS

On 28 July 2019, the opaque operations of Crown Resorts casinos, controlled by multi-billionaire James Packer, were exposed in a *60 Minutes* report featuring a whistleblower whose only power was to speak up. Jenny Jiang was employed by Crown in China on the paltry salary of A$27 000 to persuade wealthy gamblers to travel to the company's Australian venues in potential contravention of China's strict anti-gambling laws. However, the company assured her that the work did not involve any illegal activity, only advertising luxury stays in Crown's Australian facilities in Melbourne and Perth. She was operating in a culture 'uniquely steeped in gambling'. The Chinese, especially males, have a reputation for being among the world's most enthusiastic gamblers.[1] With ballooning numbers of wealthy Chinese, Crown was part of an international scramble for their business.

Packer was the largest single shareholder in Crown through his private company, Consolidated Press Holdings. He stood down as chair of the company in August 2015, yet he remained its most influential figure and returned to the board briefly in 2017. He set the company's high-risk direction and deferential culture.

Packer was fortunate that ASIC continued to be dogged by the same old problem of shying away from going after the big boys. In the previous few years, it had become the 'problem child of regulators', beset by its own boardroom squabbling and internal power plays. It had been an underperforming regulator that had lost its way.[2]

This seemed to be the consensus inside the Morrison government.

However, with an organisation as large as Crown, it's impossible to determine how many of the company's senior management were aware of the risks Crown was exposing its staff to in China. As both the Bergin and Finkelstein inquiries found, the company suffered from a systemic failure of governance and an organisational culture that drove its fixation on the continued growth of profits. Highlighting its risky culture, all the evidence indicates that some members, at least, of Crown management knew that it was placing employees like Jiang in potential jeopardy. As far back as 2013, Crown executive Michael Chen, the president of international marketing, wrote to Crown Melbourne CEO Barry Felstead, with a copy to the executive general manager of VIP international gaming, Jason O'Connor, that the China team were 'living in constant fear of getting tapped on the shoulder … it is a risky place to be for all of our team'.[3] At the time, Chen was aware people working in China to promote foreign gambling trips had been detained for questioning by the police.[4]

But Chen also thought everything was fine. In an email sent to O'Connor and Felstead in 2013, he stated that 'We [the China-based staff] have received definitive advice that the activities that we undertake in China do NOT [Chen's capitalisation] violate any criminal laws'.[5] Although Chen didn't detail the exact nature of the legal advice, he clearly believed that he was acting within the confines of China's opaque legal system. He continued to liaise with the legal firm WilmerHale into 2015. O'Connor, too, thought that he had taken appropriate action to deal with the risks associated with Crown's operations in China. In October 2013, he managed to get Crown's Risk Register to acknowledge Chinese political action as a significant risk to the performance of Crown Melbourne. But, as the Victorian Royal Commissioner, Ray Finkelstein, noted of this development, 'No further action was taken by Crown Melbourne'.[6] With both Chen and Johnson believing that they had separately identified the risk of Crown's operation in China and taken appropriate action to mitigate them, Chen went about building a team in China to lure wealthy gamblers – high rollers – to Crown's Australian casinos, either through direct marketing or by recruiting them through so-called junket operators, who charged high commissions for delivering gamblers with money to burn.[7]

The term 'junket operator' is linked to the casino industry like an umbilical cord. Junket operators are a mix of travel agents, VIP hospitality service providers and financiers who reach out to, and pull together, groups of rich gamblers and arrange for them to fly to foreign gambling destinations. Gamblers are lured by free flights, booze, limos, ritzy accommodation and lavish meals. To get the full VIP treatment on one of Crown's three Bombardier Global Express XRS jets operating out of China, a high roller had to commit to gambling a minimum of $500 000 to $1 million.[8] Crown also extended credit to Asian high rollers and was sometimes faced with the challenging job of calling in gambling debts when they were due.[9] Thus, the risks of luring such gamblers to Australia were manifold.

The high-roller gambling market was essentially a 'dirty game'. It was principally focused around attracting 'hot' – corrupt – Chinese money. Crown had made massive investments in its Melbourne and Perth casinos to attract this clientele. But such investments were required. Super-rich Chinese were drawn to extravagantly styled facilities. The bigger the facilities, the more high rollers would come, and the more they'd lose.[10] Operating in such a dicey but potentially lucrative market, Chen was thought to be under pressure to meet high targets set by Crown to justify the outlay of considerable company resources and the gold-plating of its Perth and Melbourne casinos.[11] Added pressure came from Crown's declining share of high rollers; it was losing out to Singapore's flashy new facilities. The company was spending big to claw back market share.[12]

But Chen looked like he was equal to the challenge. The Harvard-educated Taiwanese-American had joined Crown from Las Vegas' Caesars Entertainment in February 2012. Ambitious, he had all the chutzpah of a self-promoter. According to his LinkedIn page, Chen claimed to be a 'visionary leader', a 'driver of change' and a 'fanatic about results'.[13]

With so much at stake, Crown had to assure itself that it didn't draw the attention of Chinese officials. As mentioned, legal advice had been sought that showed Crown's China staff were not contravening any Chinese anti-gambling law because their promotional activities were not being organised through an official Crown-staffed office and occurred only in small groups. Staff were operating under the radar from their own homes in order to comply with the law. Targeting China's new rich, often in the clubs that had sprung up to cater for them, the sales staff arranged dinners or karaoke nights and asked them to bring friends. Then came a direct pitch: 'Would they like to visit Melbourne?'[14]

Crown seemed to overlook the reality that it was operating in a totalitarian state where the law is a grey area. And Crown was deliberately pushing the boundaries of its operations. In an attempt to disguise the company's promotional activities from the Chinese authorities, the company had been operating an 'unofficial' office in Guangzhou since 2012, the existence of which wasn't a secret at Crown Melbourne.[15] To further foil police, the office carried no Crown signage. Macau-based Ben Lee, a consultant to international companies on Asian gambling strategies, believed Crown had insulated themselves with the myth that they were marketing a resort: 'This was the height of folly'.[16]

Not surprisingly, things began to heat up. In March 2014, Veng Anh, the Vice President of International Operations at Crown, warned O'Connor that he had inside information from China that authorities would soon begin a crackdown on foreign gambling operations in China. He suggested staff be removed for at least a month, but his advice was either overlooked or ignored.[17]

On 6 February 2015, the Chinese Ministry of Public Security announced that China was cracking down on foreign casinos seeking to recruit Chinese citizens to travel abroad for gambling. In reality, it was a public reminder of the existing hard line, but it carried the imprimatur of President Xi Jinping. The day after the announcement he 'officially declared war on the global gambling industry' and warned casinos that Chinese citizens would be gambling much less in China, neighbouring countries and in the United States.[18] The President had reason to be concerned. His true character as a ruthless dictator was only beginning to emerge, but on matters of vice, the Chinese leader was a puritan. And, money laundering networks were haemorrhaging staggering sums of money out of China.[19] Casinos have long been used to convert 'dirty' money into 'clean' money. Criminal elements simply purchase chips, play for a designated period, cash in the remainder and transfer the funds into one or more bank accounts.[20]

Jiang and her colleagues were no longer simply nervous, they were scared.[21] Some of Crown's competitors pulled their entire teams out of China. Such a cautionary approach proved to be crucial to protect employees of foreign-based casino companies.

Against this backdrop, media reports of the Crackdown on Foreign Casinos Announcement were sent to a number of Crown executives and directors,[22] which prompted inquiries from some senior executives within Crown. But an internal memo written by O'Connor, who was also a Crown director, explained why nothing was done to protect staff from arrest: 'Our challenge will be convincing our masters that they need to temper their expectations, but with the development plans ahead, talk of conservative expectations won't be well received'.[23] He implied that profits were the priority. Of course, executives like O'Connor had convinced themselves that they were sensibly managing the risks of Crown's operation in China.

In February 2015, Chen summoned dozens of Crown employees to a sales meeting at Shanghai's glittering sixty-storey Shangri-La Hotel. Chen rallied the salespeople like a military commander about to go into battle: 'Sell to the end', 'fight every battle', and 'destroy the opposition'. And, like a military commander, he kept a close eye on the field of operations. He remained nervous about the situation in China.

In March 2015, Chen received advice that it was prudent to limit travel of senior executives to China and that Crown might consider the option of moving some key employees from mainland China to Hong Kong.[24] He again told Felstead that some workers were growing increasingly concerned with the company's activities in the People's Republic. Asked why he didn't take any action on the matter, Felstead later explained that he was 'of the view that the risks were being managed adequately in China'.[25]

Felstead's confidence was soon revealed as being misplaced. In mid-2015, Chinese police questioned two Crown employees about organising illegal gambling tours. The incidents were hushed up by Crown and full details only emerged in 2019 when Crown was required to produce documents to the Victorian Commission for Gambling and Liquor Regulation.[26] Then, in October 2015, Chinese police enforced their anti-gambling crackdown by arresting thirteen Korean casino operators for luring Chinese citizens into gambling in South Korea. The arrests spurred a frenzy of activity at Crown. Again, Chen sought advice from Crown's legal team, who warned: 'do not get involved in any activities which may potentially raise money-laundering or foreign exchange evasion issues'.[27]

Knowledge of the Korean arrests reached the board but 'not as an escalation of risk but rather to advise them that there was no cause for concern because Crown's operations could be distinguished from the South Korean operations', which were more aggressively promoting gambling.[28] Crown management decreed that the company should be on high alert for similar Chinese regulatory action.[29] However, no one thought it necessary to inform the board's risk management committee.[30] Crown appeared to be stumbling headlong into a crisis.

In April 2016, Crown decided to accelerate and deepen its connections to junket operators, a move that was outlined in papers presented to the board.[31] This gave Chen the go-ahead to go for broke. He had an added incentive because President Xi's wider drive against corruption had seen a slump in gaming revenues in Macau, the only Chinese province where gambling was tolerated, driving high-stakes gamblers to overseas destinations, including Australia, to avoid Chinese authorities.[32]

Chen wrote to the sales staff urging resumption of an aggressive marketing approach. It was 'crunch time', he said, advising that they were 'far behind' the budgets and requested that they focus on their target lists to make sure that everyone is 'called and called regularly'. He also suggested that they should not take 'no' for an answer and that there was 'always a way'.

On 13 October 2016, Chen wrote again to the sales team advising that it was 'time to go after our biggest customers'.[33] Sales staff like Jiang were told to divide Chinese gamblers into four categories: minnows, catfish, guppies and whales. To 'reel them in', sales staff redoubled the offers of luxury gifts and flights to Australia. The 'whales' were extended golden opportunities to secure immigration to Australia, along with children's schooling and property investments. Jiang had never heard such terms. Nor could she have imagined the amounts of money high rollers were expected to gamble. Jiang felt as if she were peering into a parallel universe. She would later call it a 'Wow world'.[34]

Several years earlier, Crown had successfully helped lobby the Gillard Labor government to introduce an 'express visa' for big-spending Chinese gamblers, jeopardised the undermining of the government's own anti-money laundering laws.[35] Known as 'golden ticket' visas, more than 80 per cent have been granted to Chinese nationals and were criticised for being vulnerable to being rorted by organised crime.[36] Crown enlisted the services of several senior politicians to help 'smooth out' visa entry for Crown's big Chinese gamblers.[37] Packer argued that the introduction of the visas was necessary to maintain Australia's competitiveness in the tourism market, but they carried risks that were seemingly overlooked. According to long-time anti-gambling campaigner and federal independent politician Andrew Wilkie, 'high rollers would disembark from private jets at Melbourne, come with as many as 15 bags unchecked by customs, and be taken straight to the casino, where they were provided with sex workers and drugs'.[38]

After the Chinese government crackdown, Crown attempted to further deceive authorities. Packer's operational team removed the Crown logos from the casino company's collection of Global Express private jets used by Chinese high rollers because of the crackdown.[39]

Crunch-time arrived. At midnight on 13 October 2016, Jiang, who was relaxing in her Shanghai apartment watching TV with her husband, US-born businessman Jeff Sikkema, heard a heavy knock at the door accompanied by a loud male voice claiming that a water pipe had burst. Opening the door, she was confronted by four men and one woman who flashed cards confirming they were from China's secretive Ministry of Public Security. Bursting into her apartment, they immediately began interrogating Jiang: 'What was her position at Crown? Did she have any work computers at home? Or phones? Or Crown documents?'[40]

The grim-faced Ministry officials wanted to know how Crown lured high rollers to spend their millions in Australia. They believed Crown had been promoting gambling and paying sales staff large bonuses to entice high rollers to Crown's casinos. After searching her home, the security team placed the quietly spoken thirty-six-year-old under arrest and drove her to a police holding cell, where the questioning continued. That night and into the early hours of the next morning, police staged twenty raids across four cities in one of the biggest moves against the employees of a foreign company ever seen in China.

Jiang sat in a Shanghai jail cell for several months awaiting trial. She was interned with drug traffickers, prostitutes and pickpockets. She had only limited contact with her husband.

Jiang was eventually sentenced along with eighteen of her Crown colleagues.[41] Included in the nineteen was Jason O'Connor, who was swept up in one of his occasional visits to China. He is thought to have flown to Shanghai on one of Crown's corporate jets to negotiate a debt with a high roller who had left the country without paying up.[42]

O'Connor was taken to the Shanghai No. 1 Detention Centre, where inmates slept on a concrete floor. Eighteen to twenty prisoners shared a single squat toilet and one tap with only cold water.[43] Despite the harsh conditions, the sentences for the nineteen Crown employees were lighter than expected: months rather than years. Michael Chen was lucky; he was at his home in Hong Kong when the raids occurred.

When Jiang emerged, traumatised from her stint in prison, she approached Crown for compensation of $1 million. A criminal conviction is a serious impediment to rebuilding a life in China. Crown offered her $60 000 in return for her silence; she refused. In early 2019, Jiang decided to speak to *60 Minutes* in the course of its six-month investigation into Crown. The program publicised the company's involvement in money laundering through its Melbourne casino and its links to organised crime through its partnership with Chinese junket operators. According to one of the journalists working on the investigation, Jiang's testimony 'formed the backbone' of their story.[44]

In the wake of the *60 Minutes* exposé, the New South Wales Independent Liquor and Gaming Authority established an inquiry, headed by New South Wales Supreme Court Justice Patricia Bergin, who had made her name as a counsel assisting the Wood police corruption royal commission in the mid-1990s. The Bergin Inquiry was set up to investigate whether, in light of the media revelations, Crown was a fit and proper organisation to hold the licence for the yet-to-be completed Barangaroo casino, a controversial $2.2 billion project being developed by James Packer in Sydney.

The quiet capture of government

The Barangaroo project had been approved by the New South Wales government in 2012 amid allegations of political favouritism: the project wasn't put out to competitive tender; it was backed by a shadowy campaign of political insiders; and it was given an easy ride through NSW planning laws.[45] The Barangaroo saga revived Sydney's reputation as 'a corrupt old town' going back to its buccaneering convict origins and cemented in a culture where problems could be fixed with the right contacts and the right sum of money.[46] Scandal followed scandal. The Independent Commission Against Corruption was established in 1989 to stamp out this culture, only to reveal further incidents.

The Packers had largely stayed clear of any hint of corruption. James' father, Kerry, had faced allegations of links to the criminal underworld during the course of the Costigan Royal Commission into the Painters' and Dockers' Union in the mid-1980s, allegations he emphatically denied and which were dismissed. James, like his father and grandfather Sir Frank, proved adept at schmoozing politicians and, by the time he inherited the family empire, the family's power was already well established. The Packers were feared by the political class: 'you take them on at your peril', notes journalist and shareholder activist Stephen Mayne.[47]

Barangaroo was 'an extraordinary story of big money, back room lobbying and political influence'.[48] It was a high point of the model of crony capitalism that, for decades, has infiltrated Australian governments – a manifestation of the wealth of the Packer family and the mateship network that continued to facilitate their access to the corridors of power. Crown had given over $1.2 million to both major political parties in Victoria, New South Wales and Western Australia between 2010 and 2020.[49] And Packer's companies have been among the most active and well-organised lobbyists in Canberra. James had a designated regulatory affairs manager who was frequently in Canberra, meeting with senior politicians, advisors and bureaucrats and, whoever occupied the role over the years, was generally regarded as one of the best in the business.[50]

Over many years James had cultivated a high-powered personal network of influence with deep connections to state and federal governments. The board of Crown included former federal Liberal Communications Minister Helen Coonan and former senior federal bureaucrat Jane Halton. Two senior federal Labor party figures, Mark Arbib and Karl Bitar, left politics for senior positions at Crown. Foreign Affairs Minister Julie Bishop was a key guest at a 2015 New Year's Eve party at Crown, along with former Victorian Premier Jeff Kennett, who had granted the original Crown licence two decades earlier. Surveying this elite network of influence, journalist John Kehoe, writing for the *Australian Financial Review*, observed that while 'there's no suggestion the aforementioned individuals have done anything wrong ... their close ties ... to Crown or Packer himself convey an underlying message to authorities overseeing Crown that it is an upstanding company and well connected to power'.[51] Establishing such networks is common practice among big corporations, as most of the case studies in this book show. They are simply part of how elite power works all over the world.

Packer was also adept at keeping other corporate power brokers onside. In particular, he maintained close relations with media moguls Kerry Stokes, owner of Channel 7, and his old family friend, Lachlan Murdoch, who was in the process of taking control of News Corp from his father, Rupert. As *Australian Financial Review* journalist James Chessell noted, Packer was taking a strategic approach to his media mates because they exerted considerable influence over the media in Perth, Melbourne and Sydney where Crown either owned casinos and hotels or wanted to build them.[52]

Positive media coverage was crucial to realising Packer's Barangaroo casino project. The planned phallic-looking glass tower, set to rise 271 metres out of prized public land close to the heart of Sydney, was, James explained, his 'chance to do something special' and leave a legacy comparable to that of his father.[53] But, it was also seen as 'a make-or-break development for Crown Resorts'.[54] Crown needed to expand its operations into New South Wales.

Crown dragged its feet in accepting responsibility for the revelations in the *60 Minutes* program. Crown's board issued a statement absolving itself from any blame for the arrests. But, in reality, the company's reputation was sinking faster than a leaky boat.

Packer faces the music

Packer fronted the Bergin Inquiry in October 2020. It was an extraordinary occasion. It was rare for billionaires to be subjected to the public grilling that he was about to face.

James' appearance over several days – some of it relayed on the nightly news – confirmed widespread speculation that he was suffering from a mental illness. The visuals told the story. Zoomed remotely from his 108-metre 'yacht', an Italian-designed floating palace, moored somewhere in the South Pacific, James, once a physically robust figure, appeared more like an inpatient at a specialist medical facility – his face was puffed, sweating and sad. In fact, some say James was in the midst of his fourth nervous breakdown – the first occurred after the collapse of One.Tel; the second after Crown was saddled with crippling debt prior to the Global Financial Crisis in 2008; and the third in the wake of the China arrests, which coincided with Israeli investigations probing his relationship with the country's Prime Minister, Benjamin Netanyahu.

Throughout his years of emotional turmoil, the chain-smoking James Packer had battled obesity and alcohol abuse while also dealing with a chaotic personal life. Dabbling in the cult-like world of Scientology provided only temporary relief. He once admitted that he didn't handle pressure well. And now, James confirmed that he was also living with bipolar disorder, which, he claimed, had impaired his memory.[55]

Understanding how both James and his company had reached such a low point begins with the Packer family's business culture.

A dynasty of bullies

James was given an early lesson in the brutal power of the Packer family. In the early 1990s, aged in his mid-twenties, he had been tasked by Kerry to phone the office of the New South Wales Premier, John Fahey, with an intimidating message about the state's impending first casino licence: 'The old man told me to ring … this is the message. If we don't win the casino, you guys are fucked'. The licence didn't go to the Packers, and the Fahey government folded not long afterwards.[56]

Much has been written about the rise of the Packer media empire, starting with Robert, James' great-grandfather, and extended by his grandfather, the legendary Sir Frank, who owned the *Telegraph,* the *Women's Weekly* and Channel Nine. James' father Kerry inherited an already politically powerful empire, which he extended by creating additional, highly profitable, magazine titles.

Undoubtedly, the Packers were astute businessmen: innovators and risk-takers. But behind the power and the glamour lies a trail of intergenerational psychological damage. This, too, has been widely written about and doesn't need re-telling here other than to make some general points pertinent to James' career.

The Packer empire was built on an authoritarian, alpha-male culture established by Sir Frank, who ruled both the company and his family with an iron fist. He bullied, belittled and intimidated his way to wealth and power. A former heavyweight boxer, he liked to throw his weight around. He once reportedly punched his chauffeur in the ear when he 'refused to obey the boss's order to ignore a traffic cop'.[57]

But behind the façade of the Sydney mansion, the yachts and the establishment connections lay a man with a sadistic streak. As Paul Barry observes in his biography of Kerry, Sir Frank was 'a dictator and tyrant at the best of times'.[58] Kerry was on the receiving end of his father's abusive temperament, which included being lashed by his father's polo whip. Derided by Sir Frank as a 'boofhead', Kerry lived in fear of the old man's menacing presence. He was relieved when his father died.[59]

The effects on Kerry were profound. Although he developed close bonds with James and daughter Gretel, Sir Frank cast a dark shadow over his life. Kerry, the larger-than-life, authoritarian media baron, aped much of his father's personality and leadership style: outbursts of volcanic rage, abusive treatment of staff and meting out to James physical punishment and verbal dressing-downs, the latter often in public. Although possessing charm and capable of spontaneous generosity, Kerry could also echo Sir Frank's cruel streak.

Irritated one day about falling ratings at Channel Nine, Kerry pulled out a pistol and, pointing it at a hapless executive, said: '"If we don't see an improvement, son, this is how you'll end up", and clicked the trigger'.[60] Even though the gun was obviously empty, the executive went white as a sheet. And James wasn't spared his father's callous streak. Some close observers of the family believed that Kerry 'brutalised his son in a way that left deep psychological scars'.[61] One of the most obvious was James' legendary 'bouts of explosive rage'.[62]

Some of the dynamics of James' complex relationship with his father are known. Even as a teenager, James was conscious of the dynastic burden he carried.[63] And Kerry openly confided that James needed 'toughening up' in preparation for his destiny. Broadcaster and author Phillip Adams saw this process at close hand. A friend of Kerry's during the 1980s, he witnessed an induction process that appeared to be straight out of military training school:

> Jamie was the sweetest, softest, and most shy little kid but then Kerry decided that he had to toughen up Jamie and make him into James so he decided to do a very Packer thing. He brought to Australia a notorious businessman called Al 'Chainsaw' Dunlap and Dunlap was given the job of turning Jamie into James. I watched this transformation as the quiet, soft, gentle boy was turned into an iron-clad Packer and I've always felt sorry for Jamie that he had to go through that process.[64]

Al Dunlap had gained the reputation as a business guru by being a ruthless asset stripper and profits-at-all-costs devotee to revive troubled companies. His biographer, John Byrne, said that Dunlap 'sucked the very life and soul out of companies and people … and replaced those ideals with fear and intimidation'.[65] James later admiringly described Dunlap as 'emotionless'; he had shown him 'how hard you can push people'.[66] It was as if he were admiring a psychopath, which is what some thought Dunlap to be.[67]

Adams said that he met up with James several years after his tutelage at the hands of Dunlap and what came across in conversation was 'pseudo Kerry', someone who had been 'worked over and turned into something he wasn't'.[68] The transformation would prove critical to James' rise and spectacular fall as a gambling mogul.

Nevertheless, the ruthless training process has risked making James a victim, even though there is more than a hint of Stockholm syndrome in James' need to identify with his father. 'The key to James Packer', a former Packer executive explained, 'was all about proving himself to Kerry'.[69] Thus, the collapse of One.Tel came as a hammer blow to James; he found himself stereotyped as 'the idiot son – the kid who lost $375 million of Dad's money'.[70]

Yet, as a fully conditioned 'iron-clad' Packer, James absorbed key lessons about the family's corporate ethos. The most obvious was that the acquisition of immense wealth was an end in itself. Kerry established the expectation that each generation of the Packers should be wealthier than the previous one, as he himself had achieved. As journalist Geoff Kitney observed, money would be 'the ultimate scorecard' for James' life.[71] And with that came the brashness of the Packer family wealth and notoriety. As a young businessman around town, James shocked colleagues by the cavalier manner in which he parked his Mercedes, instructing any passing parking officer just to place the fine on the car windscreen, often amounting to hundreds of dollars at a time.[72]

It was a small insight into James' transformation into an entitled tycoon. In 1996, and not yet thirty years old, James commanded the attention of the powerful like an emperor holding court. This at least was the impression conveyed by one of his advisors invited to sail the Greek islands on the Packer family mega-yacht, with Victorian Liberal party powerbroker Michael Kroger also on board for the trip.[73]

But such wealth, and the power that came with it, could only be realised by being a tough, ruthless and menacing operator who was prepared to throw the weight of his company around to achieve his ends. And the Packers played by their own rules, unconstrained by conventional social norms. And why wouldn't they? Both Sir Frank and Kerry knew that when it came to displays of corporate power most politicians were fawning creatures who were especially fearful of the Packers using their media power as a weapon.[74] Kerry was said to be the second most powerful person in Australia – after the Prime Minister.[75]

Kerry demanded feudal-like loyalty from his senior employees, including from those he often terrorised. Loyalty reached its apex in executive and board appointments, which typically went to Kerry's mates.[76] And, as Paul Barry wrote, when you worked for the Packers, 'you were their property'.[77]

Kerry's elder brother Clyde, who was anointed heir apparent until he broke with his father and struck out on his own, believed that the price of dynasty is the 'billionaire syndrome', a self-destructive mindset of mega-wealth. Some psychologists think he has a point. Joel Curtis, whose practice is located in Sydney's ultra-wealthy suburb of Double Bay, observes that for many of the uber-rich, 'Nothing is ever enough'.[78] Clyde opted for wearing kaftans and a free-wheeling life in California.

Building a global casino media brand

James Packer has explained that his interest in gambling was sparked as a child accompanying his father to casinos around the world and watching him lose staggering amounts of money; he thought it must be a good business to be in. In 1999, in his first big deal as chair of Publishing and Broadcasting Ltd (PBL), the Packers' publicly listed company, James snapped up the ailing Melbourne-based Crown when it was loaded with debt and vulnerable following a run of losses to high rollers.[79] James developed Crown Melbourne into a massive gambling precinct. Successive Victorian governments – both Labor and Liberal – turned a blind eye to the growing problems at the casino. Crown was the casino 'that ate Melbourne'; a two-city block gambling mecca that became the largest single-site employer in the country. Sitting on the banks of the Yarra River in the heart of the city's thriving Southbank precinct, the complex was soon regarded as too big to fail. According to anti-gambling advocate Tim Costello, over the next twenty-five years, Crown Melbourne captured the city's cultural and political torchbearers: 'its donations have corrupted people'.[80]

In 2004, the year before his father's death, James further put his stamp on PBL's move into gambling. He urged the board to examine gaming prospects in Macau, the former Portuguese colony of which China had resumed control in 1999. China inherited a fully-fledged gambling industry developed in the 1960s by casino mogul Stanley Ho, whose glitzy gaming houses catered to property tycoons and media moguls helicoptered in to splurge eye-watering amounts of cash on high-stakes games.[81]

Criminal gangs, known as triads, moved into Macau and, as Portugal began withdrawing for a handover to China, powerful criminal groups began arm-wrestling each other for power. Lawlessness reigned. When China stepped in, it reimposed order but otherwise left the gambling industry to flourish under its 'one country, two systems' policy, hoping to channel Chinese gambling money into the one location which it controlled.

Admired for his ability to seize on business trends, James saw the opportunities provided by China's rapidly rising middle class who were flocking to Macau to gamble.[82] But he was entering a viper's nest of organised crime.

Stanley Ho continued to thrive under Chinese rule, but for years he was dogged by allegations of ongoing links with triads. In the 1980s, he was banned from having any involvement in New South Wales casinos.[83] American gaming officials maintained that Ho was an associate of known and suspected triads and had permitted organised crime to operate and thrive within his casinos. In large part this resulted from a change he introduced to the industry's business model. Rather than simply attracting high-roller gamblers, Ho allowed the junket operators to run their own private rooms, which facilitated money laundering.[84] Ho did not deny the allegations and, prophetically, warned many times during the 1980s and '90s that 'anyone involved in gaming was vulnerable to such accusations'.[85]

Packer deepened his involvement with both Macau and the Ho family when, in 2004, he met Stanley's son, Lawrence. As the sons of legendary fathers, they had much in common, which was soon formalised in a joint venture between PBL and Ho's Melco. Stanley had effectively handed the keys of his empire to his son and supposedly backed away, but sceptics believed that 'he never really left the fold'.[86]

But as lucrative as the relationship was, it was also one of the origins of James Packer's long-term implosion. Packer harboured an underlying grandiose drive to be a world-leading casino mogul. Stephen Mayne has been a long-term observer and critic of Crown and the Packer family. He describes the insatiable ambition driving James Packer's casino ambitions:

> He loved the adrenalin of the casino industry. He loved building big buildings. He oversaw the construction of $12 billion worth of casinos. He used to gloat that he'd built 3 of the world's 10 biggest buildings. He had a fetish for building the great monuments of the world … he wanted to prove that he could be the biggest casino mogul in Asia and the world.[87]

And casinos offered James the opportunity to find a space that wasn't linked to his father's exalted business reputation.

But Packer's grandiose vision also masked the reality of the casino industry and its links to the Ho family. As Mayne says, Packer 'consciously chose to go into business with a family that had mob links', although he and Lawrence paid US$900 million for a sub-licence from Wynne Resorts in order to be independent of Stanley. While charting their own course, the business model was tainted by the association with Stanely Ho. 'If Stanley Ho was so toxic', Mayne notes, 'why is he [Packer] going into business with his son?'.

With the wealth inherited from his father, and the quick sale of the old Packer media empire, James hurtled headlong into a high-risk industry, somehow distancing himself from the pitfalls. And as he did so, Mayne notes, the uniqueness of James' inheritance meant that he had no one close to him to question his actions: 'his kids are too young to influence him; his dad's dead; and his mum is hands-off'. He was like 'an unguided missile'.[88]

Packer and Ho were incredibly successful in building and operating casinos in Macau. Together they built three mega venues through their separately listed Crown Melco Resorts, and Crown itself made $2 billion in profit on selling its shares in Crown Melco. Packer then doubled down on Crown casinos in Melbourne, Perth and the planned venue at Sydney's Barangaroo.

Crown's business model

On his first day of evidence to the Bergin Inquiry, the vacant expression on James Packer's face was unmistakable. But, by the third day, the glazed look was gone. He gave explosive evidence about Crown's involvement with organised crime and his own role in facilitating it. He acknowledged that he had always understood the risk of infiltration by organised crime groups and he agreed he had been one of the 'key' driving forces in negotiating tours to Crown casinos in Australia by

Suncity, a junket tour operator. He said that in Macau around 2014, he'd once met with Alvin Chau, alleged to be a triad gang member, whom he understood to be the head of Suncity. Chau was banned from entering Australia and also alleged to have been involved in a money laundering group known as The Company.

'So your meeting was to build a business relationship with him?' counsel for the inquiry asked Packer. 'I believe that's fair,' he replied.[89] Chan is now serving a long jail sentence in China.

At its core, Packer's evidence looked like an open-and-shut case of deliberately building Crown's business model, at least in part, on facilitating money laundering. Bergin found that Packer was the real power at Crown, with the capacity to 'remotely manoeuvre' the company even after he had left the board.[90] Thus, it was Packer who forged Crown's culture: the thirst for profits; the willingness to push staff; the demands for loyalty; and a willingness to act by its own rules. It's no wonder that Bergin found that the biggest problem at Crown was its culture.

But despite his domineering presence, Packer wasn't going to accept all the blame for the implosion of the company's reputation. He claimed that several former chairmen 'let the side down' when it came to managing the risks.[91] He also lambasted the board. He told the inquiry it was the job of Crown's board to set the company's risk appetite for junkets: 'I was assured they were junkets of good repute,' he said.[92] In throwing his loyal lieutenants under a bus, Packer gave a telling reminder of the family's brutal culture – they 'are famously loyal to their royally rewarded retainers, except when they're not'.[93]

What actually happened at Crown took the Bergin Inquiry and two royal commissions held in 2021 – one in Victoria and the other in Western Australia – time to flesh out. But first we need to document how Crown's operations facilitated money laundering by triad-infiltrated junkets.

Packer's *modus operandi* for Crown was to attract high rollers through direct promotion in Asia, including, as we have seen, in

China and through direct contacts with junket syndicates, as Packer himself acknowledged. Both carried risks for Crown as the arrests in China testified. But junket operators carried an especially high risk due to the involvement of triads among some of them. And triads were masters of the dark arts of business – extortion, human trafficking, drugs and money laundering.

But how did Crown get so tangled up with the bad elements of junket operators? In essence, Macau and the Ho family were Packer's gateway to junkets and a potential El Dorado of multi-billion-dollar turnovers. Driving the connections to junkets was Packer's obsession with building the Barangaroo casino and the financial pressures involved in the project. Its future success, Bergin found, was reliant on luring high rollers from China: 'Packer intended to leverage the success of the Junket operator model in Macau and implement the same model to Crown Sydney'.[94] Risk was therefore built into the Packer casino model.

However, the entire Crown senior management – executives and board members – had convinced themselves that junket operators were an established part of the global casino industry and represented a manageable risk.[95] Fair enough, perhaps, but how does a casino operator weed out the good from the bad?[96] Drug traffickers can swap ill-gotten cash for gambling chips and deposit their 'winnings' into a bank account. In fact, on at least one occasion a junior staff member at Crown Melbourne wired $500 000 to a drug trafficker.[97]

Deepening ties with triads

The financial regulator, AUSTRAC, found that Crown formed partnerships with a number of junket groups, including: Suncity, Neptune, Chinatown, Song, Meg-Star, Tak Chun and Oriental.[98] Most had deep criminal connections.

Zezhai Song became a junket operator at Crown Melbourne in May 2009, and at Crown Perth in October 2010. On 28 May 2013,

Zezhai Song's risk rating was recorded by Crown as 'Significant'. As Bergin wrote: 'There is no issue that the Song Junket was important to Crown and Mr Packer met with Zezhai Song in 2015 in order to strengthen their business relationship'. But Song had a shadowy background in crime. He was named in a Chinese court in 2003 as running a large illegal gambling syndicate in eastern China that engaged in extortion. He was convicted and imprisoned.[99] Between December 2018 and June 2019, Crown conducted several due diligence reports on Song which identified his criminal background, but, as Bergin found, on each occasion Zezhai Song was approved as a junket operator.

Meg-Star, according to AUSTRAC, brought customers to Crown Melbourne who were 'likely to be involved in serious criminal activity', including human trafficking and sex slavery.[100] The Neptune Group had financial connections with Cheung Chi-tai, an alleged leader of the Wo Hop To triad gang, as far back as 2010.[101]

The Chinatown junket was run by Tom Zhou, who held joint Chinese–Australian citizenship and who owned a mansion in Melbourne's elite suburb of Toorak. He was treated like royalty at Melbourne Crown. Crown developed 'a deep business partnership' with Zhou,[102] paying him tens of millions of dollars to funnel Chinese gamblers to its Australian operations. There was just one problem with Zhou that Crown, the casino regulator and the federal government conveniently overlooked: he was implicated in 'foreign influence operations, extortion, money laundering and had associations with drug and human traffickers'.[103] But he was a lucrative partner. Crown's internal accounts revealed that clients of Chinatown junket gambled $1.5 billion at Crown.[104] In late 2019, he was arrested in Vanuatu and deported to China under a long-standing arrest warrant.[105]

Alvin Chau's Suncity junket also exploited the lax regulatory environment surrounding Australian casinos. His was a rags-to-riches story; he built an empire around servicing Macau's casinos while leveraging its profits into legitimate businesses. But he had deep ties to senior triad gang members. Chau also had links to elites within the Communist Party, some of whom, it was speculated, 'wanted to quietly move large amounts of money to Australia'.[106]

Suncity was given its own private gambling room at Crown Melbourne, complete with arrangements to store cash in cupboards. At one point more than $5 million was stashed at the Suncity desk. One Suncity client had been given money 'in a backpack in the valet parking area of Crown Melbourne by a Suncity junket representative who had retrieved the money from behind a curtain in the Suncity room inside Crown Melbourne'.[107] The money could have ended up anywhere.

Crown Perth also approved Chau as a junket operator in June 2010 – even though it was in possession of information that Chau had been the subject of multiple requests for information from the Victorian Police, AUSTRAC and the Australian Crime Commission, and that he had been reported by the United States government as an organised crime figure. Crown did not inform the WA Gaming and Wagering Commission that it was in possession of this information.[108] Crown was deeply involved with criminal figures and concealed information about them from authorities.

Crown even allowed some junket operators to access Crown-linked bank accounts to launder their funds, leading to junket insiders crowing that laundering money through Crown was 'easier than using a bank'.[109] Bergin found that some of these accounts 'were infiltrated and used for years by organised criminals'.[110] Crown did not report such transactions to AUSTRAC.[111] The federal government's anti-money laundering laws were being grossly compromised, and either the government didn't realise what was happening, or more likely, didn't want to know.

A self-regulating criminal enterprise

Packer, in true dynastic fashion, had managed to keep gambling regulators in both Melbourne and Perth at arms-length. The tight regulatory control over casinos that accompanied their arrival in Australia from the 1970s in order to prevent criminal activity was whittled away from the late 1990s onwards. Under a framework of 'risk-based' regulation, casino companies assumed responsibility for managing their own regulatory duties, the assumption being that companies like Crown would be motivated to comply to protect their corporate reputations. Bergin described the approach as 'naïve'.[112] But it emerged out of Australia's easily compromised political system; in this case, Crown and other casino operators lobbied for the change and found receptive state governments eagerly eyeing-off revenues from gambling.[113]

In fact, Crown 'spent a fortune on political donations and hiring powerful lobbyists to influence the decision makers'.[114] But experts have described the *laissez-faire* approach to donations in Australia as problematic in terms of accountable standards of governance.[115] And researchers into political donations have found that Crown is the beneficiary of major regulatory concessions in comparison to other gambling operators.[116]

Crown's links to governments had slowly morphed into yet another example of the dark stain of crony capitalism that has infected Australia's political system: the symbiotic relationship forged through political donations, lobbyists, the revolving door between retiring politicians and industry that advantages both sides. It is a system that neither side wants changed because of the advantages it accrues to each. Occasionally the system is busted open by a blockbuster scandal, leading to an official inquiry.

Over decades, the Packers had perfected the art of crony capitalism. In Crown's case, management responded to the relaxation of controls over casinos by overseeing a weak risk culture to allow it to tolerate and facilitate misconduct. Because of its sheer size and economic impact, Crown became virtually impossible to effectively regulate, enabling the company to capture the regulators to pursue high profits.[117]

Peter McCormack, an inspector with Victoria's gambling watchdog, was one of five retired inspectors who spoke to ABC's *Four Corners* in 2021 about their experiences of being reduced to 'Clayton's inspectors' at Crown Melbourne. He felt that 'Crown were running our office ... When they wanted things changed, things changed'.[118]

Stephen Mayne aptly summed up how compromised casino inspectors had become under the model of crony capitalism. Inspectors, he said, could have the best of intentions, but the political culture at Crown undermined their efforts. Mayne described that culture as:

> don't rock the boat, don't trouble Crown, and if the budget of the regulator is too small and if you know that Crown is going to make political donations and use all their political influence, then it's pretty tough being an inspector trying to get some significant reform and change happening at Crown.[119]

In fact, police were said to refer to Crown as The Vatican, 'an independently-governed state where the laws of Victoria and the Commonwealth do not apply'.[120]

But it wasn't just the inspectors who became compromised by the model of crony capitalism. The Victorian Commission for Gambling and Liquor Registration was similarly turning a blind eye to the nefarious activities at Crown. It had produced six reports on Crown in the years leading up to the scandal, without mention of any of the money laundering concerns raised by Bergin.[121] At Crown Perth, the inspection process had also been compromised.[122]

In its 2022 court statement to bring legal action against Crown, AUSTRAC castigated the almost complete lack of risk-based procedures, systems and controls to prevent money laundering. At Crown, it was a case of open slather for criminals to launder money:

> Junket operators may provide cash to players, in circumstances where the source of funds and the purpose for which the cash is used is unknown. There was a lack of transparency and level of anonymity created by the pooling of all players' funds and transactions under the name of the junket operator. The financial arrangements between the junket operators and junket players were not disclosed to Crown Melbourne or Crown Perth ... The features of junkets ... created layers of obscurity around the identities of persons conducting transactions through junket programs and the source and ownership of funds of customers. Money deposited with a junket account and then withdrawn with minimal gaming activity can give the funds the appearance of legitimacy.

The entire system, commented the agency, circumvented international funds transfer reporting requirements.[123] AUSTRAC found that Crown made over $1 billion in revenue from junket operations between July 2015 and June 2020.[124] The figure would be higher still, taking in the entire period of Crown's involvement.

Crown's board: Asleep at the wheel

Crown's was another in a long line of boards that had failed in their basic duties. Yet as the journey through corporate scandals in this book has shown, every dysfunctional board is dysfunctional in its own way, to paraphrase Tolstoy on unhappy families. So why did the Crown board fail? The short answer seems to be that it was meant to fail; not in an obvious way, of course, but it was structured by Packer to be compliant and ignore the risks. Packer, according to Anne Hyland at the *Australian Financial Review,* maintained that

Crown, quite apart from being a public company was 'his casino and his fortune'.[125] It was the Packer way. As Stephen Mayne notes, because Packer knew he was in 'a dodgy business', he personally hand-picked board members who would provide him 'with prestige, establishment acceptance and political influence; plus mates he could trust'.[126] The latter arrangement was supposed to be long dead. No less a figure than respected businessman David Gonski told a business lunch in 2009 that the 'era when mateship dictated whether the boardroom door was open or not was well and truly over'.[127] But not at Crown.

Not surprisingly, Packer dominated the board, even after he resigned in 2015. He created a 'cult of personality' at Crown that shaped the culture of the company. Counsel assisting the Bergin Inquiry argued that Crown 'demonstrated a culture that pursues profit-at-all-costs'.[128] It was in the Packer blood to do so.

Surrounding himself with a loyal executive team, Packer ensured that Crown reflected his corporate values. As one observer noted, Crown's problems may have started by having too many 'yes men' running the group.[129] And the core value was not just profit, but 'profit above all else', as Victorian Royal Commissioner Ray Finkelstein also noted.[130] Only one director had ever been appointed who had a background in the gaming industry, and none received any formal induction on casino regulation. An online training course became available just prior to the scandal erupting, taking just half an hour to complete.[131]

Bergin systematically examined the performance of the Crown board. She found most board members were, to a greater or lesser extent, Packer loyalists, although there were exceptions. Finkelstein also found that directors and executives were committed and steadfast in their devotion to assisting Packer achieve his business pursuits.[132] There were a few commercial hard-heads and smart operators at both board and executive levels, but, as a whole, the company's leadership team lacked expertise in the global gambling industry; there was no one who could raise red flags with Packer.[133] And, crucially, Packer set the tone that 'bad news went nowhere'.[134]

The Bergin Inquiry uncovered one indicator of how far the board fell short of high governance standards. Andrew Demetriou had been a director of Crown for four years prior to the scandal erupting. The former head of the Australian Football League displayed an alarming level of ignorance in his appearance before the inquiry: he had not had any formal training in casino regulation; he had never undertaken any money-laundering training prior to joining the Crown board; and he had only recently completed the Crown online AML training, which he agreed was not extensive. He further admitted that he lacked familiarity with junket operators, and the background briefings supplied to the board didn't give him any information on what Crown was doing in China. He didn't even have any understanding of the legal framework in China. Moreover, he spent little time thinking about the operations in China because he assumed that Chinese gamblers were travelling to Perth and Melbourne 'to enjoy the facilities that Crown has to offer'. Thus, he was 'shocked' when the China arrests occurred.

Such ignorance was disturbing enough for a board member, but Demetriou attracted a barrage of criticism when the Bergin Inquiry released an email he had written to Packer in which he said that he remained 'committed to serving the best interests of Crown and, most importantly, you'. Counsel assisting then asked the obvious question: 'Mr Demetriou, how can such a statement be consistent with you claiming to be an independent director of Crown?'[135] He was one of several directors who resigned in the wake of the Bergin Report. But he was annoyed about comments directed towards him in the report, claiming they were 'unfair and unjust'.[136]

This loyalty to Packer led to what counsel assisting the Victorian royal commission, Penny Neskovcin QC, argued was Crown's 'wilful blindness' to the risks associated with junket operators. Crown, she said, did the 'bare minimum' to monitor the risks because it was driven by 'a culture of not looking too hard'.[137] One after the other, board members deflected responsibility for doing nothing about the implosion of Crown by claiming that the risks were being handled on the ground in China.

Director Helen Coonan, who had been a board member since retiring from federal politics in 2011, was pressed under questioning to admit that it was 'unsatisfactory for boards of Australian publicly listed companies to simply say they were not informed of important matters; and boards of listed companies have an obligation to constructively challenge management and ask the hard questions'.[138]

Off scot-free

Victorian Royal Commissioner Finkelstein described Crown's operation as 'variously illegal, dishonest, unethical and exploitative'.[139] Crown was fined $80 million for its breaches of money-laundering legislation in the action brought by AUSTRAC. The agency alleged that the company failed to assess the risk of sixty high rollers who had together bet more than $70 billion since 2016.[140] But such fines are a drop in the ocean of Crown's profits.

Packer lost his licence to operate Barangaroo but sold out for $3.3 billion and recovered his health. His brighter outlook was conveyed in a front-page feature article in the *Weekend Australian,*[141] owned by his old friend Lachlan Murdoch. Whether or not he's happier because he's finally freed himself from his father's malevolent shadow would probably test a psychoanalyst. Many think that he tarnished, if not destroyed, his own reputation. No doubt a few billion helps ease the pain.

A clutch of executives and board members resigned in the wake of the Bergin Inquiry. Yet they walked away with handsome payouts, collectively in the millions of dollars, such that, arguably, they suffered no financial penalty. Three of the top executives received nearly $10 million in payouts. All were free to go and run other companies, despite their failings at Crown. Helen Coonan, who managed to escape Bergin's wrath, stayed on to chair Crown on a salary of $2.5 million.

Crown kept its Melbourne licence. Despite the alarming findings of the royal commission, Commissioner Finkelstein recommended the company be given a two-year grace period under the control of a 'special manager' to correct its 'catalogue of wrongdoing'.[142]

To compound the lack of real accountability for Crown's failure of governance, ASIC refused to mount a case that directors breached their legal duties. ASIC later explained that it did not have sufficient evidence to build an actionable case against them. But how is it that AUSTRAC successfully prosecuted Crown and ASIC didn't even try? And there are the three damning reports – the Bergin Inquiry and the two royal commissions – all pointing to the same failures of governance.

In December 2022, ASIC brushed aside its detractors with a surprise announcement that it was taking legal action against eleven directors and executives at Star Entertainment for significant money-laundering and criminal risk failures at its casinos (briefly mentioned in the Introduction to this book). This decision makes the inaction against Crown, for very similar breaches, even harder to fathom.

The capitulation by the regulator caused public outrage and a revival of the claim that it is 'weak and/or captive to the big end of town'.[143] As experts in governance warned at the time, only by naming and shaming board members and executives who have engaged in failures of governance would they as a group sit up and take notice.[144]

Legalising casinos is no doubt preferable to the old days of underground venues that entrap police into corruption. But Crown, aided and abetted by governments, turned its venues into an even greater evil. It imperilled the nation's anti-money laundering system, undermined its core values and presented a risk to its national security. And, the stark reality about casinos everywhere is that the business model is based around construction of glitzy-tower venues and over-the-top service to attract high rollers. And high rollers expose casinos to organised crime. It's a vicious circle.

13

VANDALS: RIO TINTO AND JUUKAN GORGE CAVES

On 25 May 2020, Western Australian Aboriginal Affairs Minister Ben Wyatt was sitting in his Perth office at the height of the COVID-19 pandemic mulling over a cabinet meeting set to consider the ongoing drastic decision by the McGowan Labor government to keep the WA border shut. All of a sudden, a staff member rushed in bearing disturbing news that quickly reverberated around the world. Twenty-four hours earlier – and over 1000 kilometres to the north in the Pilbara region – mining giant Rio Tinto had ignited 66 tonnes of high explosives to blow up the 46 000 year-old Juukan Gorge caves on its Brockman 4 mine site. This was the traditional lands of the Puutu Kunti Kurrama people and the Pinikura people,[1] and the caves contained a treasure trove of cultural artifacts. But Wyatt had known nothing about the impending disaster. As he later explained: 'There wasn't any lead up in terms of my office'.[2]

At forty-six, Wyatt already had an accomplished career. A former lawyer, he was a graduate of the London School of Economics and the Royal Military College Duntroon. Highly intelligent and politically smart, Wyatt is well grounded, with an outgoing and inquiring manner.[3] He had broken new ground to become the state's first Indigenous Treasurer, in addition to being Aboriginal Affairs Minister.[4] He'd been in these two demanding roles since Labor's 2017 landslide victory.

Wyatt was thus on the front line of a complex balancing act.

On the one hand he had to protect and promote Indigenous interests generally, and specifically in the mining industry, which was a leading employer of Indigenous people in Western Australia. At the same time, he had to protect the revenue flows from the mining industry into state coffers. Historically, mining industry interests had prevailed. The destruction of Juukan caves was a shocking reminder of this history.

Juukan Gorge is a culturally significant place for the Puutu Kunti Kurrama people and the Pinikura people. The caves contained flaked stone artifacts, middens and faunal remains, and are especially significant because they reveal that the caves had been in continual use by Indigenous people for 46 000 years.

The caves are also where the spirits of the deceased have gone to rest for millennia. Burchell Hayes, a proud member of the Puutu Kunti Kurrama people and the Pinikura people, told a federal parliamentary inquiry, led by a joint standing committee, held in the wake of the destruction, headed by Liberal MP Warren Entsch, that Juukan Gorge is an 'anchor of our culture' comprising a string of rock shelters constituting a museum of heritage. It also features a rock pool: 'a very spiritual place, which is still visited by the spirits of our people'.[5] Members of the standing committee visited the site and came away deeply moved: 'The grief of the Traditional Owners was almost overwhelming for everyone who witnessed it. They had lost more than a piece of heritage – they had lost part of themselves'.[6]

Wyatt also hadn't known that five days before the explosion, advisors for the Puutu Kunti Kurrama people and the Pinikura people had met with his heritage department raising Traditional Owners' dismay about the impending explosion; could it be stopped, they asked? The heritage officers said that it could not, and later contacted Rio to advise them of the meeting. Wyatt later acknowledged that, had he known, there was not much he could have done.[7]

How could such a catastrophic breakdown of process have occurred? And how could Rio, advised of the cultural importance of the caves, still go ahead and destroy them? The answers to these questions are confronting. Juukan caves opened a Pandora's box of corporate power run amok and a state long in the thrall of big mining companies. In fact, Rio wasn't the only mining company routinely destroying Indigenous sacred sites. BHP and Fortescue Metals Group (FMG) were also accused of participating in the same destructive practice. In fact, the destruction of Juukan caves shone a light on the mining industry's lack of commitment to protecting Indigenous heritage.[8]

State-sponsored vandalism

From the early 1960s, Aboriginal sacred sites in remote Australia were in the cross-hairs of the mining industry as it eyed the prospects of a mining boom precipitated by the rise of Japan. By the mid-1970s, Japan led the world in iron and steel production, exports and efficiency.[9] The iron ore-rich Pilbara became the industry's El Dorado. Yet, the Pilbara is also one of the great heritage estates in the world, about which Australians at the time remained largely ignorant.

The Australian economy was transformed during the sixties by giant mining companies, financed by international capital. A drum-beat of announcements heralded new projects, and Australians became hypnotised by the mining industry and the wealth and jobs it created.[10] We had created a 'dream economy', as one newspaper enthused.[11] However, Aboriginal sacred sites were routinely destroyed in the mining bonanza.

In response, the Western Australian Tonkin Labor government introduced the *Aboriginal Heritage Act 1972.* It promised a new era of recognition of Indigenous people's cultural rights. This was historically important legislation, the first of its kind anywhere in Australia. Introducing the bill, WF Willesee, the Leader of the House of Assembly, noted the great significance of Indigenous heritage: 'many sites, especially those with outstanding rock art, are of very great historical and aesthetic importance to mankind. Their preservation is regarded as a matter of world concern'.[12] The Act made it a criminal offence (Section 17) to damage or destroy Aboriginal heritage. Developers had to apply for special approval to damage or destroy a site. The application was then assessed by the Aboriginal Cultural Materials Committee, which advised the Minister.

These high-minded aspirations soon hit political reality: the mining industry grew too powerful and Western Australian governments came to depend on the rivers of royalties flowing from a buoyant industry. Western Australia is Australia's most mineral-dependent state. A clash of cultures was inevitable.

In response to the power of the industry, the Act gave mining companies, or other developers, a free pass to engage in destruction of sites. Section 18 allowed the Minister for Aboriginal Affairs to overturn any proposal for heritage protection, without any accountability. Importantly, once granted, developers were spared criminal sanction. And a Section 18 approval could not be rescinded other than by the applicant; that is, on the good will of a mining company.[13] There was no provision for Indigenous people to appeal, and they have been subject to 'gag clauses' insisted upon by mining companies in land use agreements struck with Indigenous communities, preventing them from speaking out about Section 18 approvals.[14] The mining industry insisted on these clauses as a way to protect their investment decisions. Having gained finance for projects, they did not want Indigenous people to be able to reconsider their position regarding development.[15] But the gag clauses remained a draconian instrument denying Indigenous rights, especially given the power imbalance involved in many of the land use agreements and the possibility that new information about the significance of archaeological sites might come to light. After the Juukan scandal they were dropped.

The tables have been further stacked against Indigenous landowners in more subtle ways. Agreements can run to hundreds of pages and can be sprung at short notice on Traditional Owners, sometimes years after they were signed. They are written in inaccessible prose, and many Indigenous owners do not fully understand the meaning of dry legal documents – as would few other people – and most struggle with the lack of transparency around the process run by mining companies, which employ a raft of lawyers.[16]

As for Section 18 applications, approval has been based on the political imperatives of the government of the day and, historically, decisions have favoured development over heritage protection.[17] Consequently, Aboriginal heritage sites have, over the years, been routinely destroyed.[18]

This struggle over Indigenous land and heritage was, mostly, an unquestioned component of mainstream Australian politics until the federal *Native Title Act 1993*. This was introduced by the Keating Labor government following the ground-breaking High Court decision of the previous year which ended the legal fiction that Australia was a land belonging to no one at the time of British settlement in 1788. The Act allowed those Indigenous people who could pass the legal bar of continuity in the practice of traditional law and customs with their traditional land to regain their rights.

Through an often torturous legal process, the *Native Title Act* gradually paved the way for a new era in the relationship between companies and Indigenous communities. Rio pioneered this change, and news of its destruction of Juukan caves shocked the mining industry. But Rio's past shadowed the company. Like a dog on a leash, it strained to be well behaved.

The rise of the bad boy of international mining

Rio Tinto's reputation as 'the worst of the worst' of mining companies in relation to the rights of Indigenous people was forged at the dawn of the company. In 1962, Rio Tinto was created out of the merger of Consolidated Zinc Company and Rio Tinto Mining to form Conzinc Rio Tinto (CRA – later Rio Tinto, and referred to hereafter as Rio). The newly merged mining giant was headquartered in London.

A few years later the company was in the jungles of the island of Bougainville acting like a colonial overlord in its effort to build one of the world's biggest copper mines. Strong objections to the mine from local people were brushed aside and no effort was made to channel any of the profits to them. As one New Guinea-based correspondent noted in an article for an Australian newspaper, Rio appeared to 'regard minerals anywhere as its own if it can get its hands on them'.[19]

Tensions rose in local communities, but the mine went ahead. Rio treated the local environment simply as a sewer, discharging over a billion tonnes of mine waste into local river systems, 'devastating the environment and the health and livelihoods of local communities'.[20] Anger over the company's indifference led to an insurrection by locals in 1989 which forced the closure of the mine. Rio divested itself of ownership and simply walked away without rehabilitating the environment. Its actions remain a deep stain on the company's reputation.

Rio brought the same arrogant mentality to its operations in Australia. These commenced against a backdrop of rising protest by Traditional Owners across the country. The flashpoint was the remote Gove Peninsula in Arnhem Land in the Northern Territory, the ancestral home of the Yirrkala people. Early in 1963, and eying the bauxite riches of the region, the Commonwealth government announced that it would grant mining leases excised from the Arnhem Land Aboriginal Reserve.

The anger felt by the Yirrkala people led to a historic petition to federal Parliament written on bark. In part, the petition read that:

> the procedures of the excision of this land and the fate of the people on it were never explained to them beforehand, and were kept secret from them … That places sacred to the Yirrkala people, as well as vital to their livelihood, are in the excised land …[21]

A long legal battle ensued, leading to a High Court case in which the Yirrkala people's legal representative, AE Woodward QC, advanced the then 'sensational' argument that the Commonwealth had to recognise 'title held by native land owners, even of a kind unknown to common law'.[22]

The Yirrkala failed in their effort to achieve justice and by 1968 a massive bauxite refinery was built at Gove. Comalco and Rio were entwined in the development of Gove, the latter having a 45 per cent stake in the company during the 1960s. Hand in hand, they bulldozed ancestral lands of the Yirrkala people in the development of the refinery.[23] Convinced they were unable to achieve justice under existing law, Indigenous groups throughout the country converged on Canberra in 1972 to demand land rights and erected a tent embassy on the lawns of Parliament House as a statement of their claims to sovereignty.

After its Gove operations, Rio drew up plans for the virtual invasion of remote Australia. In 1976, it commissioned a report listing Aboriginal reserves throughout the country as 'exploration targets'. The report was kept confidential. When Aboriginal groups in North Queensland organised themselves into the North Queensland Land Council to challenge Rio, the company simply refused to acknowledge the body.[24]

In a limited number of instances, Rio employed Aboriginal elders in the exploration ventures but only when it suited them.[25] Thus, in 1979, the Gija Traditional Owners of the East Kimberley came across Rio staff exploring in culturally sensitive areas of the Lissadell pastoral lease, south of Kununurra, without their knowledge or consent.

In its operations on the lease, Rio dug one large trench within a sacred site area and rummaged around another. It was the beginning of what became the Argyle diamond mine. After tense negotiations, an agreement with the Gija was signed in 1980. Even agreeing to negotiate with Indigenous people was a significant concession for Rio, but the company ensured that it controlled the outcome. One observer of the dispute noted that Rio had acted with 'indecent haste'. The agreement was shrouded in secrecy and was not made public.[26]

At Rio's 1980 annual general meeting, chair Sir Roderick Carnegie was asked if he would pledge to protect Aboriginal sacred sites; he refused to do so.[27] Thereafter, Sir Rod authorised a major publicity campaign that argued against granting Aboriginal rights to land, claiming that doing so would 'exacerbate racial divisions'.[28] The publicity materials were widely used in schools.

At much the same time, Rio was operating a gold mine in the rugged hills on the eastern part of the island of Borneo. It owned 90 per cent of Kelian Equatorial Mining (KEM), which ran the mine. The area was inhabited by a local Indigenous Dayak community. Operations commenced in 1985 and were immediately engulfed in protests from the Dayak, who claimed that KEM evicted local people from their cultivated lands, refused to pay them compensation for their livelihoods, destroyed grave sites and polluted local rivers. Relations became so tense that KEM was forced to fly in security guards. The mine closed in 2004.[29]

Rio's dark history of flouting heritage laws continued. In the early 1990s, the company's new mine at Marandoo, in Western Australia's Pilbara region, threatened the destruction of extremely significant sites of the Eastern Guruma Traditional Owners. These sites formed 'a key location for the origin and ongoing maintenance of important elements of Pilbara Aboriginal law'.[30] The Eastern Guruma people were angered by Rio's refusal to undertake any investigation of heritage in the area because of the large number of heritage sites that would be destroyed. In a show of the power mining companies wielded in the state, the Labor government, led by Dr Carmen Lawrence, granted Rio a Section 18 approval, and the mine commenced. A subsequent piece of legislation – the *Marandoo Act 1992* – was rushed through the Western Australian Parliament in two days, effectively preventing any legal challenge by Traditional Owners. Cultural artefacts from the Marandoo site were removed and later trashed. The company failed to disclose this trashing of heritage material to the East Guruma people.

Rio's uncompromising stance on Aboriginal land rights was carried over to the mining industry's peak body – the Minerals Council of Australia (MCA) – where it was a dominating presence. For many years, the MCA spear-headed political opposition to native title; it vehemently opposed the vesting of mineral rights with Aboriginal land owners.[31] Consequently, Rio instilled a policy of constant conflict in every encounter with Indigenous people, as if it were a prizefighter bent on winning every bout.[32]

Rio's change of culture

In March 1995, after decades of belligerence towards Indigenous people's rights, Rio announced a change of heart. The occasion was a speech delivered to an industry audience at Melbourne's Grand Hyatt Hotel by the newly appointed Rio CEO, Leon Davis. The *Native Title Act* had been in force for several years, but the dust had barely settled on the bitter conservative reaction to the legislation, especially in Western Australia where mining interests had waged a vociferous campaign of misinformation about the Act, egged on by conservative politicians and public commentators.[33]

So, when Davis, who has been described as a 'slightly awkward businessman',[34] fronted an audience of his peers, little did they know he was about to lob a rhetorical hand grenade. He declared that Rio was 'satisfied with the central tenet of the Native Title Act'. His speech was designed to end the deadlock between the mining industry and Indigenous Australia. Davis was foreshadowing that Rio would work with native title, not against it. His speech quickly became known as 'the sensitive new age miner's speech'.[35]

For Davis, however, the speech also had a very pragmatic purpose. He was focused on opening up new markets in Asia, and he saw the need to create a fresh image away from the company's reputation as 'Australia's hardball corporate player'.[36] And, according to Glynn

Cochrane, who was hired by Rio in 1995 and spent twenty years with the company working in community relations, the change Davis oversaw was designed 'to counteract the effects of Bougainville and to make sure that that kind of thing never happened again'.[37]

The change of heart on native title led to a new, and constructive, era of cooperation between mining companies and Indigenous communities around the country through the mechanism of land use agreements.

So, why in 2020, would Rio risk putting this hard-earned reputation in jeopardy? Was Rio really the sensitive new age miner of corporate folklore?

More than a hint was revealed the year following Davis' groundbreaking speech when Rio entered an arrangement with controversial US mining company Freeport to finance an expansion of the enormous copper and gold mine in West Papua in return for a share of the profits. Freeport had had a history of causing grave environmental damage and destroying local livelihoods. Facing stiff opposition from the people of West Papua, the mine site was subsequently militarised.[38] It all looked a bit like a repeat of Bougainville.

Rio: A global giant

Following Davis' speech, Rio's iron ore sales climbed steadily on the back of China's economic boom. But there remained a contradiction. Global in its ambitions and reach, the company had operations in North and South America, West Africa and India. With customers around the world, Rio had, for decades, located its head office in London, the hub of international finance. Yet the backbone of the company's profits was the iron ore from the Pilbara; 76 per cent of its $31 billion total revenues (2019) came from the one region.[39] It was more accurate to call Rio a Pilbara company. By 2020, of the twenty-five industrial-scale iron ore mines in the region, Rio owned sixteen of them.

Pressures were growing. Iron ore tenements littered the ancient landscape. Indigenous sacred sites were increasingly affected. Ancestral paths were being 'boxed up' and cut off from one another, disrupting the interconnected spiritual journeys known as Dreaming Tracks and Songlines.[40] Labor Senator and Indigenous leader, Pat Dodson described this industrialised assault on the Pilbara's cultural landscape as 'incremental genocide'.[41]

Nevertheless, Rio continued to hang onto its reputation of being the industry leader in building relationships with Indigenous people. It employed senior, experienced archaeologists and anthropologists, and, according to Bruce Harvey, the global practice leader at Rio between 2007 and 2014, acknowledgment of culture had become embedded in the company.[42] But just how firmly embedded was this culture?

The Puutu Kunti Kurrama people and the Pinikura people: 'We never win'

The Puutu Kunti Kurrama people and the Pinikura people's negotiations with Rio over Juukan caves began in earnest in 2013, at the time Rio's Section 18 application was granted. The community had been going through the process of a native title claim, which had not yet been determined. They lacked the resources to negotiate on their own behalf and were represented by the Yamatji Marpla Aboriginal Corporation (YMAC).[43]

The Puutu Kunti Kurrama people and the Pinikura people's experiences with Rio are set out in a lengthy submission and oral interviews the community presented to the parliamentary inquiry. Not surprisingly, this material tells a story of a very unequal partnership between Rio and the community. It can't be replicated here in the detail it deserves, but key points clearly emerge – the Puutu Kunti Kurrama people and the Pinikura people were conscious of their 'inequitable negotiating position',[44] and Rio was aware of this power imbalance. The community was also fully appraised of the various experts' reports attesting to the significance of the site and they trusted that Rio would act in good faith. From early on in negotiations, the Puutu Kunti Kurrama people and the Pinikura people 'thought they had a shared understanding with Rio Tinto that the sites would be protected'.[45]

But at the time, did Rio really gain their informed consent? Donna Meyer, representing the Puutu Kunti Kurrama people and the Pinikura people Aboriginal Corporation, told the parliamentary inquiry that informed consent had not occurred. Because they were meeting with Rio all the time, Meyer said,

> people had a little bit of an understanding. But, when it came down to talking about the agreement … I don't think they did understand it when it came to signing it. A lot of people came along to the meetings and sat and listened, but, at the end of the day, we were told: 'This is the best agreement you're going to get. You're not going to get anything better out of it … I think the people that represented us [the YMAC] didn't present it to us properly for the people to understand … When they [Rio] came to us and told us about the Juukan Gorge, they were really happy that they had found something significant and that we should be happy … but it just disappeared. We didn't see any more about it. They only came back and told us that they had a section 18 on it. That was it. We wanted to approach them and talk to them about it … We couldn't talk to anybody, not even Rio, because there's a clause in there that says that we cannot talk about anything to anyone.[46]

When the original Section 18 approval was granted, Rio had considered four options for the Brockman 4 site – three of which would have avoided affecting Juukan caves. The company chose the option likely to have most impact in order to access higher grade ore. Rio convinced itself that the Puutu Kunti Kurrama people and the Pinikura people understood that there would be disturbance to the site in the future.[47]

The only condition imposed on Rio in return for a Section 18 approval was to report on any sites impacted and any salvage that was conducted. In other words, the company could reduce to rubble a prehistoric site twice as old France's world-famous Lascaux Caves and just report back on how it all went. How did Rio ever think this flawed process was acceptable?

For years Rio sat on its Section 18 approval on the Brockman 4 mine site without activating it. According to Sam Walsh, Rio's CEO at the time, he gave an assurance shortly after the Section 18 approval was granted that 'Juukan wouldn't be touched'.[48] He said he made the chief of the iron division, Greg Lilleyman, aware of the need to protect the caves.[49] Walsh's claim, however, is contested by Rio management in charge at the time of the disaster, who said they could find no evidence of his assurance.[50] Some thought the stand-off between Rio and Walsh was a stoush over their respective reputations.[51]

Walsh tried to make Rio live up to its image of a good corporate citizen. Quietly spoken and thoughtful, he had a grandfatherly appearance with a portly figure, rimless glasses and wispy grey hair.[52] But as a former car company executive he had plenty of business acumen. He also had an instinctive empathy for Indigenous people and the rugged, red-earth Pilbara country they inhabited. Crucially, he lived in Western Australia and was able to keep his finger on the state's pulse.[53]

In 2015, as part of its commitment to Juukan, Rio funded a documentary featuring members of the Puutu Kunti Kurrama people and the Pinikura people expressing their heartfelt attachment to the site. But Walsh's reassurances raise the question of why Rio sought a Section 18 approval in the first place. And, if Juukan's preservation depended, precariously, on one man's word, then it was a Clayton's protection. As the parliamentary committee inquiring into the disaster found, 'it would appear that Juukan Gorge was effectively destroyed from the moment Section 18 consent … was granted'.[54]

The arrival of a high-flyer

If Juukan caves were safe while Walsh was at the helm, his departure in 2016 opened the way for the Section 18 to be dusted off. His replacement, forty-four-year-old French-born Jean-Sébastian Jacques, would prove disastrous for Rio and for the Puutu Kunti Kurrama people and the Pinikura people. He instigated an ill-conceived corporate restructure which, combined with his own flawed leadership style and a compliant board, lit the fuse on Juukan caves.[55]

A product of elite French schools and universities, Jacques had a stint with iconic French personal care corporation L'Oréal, before finding his way to Rio's London office where he was credited for his able handling of the company's troubled Oyu Tolgoi gold and copper mine in Mongolia.[56] He was plucked out of relative obscurity by retiring Rio chair Jan du Plessis, and wowed the board headed by the incoming chair, Simon Thompson. They were said to be 'unaccountably stricken' by the fresh-faced, silky communicator.[57] Jacques was regarded as 'a tier one sort of guy' – an assessment made without Jacques having to put himself through the hoops of a boardroom sales pitch.[58] It is an old story in the annals of corporate history – the arrival of a *wunderkind* – the 'bright young saviour',[59] who turns out to be a flop.

Jacques was the antithesis of Sam Walsh. He carried himself with the fashionable air of a corporate high-flyer. In equal measure ruthless and charming, he was high on the scale of self-regard, ambition and restless energy, with a fondness for peppering his conversations with 'management speak'. Jacques liked to see himself as accessible and down-to-earth; he was known to his colleagues simply as 'JS'.[60] But some detected a reckless side to him – he could be 'blunt, unscripted and single-minded'.[61] A bit of a maverick, in other words. He was neither from a traditional mining background nor had he ever worked in the Pilbara. And he chose to live in Sydney with his French wife, so he was not as connected to Pilbara issues as was Walsh.

Like any CEO of a large mining corporation, Jacques faced

competing challenges: pleasing investors, growing the company, keeping costs in check and maintaining its social licence. The latter, which Walsh had fostered, was the vague but important notion that mining companies, especially, had to actively maintain the support of the local communities in which they operated. But Jacques harboured ambitions to take on BHP as Australia's biggest miner.[62] He was a man in a hurry.[63] Nevertheless, Jacques faced stiff headwinds. Commodity prices had been dismal for three years; dividends were under pressure.[64] The halcyon days of the China boom had dimmed.

Early on, Jacques got offside with sections of the press. His fondness for spin attracted critics, including Joe Aston from the *Australian Financial Review,* who, by his own admission, had been 'going pretty hard' on the new CEO for several years before the Juukan disaster. Aston had a reputation for being 'abrasive, effective and popular', his columns said to be compulsory reading in the tradition of Trevor Sykes and Stephen Mayne.[65]

Jacques, Aston explains, 'liked to talk about Rio being a more ethical company than its rivals because it had divested from coal'. But, at the same time, Aston points, out 'it was running around basically trying to blackmail state and federal governments for subsidies for its alumina and refineries otherwise they'd shut them down'. Aston highlighted the contradiction that Jacques was 'pretending Rio was a sustainable company without being one at all'.[66] It was a portent for how the company later approached the Juukan issue.

Rio's culture: Profits come first

From the time of his appointment as CEO, Jacques was driven by a mission for Rio to be the 'most envied mining company in the world'. He told London's *Financial Times* that he wanted to deliver 'superior cash returns' so that the company could 'recapture its former glories'.[67]

To achieve these ambitions, Jacques restructured the company. He showed a talent for the sort of corporate strategic shake-up that delivered high shareholder returns. But a key part of Jacques' restructure was a smoke and mirrors exercise: to make it appear that the company was maintaining its social licence with Indigenous communities while putting in place a downgrading of that licence in order, it appeared, to pursue higher growth. Of course, the restructure was never announced as such, but the building blocks put in place show it to be the case. Jacques' strategy was clearly risky. What motivated him to pursue it? Boosting growth was one reason. But another was Jacques' grandiose desire to make Rio the greatest mining company.

The first task Jacques addressed was getting the company's 20 000 employees behind his vision. Even before he formally took on the role, he delivered a blunt message to a town hall meeting of staff in Brisbane. Playing to his reputation as a 'tough guy',[68] he told the gathering that 'If someone was stuck in the past, they can fit in or f--- off'.[69] An audible gasp rippled around those assembled. Who was Jacques referring to? It wasn't made clear at the time, but in part, Jacques meant those who worked building the company's relationships with Indigenous people; these teams were set to be dismantled. Henceforth profits were to come before culture.

But Jacques realised that a very different message had to be given to the public. So he set about updating the company's mission statement published in a manual called *The Way We Work*. Included in it was a specific commitment to Indigenous people:

> We respect the special connection of local and Indigenous people to land and waters … We strive to achieve free, prior and informed consent of Indigenous communities … We work with communities to understand any impacts from our activities …[70]

It was as if a box had been ticked so that the company could move on and forget the past. But how Juukan fitted into the company's plans still appeared to trouble Jacques. In 2018, Rio management commissioned archaeologist Michael Slack to conduct a report on the caves, an update of a report he produced in 2014. The later report went even further than his initial one in highlighting the uniqueness of the site: 'Juukan 2 is of the highest archaeological significance in Australia. It has the amazing potential to radically change our understanding of the earliest human behaviour in Australia'.[71]

In his evidence to the parliamentary inquiry, Jacques claimed that he and his executive team had been unaware of the site's significance, until after it had been destroyed, even though, he said, they should have been.[72] He stunned committee members when admitting that neither he nor his top executives had even read the Slack report. Here is yet another example of a senior corporate executive claiming not to know about the very origins of the scandal that engulfed a corporation. And there is always some plausibility about such denials because of the lack of public accountability that surrounds sensitive corporate deliberations. Jacques mightn't have known about the most recent Slack report, but he should have, if he was to live up to Rio's own mission statement.

A key part of revamping Rio was to move the Communities and Social Performance function, whose principal task was building relations with Indigenous people, to a new division named Corporate Affairs and Communications Division, located in London. The new division was headed by Simone Niven, who'd been with the firm for eleven years and who was a close confidante of Jacques. Her responsibilities covered external affairs, sustainability, communities, brand, media, government affairs and employee communications. She also oversaw communications teams around the company's global operations.[73] Jacques had created a PR empire for Niven, who was paid over $3 million a year in salary and given a seat at the big table as an executive. Nevertheless, the downgrading of Indigenous issues was jarringly obvious: they had been shunted into an overseas PR department to quietly wither away.

Jacques idiosyncratic leadership style started ruffling feathers at the company. He didn't model an open decision-making style, preferring instead to keep important things close to his chest. He seemed to be always on a plane travelling the world issuing 'stream of consciousness' messages to staff about his big picture views via social media apps.[74]

It was a slow-drip disaster. Niven, who had no expertise and no experience in Indigenous relations, was located on the other side of the world.[75] She appeared to lack curiosity about Indigenous people and the history surrounding their struggles with mining companies. She never sought out a meeting with the Puutu Kunti Kurrama people and the Pinikura people until just before the parliamentary inquiry commenced. As she told the members: 'I really regret not having the chance to meet with them over the years and during the recent events, and I really should have, and I am sorry for that'.[76]

After the restructure was implemented, experienced archaeological and anthropological staff read the writing on the wall. They steadily resigned from the company. Rio executive Bruce Harvey explained their reasons for doing so to the parliamentary committee: they 'left out of a sense of frustration that the restructuring meant that they were no longer recognised as having the authority they deserved'.[77] Harvey further explained that these were world-class experts, 'who had the necessary seniority in Rio Tinto and sufficient forthrightness to have spoken up on the folly of the proposed destruction'.[78]

Jacques silenced the past in another, crucial way. Executives with corporate knowledge of the importance of Indigenous cultural matters were moved on. As Sam Walsh told the *Australian Financial Review,* Jacques

> had no one to ask about my instruction as he had removed [from the company] Andrew Harding, CEO of iron ore, Greg Lilleyman, who was MD of iron ore operations at the time, and Michael Gollschewski, who was general manager of Greater Brockman – the entire iron ore management team with responsibility for Brockman and Juukan Gorge.

The only person Jacques had to ask, said Walsh, was Chris Salisbury, the current head of iron ore, who was in coal in 2013.[79] Within nine months Rio had lost six of its nine senior executives. Jacques had, effectively, diluted the company's Australian presence.[80]

Glynn Cochrane, an advisor at Rio until 2015, confirmed to the joint committee that the company had sidelined anthropologists and archaeologists in recent years and had instead hired people with more of a focus on 'branding, marketing and media'. These people were all imbued with Jacques' mantra of doubling down on profits. In implementing these changes, the company had followed its own 'stripped-down version of cultural resource management' in the Pilbara in order to secure quick clearance and the removal of impediments to mining. It was a practice that 'too frequently results in the destruction of sacred sites', Cochrane said. Rio was engaged in 'simply a lot of box ticking and complying with regulations and legislation in order to get quick clearances'. Cochrane said that this was an intentional change on the part of senior management: 'Had there been a well-qualified heavyweight archaeologist in the Pilbara who was working closely with the head of iron ore and a person that the iron ore head was familiar with, he would've listened to their advice. That did not exist'.

On 5 October 2018, Cochrane asked Rio chair, Simon Thompson, why it was that Rio Tinto was no longer employing archaeologists and anthropologists: 'I did not get a reply and I still haven't had one'.[81]

The restructure, according to Bruce Harvey, also diminished the role of individual mine site leaders. Jacques 'also apparently authorised the change of direct accountability from asset senior leaders to someone in a centralised role with no skin in the game'. Under the previous controls, the Juukan Gorge blast 'would not have occurred', according to Harvey.

Rio management remained blinkered about its downgrading of expert advice on Indigenous matters to guide its operations. Its submission to the inquiry contained the telling comment that modern mine management was 'no longer about anthropologists running around a field'.[82] Right until days before the blast, Rio management maintained that Juukan Gorge was not a site of archaeological significance and that only a 'wildcat' group of the Puutu Kunti Kurrama people and the Pinikura people was trying to stop it.[83]

But Jacques had kept his eye on the main prize. Within a few years, he'd turned Rio into 'a money-printing machine'.[84] His real talents were beginning to shine as he presided over the largest dividends in Rio's history.[85] And he was rewarded handsomely. In fact the blowing up of Juukan cannot be separated from the debate over executive salaries and how Jacques' remuneration mirrored this debate.

Since at least the early 2000s, the Australian community has waged an ongoing skirmish over the excesses of CEOs' salaries. Between 2001 and 2016, the average CEO salary rose from seventy-six times the average worker's salary to eighty-five times. But the averages don't reveal the excesses that had crept in to the top of the scale where the highest paid CEO in Australia earned 435 times the average worker's wage.[86] Occasionally, community outrage was directed at governments failing to rein in boards that signed off on excessive salary packages. A 2017 survey by the Governance Institute of Australia found that 55 per cent of Australians believed that a salary of $600 000 for a CEO was unethical and 77 per cent believed that a $3 million salary was unethical.[87] In 2019, Jacques was paid $11.3 million, 27 per cent more than the previous year, an increase the company justified as reward for him 'achieving high profits, safety rates and share growths'.[88] Jacques was being reward for chasing short-term returns, but there was no proper regard for long-term risks. It was the same corporate trap that had played out numerous times over the decades.

The Puutu Kunti Kurrama people and the Pinikura people bore the consequences of Jacques' short-term focus and his longer-term grand, glossy vision to outgrow BHP. But just how expediently they had been treated was not revealed until the Indigenous community was given a voice through the parliamentary inquiry. Rio agreed to lift their gag order. Only the embarrassment of an inquiry prompted the removal of such a draconian control.

In the lead-up to the start of the inquiry, Jacques fell silent. Weeks went by and he'd made no statement about the company's disaster. Joe Aston, who fearlessly covered the story of the blast for the *Australian Financial Review,* accused Jacques of hiding.[89]

Aston also revealed just what the executive team thought about the disaster. In June 2020, he received a recording of an internal company meeting where the head of iron ore, Chris Salisbury, faced a complaint from a staff member that 'people have seen how we've positioned our response with an apology for the distress caused, not for doing the wrong thing'. As Aston reported: 'Answering, Salisbury gave a lengthy explanation of the events leading to the detonation of the sacred Aboriginal site last month and clarified that "that's why we haven't apologised for the event itself, *per se*, but apologised for the distress the event caused".'[90] The leak of the comment was fatal for Rio and not just because of its obvious inappropriateness, even though it's unclear what role Salisbury had in the decision-making that led to the detonation of the caves. But his comments were seen to represent the attitude of the company right to the top. According to Aston, 'they [directors and executives] all wanted to appear to be sorry and learning from their mistakes without doing that at all, and that's what killed them'.[91]

Rio's real motives

Spooling through Jacques' mind as the parliamentary inquiry got under way was his conviction that the destruction of Juukan caves was just a terrible mistake; a series of missteps and miscommunication. He outlined as much in a detailed submission to the inquiry: Rio had obtained prior informed consent; the Puutu Kunti Kurrama people and the Pinikura people's growing awareness of the significance of the site had happened late – early in 2020; and their request to cease mining was also inopportune – the dynamite was locked into place and too dangerous to remove.[92] But was this rationalisation more convenient than convincing?

When Jacques negotiated his way around several tortured sessions of evidence before the parliamentary inquiry – in turn contrite, apologetic, deflecting where he could – he offered a surprising, almost throwaway acknowledgment. Rio, under his leadership, he admitted, 'were of the view that these sites [Juukan caves] would be mined eventually'.[93] Rio was not for backing down. It continued to load blast holes following a meeting with Puutu Kunti Kurrama people and Pinikura people on site on 14 May 2020, with a further sixty-two holes loaded on 16 May, seventy-two holes loaded on 17 May and twenty-two holes loaded on 19 May. During these last desperate days in which Traditional Owners tried to save the caves, Rio's lawyers warned them that they had to abide by the gag clause.[94] As Puutu Kunti Kurrama people and Pinikura people's Aboriginal Corporation CEO Carol Meredith told the parliamentary inquiry: 'we were hamstrung'. Documents obtained by the parliamentary inquiry also showed that Rio had engaged and briefed a legal firm in preparation for an attempted injunction by Puutu Kunti Kurrama people and Pinikura people.[95]

It was just what the community had feared all along. They had been trapped by the uncertainty surrounding the Section 18 approval – mining might or might not go ahead – and their inability to respond to new concerns under the gag order. Community member Sandra Hayes later bitterly admitted: 'we never win'.[96]

Jacques wanted to pull the trigger on the agreement; the high-end ore at Brockman was irresistible. It formed a crucial part in a high-value product Rio had been selling since 2007 called 'Pilbara Blend'. Like premium coffee, it was a mix of the best ores from several Rio mines. In mid-2019, Jacques described Pilbara Blend as the company's 'flagship product in China, reflected in the price it commands'. It was a key component in Jacques' overall strategy to focus on 'value-over-volume' to lift the company's profits.

But by mid-2019, the availability of Pilbara Blend was under threat. Rio acknowledged that a higher proportion of lower grade products were going into the mix. In what seems to have been a clear intention to grab the ore surrounding Juukan caves, Rio announced that, 'in light of these challenges, there has been a review of mine plans'.[97]

It's likely that Rio felt mounting threats to its rights to this ore under the outdated Section 18 approval. In 2018, Ben Wyatt had announced a review of the *Heritage Act 1972*, which was lumbering along with an uncertain outcome.[98]

Jacques could put a precise figure on the revenue derived from blowing up Juukan. Joe Aston witnessed Jacques' answer to one parliamentary committee member, Nationals Senator Matt Canavan, who asked about the value of the ore surrounding Juukan caves: 'Jacques could barely stifle his glee reeling off the damning numbers: "eight million tonnes of high-grade iron ore. The value at the time of that decision was around $135 million"'.[99] It was a piddling amount, given Rio's overall revenue.

As prominent Indigenous leader Noel Pearson argued, Rio undertook the destruction of Juukan caves 'with full understanding and cold deliberation'.[100]

Pearson was critical of the findings of the parliamentary committee when it handed down its final report in October 2021. While Pearson acknowledged that the committee had grasped the gravity of the issue, it had 'squibbed' in uncovering the truth and holding to account those 'responsible for the crime committed against Australia's cultural heritage'.[101]

It's not the place here to fully analyse the findings of the committee other than to say two things. Firstly, it found that 'the destruction of Juukan Gorge was the result of Rio's failures'.[102] Secondly, it recognised that the Puutu Kunti Kurrama people and the Pinikura people and the company had legitimate rival 'perspectives' about the events leading up to the blast. For Pearson, this amounted to the offering of 'perspectives on the truth'. Pearson was right. While the committee generated reams of crucial information into what had occurred at Juukan and especially the flaws in Rio's processes, it was simply not enough to have shone a light into the dark corners of Rio's culture.

And what about the Rio board?

The tragedy of Juukan caves represents another catastrophic failure of a board to prevent a corporate implosion. Yet Rio had a highly credentialled board comprising nine directors – four of whom were women and each of whom brought with them a range of specialised expertise.

How, then, did the board collectively fail to stop the Juukan disaster? While there is no definitive answer to this question, because of the veil that covers boardroom deliberations, one possible explanation is structural: six of the nine directors are located in London with no expertise in Australia, let alone the Pilbara. The Rio board was managing complex Indigenous relations by remote control. Add in Simone Niven's own disconnect from heritage issues, and it's not hard to understand how the board failed to appreciate the risks.

But, as in other board failures examined in this book, the relationship between the board and the CEO often militates against good corporate governance. And, in Rio's case, it appears that the board continued to be seduced by Jacques' perceived capabilities. They signed off on his ill-considered restructure that downgraded the company's expertise in Indigenous heritage, which led to the catastrophe. Liberal Senator Dean Smith, a committee member, believed that:

> Mr Jacques' management style created a poor culture at Rio Tinto that was endorsed by the board … Mr Jacques enabled a culture to develop at Rio Tinto where non-executive level management did not feel empowered to inform the executive of the significance of the rock shelters.[103]

And the strategy developed by the board to handle the crisis was self-serving and ultimately worsened the company's position. Noel Pearson described Rio's strategy as a 'two-faced act of feigning contrition on the one hand while exonerating itself on the other'.[104] The record bears out his critique. It was manifest in the company's internal review of the disaster and the decisions taken after its release.

It wasn't until 19 June 2020 – nearly a month after the disaster – that the board decided on the need for an internal review. Aston is sanguine about the failing of the Rio board and boards in general: 'Most boards look good on paper and are weak … Nobody on boards wants to rock the boat … it's all set up for everyone to shut up and just nod'.[105]

But there was another disturbing reality about board culture that likely played into the disaster at Rio. After decades of intermittent, but persistent, criticism that board membership in Australia continued to function like a cosy club, nothing much seemed to have changed to alter this culture. An investigation by the *Australian Financial Review* in 2022 discovered 'an invisible network' that bound the country's most powerful and influential directors.[106] Such connections, the paper went on, were 'essential for advancing a director's career'. Board membership had become a *career*: directors at top ASX companies earning several hundred thousand dollars a year and typically participating in multiple board memberships linked in overlapping directorships between the corporate, arts, university and sporting sectors.

Cementing these cross-linkages are memberships of associations such as the Business Council of Australia, Chief Executive Women and the Australian Institute of Company Directors. These peak bodies remain 'potent hubs' for directors; a consolidation of the 'directors club'. In such a tight-knit, elite circle, who would risk rocking the boat to stand up for, say, Indigenous rights? Conservative News Corp columnist Janet Albrechtsen said as much when, in a 2018 article, she described boardroom Australia as 'often a dozy kind of place' where few want disagreement and where '[E]ven fewer would front up in a fight'. She offered the backhanded comments as a lead-in to arguing that the culture of complacency was about to end. Directors, at least those she had spoken to, were in 'rebellion' over the pressure being exerted by social activists to comply with their progressive social agenda, risking changing the very purpose of a corporation.[107]

We don't know whether the Rio board was quietly sparring for a culture war that the feisty Albrechtsen believed was unfolding. But whatever complacency distracted board members over the slow-moving Juukan disaster rudely ended as the scandal engulfed the company. According to reports, the board came under such intense pressure that directors turned on each other, 'pointing fingers across the board table at fellow directors that they considered had misread the magnitude of the crisis and the response it required'.[108]

Calmer heads eventually prevailed. Board member Michael L'Estrange was given the task of preparing a review, but this simply worsened the company's problems. A former senior bureaucrat, L'Estrange was also a career-long Liberal Party insider and conservative intellectual.[109] He drowned the document in management-speak. He wrote about oversights in 'systems and processes', failures in 'linked up' decision-making, deficiencies in 'inclusive work culture' and the lack of a 'fit-for-purpose management system at the mine'.

And when it came to pinpointing who was responsible and why for the Juukan disaster, L'Estrange's report left this to a brief comment at the end. The failings of the company occurred over an extended period of time, he wrote, therefore the role played by Jacques, Niven and Salisbury – the three most senior executives involved – 'represented acts of omission, rather than commission … Nevertheless … they bear partial responsibility for the failings'.[110] Therefore, L'Estrange argued that penalties on the trio should be proportionate. He settled on docking their annual bonuses for the year. Chair Simon Thompson backed the plan and committed to Jacques' future at the company. This was yet another example of Rio's bungled management style.

Public and investor outrage erupted over the findings of the company's internal review. It was widely seen as a whitewash.[111] Journalist Jennifer Hewett dismissed the report as 'another instance of corporate blather'.[112]

As Thompson and the board flailed about trying to find a way to save the executive, outrage continued to ripple through Australian investment funds. Like Lindsay Maxsted at Westpac, Thompson tried to head off trouble through a series of meetings between the board and industry-based superfunds – the very ones that had helped bring the bank to account. When the heads of AustralianSuper, HESTA, UniSuper and Aware Super (formerly First State) were told that accountability for Rio's executive over the Juukan disaster would be limited, they ramped up pressure on the board to take more concerted action.[113]

Thompson thought he had the measure of the industry-based investment funds. He appeared to have reasoned that as they accounted for less than 20 per cent of the stock held in the company, it was the big investors in the United States, Britain and Europe that held greater sway.[114] Thompson told the press that the overseas investors were happy with how the company was handling the situation.[115] But he had overplayed his hand. The deaf ear shown to Australian investors forced them to go public. The first to do was AustralianSuper, which issued a statement on 26 August saying that 'the proposed penalties fall significantly short of appropriate accountability for those responsible'.[116] Other funds weighed in, including the Church of England Pension Fund and the influential Future Fund, headed by the former Howard government Treasurer, Peter Costello. The tactic of going public worked; Thompson got the message. As one newspaper summed up Rio's capitulation, the 'Aussie rabble rousers' outfoxed the big investors around the world.[117] It was another reminder to corporations of the changed investment climate in Australia engineered by industry-based super funds, which were spearheading the calls for corporations to heed their social licence through enhanced corporate social responsibility.

Rio parted ways with Jacques, Salisbury and Niven. But, having been exonerated by the board in its internal review, each had to go on their own terms or the company risked extended legal action. All carried away with them bags of money – $40 million between them – in the form of severance pay, long-term bonuses and Rio shares, prompting Joe Aston to quip: 'Isn't life tough in the naughty corner?'[118]

Later on, both Thompson and L'Estrange announced their retirement from the board. It was left to two conservative senators on the parliamentary inquiry – Dean Smith and George Christensen – to spell out the truth: 'Rio Tinto and its board have fundamentally been let off the hook'.[119]

The Juukan disaster has potent lessons not just about the failings of boards but also why CEOs so frequently suffer the same fate. The exact reasons differ from case to case, but common reasons can be discerned. These were crisply summed up in journalist Sally Patten's 2021 investigation into CEO performance for the *Australian Financial Review*'s *Boss* magazine: 'Too many [CEOs] fail to grasp the nature of the job, fail to listen and learn, fail to shed their biases and keep their ego in check and think culture is easy'.[120] But for some, like Alan Bond, Christopher Skase and Ray Williams, Patten's analysis fails to capture the worst possible features of CEOs. How do such people keep getting appointed to top jobs of major corporations or remain as founders of publicly listed corporations? Charm somehow overwhelms board members, as appears to have been the case with Jacques. Such people go on to dominate boards, which are often stacked with either loyalists or directors disinclined to challenge the direction of a company. How such poor standards of governance prevail unchecked says much about the power wielded by society's economic elites.

As the Juukan disaster fades from memory, there will be no let-up for the revamped Rio board in its ongoing task of rebuilding its relationships with Indigenous people. Recently retired from Western Australian politics, Ben Wyatt joined the board. Wyatt will no doubt provide much-needed Indigenous and political perspectives at the board level as Rio's post-Juukan controversies continue: renewed calls from Bougainvilleans for the company to clean up its abandoned mine site; a tense set of negotiations with the Gija over the clean-up of the recently closed Argyle diamond mine; and a potential confrontation with the San Carlos Apache group over a planned copper mine on its traditional land in Arizona, which threatens to destroy their sacred sites.

History is relevant to understanding how the Juukan caves disaster unfolded and how Rio might conduct itself in the future. Put simply, 'good' Rio and 'bad' Rio have always co-existed in both the company's Australian and global operations.

Will the lessons of Juukan slip between the two sides of its culture?

CONCLUSION: TAMING THE BEAST

Corporations bring many benefits to society; that is a given. Yet the reverse is also true: corporations have left a trail of damage around the world, and especially in the era of global capitalism. The damaging side of corporations has been especially acute in Australia. Corporate scandals have for decades blown across Australian society like a toxin-laden wind; they creep up on us all too often with ruinous consequences. As a society, we've failed to acknowledge the long-term trauma associated with being a victim of a major corporate scandal.

The sheer regularity of scandals reflects a long-running ethical breakdown inside too many of Australia's corporate glass towers. This is a crisis of corporate culture aided by government inaction. As the case studies in this book have demonstrated, corporations have too much power, are often badly run and are largely unaccountable. They can capture the heart of government decision-making processes.

If yet another reminder is needed of the lack of ethical standards at the heart of Australia's corporate culture, then PricewaterhouseCoopers (PwC) provides a graphic example. During May 2023, as this book was being finalised, the Australian office of the global giant auditing and consultancy firm was mired in scandal. Labor Senator Deborah O'Neill had secured the release of a tranche of emails sent in 2015 between senior people at the company showing that it had used privileged information derived from government consultancy work to drum up new clients – but not just any new clients.

PwC was paid to advise federal Treasury about boosting government capacity to prevent global corporations from minimising their tax in Australia. Billions were potentially at stake. PwC then allegedly shared that information with some of these corporations, earning millions in the process. Commentators piled on that PwC had engaged in a massive conflict of interest and, hence, a major lapse of ethical standards.

The scandal has already led to departures of senior people at PwC and there is talk of further action against the company. But the scandal has shone a light on a bigger problem: the reliance of Australian governments on the 'big four' consultancy firms – Deloitte, EY, KPMG and PwC – in providing advice. The reliance grew exponentially when the federal Liberal Party was in power (2014–22), rising 400 per cent over the past decade.[1] In return, the big four handed out millions in political donations, mainly to the Liberal Party.

The big four are spoken of in Canberra as a 'shadow public service'.[2] With the scandal at PwC still unfolding, it's not known whether similar appropriation of government information for commercial gain has occurred in other parts of government involving other big four firms.

Warnings about poor ethical standards among the big four's global operations go back at least to the collapse of US energy giant Enron in 2002, which took consultancy firm Arthur Andersen down with it, and which was discussed in chapter 5. Since then, and across their global operations, the glittering success of the big four has been dogged by recurring crises: botched audits that dudded investors and scandals around devising tax minimisation schemes for global corporations.

In 2018, two Australian academics wrote an exposé of the excessively profit-driven culture across the entire group: 'The firms have been accused of short-termism and in trading off integrity and quality against profitability'.[3]

As the unfolding crisis at PwC illustrates, too many corporations succumb to greed and feel too little obligation to society. Some might argue that this is the price society has to pay for the creative destructiveness of capitalism. But all the scandals examined in the book were avoidable; they arose from structural failures in both government and corporations.

Consequently, scandals and inquiries come and go like a travelling circus. The frequency of scandals raises the fundamental question of where the primary causation lies: the downside of a deregulated economy; deficiencies in corporate culture; inadequate legislation governing corporate behaviour; timid regulators; and/or political complacency. There are problems in all five areas.

Deregulation

Promoting the supposed benefits of a deregulated economy was at the forefront of corporate interests when the Hawke and Howard governments pursued this policy. But deregulation has been a double-edged sword; it has delivered higher economic growth (and greater concentration of wealth) but created the conditions for riskier corporate behaviour. As the economist and long-time campaigner against the abuse of power by the big four banks, Evan Jones, argues: 'The political class assented to comprehensive financial deregulation during the 1980s, and it has never since had the intelligence and the courage to revisit that decision'.[4]

In many of the scandals discussed in this book, the public interest has been knowingly forsaken for the interests of either a particular corporation or a set of corporate interests, often relying on the ideological rationale of free markets. For examples, look no further than the sweetheart deals done over gambling licensing and the deregulation of aged care.

The 1980s corporate cowboys exposed the dangers of too little regulation of the financial system, producing a string of devastating collapses. These collapses should have been a warning that light regulation of the financial markets and corporate behaviour could harm society, but no effective action was taken. Light-touch regulation prevailed in ensuing years, leading to the collapse of HIH Insurance and Storm Financial. So, too, the serial bad behaviour of banks: calls for a royal commission into the banks were steadfastly refused by the federal Liberal government until Prime Minister Malcolm Turnbull backtracked in 2017, having previously described such demands as 'risky and unnecessary'.[5]

The ongoing political negligence around the damaging impacts of deregulation has been staggering. A particularly disturbing case was the Howard government's deregulation of the aged care sector at the behest of corporate interests. Warnings fell on deaf ears. Highly vulnerable people suffered; some died. The inaction while corporations reaped great profits revealed a nation that had lost its moral bearings. It took a royal commission to get to the truth: that the policy itself had let greed rip. There are other cases, such as the child care industry, not covered in this book, where deregulation under Howard had damaging impacts on the provision of an essential service.

It's time to ask a fundamental question: how much regulation does the economy need to protect society from corporations that go rogue?

Regulation

Only a handful of CEOs or directors have ever faced criminal or civil charges arising from big corporate scandals. Regulators, with the exception of AUSTRAC, have shied away from most of the significant cases of corporate malfeasance. Regulators operate within a framework of legislation but also develop their own individual organisational cultures. ASIC highlights this issue of regulatory culture. The lame excuses it has used for not consistently taking a 'tough cop' approach have, on occasions, infuriated the public. The popular cry that the 'big end of town' receives little more than a slap on the wrist is borne out by continual examples of unethical corporate behaviour being rewarded with large severance payouts.

In recent years ASIC has claimed that additional funding has enabled it to increase the number of civil and criminal proceedings it undertakes, but in terms of preventing and dealing with large-scale corporate scandals it's proved to be ineffective. As a corporate watchdog it has lacked bite, as the 2014 Senate inquiry into the agency noted: 'ASIC has limited powers and resources but even so appears to miss or ignore early warning signs of corporate wrongdoing or troubling trends that pose a risk to consumers'.[6] And even if its activity has increased lately, this hasn't stopped the persistent criticism that it has been reluctant to go after the big corporations. One critic said: 'Some little guys are put through the wringer to salve everybody's conscience, but the big guys remain untouched'.[7] The recent charges brought against Star Casino may signal the onset of a tougher approach. Maybe.

At the time of writing, a Senate inquiry into ASIC was underway. It's been inundated with claims that the agency has been asleep at the wheel; that it has a 'sick' culture; that radical change is needed to fix it.[8] The Albanese government will likely be under pressure to come up with a meaningful set of reforms to ensure that thousands more Australians don't suffer from the lack of proper scrutiny and enforcement of the *Corporations Act* that has plagued the organisation's history. As Nationals Senator John Williams once proclaimed: 'I want a regulator that is feared not a wimpy group of bureaucrats'.

Clearly, the shift from a command-and-control style of regulation towards greater reliance on corporate self-regulation has been a dismal failure. The problem has been exacerbated by the slap-on-the-wrist approach to ethical failures in corporations – those where the public interest has been clearly damaged but no effective action was taken against corporations.

It's not just ASIC's performance that has been under scrutiny. Other regulators established under legislation – notably in the casino industry and the media – have been captured by corporate interests. It's time to rethink the purpose of regulation. As matters stand, the answer appears to be to placate corporate interests as much as possible.

Consequently, not only has there been no message of deterrence sent to corporations, but the reverse is true: they can get away with unethical behaviour. Directors sometimes sign off on shareholders' funds to pay fines imposed on corporations without incurring any penalty to themselves.

Corporate culture

The record of James Hardie is a reminder that corporations are capable of turning a blind eye to inflicting serious ill health and death caused by their operations in order to generate profits. Allegations raised against Bupa Aged Care for contributing to deaths among residents in their care didn't shift the company's business model until it was compelled to change. Other corporations conveniently minimise the social devastation they cause. The harm caused by problem gambling in Crown and the Federal Group's venues has gone largely unaddressed. Ethics and capitalism have long been uneasy bedfellows; profits rule the day.

It's time that corporations moved beyond the simplistic model of maximisation of shareholder value to embrace the stakeholder model; that is, one that takes into consideration the broader societal impact of corporations. There have been repeated calls for such a change, and the executives of many well-run corporations would argue that they have responded with a greater commitment to their responsibility to society. The push-back against bad corporate behaviour described in this book shows that expectations of CEOs and the companies they lead is changing: they are expected to act ethically, to operate sustainably and to speak out on key social issues. This is a far cry from Milton Friedman's edict that only profits matter.

Unfortunately, no one is compelling corporations to be good corporate citizens or holding them accountable for their respective performances. For some corporations, attending to corporate culture has been simply a compliance exercise – a form of ticking the box – as witnessed in the cases of Westpac and Rio Tinto. Both had shiny mission statements that failed to save them from reputational implosion and societal damage. A review of the *Corporations Act* should consider meaningful ways to make corporations more accountable.

The balance between the shareholder versus the stakeholder model of corporate behaviour remains a contentious issue. 'Today', argued *The Economist*, 'shareholder value rules business'.[9] Others, such as Harvard economist Rebecca Henderson, argue that the current focus on maximisation of shareholder value is 'an exceedingly dangerous idea, not just to society and the planet but also to the health of business itself'.[10]

The case studies in this book add further weight to the critics of corporations maximising shareholder value. Too many corporations have a singular focus on profits, which, in turn, fosters poor organisational cultures that can precipitate scandal. And shareholders can be badly damaged by corporations that chase profits at all costs. While some investors want quick returns, many invest in corporations for the long haul and want sustainably run corporations.

'Attending to corporate culture' has become one of the buzz words of the business community, especially in light of the 2018 banking royal commission, which exposed such egregious deficiencies at the very epicentre of Australia's capitalist system. Of course, corporate culture starts at the top with CEOs and boards.

Identifying CEOs with a propensity to drive corporations into scandal is a fraught exercise. Drive, ambition and self-confidence are seen as desirable qualities for CEOs. Yet when these morph into narcissistic behaviour – high ego, over-estimation of abilities, grandiosity and a feeling of entitlement – problems arise. Complicating matters further, some CEOs also have characteristics associated with psychopathic behaviour – a capacity for charm, ruthlessness and domination, and a lack of empathy. It's not always clear which constellation of characteristics CEOs possess. Yet the need to have a clearer grasp on what makes a dangerous or lethal CEO remains an important undertaking because of the role they play in setting corporate culture. Poor corporate culture is a fairly good indicator of the likelihood of a corporation going rogue.

Over the past decades, too many CEOs have become privileged, entitled, prince-like, fuelled by eye-watering remuneration packages. Every CEO involved in the scandals examined in this book enjoyed among the most opulent lifestyles in the country. But it's a trap most don't seem to know they're getting into. To attain the lifestyle, CEOs have typically been required to meet short-term goals.[11] But international research has shown a connection between excessive CEO remuneration and unethical and illegal corporate behaviour.[12] Equally, there's no real evidence that highly paid, 'celebrity' CEOs are a key determinant of a corporation's long-term success; that lies in its management culture.[13]

The elites who run the corporate sector have pulled the wool over the eyes of the public, insinuating that celebrity-type CEOs are the vital cog in a corporation's success. The arms race that has ratcheted up remuneration packages over the past thirty years has become normalised. However, there has been too little acknowledgment that these packages are a key driver of many corporate scandals, including those described in this book. Society has ended up with a whatever-it-takes culture to generate profits and meet performance targets. The culture is quite ruthless and threatens the interests of both shareholders and the public.

Despite the flaws demonstrated by many of the CEOs discussed in this book, there's no easy way to address the problems posed by their personalities. Their talents and flaws can coexist in mysterious combination. That Alan Bond was both national sporting hero and villain highlights this complexity. The lack of a consistent ethical core among many CEOs heightens the risk that some corporations will abuse their power and/or descend into scandal. The only real antidote to bad behaviour among CEOs and senior executives is a stronger system of penalties like that, for example, which exists in America, but has been absent in Australia.

CEOs with dangerously grandiose ambitions and ruthless business strategies can be very hard to stop before scandal erupts. Such leaders can overwhelm boards. Despite all the warnings from recent literature about the presence of corporate narcissists and psychopaths, few people are in any position to know how to weed out potentially flawed corporate leaders. By the same token, there's little or no evidence that boards even try to grapple with this problem. There's obviously a role to play on this issue for peak bodies such as the Australian Institute of Company Directors. They could provide directors with better selection process procedures for appointing CEOs and strategies for managing those with difficult personalities.

Various suggestions have been made to temper the potential recklessness of corporate leaders: capping CEO salaries at twenty or thirty times the average wage, taxing heavily the higher end of the salary scale and empowering shareholders to have a greater say over executive salaries. Just like society imposes a minimum wage, it's time to consider a maximum wage. Often framed as a measure to combat inequality, it is equally relevant to protecting society from corporate excess. Any Google search will show that this is a lively debate. The reason it stays off the government agenda attests to the power corporations wield.

The role and performance of boards remain as problematic as that of CEOs. Since the Hilmer report was published in 1993 too little has changed. Professor Fred Hilmer highlighted the problems boards had in meeting their conflicting responsibilities: monitoring the executive and enhancing the profits of a company while protecting its reputation. Hilmer found too often that a board's response to management was passive and acquiescent.[14]

While education programs for directors have become available since the Hilmer report was published, the behaviour of many boards remains well below the required standard. Too many directors are lazy, overly obliging, sycophantic or ill-informed – sometimes in combination. Being a board member of a large corporation is like membership of an elite club; directors can rub shoulders with the rich and famous and have little expected of them. A strange group mentality permeated the boardrooms examined in this book. Rigorous debate was the exception rather than the rule. The board members of Crown Resorts were aware of the risks of promoting gambling in China and the existence of triad gangs but thought management on the ground was handling these issues. What the company's risk management committee actually did remains a mystery.

Have boards really changed? Despite some advances in diversity of membership, notably an increase in female appointees, boards are too often stacked with cronies, family members, ex-politicians, fawning company executives and the ill qualified, as if corporate decision-makers are emulating party-political branch stacking. 'Dud directors keep filling up boardrooms', Sarah Danckert, business reporter for the *Sydney Morning Herald*, recently lamented.[15] In other words, the board system, at least at the big end of town, is not far off being broken.

Somehow, the failure to ask hard questions of executives doesn't constitute a lack of due diligence under the *Corporations Act* as interpreted by ASIC. This is an obvious area in which the Act could be toughened up. It should be made very clear that directors must scrutinise executive decisions and that this should be made transparent in board minutes. This should especially be the case with risk management. Too often, risk blindness has prevailed on the boards of corporations that have gone rogue.[16] Problems are simply ignored. Otherwise, many directors enjoy a gravy-train existence, raking in hundreds of thousands of dollars a year in fees to rubber-stamp management.

The list of catastrophic board failures is a long one. It's time to think about legally imposed minimum standards for boards in terms of diversity, experience, education and training, and limits on the number of board appointments any individual can accrue.

Is the *Corporations Act* fit for purpose?

Given the problems associated with deregulation and poor corporate culture, the inevitable question arises: are corporate activities embedded in adequate legislation? At one level the *Corporations Act* suffices as a guide to good corporate behaviour. The Act spells out that directors and executives should act in good faith; with care and diligence; avoid improper use of information and position; and disclose conflicts of interest. The fact that the Act has been so rarely used to address the big corporate scandals suggests that the main problem is the enforcement of the Act, not the Act itself.

However, there are areas where the Act appears to lack adequate definition: ensuring a proper information flow between the executive and the board; ensuring risk management is taken seriously; balancing the long-term reputation of a corporation with its search for profit; and taking into account the wider societal impact of its operations. Corporate law is notoriously complex and the preserve of experts. I therefore don't presume to have prescriptive solutions to these problems other than to state the obvious: it's time to examine whether the *Corporations Act* is still fit for purpose. As Suzanne Corcoran, Emeritus Professor of Law at Flinders University, has argued: 'much of our corporate law historically, and currently, supports ordinary corporate vices, and only discourages bad conduct when it becomes extreme'.[17] This lax approach is a product of the ideological view that corporations are self-regulating, which has proved to be disastrous.

There is a strong case to be made that the Act should also be changed to make it compulsory for corporations to consider the public interest. At the very least, they should be required by law to report on the triple bottom line; that is, on their financial, social and environmental impacts. Such an approach is a fair trade-off for corporations being handed the legal protection of limited liability; that is, protection of the private assets of investors and owners from the consequences of corporate behaviour.

Political complacency

Why aren't corporate excesses stopped? The answer is as simple as it is uncontroversial: corporations have just got too powerful. Kowtowing to corporate interests is the way the game of politics has been normalised. It confirms how the political process has been corrupted by powerful vested interests. Evan Jones refers to 'the natural leverage of corporate capital': that, 'when in Opposition, some Parliamentarians feel free to engage in a bit of dissenting bluster. When in government and tied to strict party solidarity, they go to water'.[18]

It's not just the rivers of political donations and dark money that have driven politicians into a cowered attitude towards big corporations, it's the unquestioning reliance on corporations to produce endless growth – jobs, jobs, jobs. And, the secretive world of government–business relations provides benefits to the post-political careers of many politicians, who would otherwise go unnoticed in the corporate world. They trade on their connections to those still in the corridors of power. With both sides playing the corporate game of politics, real reform of the system has been stymied.

Over the decades, this symbiotic relationship between governments and corporations has morphed into a mindset of corporate entitlement. Not only do powerful corporations expect their interests to be serviced, they assume that there will be no accountability, that the 'system' will protect their arrangements. It is this culture of corporate arrogance and government deference that so easily slips into scandal.

Governments have continually chosen to turn a blind eye to the nefarious activities of corporations because corporations have proved adept at playing the political game. Financial commentator Martin

Wolf has written that 'corporations are not rule-takers but rule makers … via politics'.[19] In her study of corporate power in Australia, University of New South Wales academic Lindy Edwards concluded that, across key sectors of the economy, 'our democracy was not able to rein in the mega-corporations and defend the public interest'.[20]

The ability of corporations to capture the state – as many in this book have done – should be a key area of reform. The goal should be to curtail the political influence that corporations exercise. This can be achieved through democratic-enhancing measures that have repeatedly been called for: banning corporate political donations, opening up the lobbying industry to full transparency, and enhancing regulation. Loading corporate leaders up with perverse incentives – alongside weak regulation – has proved to be detrimental to society. It has also proved detrimental to the reputations of many corporations.

Nonetheless, a counterweight to corporate power has come from an unexpected quarter. As the latter case studies examined in this book show, Australia's system of compulsory superannuation has helped create an increasingly powerful counterbalance to corporate abuse of power by insisting on greater compliance with higher ethical standards (commonly referred to as environment, social and governance risk, or ESG). The financial power now wielded by industry-based super funds gives the collective voice of ordinary Australians a seat at the table of capitalist enterprise. The game is changing. But how far the big superannuation funds will go in trying to enforce higher ethical standards in corporations remains unclear. And it shouldn't be left to third parties to clean up corporate excesses.

The debate about why corporations are scandal-prone has been too fragmented; public outrage dies down and, like a fireworks display, new scandals shoot off sparks of anger in all directions. The question, then, is what should be done to ensure that all corporations operating in the country act within an ethical and effective legal framework?

A big rethink

But, perhaps, the biggest challenge is to rethink the place of capitalism in society in an age dominated by corporations. When the philosopher of capitalism, Adam Smith, wrote *The Wealth of Nations* in 1776, he perceived capitalism as both an economic and a moral system; one capable of generating wealth for freely competing individuals, but which spread its benefits across society. Smith, of course, was writing in an age dominated by small businesses. But he could also see change on the horizon. He harboured deep reservations about a new entity – the joint stock company – that was emerging in the late 18th century. As one commentator noted, 'it was no accident that he spoke of the "wealth of nations," not the "wealth of corporations"'.[21]

The more recent arrival of large-scale, often monopolistic, companies that have the power to shape the destiny of society requires us to revisit the critiques of modern capitalism to preserve what Smith saw as the inherent benefits of competitive markets, while addressing the dangers associated with the concentration of capital.

To protect the public, we have to change the way corporations operate. In the broadest sense they should serve society and not just the interests of shareholders and executives. Just ask the victims of Bell Resources, Bond Corporation, James Hardie, Storm Financial, the big four banks, the Federal Group, Crown Casino, Bupa and Rio Tinto. And what about News Corp? Can it continue to pretend that many Australians are not angered by its efforts to marginalise climate change? Sure it can. Freedom of expression trumps facts in a system designed to protect the interests of the powerful.

The next corporate scandal is likely just around the corner.

ACKNOWLEDGMENTS

I have a wonderful publisher in NewSouth. Executive Publisher Elspeth Menzies backed the project from the outset and provided a continual stream of editorial advice and constructive feedback which made a real difference to the book. The entire team at NewSouth are a delight to work with – their professionalism was extremely helpful and much appreciated.

I would like to thank the following for providing extended interviews: Joe Aston, Stewart Levitt and Stephen Mayne. Each has had a long history in dealing with corporations, and I benefited from their knowledge, insights and store of good stories.

I had conversations and interviews with a select number of other people who wished to remain anonymous. I thank them nonetheless for their contribution.

Garry Bailey provided helpful feedback on chapter 8 and Dr Shino Konishi added her cultural knowledge to chapter 13. I thank them both for their time and expertise.

The book benefited from John Mapps adding his editorial expertise to the final draft of the manuscript. I thank him for his contribution.

Of course, the author is fully responsible for the contents of the book.

I would like to thank my family for their interest in my projects and especially my wife, Marilyn. As she has done for all my books, she acted as a sounding board for ideas, a constructive critic and a source of continual encouragement. I am very privileged to have a partner who not only takes an active interest in my writing projects but who adds significantly to them.

NOTES

Introduction

1 *Australian Financial Review*, 15 November 2020.
2 This term is used to focus on four criteria of bad corporate behaviour:
(1) Where a corporation goes bankrupt from a risky business model with major social consequences.
(2) Where the CEO and/or executives are charged with either criminal conduct or breaches under the *Corporations Act 2001*.
(3) Where a corporation breaches accepted standards of ethical behaviour and attracts widespread public criticism.
(4) Where a corporation uses its power to pursue disproportionate influence over public policy outcomes.
3 Beresford, 2018.
4 Beresford, 2018.
5 Padayachee, 2021.

Ripping off Medibank and Medicare: The rise of corporate medicine

1 ABC *7.30*, 17 October 2022.
2 This was the title of his 2012 autobiography; see Edelsten, 2012.
3 Cadzow, 2010a.
4 Wynne, 2005.
5 Edelsten, 2012, p 60.
6 Edelsten, 2012, p 60.
7 Rice, 1985.
8 *Canberra Times*, 10 December 1970.
9 *The Bulletin*, 17 April 1971.
10 *The Bulletin*, 8 August 1970.
11 *The Bulletin*, 15 May 1971.
12 Flynn, 2004.
13 *The Bulletin*, 17 April 1971.
14 Flynn, 2004.
15 Wilson, 1989.
16 Edelsten, 2012.
17 Cited in Cadzow, 2010a.
18 Edelsten, 2012, p. 70.
19 Tayan, 2021.
20 Edelsten, 2012, p 74.
21 Edelsten, 2012, p 73.
22 New South Wales Medical Tribunal, 2000.
23 Edelsten, 2012, p 79.
24 Moffitt, 1974.
25 *Canberra Times,* 23, 26 May 1992.
26 Edelsten, 2012, p 86.
27 *Australian Jewish News*, 8 August 2008. This was a review of Saffron's son's memoir of his father titled *Gentle Satan*.
28 Steketee, 2021; McClymont, 2021.
29 Molloy, 2021.
30 Rice, 1985.
31 *Canberra Times,* 21 August 1976.
32 Flynn, 2004.
33 Wilson, 1989.
34 Armstrong, 1977; Germov, 1995.
35 Joint Committee on Accounts, 1982.
36 Flynn, 2004, p 58.
37 Joint Committee of Public Accounts, 1985.
38 Rice, 1985.
39 *Canberra Times,* 28 October 1984.
40 *Canberra Times,* 29 April 1976.
41 Armstrong, 1977.
42 Mann, 1987.
43 Edelsten, 2011, p 140.
44 Kurukchi, 2009.
45 *Canberra Times*, 15 June 2021.

46 *Tribune*, 22 April 1987.
47 Mann, 1987.
48 Mann, 1987.
49 *Tribune*, 27 November 1985.
50 *Canberra Times*, 15 June 2021.
51 New South Wales Medical Tribunal, 2000.
52 Kurukchi, 2009.
53 Cited in Cadzow, 2010b.
54 Flynn, 2004.
55 Blake, 1996.
56 Cited in Cadzow, 2010b.
57 News.com.au, 2 June 2014.
58 Lynch, 2021.
59 Bongiorno, 2021.
60 Tugwell, 2006.
61 Bongiorno, 2021.
62 New South Wales Medical Tribunal, 2000.
63 ABC *Four Corners*, 'Branded', updated version 10 August 2011.
64 Flynn, 2004, p 253.
65 Flynn, 2004, p 254.
66 *Canberra Times*, 12 November 1985.
67 *Sydney Morning Herald*, 4 July 1998.
68 Flower, 2021.
69 Edelsten, 2011, p 149.
70 *Sydney Morning Herald*, 12 September 2009.
71 Lambert, 2017.
72 Cited in Tugwell, 2006.
73 Edelsten, 2011, p. 162.
74 *Canberra Times*, 3 February 1994.
75 Flynn, 2004, p 254.
76 Joint Committee of Public Accounts, 1985, p 90.
77 Joint Committee of Public Accounts, 1985, p 92.
78 *Canberra Times*, 12 September 1985.
79 *Canberra Times*, 26 November 1989.
80 *Canberra Times*, 26 November 1989.
81 Medical Tribunal of New South Wales, 2000.
82 *Canberra Times*, 14 March 1988.
83 Edelsten, 2012, p 213.
84 Medical Tribunal of New South Wales, 2000.
85 Edelsten was not deregistered in either Queensland or the Australian Capital Territory.
86 *Canberra Times*, 15 August 1990.
87 Edelsten, 2011, p 253.
88 Molloy, 2021.
89 Cited in Flynn, 2004, p 296.
90 Molloy, 2021.
91 Molloy, 2021.
92 *Daily Mail*, 13 October 2015.

Empire of debt: Bond Corporation

1 See obituary, *Canberra Times*, 3 September 1990.
2 Haigh, 1991.
3 McGlue, 2018.
4 Sykes, 1996.
5 Sykes, 1996.
6 *Daily Telegraph*, 7 August 2004.
7 *The Australian*, 28 September 2004.
8 Maiden, 1996.
9 *Daily Telegraph*, 5 August 2004.
10 Sykes, 1996.
11 Frith, 2003.
12 Barry, 1991, p 336.
13 See Barry, 1991; Maher, 1990.
14 Identified by Professor Peter Kramer, Professor of Psychiatry, Brown University, in an interview with Finocchiaro, 2011.
15 Barry, 1991, p 44.
16 Maher, 1990, p 19.
17 Cited in Maher, 1990, p 24.
18 Maher, 1990, p 35.
19 Sykes, 1996.
20 Sykes, 2015.
21 Chenoweth, 2011.
22 Hornery, 2015.
23 Hornery, 2015.
24 Maher, 1990, p 76.
25 Sprange, 2015.
26 *Canberra Times*, 27 December 1977.
27 Babiak and Hare, 2006.
28 Verrender, 2015.
29 *The Bulletin*, 15 November 1983.
30 *Papua New Guinea Post Courier*, 23 October 1974.
31 *Tribune*, 29 October 1974.
32 Lipscombe, 1976.

33 Barry, 1991.
34 Lipscombe, 1976.
35 *Sydney Morning Herald*, 11 October 1997.
36 Ryan, 2003a.
37 Sykes, 1996, p 17.
38 Stoller, 2019.
39 Cited in Sparrow, 2015.
40 Button, 2003.
41 Pilger, 1991.
42 Cited in Pilger, 1991.
43 *Canberra Times,* 29 May 1989.
44 Kramer, interview with Finocchiaro, 2011.
45 Haigh, 1991.
46 Cited in Sparrow, 2015.
47 *The Bulletin,* 15 November 1983.
48 *WA Today,* 10 August 2017.
49 Barry, 2000, p 7.
50 Dunn, 2015.
51 Dunn, 2015.
52 Verrender, 2015.
53 Verrender, 2015.
54 Barass, 2015.
55 Stannard, 1983.
56 Waller, 1989.
57 Burke was jailed twice but had his convictions overturned on appeal; see Beresford, 2008.
58 Beresford, 2008.
59 Beresford, 2008.
60 Cited in the *West Australian*, 8 June 2015.
61 Toohey, 2015.
62 Maiden, 2015.
63 Maiden, 2015.
64 Maiden, 2015.
65 Brailsford and Knights, 1998.
66 Sykes, 1996.
67 Partridge, 2020.
68 Egan, 2005.
69 Buttery and Shadur, 1991.
70 Kramer, interview with Finocchiaro, 2011.
71 *Canberra Times*, 28 November 1987.
72 AAP, 5 September 2005.
73 Cited in Egan, 2005.
74 Koch, 2015.
75 O'Donnell, 2011.
76 Cited in the *Australian Financial Review*, 23 December 2020.
77 Thomson, 2011.
78 Davies, 1990.
79 McGlue, 2018.
80 Davies, 1990.
81 *Canberra Times*, 19 July 1994.
82 Tully, 2015.
83 *Canberra Times*, 12 August 1992.
84 *New York Times*, 23 December 1988.
85 Lane, 2016.
86 *Australian Financial Review*, 24 June 1995.
87 Barry, 1991, p 356.
88 Kaye, 2017.
89 Kay, 1991.
90 Sykes, 2015.
91 Barry, 2000.
92 *Canberra Times*, 13 April 1989.
93 Barry, 2000, p 291.
94 ABC *PM*, 14 August 2000.
95 News.com.au, 22 October 2009.
96 Cited in Laurence, 2002.
97 *Canberra Times*, 18 June 1999.
98 *Australian Jewish News*, 20 September 1991.
99 *Sydney Morning Herald*, 2 November 1998.
100 News.com.au, 21 October 2009.
101 Verrender, 2015.

Dreams of Hollywood: Christopher Skase and Qintex

1 Verrender, 2001.
2 McCrann, 2001.
3 Van der Plaat, 1996.
4 Salis, 2016.
5 Cited in Hewett, 1990.
6 Hewett, 1990.
7 Hoyte, 2004.
8 Beveridge, 2001b.
9 Blue, 2001.
10 Van der Plaat, 1996.
11 Van der Plaat, 1996, p 28.
12 *Canberra Times*, 29 May 1990.
13 Van der Plaat, 1996.
14 Bentley, 2004.

15 Hoyte, 2004, p 11.
16 Haselhurst, 1984.
17 McCrann, 2001.
18 *Herald Sun*, 14 September 2005.
19 Sykes, 1996, p 294.
20 Van der Plaat, 1996, p 16.
21 Van der Plaat, 1996.
22 *Herald Sun*, 7 August 2001.
23 Van der Plaat, 1996, p 27.
24 Van der Plaat, 1996.
25 Hewett, 1990.
26 Haselhurst, 1984.
27 Haselhurst, 1984.
28 Gottliebsen and Cromie, 1989.
29 *Australian Financial Review*, 21 April 1989.
30 Hoyte, 2004, p 14.
31 Walsh, 1997.
32 Hoyte, 2004, p 48.
33 Colebatch, 2019.
34 *Australian Jewish News*, 15 February 1991.
35 Armstrong and Gross, 1995.
36 Blue, 2001.
37 *Canberra Times*, 16 October 1991.
38 Fredericks, 1992.
39 Hewett, 1997.
40 Hoyte, 2004, p 49.
41 Gottliebsen, 2001.
42 Grenning, 2003.
43 *Canberra Times*, 12 February 1994.
44 Childs, 1994.
45 Beveridge, J, 2001a.
46 Bentley, 2004.
47 Bentley, 2004.
48 Van der Plaat, 1996.
49 Blue, 2001.
50 Van der Plaat, 1996.
51 Gottliebsen and Cromie, 1989.
52 *The Australian*, 8 August 2001.
53 Van der Plaat, 2004, p 39.
54 Fagan, 2001.
55 *The Age*, 7 August 2001.
56 *Herald Sun*, 4 November 2018.
57 *The Age*, 7 August 2001.
58 Hoyte, 2004, p 144.
59 Van der Plaat, 2004, p 30.
60 Hoyte, 2004.
61 Hewett, 1990.
62 Hoyte, 2004, p 115.
63 Hinch, 2001.
64 Beveridge, 2001a.
65 Verrender, 1998.
66 *Gold Coast Bulletin*, 23 November 2004.
67 Lalor, 2001.
68 Hewett, 1990.
69 Hewett, 1990.
70 Grant-Taylor, 2001.
71 Bentley, 2004.
72 Hewett, 1990.
73 Hoyte, 2004.
74 *Australian Woman's Weekly*, 30 June 2010.
75 Haigh, 2006.
76 Gottliebsen, 2001.
77 Gottliebsen, 2002.
78 Dodson, 1990.
79 Beveridge, 2001a.
80 Fagan, 2001.
81 *Australian Financial Review*, 24 July, 1995.
82 *Herald Sun*, 9 September 2012.
83 ABC *News*, 21 March 2020, <www.abc.net.au/news/2020-03-22/brisbane-bears-and-how-afl-came-to-the-gold-coast/11769818>.
84 Massey, 1991.
85 *Australian Financial Review*, 9 June 1988.
86 *Canberra Times*, 29 May 1989.
87 *Canberra Times*, 8 August 1987.
88 Beveridge, 2001a.
89 Hinch, 2001.
90 Beveridge, 2001a.
91 Hinch, 2001.
92 Hewett, 1990.
93 *Australian Financial Review*, 3 June 1988.
94 *Courier-Mail*, 20 January 2001.
95 Hoyte, 2004.
96 Grenning, 2002.
97 Sykes, 1996.
98 Donnelly, 1994.
99 Hoyte, 2004, p 162.
100 Hoyte, 2004, p 71.
101 Hoyte, 2004, p 112.

102 Hoyte, 2004, p 62.
103 Van der Plaat, 1996.
104 ABC *News*, 21 October 2017.
105 Van der Plaat, 1996.
106 *Australian Financial Review*, 26 April 1988.
107 *Herald Sun*, 4 June 2000.
108 *Herald Sun*, 4 June 2000.
109 Shand, 2003.
110 Van der Plaat, 1996, p 75.
111 *The Age*, 1 September 2010.
112 *Australian Financial Review*, 16 October 1991.
113 Gottliebsen, 1990.
114 Owen, 2001.
115 Peers, 1993.
116 Van der Plaat, 1996, p 57.
117 This story came from a reliable anonymous source who knew the particular executive, who used to dine out on the story.
118 Byrge and Barnes, 2015, and Retter, 2020.
119 *Australian Financial Review*, 6 October 1989.
120 Van der Plaat, 1996.
121 Sykes, 1996.
122 *Australian Women's Weekly*, 30 June 2010.
123 Gottliebsen, 2001; Frith, 2001.
124 Cited in Verrender, 1998.
125 *The Age*, 19 December 1994.
126 *Australian Financial Review*, 4 September 1992.
127 Verrender, 1998.
128 Cameron, 2001.
129 *Canberra Times*, 18 August 1990.
130 *Australian Jewish News*, 21 December 1990.
131 *Canberra Times*, 15 April 1990.
132 *Canberra Times*, 15 April 1990.
133 *Canberra Times*, 5 December 1990.

'The shambolic journey to oblivion': HIH Insurance

1 *Sydney Morning Herald*, 15 Marcy 2003.
2 *Green Left Weekly*, 29 January 2003.
3 *Daily Telegraph*, 18 January 2003.
4 Clark, 2022.
5 Duarte, 2006.
6 Royal Commission, 2003.
7 *Daily Telegraph*, 16 April 2005.
8 Kelly, 2015.
9 Ferguson, 2019, chapter 3 (online edition).
10 Bakir, 2003.
11 *Australian Financial Review*, 11 April 2001.
12 Cooper, 2006.
13 *Weekend Australian*, 7 January 2022.
14 *Weekend Australian*, 12 May 2001.
15 *The Age*, 20 January 2003.
16 *Australian Financial Review*, 17 January 2003
17 Main, 2003.
18 *Courier-Mail*, 12 May 2001.
19 *The Australian*, 20 March 2001.
20 Korporaal, 2022 (Hockey did not face any adverse findings in the HIH Royal Commission).
21 *Daily Telegraph*, 17 April 2003.
22 Royal Commission, 2003, 'A Corporate Collapse and its Lessons', p x111.
23 *Australian Financial Review*, 1 March 2003.
24 Main, 2003.
25 Brearley, 2003b.
26 ABC *PM*, 8 August 2002.
27 Cited in Main, 2001.
28 Main, 2001.
29 Brearley 2003.
30 *Daily Telegraph*, 7 September 2002.
31 Chenoweth, 2004.
32 Brearley, 2003b.
33 Main, 2003, p 24.
34 *Australian Financial Review*, 10 August 2002.
35 Chenoweth, 2004.
36 Ansley, 2003.
37 Seiler, nd.
38 Marks, 2014.
39 Azarian, 2018.
40 *Daily Telegraph*, 26 July 2004.
41 Shand, 2003.
42 Chenoweth, 2004.

43 ABC *7.30 Report*, 15 October 2004.
44 Saville, 2002b.
45 *Australian Financial Review*, 10 August 2002.
46 ABC *7.30 Report*, 15 October 2004.
47 Sexton et al., 2003.
48 News.com.au, 17 March 2009.
49 *Sydney Morning Herald*, 22 October 2009.
50 *Australian Financial Review*, 8 June 2007.
51 Main, 2003, p 54.
52 Haigh, 2003.
53 *Sydney Morning Herald*, 30 April 2003.
54 *Sydney Morning Herald*, 20 September 2002.
55 InsuranceNews.com.au, 5 August 2019.
56 *The Age*, 21 January 2003.
57 *Sydney Morning Herald*, 6 March 2007.
58 Slosar, 2009.
59 Main, 2003.
60 Shand, 2003.
61 Kitney, 2003.
62 Spender, 2016.
63 *The Age*, 8 August 2003.
64 *The Age*, 8 August 2003.
65 Shand, 2003.
66 Chenoweth, 2004.
67 Shand, 2003.
68 *The Age*, 14 January 2003.
69 *Daily Telegraph*, 14 May 2001.
70 Ryan, 2002.
71 *The Economist*, 25 May 2002.
72 Ryan, 2002.
73 Wooley, 2001.
74 Elias, 2003.
75 White, 2001.
76 Elias, 2003.
77 *Sydney Morning Herald*, 19 February 2005.
78 ABC *PM*, 13 May 2001.
79 *The Age*, 9 April 2002.
80 Dellit, 2001.
81 Cooper, 2005.
82 On One.Tel, see Monem, 2011, and Barry, 2002.
83 Guilliant, 2003.
84 Dellit, 2001.
85 Elias, 2003.
86 Chenoweth, 2009.
87 Chenoweth, 2004.
88 Elias, 2003.
89 Royal Commission, 2003, 'A Corporate Collapse and its Lessons', p xxi.
90 Ansley 2003.
91 Chenoweth, 2004.
92 Brearley, 2003b.
93 Sexton, 2002.
94 *Daily Telegraph*, 7 September 2002.
95 *The Age*, 8 September 2005.
96 *Herald Sun*, 20 July 2002.
97 Sharwood, 2006.
98 Royal Commission, 2003, 22.6.2.
99 *The Age*, 17 February 2005.
100 Main, 2003.
101 *Courier-Mail*, 19 September 2002.
102 Ostrow, 2016.
103 Royal Commission, 2003, 'A Corporate Collapse and its Lessons', p xv.
104 Royal Commission, 2003, 'A Corporate Collapse and its Lessons', p xvi.
105 Main, 2003, p 45.
106 Royal Commission, 2003, 'A Corporate Collapse and its Lessons', p xxviii.
107 *The Australian*, 7 August 2002.
108 Kelly, 2015.
109 Kelly, 2015.
110 Main, 2003.
111 *The Australian*, 23 April 2003.
112 ABC *7.30 Report*, 2004.
113 Head, 2001.
114 *Sydney Morning Herald*, 10 August 2002.
115 *The Age*, 8 August 2002.
116 Horan, 2003.
117 Sexton, 2004.
118 *Australian Financial Review*, 28 September 2002.

119 Cited in Kohler, 2003.
120 Cited in the *Daily Telegraph*, 3 September 2003.
121 *Sydney Morning Herald*, 22 November 2008.
122 Golis, nd, p 3.
123 *The Age*, 6 December 2002.
124 Mirshekary et al., 2005.
125 Cited in Mirshekary et al., 2005, p 90.
126 *Washington Post*, 19 July 2002.
127 Cooper, 2006.
128 *Daily Telegraph*, 18 December 2003.
129 Sexton et al., 2003.
130 Sexton et al., 2003.
131 *The Australian*, 4 August 2005.
132 News.com.au, 15 January 2008.
133 ABC *PM*, 16 April 2003.
134 Korporaal, 2022.
135 *Sydney Morning Herald*, 7 August 2002.
136 James, 2008, p 192.
137 *Courier-Mail*, 30 December 2003.
138 *Daily Telegraph*, 5 October 2002.

A plot from Machiavelli: James Hardie Industries

1 Sexton, 2007.
2 *The Age*, 21 August 2004.
3 Walker, 2004.
4 Hills, 2005.
5 *Tribune*, 5 October 1983.
6 Priest, 2004a.
7 Haigh, 2007.
8 *Sydney Morning Herald*, 25 September 2004.
9 Haigh, 2007.
10 Haigh, 2007.
11 Hills, 2004.
12 Hills, 2001.
13 Australian Democracy Network, 2022.
14 *Narromine News and Trangie Advocate*, 9 December 1937.
15 *Cumberland Argus*, 26 October 1938; *West Wyalong Advocate*, 10 December 1937.
16 *The Bulletin*, 1 July 1972.
17 *The Bulletin*, 10 August 1968.
18 Merrett, 2012.
19 *Tribune*, 30 November 1977.
20 Hills, 2004.
21 Engel and Martin, 2006.
22 Cited in Moerman, van der Laan and Campbell, 2014, p 985.
23 *Canberra Times*, 4 October 1987.
24 Sully, 2021.
25 See Professor Elizabeth Sheedy's survey of 2500 bankers in Australia and Canada, cited in *The Age*, 3 June 2015.
26 *The Age*, 31 July 2004.
27 Jackson, 2004, p 19.
28 Cited in Haigh, 2007, digital edition, chapter 16.
29 Parliamentary Joint Committee on Corporations and Financial Services, 2006, p 49.
30 Moerman, van der Laan and Campbell, 2014, p 984.
31 Haigh, 2007, digital edition, chapter 17.
32 Mayne, 2009.
33 Higgins, 2009.
34 Higgins, 2009.
35 Trute, 2005.
36 Trute, 2005.
37 Gosnell, 2004.
38 Higgins, 2009.
39 Gosnell, 2004.
40 *Herald Sun*, 23 September 2004.
41 *Courier-Mail*, 25 June 2002.
42 Haigh, 2007.
43 Haigh, 2007, digital edition, chapter 16.
44 Jackson, 2004, p 199.
45 *The Age*, 21 August 2004.
46 Haigh, 2007.
47 Higgins, 2006.
48 Haigh, 2007.
49 Higgins, 2006.
50 Haigh, 2007.
51 Haigh, 2007, digital edition, chapter 13.
52 McCrann, 2001.
53 Jackson, 2004, p 13.
54 Australian Securities and Investments Commission v Macdonald (No 12)

[2009] NSWSC 714, paragraph 216.
55 Research Note No. 12, 10 August 2004, Department of Parliamentary Services.
56 *The Age*, 6 July 2005.
57 Redmond, 2012.
58 Jackson, 2004, p 212.
59 Peacock, 2009.
60 Buffini and Priest, 2004.
61 *Sydney Morning Herald*, 6 August 2004.
62 *The Australian*, 30 January 2007.
63 Jackson, 2004, pp 228–9.
64 This was established to have been the case in the decision by the High Court when it overturned the New South Wales Court of Appeal's decision in the Hardie matter. The New South Wales Court of Appeal had overturned the decision of the trial judge, Justice Gzell.
65 The press release is included in full in Jackson, 2004, p 29.
66 Bouffini and Priest, 2004.
67 Jackson, 2004, p 201.
68 *Sydney Morning Herald*, 11 May 2004.
69 Priest, 2004b.
70 A copy of the strategy was obtained by Marcus Priest and analysed in an article by him in the *Australian Financial Review* (2004b), from which the quote is taken.
71 Priest, 2004b.
72 *The Guardian*, 21 July 2004.
73 Jackson, 2004, p 193.
74 Cited in Peacock, 2009, p 215.
75 *The Age*, 31 July 2004.
76 *Sydney Morning Herald*, 23 September 2004.
77 Walker, 2004.
78 Walker, 2004.
79 Comino, 2006.
80 Redmond 2012.
81 Gettler, 2005.
82 *Sydney Morning Herald*, 6 November 2004.
83 *Sunday Territorian*, 28 August 2005.
84 *The Australian*, 13 December 2006.
85 Webb, 2007.
86 Sexton, 2009.
87 Sexton, 2008.
88 Sexton, 2009.
89 Sexton, 2009.
90 Sexton, 2009.
91 Sexton, 2009.
92 Cited in ABC *PM*, 23 April 2009.
93 Australian Securities and Investments Commission v Macdonald (No 12) [2009] NSWSC 714.

The cult: Storm Financial

1 *Sydney Morning Herald*, 3 November 2000.
2 Gaynor, 2009.
3 Raggatt, 2008a.
4 Gaynor, 2009.
5 *Townsville Bulletin*, 27 February 2009.
6 Senate debates, 25 November 2009, cited in Open Australia, 'Matters of Public Interest: Storm Financial Ltd', <www.openaustralia.org.au/senate/?id=2009-11-25.33.1>.
7 Edwards, 2020.
8 Edwards, 2020.
9 Parliamentary Joint Committee on Corporations and Financial Services, 2009, p 71.
10 'In Defence of Self-managed Super Funds', https://cdn.tspace.gov.au.
11 *Canberra Times*, 19 March 1989.
12 *Sunday Mail*, 31 August 2008.
13 Raggatt, 2008a.
14 Gaynor, 2009.
15 Gaynor, 2009.
16 Gaynor, 2009.
17 Fraser, 2009.
18 Interview, Stewart Levitt, March 2022.
19 *Australian Financial Review*, 22 May 2008.
20 *Australian Financial Review*, 26 September 2012.
21 *Townsville Bulletin*, 29 July 2006.
22 Hanrahan, 2018.
23 Barry, 2009.
24 Raggatt, 2008b.

25 *Sunday Mail*, 14 December 2008.
26 Cited in ABC *Four Corners*, 2009.
27 *Townsville Bulletin*, 16 January 2009.
28 *Townsville Bulletin*, 11 April 2006.
29 Raggatt, 2018.
30 ABC *PM*, 26 September 2012.
31 Passmore, 2015.
32 Submission Jack and Frances Dale, Joint Parliamentary Committee, 2009 submission No. 121.
33 Barry, 2011.
34 Royal Commission into Misconduct in the Banking, Superannuation and Financial Services Industry, 2019 Final Report, Volume 1.
35 Cited in Raggatt, 2008b.
36 Parliamentary Joint Committee, 2009, p 19.
37 Raggatt, 2008b.
38 *Cairns Post*, 28 March 2009.
39 Schwarten, 2009.
40 Submission, Statement written on behalf of a number of ex-Storm clients, Joint Parliamentary Committee, Submission No. 1.
41 *Townsville Bulletin*, 6 May 2009.
42 Interview, Stewart Levitt, March 2022.
43 *Sydney Morning Herald*, 4 September 2009.
44 Washington, 2009b.
45 *Townsville Bulletin*, 16 January 2009.
46 Submission, Jo-Anne and Alan Harding, Joint Parliamentary Committee, 2009, Submission No. 171.
47 Joint Parliamentary Committee, 2009, p 29.
48 Submission, Alain D'Hotman De Villers, Joint Parliamentary Committee, 2009, Submission No. 150.
49 *Australian Financial Review*, 26 September 2012.
50 Interview, Stewart Levitt, March 2022.
51 Barry, 2011.
52 Submission, name withheld, Joint Parliamentary Committee, Submission No. 9.
53 *Sunday Mail*, 14 December 2008.
54 Schwarten, 2009.
55 Submission, names withheld, Joint Parliamentary Committee, Submission No. 1.
56 *Townsville Bulletin*, 5 March 2008.
57 *Townsville Bulletin*, 5 March 2008.
58 Barry, 2011.
59 Washington, 2009b.
60 Washington, 2009c.
61 Washington, 2009a.
62 Joint Parliamentary Committee, 2009, p 42.
63 Ferguson and Vedelago, 2013.
64 Jones, 2012.
65 Joint Parliamentary Committee, 2009, p 32.
66 Davis, 2018.
67 Keane, 2018.
68 *The Age*, 15 July 2014.
69 Prior, 2018.
70 *The Age*, 15 July 2014.
71 Jones, 2012.
72 Kruger, 2009.
73 Kruger, 2009.
74 Cited in Barry, 2011.
75 *The Age*, 16 June 2004.
76 *The Age*, 28 October 2006.
77 *Crikey*, 20 August 2009.
78 Washington, 2009b.
79 *Australian Financial Review*, 11 June 2009.
80 Submission, name withheld, Joint Parliamentary Committee, 2009, Submission No. 48.
81 Brailey, nd.
82 Submission, Denise Brailey, Joint Parliamentary Committee, 2009, Submission No. 358.
83 Corporate Finance Institute, 14 October 2022.
84 Healy, 2019, pp 141–2.
85 Australian Prudential Regulatory Authority, 2018, p 11.
86 Walker, 2000.
87 Schwarten, 2009.

88 Washington, 2009a.
89 *Australian Financial Review,* 17 October 2009.
90 Interview, Stewart Levitt, 2022.
91 Interview, Stewart Levitt, 2022.
92 Interview Stewart Levitt, 2022.
93 *Sydney Morning Herald,* 5 November 2009.
94 *Money Management,* 29 October 2009.
95 ABC *News*, 3 December 2012.
96 Interview, Stewart Levitt, March 2022.
97 Joint Parliamentary Committee, 2009, p 36.
98 Cited in Ferguson, 2014b.
99 Submission by Jeff Morris, Senate Inquiry into the Performance of the Australian Securities and Investment Commission, 2014, Submission No. 421.
100 *Australian Financial Review,* 9 February 2009.
101 Senate Economic Reference Committee, 2014, 20.10.
102 ABC *News*, 18 November 2009.
103 Joint Parliamentary Committee, 2009, p 7.
104 Senate Economics References Committee, 2014.
105 Washington, 2010.
106 John Williams, Matter of Public Interest, Storm Financial Ltd, Senate debates, 25 November 2009.
107 Legg, 2016.
108 Raggatt, 2017.
109 ABC *News*, 22 September 2014.
110 *Courier-Mail,* 10 June 2015.
111 ABC *PM*, 29 May 2013.
112 *Australian Financial Review,* 5 February 2016.
113 *Courier-Mail,* 22 March 2018.
114 ABC *News*, 22 March 2018.
115 Hanrahan, 2018.
116 Walsh and Michael, 2018.
117 Raggatt, 2017.
118 Edwards, 2020.
119 Keane, 2021.
120 Edwards, 2020, p 66.
121 Hewett, 2014.
122 Collins, 2009.

Franchising exploitation: 7-Eleven

1 Fraser, 2016, p 84.
2 Ferguson and Toft, 2015.
3 Lacey, 2019.
4 Ferguson, 2015a.
5 *Herald Sun,* 2 September 2015.
6 *New Daily*, 7 October 2016.
7 Henderson, 2018.
8 Parliamentary Joint Committee on Corporations and Financial Services, 2019.
9 Buchan, 2017.
10 ACTU, 2018; Ferguson and Danckert, 2017.
11 Parliamentary Joint Committee on Corporations and Financial Services, 2019, p xv.
12 Parliamentary Joint Committee on Corporations and Financial Services, 2019.
13 *Domain News*, 28 May 2015.
14 *Australian Food News*, 28 May 2014.
15 Johnson, 2001.
16 *Australian Financial Review*, 30 November 2017.
17 Senate, 2016.
18 Senate, 2016.
19 *PR Daily*, 19 June 2013.
20 Franchise City, nd.
21 Senate, 2016, p 222.
22 Fraser, 2016.
23 *Australian Financial Review,* 1 March 2017.
24 Berg and Farbenblum, 2017.
25 Fraser, 2016, p 76.
26 Senate, 2017.
27 Senate, 2017, p 8.
28 Fraser, 2016.
29 Senate, 2016.
30 Johnson, 1998.
31 Cited in Johnson, 1998.
32 Senate, 2016, p 230.
33 *Sydney Morning Herald*, 29 March 2016, and interview with Stewart Levitt, March 2022.

34 *The Leader,* 28 March 2016.
35 Johnson, 1998.
36 Johnson, 1998.
37 Interview, Stewart Levitt, March 2020.
38 *Australian Food News,* 1 December 2021.
39 Fair Work Ombudsman, 2016, p 49.
40 Senate, 2016, p 220.
41 Ferguson and Toft, 2015.
42 Ferguson and Danckert, 2015.
43 Senate, 2016, p 253.
44 Ferguson, Danckert and Toft, 2015.
45 Fair Work Commission, 2016.
46 Interview, Stewart Levitt, March 2022.
47 Franchise City, nd.
48 Fair Work Commission, 2016.
49 Fair Work Commission, 2016, p 41.
50 Ferguson, 2015b.
51 Senate, 2015b.
52 *Sydney Morning Herald,* 20 November 2015.
53 Senate, 2015b.
54 Ferguson, 2016a.
55 Ferguson, 2015b.
56 Fair Work Commission, 2016, p 36.
57 Berg and Farbenblum, 2018.
58 Fraser, 2016.
59 Senate, 2015a.
60 Senate, 2016, p 2018.
61 Senate, 2016, p 222.
62 Fair Work Commission, 2016.
63 Ferguson, 2015b.
64 Senate, 2015a.
65 Senate, 2015a.
66 Fair Work Commission, 2016, p 14.
67 *Australian Financial Review,* 31 August 2015.
68 Senate, 2016.
69 Cited in Nunweek, 2015.
70 Nunweek, 2015.
71 *Sydney Morning Herald,* 14 April 2015.
72 Ferguson, 2013.
73 Fraser, 2016, p 75.
74 ABC *Four Corners,* 2015.
75 Cited in Senate, 2016, pp 219–20.
76 ABC *World Today,* 24 September 2015.
77 ABC *Four Corners,* 2015.
78 Fraser, 2016, p 81.
79 Ferguson and Danckert, 2015.
80 Ferguson and Danckert, 2015.
81 *Australian Financial Review,* 31 August 2015.
82 Ferguson, 2016a.
83 Ferguson, 2016b.
84 *The Australian,* 12 May 2016.
85 Lacey, 2019.
86 Bates, 2016.
87 *Australian Financial Review,* 1 March 2017.
88 *Sydney Morning Herald,* 21 June 2017.
89 *The Age,* 7 April 2017.
90 *Australian Financial Review,* 22 February 2021.
91 *The Guardian,* 2 December 2021.
92 *Sydney Morning Herald,* 30 October 2010.
93 Interview, Stewart Levitt, March 2020.

Dark money: The Federal Group

1 O'Malley, 2018a.
2 Cited in Lee, 2018.
3 Boyce, 2020.
4 O'Malley, 2018a.
5 Boyce, 2017.
6 O'Malley, 2018a.
7 O'Malley, 2018a.
8 Lester and Bolwell, 2018.
9 Beresford, 2015, p 40.
10 Beresford, 2010.
11 Beresford, 2015.
12 ABC *7.30,* 27 October 2015.
13 Lee, 2018.
14 Boyce, 2017.
15 Boyce, 2017, p 91.
16 Cited in Lohrey, 2017.
17 Lee, 2018.
18 Cited in Lee, 2018.
19 Glaetzer, 2015.
20 Boyce, 2017.
21 Cited in Way, 2006.
22 Lee, 2018.
23 Cannane, 2021.
24 Cannane, 2021; Boyce, 2017.
25 Cited in Boyce, 2017, p 107.

26 Interview, anonymous, November 2021.
27 Beresford, 2015.
28 Rundle, 2018.
29 Lee, 2018; Neales, 2008.
30 ABC *7.30*, 27 October 2015.
31 Burton, 2020.
32 Law, 2015.
33 Boyce, 2017.
34 Bevilacqua, 2002.
35 Foster, 2017.
36 *Sydney Morning Herald*, 2 March 2018.
37 Neales, 2008.
38 Lee, 2018.
39 Interview, anonymous, November 2021.
40 *The Age*, 1 October 2016.
41 *Australian Financial Review*, 13 December 2017.
42 ABC *Fact Check*, 5 July 2018.
43 *The Guardian*, 11 February 2023.
44 Lee, 2018.
45 Boyce, 2017, p 188.
46 Lee, 2018.
47 O'Malley, 2018b.
48 O'Malley, 2018b.
49 Glaetzer, 2017.
50 O'Malley, 2018a.
51 Markham, Kinder and Young, 2017.
52 ABC *News*, 23 July 2008.
53 *The Mercury*, 8 March 2008.
54 West, 2019.
55 Beresford, 2015, p 335.
56 Beresford, 2015.
57 *The Mercury*, 20 October 2016.
58 ABC *News*, 17 December 2017.
59 Glaetzer, 2017.
60 ABC *News*, 11 May 2020.
61 Bevilacqua, 2002.
62 Interview, anonymous, October 2021.
63 Altmann, 2002.
64 Goulston, 2014.
65 Lee, 2018.
66 ABC *7.30*, 27 October 2015.
67 Glaezter, 2015.
68 Glaezter, 2015.
69 Glaetzer, 2015.
70 ABC *News*, 15 September 2015.
71 Lee, 2018; Cannane, 2021.
72 O'Malley, 2018a.
73 O'Malley, 2018a.
74 O'Malley, 2018a.
75 *The Advocate*, 15 December 2017.
76 O'Malley, 2018.
77 Boyce, 2020.
78 Rundle, 2018.
79 See *Australian Financial Review*, 28 February and 1 March 2018
80 ABC *News*, 5 March 2018.
81 Boyce, 2020.
82 Boyce, 2020.
83 O'Malley 2018b
84 ABC *News*, 19 January 2018.
85 ABC *News*, 23 February 2018.
86 ABC *News*, 23 February 2018.
87 Markam, Kinder and Young, 2017.
88 Morton, 2018a.
89 ABC *News*, 19 January 2018.
90 Cannane, 2021.
91 *Tasmanian Times*, 27 September 2020.
92 ABC *News*, 7 February 2018.
93 ABC *News*, 21 February 2018.
94 ABC *News*, 21 February 2018.
95 *Australian Financial Review*, 1 March 2018.
96 Barns, 2018.
97 Lester and Bolwell, 2018.
98 O'Connor, 2021.
99 Burton, 2020.
100 Baker, 2021.
101 *The Mercury*, 24 November 2021.

'Horror stories': Bupa Aged Care

1 Squires, 2010.
2 Wynne, 2008.
3 Corpwatch, 2021.
4 Rogozenska, 2021.
5 Sheehy, 2019; ABC *News*, 12 September 2019.
6 Martin, Evdershed and Butler, 2019.
7 9 *News*, 2 September 2018.
8 ABC *7.30 Report*, 1 May 2017; ABC *RN*, 21 August 2014.
9 *Sydney Morning Herald*, 4 June 1988.
10 Wynne, 2007a.

11 *Business Review Weekly*, 10 October 1994.
12 Wynne, 2007b.
13 Wynne, 2007a.
14 Vass, 2002.
15 Saville, 2002a.
16 *Business Review Weekly*, 26 May 2000.
17 *Business Review Weekly*, 10 October 1994.
18 Mitchell and Bye, 1997.
19 Bagwell, 1997.
20 Saville, 2002a.
21 *Herald Sun*, 2 April 2000.
22 Lawson, 1997.
23 Lawson, 1997.
24 Mitchell and Bye, 1997.
25 *Sydney Morning Herald*, 23 October 1997.
26 Aged Care Crisis Inc., 2019.
27 ABC *PM*, 29 February 2000.
28 Russell, 2020a.
29 Davies, 1996.
30 Morton, 2020.
31 Horin, 2000b.
32 Lee, 2019; Morton, 2020.
33 Hull, 2021.
34 *Sydney Morning Herald*, 7 March 2000.
35 Tingle, 2001.
36 Horin, 2000b.
37 *The Age*, 10 August 2005.
38 Davies and Birnbauer, 1998.
39 *Courier-Mail*, 26 February 2000.
40 *The Age*, 7 March 2000.
41 *The Australian*, 1 March 2000.
42 Strong, 2000.
43 Button, 2000.
44 *The Age*, 29 March 2002.
45 *Sydney Morning Herald*, 15 March 2000.
46 *Sydney Morning Herald*, 15 March 2000.
47 *The Age*, 10 March 2000.
48 Wynne, 2006.
49 *The Age*, 2 May 2000.
50 *Courier-Mail*, 20 July 2019.
51 Button, 2000.
52 Wynne, 2006.
53 Hudson, 2000.
54 *The Age*, 7 March 2000.
55 Lee, 2009.
56 Davies and Birnbauer, 1998.
57 Lohr and Head, 2000.
58 Horin, 2000a.
59 *Canberra Times*, 27 August 2001.
60 Cited in *The Weekly Source: The Business of Aging*, 16 December 2019.
61 Royal Commission into Aged Care Quality and Safety, Hobart Hearing, 2019, p 27.
62 The Australian Institute of Company Directors, 2016.
63 The Australian Institute of Company Directors, 2016; KMPG, 2018.
64 Mirza, 2018.
65 Royal Commission into Aged Care Quality and Safety, Hobart Hearing, 2019, pp 14–15.
66 Royal Commission into Aged Care Quality and Safety, Hobart Hearing, 2019, p 4.
67 *The Australian*, 14 November 2019.
68 *The Australian*, 14 November 2019.
69 *Daily Telegraph*, 2 September 2019.
70 *The Australian*, 14 November 2019.
71 Martin, Evdershed and Butler, 2019.
72 Martin, Evdershed and Butler, 2019.
73 *The Examiner*, 16 November 2019.
74 *Crikey*, 15 January 2015.
75 *Daily Telegraph*, 16 September 2019.
76 *Red Flag*, 24 October 2017.
77 Ward, 2018, p 2018.
78 ABC *News*, 21 August 2019.
79 ACCC, 2020.
80 ABC *News*, 12 September 2019.
81 *Gympie Times*, 7 September 2019.
82 Russell, 2020b.
83 Aged Care Crisis Inc., 2019.
84 Blanchard, 2017.
85 Hepworth, 2019.
86 Royal Commission, 2021, Vol 1, p 74.
87 Royal Commission into Aged Care Quality and Safety, Hobart Hearing, 2019, p 22.

'Free pass to paedophiles': Westpac

1 *The Australian,* 27 November 2019.
2 ABC *News*, 24 November 2019.
3 AUSTRAC, 2019, pp 28, 29.
4 Lynch, 2020.
5 Grigg and Chenoweth, 2019.
6 ABC *News*, 26 November 2019.
7 Ferguson, 2019a.
8 Ferguson, 2019b.
9 Williams, 2019b.
10 *Australian Financial Review*, 4 February 2020.
11 *Boss*, 3 December 2018.
12 Eyres and Frost, 2019a.
13 AUSTRAC, 2019.
14 Williams, 2019a.
15 Eyres and Frost, 2019a.
16 *The Guardian*, 23 November 2019.
17 ABC *News*, 24 December 2020.
18 ABC *News*, 24 September 2020.
19 News.com.au, 27 November 2019.
20 ABC *News*, 5 May 2021.
21 *Weekend Australian*, 27 July 2019.
22 Cited in *Crikey*, 3 December 2019.
23 Hartzer, 26 July 2018, <American_Chamber_of_Commerce_speech>.
24 Cited in Patrick, 2019.
25 *The Australian,* 13 December 2019.
26 Grigg and Chenoweth, 2019.
27 ABC *News*, 22 November 2019.
28 Royal Commission, 2018, Interim Report, vol. 1, p xvii.
29 *The Age*, 22 October 2014.
30 *The Australian*, 25 September 2018.
31 Cited in Hooper, 2020.
32 Ferguson, 2019b.
33 Jones, 2020.
34 Westpac Review Team, 2019, pp 18–19.
35 *Financial Review*, 19 August 2018.
36 Ferguson, 2019b.
37 Royal Commission, 2018, Executive Summary, p 1.
38 Westpac Review Team, p 34.
39 Williams, 2019a.
40 Westpac Review Team, 2019, p 90.
41 Hooper, 2020.
42 Richardson, 2020.
43 Richardson, 2020.
44 Interview, Stephen Mayne, October 2022.
45 AUSTRAC, 16 March 2017.
46 *Sydney Morning Herald*, 19 November 2022.
47 ABC *News*, 5 April 2018.
48 *Australian Financial Review*, 20 November 2019.
49 Van Onselen, 2019.
50 *Australian Financial Review*, 20 November 2019.
51 Maley, 2019.
52 Yun, 2021.
53 Maley, 2019.
54 Maley, 2019.
55 Cited in Patrick, 2019.
56 Maley, 2019.
57 Durkin, 2016.
58 Densley, 2012.
59 Durie, 2019.
60 *The Age,* 19 November 2005.
61 *The Australian,* 2 September 2015.
62 Aston, 2019.
63 Densley, 2012.
64 *Financial Review*, 25 November 2019.
65 ABC *News*, 22 November 2019.
66 *The Australian*, 27 November 2019.
67 *Australian Financial Review*, 25 November 2019.
68 *Australian Financial Review*, 30 November 2019.
69 *The Age*, 12 May 2011.
70 Gluyas, 2019.
71 Durkin, 2019.
72 Cited in Eyres and Frost, 2019c.
73 *The Australian*, 30 November 2019.
74 *The Australian*, 30 November 2019.
75 *The Australian*, 26 November 2019.
76 See *The Guardian*, 25 November 2019; *Sydney Morning Herald*, 26 November 2019; *Daily Telegraph*, 26 November 2019; *Australian Financial Review*, 27 November 2019; Sky News, 26 November 2019; *Financial Times*, 25 November 2019.
77 Cited in Ferguson, 2019.
78 News.com.au, 12 December 2019.

79 Australian Shareholders' Association, minutes of 12 December Westpac AGM.
80 *Australian Financial Review,* 12 December 2019; News.com.au, 12 December 2019.
81 ABC *News*, 24 September 2020.
82 *The Age*, 17 April 2019.
83 Coburn, 2021.
84 Royal Commission, 2019, p 427.
85 Schmulow, 2021.
86 ABC *News*, 23 April 2018.
87 Submissions Nos 17, 20, 30, 32 Senate Standing Committee on Economics, Public Submissions, 'The Performance of the Australian Securities and Investment Commission', 2013.
88 ABC *PM*, 25 April 2018.
89 Royal Commission 2019, Final Report, vol. 1, pp 347, 396.

'The climate change hoax': News Corp

1 Purtill and Lauder, 2022.
2 *Sydney Morning Herald*, 11 January 2020.
3 Hamilton, 2007.
4 Brailsford et al, 2020.
5 Rudd, 2019; Fielding, 2022; Beresford, 2018.
6 Craufurd Smith, 2015.
7 Wolff, 2009, digital edition, chapter 2.
8 *Daily Mail*, 3 May 2012.
9 *The Guardian*, 20 February 2013.
10 Page, 2003.
11 Page, 2003.
12 Beahm, 2012.
13 Lever, 2012.
14 Wolff, 2009 digital edition, chapter 2.
15 Interview, Stephen Mayne, October 2020.
16 Senate public hearings, 12 April 2021, p 4.
17 Senate public hearings, 12 April 2021, p 2.
18 See also Tiffen, 2021.
19 Samios, 2020.
20 *Time*, 15 January 2020.
21 *Independent*, 15 October 2020.
22 *New Daily*, 15 January 2020.
23 Gebel, 2021.
24 Irving, 2020.
25 *Sydney Morning Herald*, 17 January 2020.
26 *Sydney Morning Herald*, 11 January 2020.
27 *New Daily*, 15 January 2020.
28 *Vanity Fair*, 7 September 2021.
29 Maharaj and Dargaville, 2020.
30 Bacon and Jegan, 2020.
31 Cited in Bacon and Jegan, 2020, p 55.
32 McKnight, 2011.
33 Interview, Stephen Mayne, October 2022.
34 The Australian Centre for Corporate Responsibility, 2022, 'Advertising Tricks of the Fossil Fuel Sector'.
35 Beresford, 2018.
36 Marsh, 2020.
37 Interview, Stephen Mayne, October 2020.
38 Tiffen, 2014, digital edition, chapter 11.
39 Dover, 2020.
40 Tiffen, 2014.
41 Feldman et al., 2012.
42 Hamilton, 2007.
43 McKnight, 2011.
44 Hamilton, 2007.
45 Dembicki, 2021.
46 Dembicki, 2021.
47 Dembicki, 2021.
48 Pavlus, 2011.
49 Cave, 2020.
50 Cited in *The Ecologist*, 12 October 2015.
51 Centre for Advancing Journalism, 2020.
52 Interview, Stephen Mayne, October 2020.
53 Norman, Newman and Steffen, 2021.
54 New South Wales government, 2020.
55 Brailsford et al., 2020; WWF, 2020.
56 *The Guardian*, 7 December 2020.
57 Brailsford et al., 2020.
58 Norman, Newman and Steffen, 2021, p 2.

59 Lowy Institute (2021), 'Climate Poll 2021', 26 May.
60 *The Guardian*, 21 November 2019.
61 Mocatta and Hawley, 2020.
62 Cited in Mocatta and Hawley, 2020.
63 ABC *Media Watch*, 3 February 2020.
64 Cited in Cassella, 2019.
65 'Andrew Bolt', DeSmog, <www.desmog.com/andrew-bolt>.
66 Interview, Stephen Mayne, October 2022.
67 Institute for Strategic Dialogue, 2022.
68 See Dick, 2020.
69 Richards and Brew, 2020.
70 Hale Spencer, 2020.
71 *Daily Telegraph*, 19 November 2019.
72 ABC *News*, 11 January.
73 ABC *Media Watch*, 3 February 2020.
74 Joshi, 2020.
75 Jepsen, 2020.
76 Brailsford et al., 2020, p 4.
77 Brailsford et al., 2020, p 33.
78 Bacon and Jegan, 2020.
79 Bacon and Jegan, 2020, p 10.
80 Brailsford et al., 2020.
81 Brailsford et al., 2020, p 39.
82 Brailsford et al., 2020, p 5.
83 Senate public hearings, *Media Diversity in Australia*, 12 April 2021.
84 Senate public hearings, *Media Diversity in Australia*, 12 April 2021, p 12.
85 Gregoire, 2020.
86 *New York Times*, 13 November 2020.
87 *Renew Economy*, 13 February 2020.
88 Cited in Brailsford et al., 2020.
89 Gregoire, 2020.
90 Ritter, 2020.
91 Interview, Stephen Mayne, October 2022.
92 Senate, public hearings, *Media Diversity in Australia*, 12 April 2021, p 4.
93 Finkelstein and Tiffen, 2015.
94 Cited in Finkelstein and Tiffen, 2015, p 960.
95 Finkelstein and Tiffen, 2015.
96 Environment and Communications References Committee, 2021, public hearings, 22 October, pp 19–20.
97 Podger, 2019.
98 Lord, 2020.
99 Ricketson, 2021.
100 Environment and Communications References Committee, 2021, public hearings, 22 October, p 13.
101 *The Guardian*, 16 February 2021.
102 *New Daily*, 16 January 2020.
103 *The Age*, 9 September 2021.
104 *The Guardian*, 7 August 2018.
105 *The Bolt Report*, Sky News, 10 July, 2018.
106 *Sydney Morning Herald*, 6 September 2021.
107 Mocatta, 2021.
108 Joshi, 2021.
109 *The Guardian*, 7 August 2021.
110 Australian Communications and Media Authority, 2022.
111 *The Guardian*, 27 March, 2023.
112 Wolff, 2008.

Infiltrated by criminals: Crown Resorts

1 Godot, nd.
2 Williams, 2021.
3 Bergin, 2021, p 264.
4 Bergin, 2021, p 259.
5 Royal Commission into the Casino Operator and Licence, 2021, vol 1, p 76.
6 Royal Commission into the Casino Operator and Licence, 2021, vol 1, p 76.
7 *Canberra Times*, 24 November 2016.
8 Toohey and Sainsbury, 2017.
9 Interview, Stephen Mayne, October 2022.
10 Interview, Stephen Mayne, October 2020.
11 'Man in charge of Chinese VIP strategy leaves Crown Casino', OnlineCasinoSite, <onlinecasinosite.com/man-in-charge-of-chinese-vip-strategy-leaves-crown-casino>.

12 *Australian Financial Review*, 23 March 2011.
13 *Australian Financial Review*, 26 April 2017.
14 Toohey and Sainsbury, 2017.
15 Bergin, 2021, pp 254–55.
16 *Daily Telegraph*, 4 March 2017.
17 Royal Commission into the Casino Operator and Licence, 2021, p 76.
18 Perth Casino Royal Commission, 2022, p 404.
19 Royal Commission into the Casino Operator and Licence, 2021.
20 Keaton, 2021.
21 McKenzie, Toscano and Tobin, 2019.
22 Perth Casino Royal Commission, 2022, p 404.
23 Bergin, 2021, p 273.
24 Bergin, 2021, p 404.
25 O'Connor, 2020.
26 *Sydney Morning Herald*, 18 May 2021.
27 Bergin, 2021, p 263.
28 Bergin, 2021, p 417.
29 Bergin, 2021, p 524.
30 Bergin, 2021, p 524.
31 Bergin, 2021, p 27.
32 Murray, Grigg and Smith, 2016.
33 Bergin, 2021, p 291.
34 McKenzie, Toscano and Tobin, 2019.
35 *Australian Financial Review*, 19 October 2016.
36 *The Australian*, 8 September 2022.
37 McKenzie, Toscano and Tobin, 2019.
38 Tiffen, 2019.
39 *The Australian*, 21 August 2020.
40 McKenzie, Toscano and Tobin, 2019.
41 McKenzie, Toscano and Tobin, 2019.
42 Toohey and Sainsbury, 2017.
43 *Australian Financial Review*, 17 October 2016.
44 ABC *News*, 14 February 2021.
45 Morton, 2021; Kitney, 2018.
46 Clune, 2020.
47 Stephen Mayne, interview, October 2020.
48 ABC *Four Corners*, 2021a.
49 *Crikey*, 10 February 2021.
50 *Australian Financial Review*, 27 May 2004.
51 *Australian Financial Review*, 5 August 2019.
52 *Australian Financial Review*, 18 October 2016.
53 *Sydney Morning Herald*, 10 October 2020.
54 Pyne, 2019.
55 *Weekend Australian*, 13 April 2019.
56 Cooke, 2017.
57 Williams and Kitney, 2006.
58 Barry, 2008, p 79.
59 Kitney, 2014.
60 Tippet, 2005.
61 Kitney, 2014, p 27.
62 Hornery, 2018.
63 Guilliant, 2003.
64 ABC *Australian Story*, 2014.
65 *New Zealand Herald*, 1 February 2019.
66 Barry, 2008, p 495.
67 Sheehy, 2021.
68 Cited in Kitney, 2014, p 36.
69 Dovkants, 2014.
70 Guilliant, 2003.
71 Kitney, 2014, p 63.
72 The source of this anecdote is someone working in advertising who was in Parker's orbit.
73 Barry, 2002.
74 Tiffen, 2019.
75 Clark, 2005.
76 Sainsbury, 2019.
77 Barry, 2008, p 250.
78 *Australian Financial Review*, 23 March 2018.
79 Interview, Stephen Mayne, October 2022.
80 *Australian Financial Review*, 26 October 2021.
81 Johnson, 2020.
82 Kitney, 2018.
83 Verrender, 2021.
84 Verrender, 2021.
85 *The Guardian*, 26 May 2020.
86 Verrender, 2021.
87 Interview, Stephen Mayne, October 2020.

88 Interview, Stephen Mayne, October 2020.
89 News.com.au, 8 October 2020.
90 Bergin, 2021, p 567.
91 News.com.au, 7 October 2020.
92 News.com.au, 8 October 2020.
93 *Crikey*, 23 October 2010.
94 Bergin, 2021, p 242.
95 Bergin, 2021, pp 515–16.
96 ABC *RN*, 2021.
97 *The Age*, 11 September 2020.
98 AUSTRAC, 2022.
99 Bergin, 2021, p 312.
100 AUSTRAC, 2022, p 132.
101 McKenzie, Toscano and Tobin, 2019.
102 AUSTRAC, 2022, p 130.
103 McKenzie, 2020.
104 McKenzie, Toscano and Tobin, 2019.
105 *The Age*, 7 February 2020.
106 McKenzie and Hunter, 2021.
107 AUSTRAC, 2022, p 216.
108 Perth Casino Royal Commission, 2022.
109 *The Age*, 27 July 2019.
110 Bergin, 2021, p 627.
111 *Australian Financial Review*, 24 June 2021.
112 Burton, 2021.
113 Burton, 2021.
114 *The Age*, 9 October 2020.
115 Tham, 2010, p 76.
116 Johnson and Livingstone, 2021.
117 Interview, Stephen Mayne, October 2022.
118 ABC *Four Corners*, 2021b.
119 Cited in ABC *Four Corners*, 2021b.
120 Tiffen, 2019.
121 Chenoweth, 2021.
122 Perth Casino Royal Commission, 2022, p 615.
123 AUSTRAC, 2022, p 112.
124 AUSTRAC, 2022.
125 Hyland, 2017.
126 Interview, Stephen Mayne, October 2022.
127 *Australian Financial Review*, 12 May 2009.
128 *Daily Telegraph*, 7 November 2020.
129 Fowler, 2021.
130 Royal Commission into the Casino Operator and Licence, 2021, p 147.
131 *Australian Financial Review*, 17 October 2020.
132 Royal Commission into the Casino Operator and Licence, 2021, p 99.
133 Interview, Stephen Mayne, October 2022.
134 *The Australian*, 8 October 2020.
135 Bergin, 2021, p 461.
136 ABC *News*, 12 February 2021.
137 msm.com.au, 20 May 2021.
138 Bergin, 2021, p 350.
139 Royal Commission into the Casino Operator and Licence, 2021, p 2.
140 *Australian Financial Review*, 3 March 2022.
141 *Weekend Australian*, 25–26 June 2022.
142 Royal Commission into the Casino Operator and Licence, 2021.
143 Knight, 2022.
144 Fowler and Wootton, 2022.

Vandals: Rio Tinto and Juukan Gorge caves

1 'The Puutu Kunti Kurrama people and the Pinikura people are two distinct Aboriginal socio-territorial groups, whose country lies in the West Pilbara region of Western Australia. The Puutu Kunti Kurrama people and the Pinikura people are separate peoples with discrete rights and interests in country, though we have some shared laws and customs'. Joint Standing Committee on Northern Australia, 2021, p 3.
2 Laurie, 2020.
3 I have personally know Ben Wyatt for many years.
4 The first Indigenous Affairs Minister in Western Australia was Ernie Bridge (1986–88), who was also the first Indigenous member of any Australian cabinet.
5 Joint Standing Committee on Northern Australia (2020), 'Never

Again: Interim Report', p 2.
6 Joint Standing Committee on Northern Australia (2020), 'Never Again: Interim Report', p vii.
7 Laurie, 2020.
8 Transparency International Australia, 9 October 2020.
9 Elbaum, 2007.
10 Clark, 2021.
11 *Australian Financial Review*, 21 October 2021.
12 Cited in Chapple, 2020, Appendix 7.
13 Chapple, 2020.
14 ABC *News*, 17 September 2020.
15 Interview, Howard Pedersen, September 2022.
16 Nagar, 2021.
17 Chapple, 2020, p 11.
18 Manne, 2020, p 3.
19 Cooper, 1969.
20 Adams and Kerwin, 2020.
21 House of Representatives, 1963.
22 Cited in *The Bulletin*, 24 May 1969.
23 *Canberra Times*, 9 February 1972; Comalco became a fully-owned subsidiary of Rio in 2000. The relationship between the two is outlined on Rio Tinto's website, <www.riotinto.com/en/about/we-are-150-rt-rio150–1960>.
24 Roberts, 2008.
25 Roberts, 2008.
26 Doohan, 2013.
27 Roberts, 2008.
28 Roberts, 2008, p 160.
29 Nyompe, 2003.
30 Wintawari Guruma Aboriginal Corporation, 2020.
31 Altman, 2020.
32 Fitzpatrick, 2016.
33 Beresford, 2006.
34 Stevens, 2015.
35 Stevens, 2015.
36 *Canberra Times*, 29 June 1995.
37 Joint Standing Committee on Northern Australia (2020), Public Hearings, 28 August, p 3.
38 Solly, 2018.
39 *Australian Financial Review*, 2 July 2021.
40 Holocombe and Fredricks, 2021.
41 *The Guardian*, 30 May 2020.
42 See Harvey's evidence, Joint Standing Committee on Northern Australia (2020), Public Hearings, 28 August, pp 18–26.
43 Interview, Howard Pedersen, September 2022.
44 Puutu Kunti Kurrama and Pinikura (PKKP), 2020.
45 Manne, 2020.
46 Joint Standing Committee on Northern Australia (2020), 12 October, pp 4–7.
47 Rio Tinto, 2020b.
48 *Saturday Paper*, 21–27 November 2020.
49 *Australian Financial Review*, 9 August 2020.
50 Rio Tinto, 2020.
51 Interview, Howard Pedersen, September 2022.
52 I had met Walsh several times at university functions.
53 West, 2020.
54 Joint Standing Committee on Northern Australia (2020), 'Never Again: Interim Report', p 5.
55 See Chessell's and Aston's articles below.
56 Aston, 2021.
57 *Australian Financial Review*, 24 February 2022.
58 *Australian Financial Review*, 29 April 2016.
59 Sykes, 1996, p 575.
60 Aston, 2021.
61 Chessell, 2018.
62 Chessell, 2018.
63 Chessell, 2018.
64 *Australian Financial Review*, 19 March 2016.
65 *Crikey*, 14 December 2020.
66 Interview, Joe Aston, August 2022.
67 *Financial Times*, 12 July 2017.
68 Ker, 2020.

69 Chessell, 2018.
70 *Australian Financial Review*, 2 July 2021.
71 *Australian Financial Review*, 24 August 2020.
72 *The Guardian,* 16 October 2020.
73 Sims, 2020.
74 Interview, Joe Aston, August 2022.
75 Aston, 2020b.
76 *Weekend Australian*, 17 October 2020.
77 Harvey's evidence to the Joint Standing Committee on Northern Australia (2020), Public Hearings, 28 August, pp 18–26.
78 Bruce Harvey, submission No. 19, Joint Standing Committee on Northern Australia (2020).
79 Bond, 2020.
80 Ker, 2020.
81 Joint Standing Committee on Northern Australia (2020), Public Hearings, 28 August, pp 1–3.
82 Rio Tinto, 2020.
83 Interview, Howard Pedersen, August 2022.
84 Bloomberg, 11 September 2020.
85 Ker, 2020.
86 News.com.au, 17 October 2018.
87 *Sydney Morning Herald*, 2 August 2017.
88 *Australian Mining*, 3 March 2020..
89 *Australian Financial Review*, 6 August 2020
90 Aston, 2020c.
91 Interview, Joe Aston, August 2022.
92 Rio Tinto, 2020b.
93 Joint Standing Committee on Northern Australia (2020), Public Hearings, 12 October, p 8.
94 *National Indigenous Times*, 16 October 2020.
95 Joint Standing Committee on Northern Australia (2020), 'Never Again: Interim Report', additional comments by Senator Dean Smith, p 29.
96 Puutu Kunti Kurrama and Pinikura (PKKP), 2020.
97 *Mining Mirror*, 25 June 2019.
98 A revised Heritage Act passed the Western Australian Parliament in December 2021. Among its provisions was the creation of an Aboriginal Cultural Heritage Commission comprised of a majority of Indigenous members. However, the Minister for Aboriginal Affairs retained the final say over projects in circumstances where Traditional Owners and mining companies cannot agree. And, there was no right of appeal by Traditional Owners to a Minister's ruling. For these reasons, critics argued that the Act would not necessarily prevent another Juukan caves disaster. ABC *News*, 16 December 2012.
99 *Australian Financial Review*, 11 August 2020.
100 Pearson, 2021.
101 Pearson, 2021.
102 Joint Standing Committee on Northern Australia (2021), 'A Way Forward: Final Report'), p xi.
103 Joint Standing Committee on Northern Australia (2020), 'Never Again: Interim Report', additional comments by Senator Dean Smith, p 32.
104 Pearson, 2021.
105 Interview, Joe Aston, August 2022.
106 Durkin, 2022.
107 Albrechtsen, 2018.
108 *The Age*, 9 September 2020.
109 *Canberra Times*, 3 February 2000.
110 Rio Tinto, 2020a.
111 *The Australian*, 2 March 2021.
112 *Australian Financial Review*, 10 September 2020.
113 *Sydney Morning Herald*, 19 September 2020.
114 *Weekend Australian*, 12 September 2020.
115 Interview, Joe Aston, August 2022.
116 *Sydney Morning Herald*, 19 September 2020.
117 *Weekend Australian*, 12 September 2020.

118 *Australian Financial Review*, 24 August 2020.
119 Cited in Pearson, 2021.
120 *Boss*, 10 June 2021.

Conclusion: Taming the beast

1 *Sydney Morning Herald*, 21 May 2023.
2 *The Full Story* podcast, 22 May 2023.
3 Kells and Gow, 2018.
4 Jones, 2020.
5 ABC *7.30 Report*, 1 December 2017.
6 Senate Economics and References Committee, 2014, p vxii.
7 Jones, 2013.
8 *Australian Financial Review*, 25–26 March 2023.
9 *The Economist*, 31 March 2016.
10 Henderson, 2021, p 12.
11 Cameron, Nelson and Reza, 2019.
12 Balnaves-James, 2015; Whelton, nd.
13 Cornell, 2009.
14 *Australian Financial Review*, 4 June 1993.
15 *Sydney Morning Herald*, 26 October 2020.
16 This is a term used by CEO and author Margaret Hefferman; see Riggins, 2019.
17 Corcoran, 2019.
18 Jones, 2014.
19 Wolf, 2020.
20 Edwards, 2020, p 197.
21 White, 2020.

BIBLIOGRAPHY

Books and book chapters

Armstrong, H and Gross, D (1995) *Tricontinental: The Rise and Fall of a Merchant Bank,* Melbourne University Press

Babiak, P and Hare, R (2006) *Snakes in Suits: When Psychopaths Go to Work,* HarperBusiness

Barry, P (1991) *The Rise and Fall of Alan Bond,* Bantam

Barry, P (2000) *Going for Broke: How Bond Got Away with It,* Bantam

Barry, P (2002) *Rich Kids,* Random House

Barry, P (2008) *The Rise and Rise of Kerry Packer Uncut,* Bantam Books

Beahm, G (ed.) (2012) *The Sun King: Rupert Murdoch in His Own Words,* Grant Hardie Books

Beresford, Q (2006) *Rob Riley: The Life of an Aboriginal Leader,* Aboriginal Studies Press

Beresford, Q (2008) *The Godfather: The Life of Brian Burke,* Allen & Unwin

Beresford, Q (2015) *The Rise and Fall of Gunns Ltd,* NewSouth

Beresford, Q (2018) *Adani and the War Over Coal,* NewSouth

Boyce, P (2017) *Losing Streak: How Tasmania Was Gamed by the Gambling Industry,* Black Inc.

Collins, J (2009) *How the Mighty Fall and Why Some Companies Never Give In,* Penguin

Cooper, B (2005) 'Where Were the Gatekeepers? Corporate Collapses and the Role of Accountants', in Campbell, T and Houghton, K, *Ethics and Auditing,* ANU EPress

Edelsten, G (2012) *Enigma,* New Holland

Edwards, L (2020) *Corporate Power in Australia: Do the 1% Rule?,* Monash University Publishing

Ferguson, A (2019) *Banking Bad, Whistle Blowers Corporate Cover-ups: One Journalist's Fight for the Truth,* ABC Books, online edition

Haigh, G (2007) *Asbestos House: The Secret History of James Hardie Industries,* Scribe Publications

Hamilton, C (2007) *Scorcher: The Dirty Politics of Climate Change,* Black Inc.

Healy, J (2019) *Breaking the Banks: What Went Wrong with Australian Banking?,* Impact Press

Henderson, R (2021) *Reimagining Capitalism in a World on Fire,* Penguin

Kells, S and Gow, I (2018) *The Big Four: The Curious Past and Perilous Future of the Global Accounting Monopoly,* La Trobe University Press

Kelly, G (2015) *Why Insurers Fail: The Role of Capital in Weathering Crises,* Property and Casualty Insurance Compensation Corporation of Canada

Kitney, D (2018) *The Price of Fortune: The Untold Story of Being James Packer, a Biography,* HarperCollins Publishers

Maher, T (1990) *Alan Bond: The World's Richest Debtor,* Mandarin

Main, A (2003) *Other People's Money: The Complete Story of the Extraordinary Collapse of HIH,* HarperCollins Publishers
Page, B (2003) *The Murdoch Archipelago,* Simon & Schuster
Peacock, M (2009) *Killer Company,* ABC Books
Roberts, J (2008) *Massacres to Mining: The Colonisation of Aboriginal Australia,* Impact Investigative Media Production
Spender, H (2016) *Corporate Political Expenditure in Australia,* Australasian Centre for Corporate Responsibility
Tham, J (2010) *Money and Politics: The Democracy We Can't Afford,* UNSW Press
Stoller, M (2019) *Goliath: The 100-Year War Between Monopoly Power and Democracy,* Simon & Schuster
Sykes, T (1996) *The Bold Riders,* Allen & Unwin
Tiffen, R (2014) *Rupert Murdoch: A Reassessment,* NewSouth
Van der Plaat, L (1996) *Too Good to Be True: Inside the Corrupt World of Christopher Skase,* Macmillan
Wolff, M (2009) *The Man Who Owns the News: Inside the Secret World of Rupert Murdoch,* Vintage Books

Academic journal articles

Azarian, B (2018) 'How Religious Fundamentalism Hijacks the Brain', *Psychology Today,* 10 October
Beresford, Q (2010) 'Corporations, Government and Development: The Case of Institutional Corruption in Tasmania', *Australian Journal of Political Science,* vol 45, no 2
Berg, L and Farbenblum, B (2018) 'Remedies for Migrant Worker Exploitation in Australia: Lessons from the 7-Eleven Wage Repayment Program', *Melbourne University Law Review,* vol 41, no 3, <law.unimelb.edu.au/__data/assets/pdf_file/0008/2694995/Berg-and-Farbenblum-413-Advance.pdf>
Brailsford, T and Knights, S (1998) 'The Financial and Non-Financial Effects of Corporate Takeovers', *Melbourne Institute Working Papers,* no 23/98
Buttery, E and Shadur, M (1991) 'Understanding Corporate Collapses', *Management Decision,* vol 29, no 5
Cameron, R, Nelson, J and Reza, P (2019) 'The Impact of Shareholder Activism on CEO Renumeration Structures', *Accountancy Business and the Public Interest,* vol 1
Comino, V (2006) 'Civil or Criminal Penalties for Corporate Misconduct: Which Way Ahead?', *Australian Business Law Review,* vol 34, no 6
Cooper, J (2006) 'The Integration of Financial Regulatory Authorities: The Australian Experience', ASIC
Corcoran, S (2019) 'Ordinary Corporate Vices and the Failure of Law', *Adelaide Law Review,* vol 40, no 1, <Ordinary Corporate Vices and the Failure of Law>
Craufurd Smith, R (2015) 'Rupert Murdoch: A Re-Assessment: The Ethics of Journalism: Individual, Institutional and Cultural Influences', *Journal of Media and Law,* vol 7, no 1
Davis, K (2018) 'Banking Royal Commission: Dodgy Financial Dealings Exposed Greed and Moral Vacuum', Monash University, 7 May
Doohan, K (2013) 'Transformative Practices: Imagining and Enacting Relationships in the Context of Resource Development, the Argyle Case', *Asia Pacific Viewpoint,* vol 54, no 2

Duarte, F (2006) 'Spivs, Shonks and Sharks: The HIH Collapse as a Moral Tale of Corporate Capitalism', *Social Responsibility Journal,* vol 2, nos 3 and 4

Elbaum, B (2007) 'How Godzilla Ate Pittsburgh: The Long Rise of the Japanese Iron and Steel Industry, 1900–1973', *Social Science Journal Japan,* vol 10, no 2

Engel, S and Martin, B (2006) 'Union Carbide and James Hardie: Lessons in Politics and Power', *Global Society*, vol 20, no 4

Feldman, L, Maiback, EW, Roser-Renouf, C, and Leiserowitz, A (2012) 'Climate on Cable: The Nature and Impact of Global Warming Coverage on Fox News, CNN, and MSNBC', *International Journal of Press/Politics*, vol 17, no 1

Finkelstein, R, and Tiffen, R (2015) 'When Does Press Self-Regulation Work?' *Melbourne University Law Review*, vol 38, no 3

Fraser, M (2016) 'Investigating 7-Eleven: Who Are the Really Bad Guys?', *Griffith Journal of Law and Humanity,* vol 4, no 2

Germov, J (1995) 'Medi-fraud, Managerialism and the Decline of Medical Autonomy: Deprofessionalisation Reconsidered', *Australian and New Zealand Journal of Sociology,* vol 21, no 3

Goulston, M (2014) 'Compartmentalized Versus Integrated: The Mind of Elliot Rodger', *Psychology Today,* 26 May

Gregoire, (2020) 'Morrison and Murdoch Scramble to Hide the Climate Cause of the Bushfires', *Sydney Criminal Lawyers,* 11 September

Hills, B (2005) 'The James Hardie Story: Asbestos Victims' Claims Evaded by Manufacturer', *International Journal of Occupational and Environmental Health,* vol 11, no 2

James, N (2008) 'Distracting the Masses: Corporate Convictions and the Delegitimisation of Neo-liberalism', *Macquarie Law Journal,* vol 8

Johnson, M and Livingstone, C (2021) 'Measuring Influence: An Analysis of Australian Gambling Industry Political Donations and Policy Decisions', *Addiction Research & Theory,* vol 29, no 3

Lester, M and Bowell, D (2018) 'Tasmania: Majority or Minority Government?' *Australasian Parliamentary Review,* vol 33, no 2

Merrett, D T (2012) 'Reid, Sir John Thyne (1903–1984)', *Australian Dictionary of Biography,* <adb.anu.edu.au/biography/reid-sir-john-thyne-14437>

Mirshekary, S et al. (2005) 'Australian Corporate Collapse: The Case of HIH Insurance', *Journal of Financial Services Marketing,* vol 9, no 3

Mocatta, G and Hawley, E (2020) 'Uncovering a Climate Catastrophe? Media Coverage of Australia's Black Summer Bushfires and the Revelatory Extent of the Climate Blame Frame', *M/C Journal,* vol 23, no 4

Moerman, L, van der Laan, S and Campbell, D (2014) 'A Tale of Two Asbestos Giants: Corporate Reports as (Auto)Biography', *Business History,* vol 65, no 6

Monem, R (2011) 'The One.Tel Collapse: Lessons for Corporate Governance', *Australian Accounting Review,* December

Nagar, A (2021) 'The Juukan Gorge Incident: Key Lessons of Free, Prior and Informed Consent', *Business and Human Rights Journal,* vol 6 no 2

Norman, B, Newman, P and Steffen, W (2021) 'Apocalypse Now: Australian Bushfires and the Future of Urban Settlements', *NPJ Urban Sustainability*, vol 2

Podger, A (2019) 'Fake News: Could Self-Regulation of Media Help to Protect the Public? The Experience of the Australian Press Council', *Public Integrity*, vol 21, no 1

Redmond, P (2012) 'Directors' Duties and Corporate Responsiveness', *UNSW Law Journal,* vol 35, no 1

Ricketson, M (2021) 'Why the MEAA Left the Press Council and Why that Matters', *Australian Journalism Review,* vol 43, no 1

Salis, G (2016) 'The Icarus Complex: The Influence of the Greek Myth of Icarus and Daedalus in 20th Century Literature', *Galaxy International Multidisciplinary Research Journal,* vol 5, no 4

Reports and inquiries

ACTU (2018) 'The Exploitation of Workers Is Widespread and Has Become a Business Model', Submission to Inquiry into Wage Theft in Queensland, <https://www.actu.org.au/media/1385221/d170-wage-theft.pdf>

Adams, K and Kerwin, H (2021) 'After the Mine: Living With Rio Tinto's Deadly Legacy', Human Rights Law Centre

Aged Care Crisis Inc. (2019) Submission 302, Royal Commission into Aged Care and Safety

Altman, J (2020) Submission No 22, Joint Standing Committee on Northern Australia, Inquiry into the destruction of 46,000 year old caves at the Juukan Gorge in the Pilbara region of Western Australia

AUSTRAC (2019) Chief Executive Officer of the Australian Transaction Reports and Analysis Centre v Westpac Banking Corporation, <jade.io/article/770842>

Australian Communications and Media Authority (2022) 'Investigation Report No BL-647'

Australian Democracy Network (2022) 'Confronting State Capture', <australiandemocracy.org.au/statecapture>

Australian Prudential Regulatory Authority (2018) 'Inquiry into the Commonwealth Bank of Australia'

Berg, L and Farbenblum, B (2017) 'Wage Theft in Australia Findings of the National Temporary Migrant Work Survey', UNSW Law

Bacon, W and Jegan, A (2020) 'Lies, Debates and Silences: How News Corp Produces Climate Scepticism in Australia', GetUp, <cdn.getup.org.au/2790-Lies_Debates_and_Silences_FINAL.pdf>

Bergin, P (2021) 'Inquiry Under Section 143 of the Casino Control Act 1992, Report', NSW Government

Brailsford, L, et al., (2020) 'Dirty Power Burnt Country', Greenpeace

Centre for Advancing Journalism (2020) Submission No 64. Senate Inquiry into Media Diversity in Australia

Chapple, R (2020) Submission No 65, Joint Standing Committee on Northern Australia, 'Never Again: Interim Report'

Fair Work Ombudsman (2016) 'A Report of the Fair Work Ombudsman's Inquiry into 7-Eleven'

House of Representatives (1963) 'Report of the Select Committee on Grievances of Yirrkala Aborigines, Arnhem Land Reserve'

Institute for Strategic Dialogue (2022) 'Deny, Deceive, Delay: Documenting and Responding to Climate Disinformation at COP 26 and Beyond'

Jackson, D (2004) 'Report of the Special Commission of Inquiry into the Medical Research and Compensation Fund', NSW Government

Joint Committee of Public Accounts (1985) 'Medical Fraud and Overservicing – Pathology', Parliament of the Commonwealth of Australia

Joint Parliamentary Committee (2009) 'Inquiry into Financial Products and Services in Australia', Parliament House, Canberra

Joint Standing Committee on Northern Australia (2021) 'A Way Forward: Final Report into the Destruction of Indigenous Heritage Sites at Juukan Gorge'
Joint Standing Committee on Northern Australia (2020) 'Never Again: Interim Report'
Jones, E (2013) 'Submission 295, The Performance of the Australian Securities and Investments Commission', Senate Economics Committee
Law, M (2015) 'House of Cards: Problem Gambling and Low Income Earners in Tasmania', Anglicare
Maharaj, A and Dargaville, R (2020) 'Australian Meteorological and Oceanographic Society, Submission, Senate Standing Committees on Environment and Communications, Media Diversity in Australia'
Manne, T (2020) 'Submission No 37, Joint Standing Committee on Northern Australia'
Medical Tribunal of New South Wales (2000) 'No. 40018 – in the Matter of Geoffrey Walter Edelsten for Determination'
Moffitt, A (1974) 'Allegations of Organised Crime in Clubs', Final Report of the Royal Commission of Inquiry in Respect of Certain Matters Relating to Allegations of Organised Crime in Clubs
New South Wales government (2020) 'Bushfire Inquiry Report'
Parliamentary Joint Committee on Corporations and Financial Services (2006) 'Corporate Responsibility: Managing Risk and Creating Value'
Parliamentary Joint Committee on Corporations and Financial Services (2019), 'Fairness in Franchising'
Perth Casino Royal Commission (2022) 'Final Report'
Puutu Kunti Kurrama and Pinikura (PKKP) (2020) 'Submission No. 129, Joint Standing Committee on Northern Australia, the destruction of 46,000 year old caves at the Juukan Gorge in the Pilbara region of Western Australia'
Richards, L and Brew, N (2020) '2019–2020 Australian Bushfires Frequently Asked Questions: A Quick Guide', Parliamentary Library Research Project Series, 12 March
Rio Tinto (2020a) 'Board Review of Cultural Heritage Management', 23 August, <http://www.riotinto.com/news/inquiry-into-juukan-gorge>
Rio Tinto (2020b) 'Submission 25, Joint Standing Committee on Northern Australia'
Royal Commission (2003) 'A Corporate Collapse and its Lessons', *The Failure of HIH Insurance*. [This is a separate introductory overview, by Justice Owens, which is included in volume 1 of the royal commission report]
Royal Commission into Aged Care Quality and Safety (2019) vol 1
Royal Commission into Aged Care Quality and Safety (2019), 'Hobart Hearing, Bupa South Hobart Case Study'
Royal Commission into Misconduct in the Banking, Superannuation and Financial Services Industry (2019) 'Final Report'
Royal Commission into Casino Licence and Operator (2021) 'Report', Government Printer Victoria
Senate (2015a) 'Public Hearings, Inquiry by the Education and Employment References Committee', 24 September
Senate (2015b) 'Public Hearings, Inquiry by the Education and Employment References Committee', 20 November
Senate (2016) Education and Employment References Committee, 'A National Disgrace: The Exploitation of Temporary Worker Visa Holders'
Senate (2017) Education and Employment Legislation Committee Fair Work Amendment Protecting Vulnerable Workers Bill 2017 [Provisions]

Senate Economic Reference Committee (2014) 'Final Report: Inquiry into the Performance of the Australian Securities Investment Commission

Tiffen, R (2021) 'Submission No 9 Senate, Inquiry into Media Diversity in Australia'

Ward, J (2018) 'Tax Avoidance by For-Profit Aged Care Companies: Profit Shifting on Public Funds', Tax Justice Network

Westpac Review Team (2018) 'Governance, Accountability and Culture Self-Assessment', Westpac Banking Corporation

Wintawari Guruma Aboriginal Corporation (2020), 'Marandoo: A State of Shame', Submission no. 50 to the Joint Standing Committee on Northern Australia

WWF (2020), 'Impacts of the Unprecedented 2019–20 Bushfires on Australian Animals', <assets.wwf.org.au/WWF_Impacts-of-the-unprecedented-2019-2020-bushfires-on-Australian-animals>

Electronic media

ABC *Australian Story* (2014) 'Packer's Road: Inside the Mind of Kerry Packer', April

ABC *Four Corners* (2021a) 'Packer's Gamble', 31 May

ABC *Four Corners* (2021b) 'Watchdog or Lap Dog', 5 June

ABC *Four Corners* (2015) '7-Eleven: The Price of Convenience', 30 August

ABC *Four Corners,* (2009) 'Perfect Storm', 9 February

ABC *RN* (2021) Religion and Ethics Report: 'The Dirty Business of Gambling', 17 February

ABC *Media Watch* (2023) 'Fox's Big Lie', 27 February

Theses

Flynn, K (2004) 'Medical Fraud and Inappropriate Practice in Medibank and Medicare, Australia, 1975–1995', PhD, University of Wollongong

Hoyte, C (2004) 'An Australian Mirage', PhD, Griffith University

Lane, RJ (2016) 'Unexpected Corporate Failures in Australia Through the Decades: Commonality of Causes', PhD, James Cook University

Newspaper and magazine articles

Albrechtsen, J (2018) 'Get Behind the Boardroom Rebellion Against Activists', *Weekend Australian,* 4 August

Altmann, (2002) 'Clouded Future for Golden Windfall', *The Australian,* 31 October

Ansley, G (2003) 'Greed Empire's Rise and Fall, *New Zealand Herald,* 12 April

Armstrong, D (1977) 'How to Stop Doctor Frauds', *The Bulletin,* 9 July

Aston, J (2019) 'At a Moment of Truth, Lindsay Maxsted Squibbed it', *Australian Financial Review,* 27 November

Aston, J (2020a) 'Rio Tinto Has Full Circle', *Australian Financial Review,* 9 July

Aston, J (2020b) 'More Cringeworthy Answers from Rio Tinto', *Australian Financial Review,* 8 September

Aston, J (2020c) 'Secret Recording: Rio Tinto 'Not Sorry' for Cave Blast', *Australian Financial Review,* 15 June

Aston, J (2021) 'Oyu Tolgoi Another Jacques Scandal for Rio Tinto, *Australian Financial Review,* 9 August

Australian Institute of Company Directors (2016) 'The Role of the Board in Corporate Culture'

Bachelard, M (2017) 'Is This How it Ends?', *The Age,* 23 September

Bagwell, S (1997) 'How Doug Moran Looks After Himself', *Australian Financial Review*, 18 October

Baker, E (2021) 'Tasmania's Gaming Legislation Passes Upper House', ABC *News*, 22 November

Balnaves-James, A (2015) 'The Ethics of Executive Compensation: A Matter of Duty', Seven Pillars Institute, 15 June

Barass, T (2015) 'WA's Cup Ran Over with Champagne' *West Australian*, 10 June

Barns, G (2018) 'Questions on Election Transparency a Matter for Democracy', *The Mercury*, 18 June

Barry, P (2011) 'In the Eye of the Storm', *The Monthly*, February

Bates, D (2016) '7-Eleven Wage Scandal a Classic PR Disaster', *Switzer Daily*, 17 May

Bentley, D (2004) 'Flight of the Pixie Queen', *Courier-Mail*, 4 December

Beveridge, J (2001a) Skase's Dream Was More than A Mirage', *Herald Sun*, 7 August

Beveridge, J (2001b) 'Say Goodbye to Hollywood – Movie Star Life Became Real Drama', *Courier-Mail*, 7 August

Bevilacqua, S (2002) 'Dealing Hearts, Holding Aces', *Sunday Tasmanian*, 22 September

Blake, E (1996) 'Dr Who?', *The Age*, 13 September

Blue, T (2001) 'A Career that Built a House of Cards', *The Australian*, 7 August

Bond, T (2020) 'Rio's Tinto's Culture of Indifference', *Australian Financial Review*, 8 August

Bongiorno, F (2021) 'Dr X', *Canberra Times*, 15 June

Bouffini, F and Priest, M (2004) 'Reputations on the Line', *Australian Financial Review*, 19 June

Boyce, J (2020) 'Pokies Plunder: The Final Chapter? Background Notes to the Tasmanian Government's Proposed 2020 Poker Machine Legislation', TasmanianTimes.org, <tasmaniantimes.com/2020/06/pokies-plunder>

Brailey, D (nd) 'Four Key Questions MPs Should Ask the Big Banks (and the Big Banks Should Answer)', TasmanianTimes.org, <tasmaniantimes.com/2020/06/pokies-plunder>

Brearley, D (2003a) 'Moral Hazard', *Weekend Australian*, 19 April

Brearley, D (2003b) 'The Emperor Stands Proudly Bared', *The Australian*, 17 April

Buchan, J (2017) 'What Is Going Rotten in the Franchise Businesses Plagued by Scandals?', *The Conversation*, 13 December

Buffini, F and Priest, M (2004) 'Reputations on the Line', *Australian Financial Review*, 19 June

Burton, B (2020) 'Tasmanian Poker Machine Losses Surge to Almost $600,000 Per Day', *Tasmanian Inquirer*, 28 September

Burton, T (2021) 'Odds Are Light-Touch Regulation of Casinos Is Over', *Australian Financial Review*, 18 February

Button, J (2003) 'The Ascendancy of Bob Hawke', *The Age*, 1 March

Button, V (2000) 'A Call that Took a Month to Answer', *The Age*, 26 February

Byrge, D and Barnes, M (2015) 'Kirk Kerkorian Three Times Owner of MGM, Dies at 98', *Hollywood Reporter*, 16 June

Cadzow, J (2010a) 'This Glamorous Life', *Sydney Morning Herald*, 3 July

Cadzow, J (2010b) 'The Fall and Rise to Riches of Edelsten and His Young Bride', *Sydney Morning Herald*, 5 July

Cameron, P (2001) ' How Skase Fled Queensland', *Sunday Mail*, 12 August

Cannane, S (2021) 'The Secret Deals that Allowed Tasmania's Pokies Profits to Go to One Family for Decades', ABC *News*, 11 September 2021

Cassella, C (2019) 'Climate Deniers Are Spreading a Totally Unscientific "Paper" with no Basis in Reality', *Scientific Alert,* 16 July
Cave, D (2020) 'How Rupert Murdoch Is Influencing Australia's Bushfire Debate', *New York Times,* 13 January
Chenoweth, N (2004) 'Fiddling While the Firm Was Burning', *Australian Financial Review,* 16 December
Chenoweth, N (2009) 'Turnbull's Great Escape – He's Off the FAI Hook', *Australian Financial Review,* 9 July
Chenoweth, N (2021) 'How Packer Wins at Crown', *Australian Financial Review,* 12 February
Chessell, J (2018) 'Rio Tinto's Jacques Looks to Growth', *Boss,* 9 March
Childs, K (1994) 'Skase's Loyal Defender Pixie Has Her Own Share of Troubles', *The Canberra Times,* 12 February
Clark, A (2005) 'Power and Persuasion', *Australian Financial Review,* 11 December
Clark, A (2021) 'Australia in the 1960s: The Making of a Mining Boom', *Australian Financial Review,* 22 October
Clark, A (2022) 'Why This Was Australia's Most Significant Corporate Collapse', *Australian Financial Review,* 25 March
Clune, D (2020) 'The Long History of Political Corruption in NSW …', *The Conversation,* 15 October
Coburn, N (2021) 'Westpac Executives Escape AML Liability', Bond University News, <bond.edu.au/news/westpac-executives-escape-aml-liability>
Colebatch, T (2019) 'John Cain Was a Leader of Integrity, Courage and Vision', *Inside Story,* 28 December
Cooke, R (2017) 'James Packer Has Been Down But He's Not Out', *The Monthly,* February
Cooper, J (1969) 'Conzinc RioTinto Makes Enemies on Bougainville', *Tribune,* 7 May
Cornell, A (2009) 'When Good Companies Go Bad', *Australian Financial Review,* 20 June
Corpwatch, (2021) 'Bupa Aged Care Homes in Australia and the UK Regularly Rated "Inadequate"', European Network of Corporate Observatories
Davies, J-A (1996) 'Crisis in Nursing Homes', *Sunday Age,* 13 October
Davies, J-A and Birnbauer, B (1998) 'Nursing Homes in Crisis – Terminal Neglect', *The Age,* 24 August
Davies, N (1990) 'Tiny Rowland: Portrait of the Bastard as a Rebel', *The Guardian,* 1 August
Dellit, A (2001) 'Corporate Collapses: Make the Rich Pay', *Green Left,* 20 June
Dembicki, G (2021) 'Rupert Murdoch Has Known We've Been in a Climate Emergency since 2006, Documents Show', *Vice News,* 23 September
Densley, J (2012) 'Most Powerful Person in Australian Boardrooms: Lindsay Maxsted', SmartCompany, 11 December
Dick, S (2020) 'News Corp Employee Lashes Murdoch's Reporting of Bushfires', *New Daily,* 10 January
Dodson, L (1990) 'Quiet Survivors Who Pull Canberra's Strings', *Australian Financial Review,* 19 November
Donnelly, A (1994) 'Lessons from the Failure of Qintex', *Canberra Times,* 25 December
Dover, B (2020) 'The Foxification of the Murdoch Media in Australia', *Pearls and Irritations: John Menadue's Public Policy Journal,* 22 January
Dovkants, K (2014) 'Jamie Packer: The Polo Playboy', *Tatler,* 6 May
Dunn, M (2015) 'The Roaring 80s', *Gold Coast Bulletin,* 6 June
Durie, J (2019) 'Numbers Run in Maxsted's Veins', *Weekend Australian,* 27 July

Durkin, P (2016) 'Ceasefire Called in Banking Culture Wars', *Australian Financial Review,* 7 April
Durkin, P (2019) 'The Action Women Who Felled a Bank', *Australian Financial Review,* 28 November
Durkin, P (2022) 'The Invisible Networks that Bind the Directors' Club', *Boss,* 3 June
Elias, D (2003) 'Rocket Rod Forgot that What Goes Up …', *The Age,* 14 January
Eyres, J and Frost, J (2019a) 'Westpac's Failures: How Did They Happen?', *Australian Financial Review,* 20 November
Eyres, J and Frost, J (2019b) 'Westpac Hit by AUSTRAC for Systemic Failures', *Australian Financial Review,* 20 November
Eyers, J and Frost, J (2019c) 'The Short Walk that Sealed Hartzer's Fate', *Australian Financial Review,* 27 November
Fagan, D (2001) 'All that Glitter, Just a Mirage', *The Australian,* 7 August
Ferguson, A (2013) 'CBA Sent Spies to Coalition Function', *Sydney Morning Herald,* 26 October
Ferguson, A (2014a) 'Big Banks Face Up to Inherent Flaw', *The Age,* 2 September
Ferguson, A (2014b) 'Hearing into ASIC's Failure to Investigate CBA's Financial Wisdom', *Sydney Morning Herald,* 3 June
Ferguson, A (2015a) '7-Eleven Stuns with New Evidence', *The Age,* 25 September
Ferguson, A (2015b) '7-Eleven Wage Abuse Scandal Has Lessons for All Directors', *The Age,* 5 October
Ferguson, A (2016a) '7-Eleven Franchisees Feel No Goodwill', *Sydney Morning Herald,* 10 September
Ferguson, A (2016b) 'Scandal-plagued 7-Eleven in New Public Relations Crisis After Panel Sacked', *The Age,* 14 May
Ferguson, A (2019a) 'Limp Apologies Were Never Going to Save Westpac Bosses', *Sydney Morning Herald,* 27 November
Ferguson, A (2019b) 'The Fateful Mistake that Westpac's CEO and Chairman Made', *Sydney Morning Herald,* 26 November
Ferguson, A and Danckert, S (2015) 'How 7-Eleven Is Ripping Off its Workers', *Sydney Morning Herald,* interactive video, <www.smh.com.au/interactive/2015/7-eleven-revealed>
Ferguson, A and Danckert, S (2017) 'Cup of Sorrow', *The Age,* 9 December
Ferguson, A and Toft, K (2015) '7-Eleven Investigation: Convenience Store Empire Built On Not Much More Than Slavery', ABC *News,* 31 August
Ferguson, A and Vedelago, C (2013) 'Targets, Bonuses And Trips – Inside the CBA Boiler Room', *The Age,* 22 June
Ferguson, A, Danckert, S and Toft, K (2015) 'Corner Sweatshop', *Sydney Morning Herald,* 29 August
Fielding, V (2022) 'Murdoch Bias Is Boiling Australian Democracy', *Independent Australia,* 21 May
Finocchiaro, P (2011) 'Is Bernie Madoff a Sociopath?', *Salon,* 2 March
Fitzpatrick, S (2016) 'Davis Bomb Fixed Indigenous Standoff', *Weekend Australian,* 27 August
Flower, N (2021 'With His Gaudy Show of Wealth …', *Daily Mail,* 18 June
Foster, T (2017) 'Battlers Pay the Price for Pokies Profits', *The Mercury,* 28 December
Fowler, E (2021) 'Crown Resorts Suffers Under Intense Scrutiny', *Australian Financial Review,* 12–13 June

Fowler, E and Wootton, H (2022) 'Experts Slam ASIC's Failure to Prosecute Crown Resort Execs', *Australian Financial Review,* 2 March

Franchise City (nd) 'Top 4 Reasons NOT to Buy a 7-Eleven Franchise', <www.franchise.city/7-eleven-franchise>

Fraser, A (2009) 'Townsville Caught in the Eye of the Storm', *Weekend Australian,* 17 January

Fredericks, K (1992) 'The Untouchables: Corporate Criminals, *Green Left*, 30 September

Frith, B (2001) 'Greed Was Slanted to Saving the Empire', *The Australian,* 7 August

Frith, B (2003) 'Bond Pushes Licence to Kill Off History', *The Australian,* 5 November

Gaynor, M (2009) 'At a Meeting of Storm Investors …', *Sunday Mail,* 1 February

Gebel, M (2021) 'Misinformation vs Disinformation: What to Know About Each Form of False Information, and How to Spot Them Online', *Insider,* 15 January

Gettler, L (2005) 'Corporate Good Guys', *The Age,* 4 April

Glaetzer, S (2015) 'Game Changer', *The Mercury,* 14 November

Glaetzer, S (2017) 'Winner Takes All?', *The Mercury,* 25 March

Gluyas, R (2003) 'Rolled Oates 'N' Porridge', *Weekend Australian,* 21 June

Gluyas, R (2019) 'What a Difference Six Days Makes for a Scandal', *The Australian,* 27 November

Godot, D (nd) 'Cultural Factors in Problem Gambling Among the Chinese', DavidGodot.com, <davidgodot.com/cultural-factors-in-problem-gambling-among-the-chinese>

Golis, C (2019) 'The Collapse of Arthur Andersen: A Failure of Emotional Intelligence', <www.emotionalintelligencecourse.com/wp-content/uploads/2019/07/Andersen-paper-2.pdf>

Gosnell, P (2004) 'Straight Talker Above the Hiss', *Daily Telegraph,* 19 August

Gottliebsen, R (1990) 'James Yonge, the Man who Fell to Earth', *Australian Financial Review,* 15 June

Gottliebsen, R (2001) 'An Old Mate Called Chris', *The Australian,* 7 August

Gottliebsen, R (2002) 'To Err Is Human, to Cover Up Is Suicidal', *The Australian,* 22 February

Gottliebsen, R and Cromie, A (1989) 'Backs to the Wall', *Australian Financial Review,* 27 October

Grant-Taylor, T (2001) 'Death of a Salesman', *Courier-Mail,* 7 August

Grenning, R (2002) 'Queensland's Sinners', *Courier-Mail*; 22 May 2002

Grigg, A and Chenoweth, N (2019) 'Westpac's Dirty Laundering Exposed', *Australian Financial Review,* 23 November

Guilliant, R (2003) 'Shadow of the Son', *Sydney Morning Herald,* 5 May

Haigh, G (1991) 'Master of the Art of Illusion', *Canberra Times,* 23 March

Haigh, G (2003) 'Bad Company: The Cult of the CEO', *Quarterly Essay*, Issue 10

Haigh, G (2006) 'Brilliant Careers', *Australian Financial Review,* 24 August

Haigh, G (2007) 'The Man Who Showed Real Ticker in Battling a Corporate Giant', *The Advertiser,* 29 November

Hale Spencer, S (2020) 'Setting the Record Straight on Climate Change and Arson in Australia's Bushfires', FactCheckorg, 17 January, <www.factcheck.org/2020/01/setting-the-record-straight>

Hanrahan, P (2018) 'Are You an Active or Passive Director', Australian Institute of Company Directors, 29 June

Haselhurst, D (1984) 'Chris Skase – Cub Reporter to TV Tycoon', *The Bulletin,* 22 May

Head, M (2001) 'Australian Government Forced to Call a Royal Commission into Major

Insurance Collapse', World Socialist Website, 22 May
Henderson, J (2018), 'What's Wrong with Australia's Franchises?' *The Conversation*, 6 March
Hepworth, K (2019) 'Lobby Groups and the Australian Aged Care Sector', *Lobby Watch*, 1 October
Hewett, J (1990) 'On the Trail of a Recluse', *Australian Financial Review*, 29 June
Hewett, J (2014) 'Corman Slips into Sinodinos's FoFA Shoes', *Australian Financial Review*, 21 March
Higgins, E (2009) 'Meteoric Career Fizzles Out', *Weekend Australian*, 25 April 2009
Higgins, I (2006) 'On a Fast Lane to Nowhere', *Weekend Australian*, 4 February
Hills, B (2001) 'James Hardie's Forgotten Victims', *Sydney Morning Herald*, 27 February
Hills, B (2004) 'Sins of the Fathers', *Sydney Morning Herald*, 2 October
Hinch, D (2001) 'A Fugitive's Fatal Flaw', *The Australian*, 9 August
Holocombe, S and Fredricks, B (2021) 'Beyond Juukan Gorge: The Relentless Threat Mining Poses to the Pilbara Landscape', *The Conversation*, 25 February
Hooper, N (2020) 'What Happened to Westpac Culture', Australian Institute of Company Directors, 1 February
Horan, M (2003) 'The Arrogance Behind HIIH's Inglorious Fall', *Sunday Telegraph*, 20 April
Horin, A (2000a) 'No Guarantee This Home is a Freak', *Sydney Morning Herald*, 7 March
Horin, A (2000b) 'Golden Oldies', *Sydney Morning Herald*, 2 March
Hornery, A (2015) 'Alan Bond: The Many Ladies of the Billionaire with More Charm than 007', *Sydney Morning Herald*, 5 June
Hornery, A (2018) 'James Packer at the Crossroads', *Sydney Morning Herald*, 21 March
Hudson, P (2000) 'History of Problems at Home', *The Age*, 3 March
Hull, C (2021) 'Howard's Way: Turning Aged Care into Profit', Crispin Hull Journalism
Hyland, A (2017) 'James Packer and Crown Resorts: The Clock is Ticking', *Australian Financial Review*, 13 January
Irving, C (2020) 'Lauchlan Murdoch is Even More of a Right Wing Ultra than His Old Man', *Daily Beast*, 10 August
Jepsen, B (2020) 'How to Have a Conversation with Someone who Believes the Bushfires Are the Greens' Fault', Mamamia, 8 January
Johnson, C (1998) 'Open All Hours', *Sunday Age*, 12 July
Johnson, M (2001) 'A Marriage of Convenience', *Sunday Herald Sun*, 8 July
Johnson, M (2020) 'Macau: The Gambling Capital of the World', *Gambling News*, 24 September
Jones, E (2012) 'The Dark Side of the Commonwealth Bank – Part 2' *Independent Australia*, 4 April
Jones, E (2014) 'CBA, ASIC and the Political Class: Partners in Crime', *Independent Australia*, 7 July
Jones, E (2020) 'The Sins of Westpac', *Bank Reform Now*, 27 May
Joshi, K (2020) 'Australia Burned Under a Haze of Misinformation Earlier this Year: The US Is Next', *Gizmodo*, 9 December
Joshi, K (2021) 'News Corp's Turnaround on Climate Crisis is a Greenwash', *The Guardian*, 12 October
Kay, T (1991) 'Is Bond Really Bankrupt?', *Australian Jewish News*, 20 September
Kaye, T (2017) 'Bond's Legacy Lives On', *Eureka Report*, 13 April
Keane, B (2018) 'The Liberal Party's Deep, Rich Connections with the Banks and Financial Planners', *Crikey*, 2 May
Keane, B (2021) 'When it Comes To Donations, the Banks Are Back', *Crikey*, 2 February

Keaton, B (2021) 'Money Laundering Explained', Casino.org, 25 November
Ker, P (2020) 'Aiming for the Stars, Jacques Failed Rio's Grassroots', *Australian Financial Review,* 11 September
Kitney, G (2003) 'Clubbing Together for a Soft Touch', *Sydney Morning Herald,* 17 January
Knight, E (2022) 'ASIC Braces for Backlash after the Great Crown Let Off', *The Age,* 3 March
Koch, T (2015) 'The Nickel Mine that Ensnared Two Tycoons', *Weekend Australian,* 12 December
Kohler, A (2003) 'HIH Chairman's Role Remains One of the Great Mysteries', *Australian Financial Review,* 24 April
Korporaal, G (2022) 'HIH Baptism of Fire for Future Treasurer', *Weekend Australian,* 1–2 January
KPMG (2018) 'Board Oversight of Corporate Culture', <boardleadership.kpmg.us/relevant-topics/articles/2018/board-oversight-of-corporate-culture>
Kruger, C (2009) '$2 Million Paid Out After Storm Directors Quit', *Sydney Morning Herald,* 21 February
Kurukchi, G (2009) 'A Corporate Practice Is Born', *Australian Doctor,* 22 May
Lacey, A (2019) 'How to Respond to a National Crisis: A Closer Look at 7-Eleven and Underpaying Wages', POPCOM, 11 September, <www.linkedin.com/pulse/how-respond-national-pr-crisis-closer-look-7eleven-wages-amanda-lacey>
Lalor, P (2001) 'Climb to Riches Led to a Fall into Hell', *Daily Telegraph,* 7 August
Lambert, O (2017) 'Christopher Flannery, Known as Mr Rent-a-Kill, Still a Cold Case', News.com.au, 9 May
Laurence, M (2002) 'A Creditor-proof Mansion', *Australian Financial Review,* 31 October
Laurie, V (2020) 'Rock and a Hard Place', *The Weekend Australian Magazine,* 3 October
Lawson, V (1997) 'Strategic Friends', *Sydney Morning Herald,* 25 October
Lee, B (2018) 'For Over 50 Years a Family Little-known in Sydney Society Has Controlled Legal Gambling in Tasmania', *Pigsfly Newspaper,* 28 February
Lee, K (2019) 'How John Howard Contributed to the Aged Care Crisis', *Australian Independent Media,* 7 May
Lever, RE (2012), 'Rupert Murdoch's Crazy House', *Independent Australia,* 15 September
Lipscombe, D (1976) 'The Great Survival Starring Alan Bond', *The Bulletin,* 28 February
Lohr, R and Head, M (2000) 'Kerosene Baths Reveal Systemic Aged Care Crisis in Australia', World Socialist Web Site
Lord, J (2020) 'Murdoch: Forever Brutal', Australian Independent Media Network, 30 December
Lynch, M (2021) 'For Edelsten it Was All About the Spectacle', *Sunday Age,* 13 June
Lynch, N (2020) 'AUSTRAC's Money Laundering Cases Exposes the Dark Heart of Financial Crime', Thomson Reuters, 17 June
Maiden, M (1996) 'Bond Verdict Spurs ASC Case', *The Age,* 7 December
Maiden, M (2015) 'Bond: Deal-making Dynamo Gone Wrong', *Sydney Morning Herald,* 6 June
Main, A (2001) 'HIH Debacle Had Genesis Long Ago', *Australian Financial Review,* 18 May
Main, A (2003) 'Directors in the Dock', *Australian Financial Review,* 14 May
Maley, K (2019) 'An Ignominious End for Hartzer', *Australian Financial Review,* 26 November
Mann, A (1987) 'Like it or Not, 24-hour Clinics Are Here to Stay', *Canberra Times,* 17 January

Markham, F, Kinder, B and Young, M (2017) 'How One Family Used Pokies and Politics to Extract a Fortune from Tasmanians', *The Conversation,* 5 April
Marks, K (2014) 'Australians Shocked by Corporate Gravy Train', *Independent,* 2 February
Marsh, S (2020) 'Compromised: Genie Energy and the Murdoch Media's Climate Denial', Michael West Media, 15 January
Martin, L, Evershed, N and Butler, B (2019) '"Something is Rotten at the Top": How Bupa's Aged Care Homes Hit Rock Bottom', *The Guardian,* 12 September
Massey, M (1991) 'The Men Who Fell to Earth', *Australian Financial Review',* 31 May
Mayne, S (2009) 'Time for Rupert to Send Spinner Greg Baxter Packing', *Crikey,* 24 April
McClymont, K (2021) 'King of the Cross …', *Sydney Morning Herald,* 16 March
McCrann, T (2001) 'From Success to Self-destruction', *Herald Sun,* 2 August
McGlue, J (2018) 'Investor Activism's Birth: Rowland, Lonrho and the Report that Felled Alan Bond', *Australian Financial Review,* 9 November
McKenzie, N (2020) 'Crown Casino's "Mr Chinatown" Arrested and Deported to China', *The Age,* 7 February
McKenzie, N and Hunter, F (2021) 'How the Screws Turned on Junket King', *The Age,* 14 December
McKenzie, N, Toscano, N, and Tobin, G (2019) 'Gangsters, Gamblers and Crown Casino', *Sydney Morning Herald,* 27 July
McKnight, D (2011) 'The Climate of Opinion at The Australian', David McKnight blog, 15 January, <www.davidmcknight.com.au/archives/2011/01/climate-opinion-australian>
Mirza, N (2018) 'Board Failures: What Makes Boards Effective – An Independent Director's Views', Bloomberg, 27 December
Mitchell, A and Bye, C (1997) 'The Moran Who Would Be King', *Sun-Herald,* 26 October
Mocatta, G (2021) 'What's Behind News Corp's New Spin on Climate Change?', *The Conversation,* 18 October
Molloy, S (2021) 'Inside the Lavish and Controversial Life of Geoffrey Edelsten', News.com.au, 18 June
Morton, A (2018a) 'Battle Over Poker Machines to Take Centre Stage in Tasmania's Election', *The Guardian,* 28 January
Morton, R (2018b) 'Profits Before Patients in Aged Care', *The Australian,* 3 April
Morton, R (2020) 'The Collapse of Aged Care (Part One)', *Saturday Paper,* 12–18 September
Morton, R (2021) 'James and the Giant Breach', *Saturday Paper,* 13–19 February
Murray, L, Grigg, A and Smith, M (2016) 'Inside James Packer's China Crown Nightmare', *Financial Review,* 21 October
Neales, S (2008) 'The Family Fortune Founded on Pokies', *The Mercury,* 19 April
Nunweek, J (2015) 'Lessons for 7-Eleven Scam', *Overland,* 22 October
Nyompe, P (2003) 'The Closure of the Kelian Gold Mine and the Role of the Business Partnership for Development/World Bank', <www.downtoearth-indonesia.org/old-site/Ckl03>
O'Connor, C (2021) 'Premier Walks Away from Electoral Reform', Tasmanian Greens, 23 March, <tasmps.greens.org.au/media-release/premier-walks-away-electoral-reform>
O'Connor, D (2020) 'Former Crown Resorts Executive Warned Company of Dealings in China That Led to Arrests', Casino.org, 18 August, <wwwcasinoorg/news/former-crown-resorts-executive-warned-company-of-dealings-in-china>
O'Donnell, V (2011) 'A "Fit and Proper" Test Case: Rating Alan Bond's Character', *Crikey,* 14 July

O'Malley, N (2018a) 'Rebecca White: The Politician Who Wants to Remove Pokies from Pubs and Clubs', *The Age,* 24 February
O'Malley, N (2018b) 'The Family Who Owns Tasmania's Gambling Industry', *The Age,* 2 February
Ostrow, R (2016) 'Rodney Adler on Jail and Redemption ... and What He Plans Next', *The Australian,* 13 November
Owen, R (2001) 'Qintex Empire Built on Magic of Skase's Spell', *Courier-Mail,* 7 August 2001
Partridge, M (2020) 'Great Frauds in History: Alan Bond's Debt-fuelled Empire', *Money Week,* 1 October
Passmore, D (2015) 'Banks Face Class Bid Over Loans', *Courier-Mail,* 10 May
Patrick, A (2019) 'Westpac Execs Driven by Status, Money and Power', *Australian Financial Review,* 3 December
Pavlus, S (2011) 'Going Green: How News Corp Cashes in on Both Sides of the Climate Fight', Media Matters for America, 21 April
Pearson, N (2021) 'No Perspective on Juukan George', *The Australian,* 22 October
Peers, M (1993) 'MGM Financial Intrigue has Makings of a Movie', *Australian Financial Review,* 19 February
Pilger, J (1991) 'Gang of Mates', *Canberra Times,* 19 January 1991
Priest, M (2004a) 'The Suburban Killer', *Australian Financial Review,* 1 July
Priest, M (2004b) 'James Hardie's Secret Plan to Spin the Media and the Politicians', *Australian Financial Review,* 15 May
Prior, N (2018) 'How Australia's Big Five Banks Have Sewn Up the Financial Advice Industry', *West Australian,* 23 April
Purtill, J and Lauder, J (2022) 'Emily Townsend and Alex Hillman Publicly Quit Their Jobs for Climate Change: Here's What Happened Next', ABC *News*, 30 August
Pyne, I (2019) 'The Broken Billionaire: Inside James Packer's Tough Mental Health Battle', *Australian Woman's Weekly,* 20 June
Raggatt, T (2017) 'A Decade On and the Storm Continues for Poor Investors', *Daily Mercury*, 4 February 2017
Raggatt, T (2008a) 'Ethics, Humble Backgrounds Drive Couple to Success: Gurus Make Richest List Townsville', *Townsville Bulletin*, 30 August
Raggatt, T (2008b) 'Tears of Financial Ruin', *Townsville Bulletin,* 26 December
Retter, B (2020) 'How Kirk Kerkorian Transformed Las Vegas', Better US Casinos, 30 October
Rice, M (1985) 'How Pathology Failed the Medicare Test', *Canberra Times,* 20 October
Richardson, T (2020) 'AUSTRAC Reaps What it Sows', *Australian Financial Review,* 29 September
Riggins, N (2019) '10 Reasons for Corporate Failure', *The CFO,* 29 March
Ritter, D (2020) 'The Fossil Fuel Industry Has Corrupted Our Democracy', *Independent Australia,* 13 May
Rogozenska, E (2021), 'Bupa Aged Care Homes in Australia and the UK Regularly Rated "Inadequate"', *Corpwatch,* 14 October
Rudd, K (2019) 'Democracy Overboard: Rupert Murdoch's Long War on Australian Politics', *The Guardian,* 7 September
Rundle, G (2018) 'Rundle: The Rotten Heart of the Apple Isle', *Crikey*, 27 February
Russell, S (2020a) 'Tone Deaf: Aged Care Providers' PR Campaign Strikes the Wrong Note', Michael West Media, 9 September

Russell, S (2020b) 'Are Political Donations Protecting Bupa's Licence?', Michael West Media, 3 February
Ryan, C (2002) 'Guilty: Rodney Adler's Career in Tatters', *Australian Financial Review,* 15 March
Ryan, C (2003a) 'A Revolution Made by Breaking a Few Eggs', *Australian Financial Review,* 4 March
Ryan, C (2003b), 'HIH: Reporter's Tale', *Australian Financial Review,* 22 July
Sainsbury, M (2019) 'Crown Resorts Board: Is Orange the New Black', Michael West Media, 1 August
Samios, Z (2020) 'From Green Papers to Toxic Denial: How the Murdoch Family Split on Climate', *The Age,* 17 January
Saville, M (2002a) 'Patriarch Strikes Back: Doug Moran's Ironclad Empire', *The Age,* 26 January
Saville, M (2002b) 'Ray's Lieutenant Knew How to Keep the Peace', *Sydney Morning Herald,* 31 August
Schmulow, A (2021) 'ASIC, Now Less a Corporate Watchdog, More a Lapdog', *The Conversation,* 14 September
Schwarten, E (2009) 'Imperfect Storm Leaves Trail of Ruin', *The Bulletin,* 28 March
Seiler, P (nd) 'The Christadelphian Cult', Christian Library, <christianlibrary.org.au/cel/documents/cults/04.html>
Sexton, E (2007) 'A Battler Who Kept the Fire to the End', *Sydney Morning Herald,* 28 November
Sexton, E (2008) 'Secrets of the Boardroom', *Sydney Morning Herald,* 25 October
Sexton, E (2009) 'Judge Ends Board Game at James Hardie and ASIC Scores a Win', *Sydney Morning Herald,* 25 April
Sexton, J (2004) 'Money No Object in Lavish Life', *The Australian,* 16 December
Sexton, M (2002) 'The Rocky Rise of Brad Cooper, Salesman', *The Age,* 20 July
Sexton, J, Harris, T, Elliot, G and White, A (2003) 'Secret Life of HIH Roller', *Weekend Australian,* 20 December
Shand, A (2003) ' The Fatal Weakness of Ray Williams', *Australian Financial Review,* 18 January
Sharwood, A (2006) 'Brad Cooper – Secrets of a Spiv', *Sunday Telegraph, 2 July*
Sheehy, B (2019) 'Bupa's Nursing Home Scandal is More Evidence of a Deep Crisis in Regulation', *The Conversation,* 17 September
Sheehy, B (2021) 'Bullies, Thieves and Chiefs: The Hidden Cost of Psychopaths at Work', *The Conversation,* 16 March
Sims, M (2020) 'Rio Corporate Relations Head Steps Down After Aboriginal Cave Blast', Provoke Media, 11 September
Solly, R (2018) 'Death and Destruction Caused by Mining in West Papua, but Rio Denies Responsibility', London Mining Network, 11 April
Sparrow, J (2015) 'Labor's Embrace of Alan Bond Was Grotesque but at Least it Wasn't Bland', *The Guardian,* 8 June
Sprange, J (2015) 'Bond Rode Roughshod through Wild West', *The Age,* 2 June
Squires, R (2010) 'This is How We Care for the Aged', *Sunday Telegraph,* 30 May
Stannard, B (1983) 'The Go-Go Plans of Alan Bond', *The Bulletin,* 15 November
Steketee, M (2021) 'Was Bob Askin Corrupt?', *Inside Story,* 9 April
Stevens, M (2015) 'Beleaguered Miners Should Remember Leon Davis' Legacy', *Australian Financial Review,* 23 March

Strong, G (2000) 'Monitors Blew Whistle on Home 10 Months Ago', 26 February
Sully, S (2021) 'All About Machiavellianism', Psych Central, 6 October
Sykes, T (2015) 'Alan Bond: Three Decades of Wheeling and Dealing', *Australian Financial Review,* 5 June
Tayan, B (2021) 'Are All Narcissistic CEOs Bad?', Harvard Law School Forum on Corporate Governance, 25 October
Thomson, R (2011), 'Profile: Trader with an Iron Grip', *Independent,* 23 October
Tiffen, R (2019) 'Last Gasp for the Packer Mystique, *Inside Story,* 27 August
Tingle, L (2001) 'Moran the Big Winner as Aged Care Goes Private', *Sydney Morning Herald,* 16 March
Tippet, G (2005) 'How "Boofhead" Made Good', *The Age,* 28 December 2005
Toohey, P (2015) 'Rich Man, Poor Man, Beggar Man or Thief', *Daily Telegraph,* 6 June
Toohey, P and Sainsbury, M (2017) 'Inside Crown's China Bust and How Australian Jason O'Connor Was Arrested', *Daily Telegraph,* 4 March
Trute, P (2005) 'Hellicar Has Fire Enough for Asbestos Fight', *Daily Telegraph,* 20 August
Tugwell, N (2006) 'It Was an Illusion: The Story Behind the Edelsten Myth', *Daily Telegraph,* 31 May
Tully, J (2015) 'Alan Bond and His Brief but Spoiled Ownership of Van Gogh's Irises', Judd Tully blog, <juddtully.net/blog/alan-bond-and-his-brief-but-spoiled-ownership-of-van-goghs-irises>
Van Onselen, P (2019) 'Arrogant Westpac Chief Symbolises Bank Industry Shame', *Weekend Australian,* 23 November
Vass, N (2002) 'They're a Weird Mob', *Sunday Telegraph,* 27 January
Verrender, I (2001) 'The Man Who Cried Wolf', *Sydney Morning Herald,* 7 August
Verrender, I (2015) 'Alan Bond: Australia's Weak Spot for the Man Behind the Biggest Heist in History', ABC *News,* 5 June
Verrender, I (2021) 'House of Cards …', *In Queensland,* 10 February
Walker, J (2004) 'Set Up to Take the Fall', *Courier-Mail,* 14 August
Walker, S (2000) 'The Great Margin Lending Gamble', *Money Management,* 17 February
Waller, L (1989) 'Bond's Private Collection', *Canberra Times,* 22 June
Walsh, M (1997) 'The Crash of 87: A 10-Year Perspective', *Sydney Morning Herald,* 11 October
Walsh, L and Michael, P (2018) 'From High Life to Brisbane Burbs', *Courier-Mail,* 17 March
Washington, S (2009a) 'Tracey Richards Trusted Storm Financial with Her Life Savings. Now She Lives in a Caravan: Are Big Banks to Blame for the Storm Pain?', *Sydney Morning Herald,* 20 June
Washington, S (2009b) 'How CBA Fuelled Storm's Grand Delusion', *The Age,* 5 September
Washington, S (2009c) 'Cap'n Manny and His Crazy Crew', *Sydney Morning Herald,* 5 September
Washington, S (2010) 'Keeping Storm's Victims in Mind', *Sydney Morning Herald,* 19 May
Way, N (2006) 'A Sure Bet', *Australian Financial Review,* 18 May
Webb, R (2007) 'Why the Actions of All 10 Hardie Directors Had to be Tested', *Sunday Age,* 18 February
West, M (2019) 'Democracy Gamed: How Tasmania Was Sold to a Pokies Family from Interstate', Michael West Media, 4 March
West, S (2020) 'Time for Rio to Right its Wrongs', Michael West Media, 12 September
Whelton, R (nd) 'Effects of CEO Pay on US Society', Saginaw State University

White, A (2001) 'Rodney Adler: To the Manner Born', *Weekend Australian*, 2 June
White, A (2020) 'The Purpose of the Corporation: Adam Smith Revisited', Corporation 2020 Workshop, 6 October
Williams, P (2019a) 'What Did Hartzer Know and When?', *Australian Financial Review*, 26 November
Williams, P (2019b) 'How Many Children Did Westpac Fail?', *Australian Financial Review*, 22 November
Williams, P (2021) 'Inside Story: How the ASIC Soap Opera Forced Frydenberg to Act', *Australian Financial Review*, 15 April
Williams, P and Kitney, D (2006) 'My Way', *Australian Financial Review*, 24 November
Wilson P (1989) 'Doctoring the Books', *Canberra Times*, 26 November
Wolf, M (2020) 'Milton Friedman Was Wrong on the Corporation', *Australian Financial Review*, 10 December
Wolff, M (2008) 'Murdoch's Secret is that He Doesn't Have One', *Spectator*, 29 November
Wooley, B (2001) 'Sparks Fly in the New Boys Network', *Weekend Australian*, 9 June
Wynne, M (2005) 'Tom Wenkart and Macquarie Health', <documents.uow.edu.au/~bmartin/dissent/documents/health/wenkart>
Wynne, M (2006) 'Illawong Retirement Equity Pty Ltd. The Riverside Scandal', <documents.uow.edu.au/~bmartin/dissent/documents/health/nh_riverside>
Wynne, M (2007a) 'The Moran Family Story', <documents.uow.edu.au/~bmartin/dissent/documents/health/moran_fam>
Wynne, M (2007b) 'Moran Health Care: The Nursing Home Empire', <documents.uow.edu.au/~bmartin/dissent/documents/health/moran_nurshm>
Wynne, M (2008) 'MFF and Domain Aged Care', <documents.uow.edu.au/~bmartin/dissent/documents/health/mfs_Domain>
Yun, J (2021) 'Exclusive Interview: Former Westpac CEO, Brian Hartzer', *Yahoo Finance*, 4 September
Zehnwirth, B (2021) 'HIH: Myths Debunked and Abrupt Collapse Explained', Insureware, <insureware.com/hih-myths-debunked-and-abrupt-collapse-explained>

INDEX

INDEX